THE PRINCIPLES

OF THE

ADMINISTRATIVE LAW

OF THE

UNITED STATES

BY

FRANK J. GOODNOW, LL.D.

EATON PROFESSOR OF ADMINISTRATIVE LAW AND MUNICIPAL SCIENCE IN
COLUMBIA UNIVERSITY

———

THE LAWBOOK EXCHANGE, LTD.
Clark, New Jersey

ISBN 9781584773481 (hardcover)
ISBN 9781616192259 (paperback)

Lawbook Exchange edition 2003, 2012

The quality of this reprint is equivalent to the quality of the original work.

THE LAWBOOK EXCHANGE, LTD.

33 Terminal Avenue
Clark, New Jersey 07066-1321

*Please see our website for a selection of our other publications
and fine facsimile reprints of classic works of legal history:*
www.lawbookexchange.com

Library of Congress Cataloging-in-Publication Data

Goodnow, Frank Johnson, 1859-1939.
    The principles of the administrative law of the United States /
Frank J. Goodnow.
        p. cm.
Originally published: New York: G.P. Putnam's Sons, 1905.
Includes bibliographical references and index.
ISBN 1-58477-348-0 (alk. paper)
        1. Administrative law—United States. I. Title.

KF5402 .G6 2003
342.73'06—dc21   2002042756

Printed in the United States of America on acid-free paper

THE PRINCIPLES

OF THE

ADMINISTRATIVE LAW

OF THE

UNITED STATES

BY

FRANK J. GOODNOW, LL.D.

EATON PROFESSOR OF ADMINISTRATIVE LAW AND MUNICIPAL SCIENCE IN
COLUMBIA UNIVERSITY

———

G. P. PUTNAM'S SONS

NEW YORK AND LONDON

The Knickerbocker Press

The Knickerbocker Press, New York

PREFACE.

SOME twelve years ago, the writer of the following pages ventured to submit to those interested in the study of political subjects a book entitled *Comparative Administrative Law*.

The great interest in administrative subjects, which is now so manifest in this country, has led him since to believe that a fuller treatment of American administrative conditions than was possible in a book devoted to a comparison of different administrative systems was desirable. This has been his excuse for preparing this work. The plan adopted in his *Comparative Administrative Law* is the one which is here followed. In a number of instances, further, the language which was used in the former work has been retained. In the main, however, the portions of *Comparative Administrative Law* dealing with American conditions have been greatly amplified, if not absolutely rewritten. In a number of instances, where the plan adopted has involved a rather technical presentation of the subject, the author has deemed it wise to state the law in the words of text-writers of acknowledged authority. He has thus been greatly indebted in this, as in the former work, to Professor Floyd R. Mechem, whose excellent treatise on *The Law of Public Officers* has been of the greatest use.

It is the hope of the author that the book now presented to students of politics will soon be followed by one consisting of cases illustrative of American administrative law, to be arranged in the same order as the one here adopted. Such a case book he feels would be of the greatest service in illustrating the conditions which are encountered by administrative officers, and thus bringing in concrete shape before the student's eyes the problems which he is studying.

FRANK J. GOODNOW.

COLUMBIA UNIVERSITY,
August, 1905.

TABLE OF CONTENTS.

BOOK I. THE SEPARATION OF POWERS.

BOOK V. METHODS AND FORMS OF ADMINISTRATIVE ACTION.

CHAPTER III. EXECUTION OF THE WILL OF THE STATE.

BOOK VI. CONTROL OVER THE ADMINISTRATION.

DIVISION I. METHODS OF CONTROL.

CHAPTER I. NECESSITY OF CONTROL

CHAPTER II. INTERESTS TO BE REGARDED

CHAPTER III. KINDS OF CONTROL AND PARTICULARLY THE ADMINISTRATIVE CONTROL.

DIVISION II. THE JUDICIAL CONTROL.

CHAPTER I. ANALYSIS OF THE JUDICIAL CONTROL.

CHAPTER II. CONTROL OF THE CIVIL COURTS.

TABLE OF CASES CITED.

TABLE OF CASES CITED.

BOOK I.

THE SEPARATION OF POWERS.

CHAPTER I.

ADMINISTRATION.

THE most striking if not the most important questions of public law and the first to demand solution are those to which the name "constitutional" is applied. To their solution the wisdom and political activity of the past have been devoted. The present age, however, is devoting itself primarily to questions which are generally referred to as "administrative." A function of government called "administration" is being differentiated from the general sphere of governmental activity, and the term "administrative law" is applied to the rules of law which regulate its discharge.

On the continent of Europe the term "administrative law" has been accepted in the vocabulary of legal writers, and no course of legal study is regarded as complete which does not devote more or less attention to this subject.

In England, however, as well as in the United States, administrative law has been generally ignored as a branch of legal study except by those authors who have been subjected directly to the influences of continental thought. Some English writers, as, *e. g.*, Mr. A. V. Dicey, even deny the possibility of its existence.[1] This general failure on the part of English writers to recognize the existence of administrative law is due to the fact that legal classification has never seemed to them to be of any importance. As Holland[2] points out, except as it has been deduced from the theory of feudal tenure, the classification of English law "is little more than a collection of isolated rules strung together, if at all, only by some slender thread of analogy."

The denial of the possibility of the existence of administrative law in countries having the English system of law which is made by Mr. Dicey, is, however, due to a misconception. His idea is that the term, which is a translation from the French, was originally and is now used by the French to indicate rules of law which provide that administrative officers are not civilly responsible to the courts, and which, on that account, are inconsistent with the spirit of English institutions. While it is, of course, true that the rules of law which the French call administrative do include rules which have no force in England or the United States, it is to be noticed that this administrative law is much broader in its scope than would appear from Mr. Dicey's description of it. It includes many matters which are and must be the subject of legal regulation in English-speaking countries.[3]

[1] *The Law of the Constitution*, 3d ed., p. 304.
[2] *Elements of Jurisprudence*, 1st ed., Preface.
[3] *Cf.* Wyman's *Administrative Law*, p. 3.

It may therefore be said with perfect safety that administrative law, using the words in their proper sense, does and must exist in all countries which have attained any political development worthy of the name.

The subject has, however, as compared with other subjects of legal study, been so recently differentiated that there is not unanimity as to its meaning and extent. This is due largely to the fact that the function of administration, whose discharge administrative law regulates, has itself only recently been differentiated from the general function of government by the theoretical writers on government who have not as yet reached harmonious conclusions as to its meaning.

What, now, do we mean by administration as a function of government, and what do we mean by administrative law? In the first place, it may be said that administration has to do with the governmental system in active operation. Theoretically, the study of administration should have little if anything to do with the organization of government. The study of the organization of government belongs to constitutional law. Constitutional law deals with the anatomy of government; administrative law and administration have to do with the functions, the physiology of government, so to speak.

In the second place it may be remarked that a study of governmental organization alone will often not give a correct idea of the real character of government. It is, of course, true that a knowledge of its organization is absolutely necessary. But it is to be remembered that the real character of a governmental system is determined just as much by the way in which its various parts operate as by the formal character of its organization. Indeed, it may happen, as in the case of an organism, that certain of its parts cease to discharge the functions which they were originally intended to discharge. Others may be called upon to discharge functions which they were originally not intended to discharge. The study of administration, being devoted to the actual operations of government, is well adapted thus to correct impressions derived from a consideration of matters of organization which from the point of view of the real character of the government are incorrect impressions.

Finally, it is to be noticed that the real character of a governmental system is determined not only by the laws in accordance with which it is supposed to act, but also by extra-legal conditions and practices. Indeed it is not infrequently the case that these extra-legal conditions and practices have more influence in giving its real character to a political system than the laws which are supposed to regulate its action. Thus, Rome became an empire, preserving for a long time the form of a republic. Thus, again, the public law of England makes provision for a crown, a privy council, and a parliament. But every one who knows anything about the English government knows that none of these institutions is to the real political life of the English people what the Cabinet is—a body absolutely unknown to the English law.[1]

The necessity of studying extra-legal political conditions and practices is most marked in the case of

[1] *Cf.* Goodnow, *Politics and Administration.*

governmental systems based on a written constitution.
No sooner is such an instrument adopted than
political forces begin at once to interpret and
amend it until the actual political system becomes in
many respects, almost without the knowledge of the
people, quite different from the system as outlined in
the written constitution. No better example of this
fact can be found than the method of electing the
President of the United States. Although, as provided by the constitution, the President is formally
elected indirectly by the people of the States, *i. e.*, by
presidential electors who are elected by the people,
hardly any one who votes for a presidential elector
gives him a thought. Every one is thinking of the
presidential candidates put in nomination by the
political parties. The party system—an extra-legal
institution—has thus come to supplement—we may
say, indeed, to amend—the written constitution.[1]

Since administration and administrative law have
to do with the governmental system in operation, or,
in other words, with the actual operations of political
life, it is absolutely necessary that the study of these
subjects take into account not merely the formal
governmental system as it is outlined in charters of
government and legal rules, but, as well, those extra-
legal conditions and practices which, it has been
shown, have such an important influence on the real
character of governmental systems. What, now, are
the actual operations of political life with which the
study of administration and administrative law has
to do? These operations group themselves naturally
under two heads. They consist either in operations

[1] *Cf.* Macy, *Party Organization and Machinery*, passim.

which are necessary to the expression of the political will or in operations which are necessary in order that that will may be executed.   The political will must be expressed before political action can be had.   The political will must be executed after it has been expressed, if that will is to result in political action.

In the case of a human being, who naturally formulates and executes his will himself, it is necessary that the will be formulated before it is executed.   In the case of political beings it is necessary not only that the will of the sovereign be formulated or expressed before it can be executed, but also that the execution of that will be entrusted in large measure to a different organ from that which expresses it. The great complexity of political conditions makes it practically impossible for the same governmental organ to be entrusted in equal degree with the discharge of both functions.

The two functions of government which we have attempted to differentiate may, for purposes of convenience, be designated respectively as Politics and Administration.   Politics has to do with policies or expressions of the state will.   Administration has to do with the execution of these policies.   It is, of course, true that the meaning which is here given to the word "politics" is not the meaning which has been attributed to it by most political writers.   At the same time it is the meaning which the word conveys when it is used in ordinary conversation.   As the *Century Dictionary* says : Politics is, "in the narrower and more usual sense, the act or function of guiding or influencing the policy of government through the organization of a party among its citizens."

The use of the word "administration" as indicative of the function of executing the will of the state needs a more extended apology. For the word, when accompanied by the definite article, is used to indicate an organization. "The administration" means popularly the most important administrative authorities. The word "administration" when used as indicative of function is apt, therefore, to promote the idea that the function of administration is to be found exclusively in the work of what are known as the executive or administrative authorities, who are in their turn regarded as monopolizing the discharge of the function of administration. This is not the case in any concrete government. For political necessity requires that there shall be harmony between the expression and execution of the state will. Lack of such harmony will result in political paralysis. For a rule of conduct, *i. e.*, a concrete expression of the state will, practically amounts to nothing if it is not executed. On the other hand, the execution of a rule of conduct which is not the expression of the state will is really an exercise by the executing authority of the right to express the state will.

The necessary harmony between the expression and the execution of the state will can be obtained only by subordinating one of these functions to the other. Popular government requires that the execution of the state will shall be subjected to the control of the organ expressing the state will. For an effective executive authority can never be so representative of the people of a state as a body which can effectively express their will. Administration must, therefore, be subjected to the control of politics. While, therefore,

the function of politics has to do primarily with
the expression of the state will, it has also to do,
secondarily, with the execution of that will. Provision may be made in the formal governmental organization for the control which politics must have
over administration. Thus, the constitution of a
state may give the legislature the power to remove
the officers entrusted with the execution of the law
and subject their actions to a continual control to be
exercised by the legislature. This is what is done in
Switzerland.[1] If no provision for such control is
made by the constitution, the control is apt, in a popular government, to develop outside of the government. This is the case in England, where, as a result
of political practice, the ministry must resign when
they lose the confidence of the House of Commons.

But however this control may be provided, whether
provision be made for it in the governmental system
or not, it should not be extended beyond what is
necessary to produce harmony between the making
and enforcement of law, *i. e.*, between the expression
and execution of the state will. If it is extended
beyond these limits it is apt to defeat the purpose for which it is established. If made use of, *e. g.*,
to perpetuate the existence of a particular party organization, it really hinders instead of aiding the
spontaneous expression of the public will, and ham-
pers its efficient execution.

The evils arising from the partial and interested
administration of the law, which are due to the too
extensive control of politics over administration, are
so great that the most progressive political communi-

[1] Lowell, *Government and Parties in Continental Europe*, ii., p. 197.

ties have felt obliged to assign by law to certain authorities entrusted with the administration of the law a large degree of independence in action. Such, for example, has been the case in England, which from a very early time has based her governmental system on the principle that no rule of conduct, *i. e.*, no expression of the state will, shall be enforced until the concurrence of some authority largely independent of the authority laying down such rule of conduct has been obtained.

The influence of this principle may be seen in all branches of the English public law. It is not, however, the same in the case of all officers entrusted with the execution of the state will. The distinction which is thus made brings up naturally the differentiation which is usually made between what are known as judicial officers and administrative officers. The former are in the main entrusted with the administration of justice the latter are in the main entrusted with the administration of government. What, now, do we mean by these terms? If we analyze the work done by officers engaged in the application or execution of the law, we find that a part of this work may be differentiated from the rest by the fact that it consists in the decision of controversies between individuals, or between individuals and government officers, as to the applicability in the cases in question of a particular rule of law. The other branch of the work done by government officers may be distinguished by the fact that the action taken by such officers is not necessarily, or even often, the result of any controversy and is not merely dependent on the solution of the question What is the law? but is made

also as a result of considerations. of expediency.
Thus, in the first kind of work, all the officer has to do
is to determine what is the law applicable to the facts
brought before him ; in the second kind of work he
must determine, of course, what is the law in order to
determine whether he is competent to act ; but furthermore he must decide whether in case, he is competent,
it is wise for him to act.   In the first case, for example,
the officer is to determine whether under the law a
given piece of property belongs to A or B ; in the
second case he is to determine, for example, whether,
conceding he has the power, it is wise for him to
grant to A a license to sell liquor or to lay out a
highway over A's property.   In these last cases, it is
true, the law may provide that before he grants A
his license he must hear the objections which A's
neighbors may have to the granting of the license, or
A's objections or the objections of other interested
persons to the laying out of the highway as proposed.
In both of these cases something in the nature of a
controversy may thus arise.   But it is not a controversy as to the applicability of the law but rather one
as to the expediency of the action which it is proposed
to take.

Now the Anglo-American law denominates the
first kind of action as judicial, and the second
kind of action as administrative.   On account of
the necessity that justice shall be administered im-
partially, that is, with regard merely to the law as it
exists, and without regard to the political position
and standing of the contestants before the court, the
English law from an early time accorded to the authorities entrusted with the discharge of the judicial

function, *i. e.*, the courts, a position of great independence. This independence was in a large part due to the jury system. It was also due to the feeling among the people that the courts must be free from all political influences. The fact that judges may be removed by Parliament does not render them politically, although it may make them legally, dependent on the body which expresses the will of the state. Their political independence is due to an enlightened public opinion. In the United States we have carried the idea of judicial independence to its utmost legal limits in that we have made it impossible for the legislature to remove judges except as the result of an impeachment trial. We also have in large, though not to the same degree, the feeling which is so characteristic of England, that judges should be politically as well as legally independent. But owing to frequent elections, party feeling, and a less enlightened public opinion, judges are not, from a political point of view, so independent.

It may be said, therefore, that English-speaking peoples have come to the conclusion that the danger of permitting distinctly political bodies to exercise a control over the administration of justice is so great that the authorities entrusted with this branch of the execution of the state will should be placed in a position of great independence, both from the legal and extra-legal or political point of view, even if this position of independence diminishes or destroys the control which politics has over this branch of the function of administration.

The rule that the concurrence of some authority independent of the body expressing the state will must be obtained before the expression of the state will shall become a rule of conduct was accepted in England in the administration of government as well as in the administration of justice. It was applied most conspicuously in the system of local government for which England was famous, and which was ultimately characterized by the great independence of the local authorities entrusted with the enenforcement of law. This system, which, it was believed, saved England from the absolute monarchy, was introduced into this country where the local administrative authorities were assigned an even greater independence than was their portion in England.

Further, the adoption of the principle of the separation of powers,[1] which was made theoretically a part of American public law, has done much to make the executive or administrative authorities, generally, independent of the legislative authority. Indeed the degree of legal independence was carried so far that it would have destroyed that harmony between the making and enforcement of law had not a control of an extra-legal character been found in the political party. The political party interested itself with the execution as well as the making of law. The control of the political party, as is natural, has been carried too far, and at the present time, notwithstanding the mandates of our formal constitutional law, our administrative authorities are subjected to an ever-present political control which aims not merely at securing the enforcement of law, but also at the perpetuation and strengthening of party organization.

[1] See *infra*, p. 24.

In extending thus their control the parties, the extra-legal political organizations, have stepped beyond the limits which, from the point of view of theory, should be set to their action ; and the result is at the present time a revolt against party rule by many persons who believe that party tyranny is making the expression of the real will of the people difficult and the execution of that will inefficient.

This condition of things, which is unquestionably bad, is to be attributed to the undue extension of the control of politics over administration. Until it is recognized that government should be administered as justice now is, without regard to the effects on the party, *i. e.*, without regard to the effects of governmental action on the future expression of the state will, it is doubtful whether we shall be emancipated from the present tyranny of party.

In other words, it is necessary to the proper conduct of government that a function which, for want of a better word may be called the function of administration, shall be granted recognition. The discharge of this function consists in the impartial and efficient execution of the law as laid down by the legislative body. If we are to be guided by the facts of history we may conclude that its recognition will be accompanied by the grant of a reasonable degree of independence —not merely a legal, but, as well, an extra-legal independence—to those to whom its discharge is entrusted. For it was only when judicial authorities were made independent in fact as in form that the administration of justice became impartial.

The **problem in the** case of the administrative is

more difficult of solution than in the case of the judicial function.   For it is necessary in the case of the former function that it should be subjected to the control of politics to an extent which will ensure harmony between the making and the enforcement of law.   Much may undoubtedly be done by laws which, like the civil service laws, remove administrative positions from politics, but much must as unquestionably be left to a sound public opinion which will insist that impartial enforcement of law is an end in and of itself.   Such, then, is what is meant in these pages by the function of administration—the execution, in non-judicial matters, of the law or will of the state as expressed by the competent authority.

It has already been shown that the function of administration, *i. e.*, the execution of the law, must in some way be subjected to the control of the law-making authority.   It is also to be noticed that in all concrete governmental systems the highest governmental authorities entrusted with the execution of the law do much towards shaping the law by the influence they exert over the legislative body.   Express provision for the exercise of such influence may be made in the law, as, for example, the power of high executive officers to initiate legislation or to send messages and recommendations to the legislature.   Where such express provision is not made it is none the less true that such an influence is exerted.[1]   While legally the shaping of legislation may thus be a part of the work of authorities whose duties are otherwise mainly executive in

---

[1] See Ford, *The Rise and Growth of American Politics*, p. 275, chapter entitled " The Presidency," on the influence of the American Executive on legislation.

character, it is none the less true that from the point of view of theory this work is political rather than administrative in character. Thus, authorities mainly political control administration, and authorities mainly administrative influence politics.

CHAPTER II.

ADMINISTRATIVE LAW.

ADMINISTRATIVE law, from the point of view which has been taken, should deal exclusively with this function of administration which has been differentiated. But from the point of view of the generally accepted legal terminology its scope is somewhat larger. Administrative law not only treats of the function of administration, *i. e.*, the execution of the law, thus determining the competence of the executive or administrative officers of the government, it has also to supplement constitutional law. For while constitutional law in theory should deal with the entire structural organization of the government, as a matter of fact it has to do merely with the general form of the government and the relations of the most important governmental authorities, one with another. Administrative law takes up this work where constitutional law leaves it, and carries out in its minutest details the general plan of governmental organization laid down by constitutional law. Thus the constitutional law provides for a chief executive; the administrative law proceeds to organize the various executive departments through which the executive authority acts.

With this important exception, however, administrative law deals with the execution of law, with the work of governmental authorities whose existence is to be presumed and whose organization is determined by the constitutional law. Administrative law treats of the powers and duties of officers whose main function is to execute the law.

It is to be remembered, however, that, in so far as the administrative law determines the competence of such officers, it indicates what are the rights of the individual which the administration must respect and the remedies to which the individual may resort in case the administration does not respect these rights. These rights may be and, as a matter of fact, are in the United States guaranteed to the individual by the written constitution. But as in the case of the organization of government, the constitutional law goes no further than to sketch out the general plan, so here the constitutional law simply states in a general way what are individual rights, leaving to the administrative law to indicate how far they are modified by the powers granted to administrative officers, and what remedies are open in case individual rights are violated.

Administrative law is therefore that part of the law which fixes the organization and determines the competence of the authorities which execute the law, and indicates to the individual remedies for the violation of his rights.

Taking up the subjects in the order adopted in this definition, we find that administrative law treats in detail of the following matters :

I.—Administrative organization.

As the function of administration is discharged in large part by the executive authorities—*i. e.*, the

authorities which execute the laws, that part of the
administrative law which has to do with governmental organization has to do primarily with the
organization of these executive authorities. But inasmuch as all states of any size are composed of various territorial divisions, many of which are at the
same time bodies corporate participating in the work
of administration, administrative law has to treat not
merely of the central, but also of the local, administrative organization. In this country, the administrative
organization, not only of the national, but also of the
state, government and of the local communities, such
as the counties, towns, cities, and villages, is then to
be fixed by administrative law, which is to be found
in the constitutions as well as in statutes and local
ordinances.

II.—Powers and duties of administrative officers.

In every government we find regularly constituted
public services whose extent and number vary according to the manners and peculiar genius of the people.
In the first place, the state occupies a position among
other states. It is a subject of international law, and
as such, has rights and duties over against other
states, and must enter into relations with them. The
management of these relations calls for certain executive action, which constitutes a branch of the general
function of administration, *viz :* the administration
of foreign relations. For the regulation of this
branch of administration, we must have a body of
law which, in addition to organizing the executive
force necessary, determines its duties, and fixes the
limits of its action.

In the second place, the state must have means at its command to repel any attempts which may be made against its existence or power by other states, or against its peace and order by its own inhabitants. In other words, it must have an army, and, in most cases, a navy. The executive action made necessary by the existence of a military force constitutes another branch of administration, *viz:* the administration of military affairs. For the regulation of this branch of adminstration again, we must have a body of law in accordance with which the peace and war effective of the army and navy are determined, the principles of mobilization established, and the rights and duties of military persons fixed.

In the third place, every government must do something to decide conflicts which arise between its inhabitants relative to their rights. This duty makes the existence of courts necessary, and they in their turn require executive action, for which we find a third branch of administration, *viz.;* the administration of judicial affairs. By this term is meant not the decision by the courts of the controversies which may arise, but the activity of the executive organs of the government to the end that the courts be in existence and in a position to discharge their duties. This is a side of what is ordinarily known as the administration of justice, which, in most cases, is easily distinguished from the rendering of judicial decisions. This branch of administration is not nearly so important in this country as on the continent of Europe, where we find a well organized department of justice, whose duty it is to supervise the action of the judges, to call upon the proper authority to exercise the disciplinary power over them when necessary, and to distribute judicial officers among the different courts in accordance with the needs of justice. In this country, most matters of this sort, outside of the appointment to judicial office, are attended to either by the judges themselves or by the legislature which alone has the power to remove judges from office. In some few instances, as in New York, the governor has powers of this character, as, for example, the power to call extraordinary terms of the courts and to assign judges from one judicial department to another in accordance with the needs of the service.[1]

In the fourth place, we have a branch of administration known as the administration of financial affairs. Every state and every one of its local corporations must have property, receipts and expenses. Inasmuch as its property is paid for by the contributions of its citizens, which also form the major part of its receipts, and inasmuch as the amount of such contributions is determined by the amount of the expenditures, it is particularly necessary that the actions of the administration in the domain of finance be in accordance with the law, which often descends into the minutest details. Thus arise a law of taxation and a law of public accountability, which are intended to be so formulated as to insure to the citizen fair treatment and exemption from arbitrary action, and to force the administration to spend only such amounts of money and for only such purposes as the legislature directly or indirectly may have provided.

---

[1] By many the management of all penal institutions is regarded as a part of the administration of judicial affairs. So far as that is so regarded, we naturally have an administration of judicial affairs in this country.

The rules of law governing the discharge of public functions relate, fifthly, to the administration of the internal affairs of the state. Here we find the greatest difference between different states; from those states whose policy is in the main to discharge simply jural and police functions, to those whose laws are saturated with the doctrines of state socialism. But even in those states where the *laisser faire* policy is carried out most thoroughly, we find certain internal affairs which are regulated by law. The laws which govern these subjects are of two kinds. They are, first, repressive in character, when they are called police laws. Such laws attempt to ward off harm of some kind by imposing restrictions on individual liberty. They limit, in many cases, the right of association, of free speech, and freedom of action. Among the numerous laws of this sort may be mentioned the whole sanitary and quarantine legislation, the building laws which are found in all of our larger cities, the excise and theatre legislation in accordance with which licenses are required before the business of selling liquor by the glass to be drunk on the premises may be carried on, or a theatrical enterprise may be conducted, and those numerous laws which, like those requiring an inspection of steam boilers and the licensing of engineers and pilots, are intended to protect the public safety.

The second class of laws governing the administration of internal affairs directly furthers the public welfare by offering to the individual the means of satisfying his various wants, either material or intellectual. Thus we find the highway, railway, postal, and telegraph legislation, which provides for the construction, maintenance, and operation of means of public communication ; the poor-law legislation, which provides for a system of public charity ; and the school law, which offers to citizens an opportunity to educate their children of which, in most cases, they are obliged by law to avail themselves.

The treatment of none of these subjects of administrative law would, however, be complete and exhaustive if it did not devote considerable space to the subject of the remedies offered to individuals against the arbitrary action of the officers of the government in the application of the administrative law.   In all branches of administrative law, but particularly in those in which, like tax and police legislation, the government steps in to abridge private rights, some means must be provided for preventing the administration from overstepping, even in the interest of the public welfare, the bounds of individual freedom which have been fixed by the law.   In many cases the administrative law finds adequate remedies by making use of ordinary judicial machinery, and by applying to officers of administration the ordinary rules of law—as, for example, when it provides that the government in its central or local organizations shall be liable to suit, or that officers who exceed their jurisdiction may, in the proper cases, be prosecuted either civilly or criminally.   In a great many cases, however, adequate remedies will not be provided by applying to the government or its officers the ordinary rules of law.   For these cases there must be formed a special jurisdiction of some sort. This is done in two ways.   Either the ordinary courts are given the power to apply special remedies, or special courts are formed for the exercise of this jurisdiction. While instances of both methods are to be found in the United States, the rule is that the ordinary courts have a special jurisdiction, by the exercise of which, on the demand of individuals, they are able both to hold the administration up to its duty and to preserve intact the sphere of individual freedom guaranteed by the law. The special courts found in this country are quite rare. Instances of them are the United States Court of Claims and the Board of General Appraisers in the national customs administration, which have jurisdiction respectively over certain claims against the United States government, and over contests with regard to the classification and appraisement of merchandise in accordance with the provisions of the customs administrative law. Among the special remedies applied by the courts are the extraordinary legal remedies—*viz :* the *mandamus*, the *certiorari*, the *quo warranto*, the prohibition, the *habeas corpus*, and certain of the equitable remedies, notable among which is the injunction, which, in a proper case, will be made use of to restrain the action of public officers where such action is not justified by the law. While some of these remedies, as, for example, the *habeas corpus* and the injunction, are remedies of the private law as well, most of them are essentially public legal remedies, and may be made use of only when questions of public law are to be determined. In addition to these remedies, which are a part of the common law, various statutes have provided special remedies in particular cases, in the nature of appeals to the courts from the decisions of administrative officers.

CHAPTER III.

THE THEORY OF THE SEPARATION OF POWERS.

THE attempt made in England, as a result of the struggles of the revolutionary movements of the seventeenth century, to separate the functions which have been spoken of as politics and administration, and to entrust the discharge of each of these functions to a separate governmental authority,[1] combined with the independence accorded to the courts, to which allusion has been made, led the great French political philosopher Montesquieu to the formulation of his famous theory of the separation of powers. In his *Esprit des Lois*[2] he distinguished three powers of government, which he called respectively the legislative, the executive, and the judicial. This differentiation of three rather than two governmental functions, was probably due to the fact that Montesquieu's theory was, as has been indicated, derived very largely from a study of English institutions. England was almost the only country of the civilized world which, at the time he wrote, made a distinction in its governmental organization between the executive and judicial authorities. This was made finally by the Act of Settlement in 1701, which prevented the Crown from removing the judges except upon

[1] On this point see Ford, *op. cit.*, p. 28.   [2] Book XI., chap. iv.

the address of Parliament.[1] It was only natural that Montesquieu should find in this independence of the judiciary the recognition of a judicial power separate from, and independent of, the executive power.

If, however, Montesquieu had carried his researches further, he would have seen that the existence of this third function of government, *i. e.*, the judicial power, could not be proven by the mere fact of the independence of the judges. A study of the powers of the judges of the higher courts, and particularly of the powers of the justices of the peace, would have shown conclusively that English political ideas were not reconcilable with the existence of three separate powers or functions of government. The laws were often executed by authorities which at the same time administered justice. Administrative and judicial authorities were not nearly so clearly distinguished in England as Montesquieu seems to have thought.[2]

Montesquieu's theory involved, however, not merely the recognition of three separate powers or functions of government, but also the existence of separate governmental authorities, to each of which one of the three powers of government was to be entrusted. This part of the theory has been proven to be impossible of application to concrete political organizations. No political organization, based on the general theory of the separation of powers, has ever been established

---

[1] The *Esprit des Lois* appeared in 1748.

[2] Montesquieu's theory of the existence of three powers or functions of government is not finally accepted by the modern political philosophy of his own country. As one of the great writers on French administrative law, M. Ducrocq, says: "The mind can conceive of but two powers—that which makes the law, and that which executes it. There is no place, therefore, for a third power by the side of the first two."—See *Cours de Droit Administratif*, 6th ed., 1881, vol. i., p. 27.

which assigns the discharge of each of the great governmental functions distinguished by this theory exclusively to one governmental authority. It is impossible, for several reasons, to make such an assignment of functions.

In the first place, it is impossible to arrive at clear definitions of legislative, executive, and judicial power in accordance with which specific powers, which it is desirable should be exercised, may be unquestionably denominated as legislative, executive, or judicial.[1]

In the second place, it is inexpedient to confine the exercise of what is unquestionably legislative power to one governmental authority. Thus it is often highly desirable that the courts shall have the power to make law through their power of declaring, in their decisions, what is often spoken of as the unwritten law. Thus again it is desirable that the executive authorities shall have the power, through the issue of what are known as ordinances or regulations, either to supplement existing statutes or lay down the law as to details not regulated by such statutes.

Finally, as political systems develop, the authorities of government become differentiated. To each of these differentiated authorities it is attempted to entrust some portion of one of what may be called the primary functions of government. Thus the expression of the will of the state on certain subjects may

[1] See the remarks of a judge of the Supreme Court of North Carolina, who says in Brown *vs.* Turner, 70 N. C., 93, 102, that while "the executive, legsilative, and supreme judicial powers of the government ought to be forever separate and distinct, it is also true that the science of government is a practical one ; therefore, while each should firmly maintain the essential powers belonging to it, it cannot be forgotten that the three co-ordinate parts constitute one brotherhood, whose common trust requires a mutual toleration of what seems to be a ' common because of vicinage' bordering on the domains of each."

be entrusted to a constitutional convention and not to the legislature.

But while Montesquieu's principle of the separation of powers is not capable of application in its pure form to concrete political organizations, at the same time this theory lies at the basis of most well-developed existing political systems. In most such systems, however, many exceptions have been made to the theory. The exceptions which are thus made to the theory are not the same in the different states which have endeavored, in a general way, to apply the theory. Even from the point of view merely of political theory, there is no agreement as to what the theory means in its detailed application. This lack of agreement, however, occasions no particular difficulty, so long as the discussion is carried on from the point of view of what ought to be. But just so soon as the general theory is formulated as a legal principle, just so soon as it becomes a part of the positive law, the difficulties that arise are legion and appear to be insurmountable.

Such difficulties do not, of course, arise where a clear statement is made as to what powers a particular authority in the government may exercise. For however inconsistent such a statement may be with the general principle which is supposed to be at the basis of the government, still it will control, since it, and not the general theory, is the law. It is only when, in addition to what is provided by such a statement, the general theory is made the law, that the difficulty alluded to will arise.

Before taking up the law of the separation of powers as it has been developed by the courts in the

United States, which has made the general theory a part of its public law, it may be well to take up the exceptions to the general theory which are made in the written constitutions.   We may consider, in the first place, the executive functions of the legislature, and, in the second place, the legislative functions of the executive authorities.   It is unnecessary for our purpose, which is to ascertain what are the powers of the authorities which execute the laws, to inquire as to what are the judicial functions of the legislature, or what are the legislative functions of the judicial authorities.   Nor need we consider in this connection the judicial functions of executive authorities, nor the executive functions of judicial authorities.   So far as these authorities may possess any such functions, they possess them as a result of a failure, in the infrequent particular instances in which they occur, to distinguish between judicial and executive action.   This failure, it may well be, is due to the theoretical impossibility of making any such distinction, to which allusion has already been made.

I.—*Executive functions of the legislature.*

Legislatures very commonly exercise powers which from the point of view of the theory of the separation of powers are executive rather than legislative in character.   Legislative power is commonly regarded as the power to lay down general rules of conduct for the persons subject to the obedience of the state. From this point of view, the action of the legislature in regulating individual cases through the passage of " special legislation," as it is called, and in appointing and removing, or in participating in the appointment and removal of officers, is not legislative in character. Still most legislatures possess all or most of these powers. Most American constitutions provide that some of these powers, at any rate, shall be exercised only with the consent of the legislature, or vest in the legislature alone the right to exercise such powers. The reason those constitutions vest such powers in the legislature is largely the necessity of providing a means by which administration may be subjected to the control of politics. This is particularly true of the financial powers of the legislature and of its powers relative to the appointment and removal of officers.

II.—*Legislative functions of the executive authority.*

The executive power is usually regarded as the power to execute rules of conduct laid down by the legislature. The executive authority, however, by most American constitutions, has the power to initiate legislation by sending recommendations to the legislature, the power to disapprove bills passed by the legislature, in which case such bills do not become law unless passed again by the legislature, and the power of issuing ordinances, which either are supplementary to existing legislation or regulate matters not regulated by such legislation.

Such powers are given to the executive authority expressly by most American constitutions, although in other respects such constitutions may be based on the theory of the separation of powers. The reason why executive authorities have these legislative powers is in ultimate analysis the same as the reason why the legislature has executive powers. This reason in the case of the legislature is that politics may have a control over administration ; in the case of the executive authority, that administration may have an influence over politics. It is only by the interac·tion of this control and influence that we can secure that harmony between politics and administration, between the making and the enforcement of the law, which lies at the basis of orderly and effective government.

It has already been pointed out that this result need not be due entirely to enactment of law, but where it is not, where, for example, a power of initiating legislation may not be granted expressly by the constitutional system, it may be secured in other ways.[1] But in all political systems the attempt is made to secure this result, either by the operation of law or by the adoption of extra-legal political practices.

[1] *Supra*, p. 14.

CHAPTER IV.

THE THEORY OF THE SEPARATION OF POWERS IN THE UNITED STATES.

I.—The theory a part of the American public law.

IT has already been intimated that Montesquieu's theory of the separation of powers was made the basis of the system of government adopted in the United States at the end of the eighteenth century. A perusal of the writings of those men who influenced most profoundly the political thought of the time will reveal a practically unanimous acceptance of the theory.[1]

The theory was accepted not, however, as a scientific theory but as a legal rule. Many of the state constitutions, which either were adopted soon after the American revolution or have been put into force since, contain clauses known as " distributing clauses," of which that contained in the constitution of Massachusetts may be taken as a most forcible example. Article 30 of the first constitution of Massachusetts provides that "in the government of this commonwealth the legislative department shall never exercise the executive or judiciary powers or either of them ;

---

[1] Bondy, " The Separation of Powers," *Columbia University Series in History, Economics and Public Law*, v., No. 2.

the executive shall never exercise the legislative or judiciary powers or either of them ; the judiciary shall never exercise the legislative or executive powers or either of them, to the end that it may be a government of laws and not of men." Other constitutions, of which the constitution of the United States is one, provide that the legislative power shall be vested in a legislature, that the executive power shall be vested in a President or governor, and that the judicial power shall be vested in certain courts.[1] Such provisions, however, are held to have practically the same legal effect as the distributing clause in the Massachusetts constitution, on the theory that " affirmative words are often, in their operation, negative of other objects than those affirmed." [2]

As a result of these constitutional provisions, it is said by the United States Supreme Court, Justice Miller giving the opinion,

" that all the powers entrusted to government, whether state or national, are divided into the three grand departments, the executive, the legislative, and the judicial. That the functions appropriate to each of these branches of government shall be vested in a separate body of public servants, and that the perfection of the system requires that the lines which separate and divide these departments shall be broadly and clearly defined. It is also essential to the successful working of this system that the persons intrusted with power in any one of these branches shall not be permitted to encroach upon the powers confided to the others, but that each shall by the law of its creation be limited to the exercise of the powers appropriate to its own department and no other." [3]

It is, however, to be noticed that the provisions of the

---

[1] *Cf.* U. S. Constitution, art. i., sec. 1; art. ii., sec. 1; art. iii., sec. 1.

[2] Marbury *vs.* Madison, 1 Cranch, 137, 174.

[3] Kilbourn *vs.* Thompson, 103 U. S., 168, 190.

United States const.tution to which reference has been made do not in any way affect the states in this respect,—do not, for example, forbid a state legislature from exercising judicial power.[1]

II.—The meaning of the rule in American law.

While it is a rule of American public law that the powers of government which are distinguished by the constitution are distributed among the legislative, executive, and judicial departments of the government, hardly any American constitution defines any one of these three powers of government. An examination of the constitution, therefore, does not enlighten us as to the exact meaning of the rule. We must go to the decisions of the courts made in their interpretation of the constitution if we would know whether the exercise of a specific power by any one of the departments of government is permitted under a particular constitution.

When we do so examine the decisions we find that they are often conflicting as to specific powers of government.[2] In order, therefore, that the student may know what the legal meaning of the principle of the separation of powers is in a given state of the American Union, he must examine the decisions of the courts of that state. This is extremely important. For the effect of the adoption of a particular view of the separation of powers by the courts of a state is that all attempts of any governmental authority to

[1] Satterlee *vs.* Matthewson, 2 Peters, 380, 413 ; Calder *vs.* Bull, 3 Dallas, 386.

[2] See remarks of Judge Chris iancy, in People *vs.* Hurlbut, 24 Michigan, 44, 63, where he frankly admits that the different powers of government differ in extent in different states.

exercise powers whose exercise is inconsistent with that view, are unconstitutional and void.[1]

But while there is conflict of opinion as to concrete points there are certain general principles which the courts of most of the states are inclined to apply. Thus it may be laid down :

First. That the action of any one of the departments of the government must, in order to partake of the nature of the department so as to satisfy the provision of the constitution requiring a separation of powers, be completely independent of the influence and control of any other department. Take, for example, the case of Gordon *vs.* United States.[2] Here the Congress of the United States passed a law providing for a Court of Claims which should have jurisdiction of certain complaints which individuals might have to make against the national government. The act provided for an appeal from the judgment of the Court of Claims in certain cases to the Supreme Court of the United States, and added that the judgment should be paid when it had been revised by the Secretary of the Treasury. When the first case came up to the Supreme Court on appeal, that body held that it could not take jurisdiction inasmuch as it was vested by the constitution only with judicial powers, and the decision of an appeal from the determination of the Court of Claims was not an exercise of judicial power since such determination was not conclusive, but might be revised by an executive officer.[3]

---

[1] *E. g.*, see Gordon *vs.* U. S., 117 U. S., 697.   [2] 117 U. S., 697.

[3] See also as to the power of the courts to review the distinctly executive action of the President and governor, *infra*, p. 92, and cases cited.

The only exceptions to this general rule that each department is to be independent of the others are to be found in those cases where appeal is made to the courts to apply or construe an act of the legislature or an act of the executive. In these cases, if the courts deem that such acts are not in accordance with the higher law of the land, in the one case the constitution and in the other case the statute law, they do not hesitate to refuse to enforce such acts on the theory that they are legally void and of no effect. In this, their action, the courts do not claim to be exercising a control over other departments of the government, but merely to be exercising their right to judge of what is law, and to apply only what they consider to be law. This rule of law was not, however, adopted so far as concerns the relation of the courts to legislation without a long struggle.[1]

Second. The principle of the separation of powers does not apply to the local governments. Perhaps as good a case as can be found on this point is the case of the People *vs.* Provines.[2] The facts of the case were as follows: The constitution of California provided in article iii. that no one exercising judicial powers might exercise executive powers. A police judge of the city of San Francisco was elected police commissioner by the people of San Francisco and entered upon the performance of the duties of his office. Information in the nature of a *quo warranto* was brought against him by the attorney-general to oust him from the office of police commissioner, into which, it was claimed, he had entered contrary to the provisions of the constitution. When the matter

---

[1] See Bondy, *op. cit.*, p. 52.　　　　　　　[2] 34 Cal., 520.

came before the court which reviewed all the other cases decided upon this point in California and actually overruled several of such cases, it was held that the distributing clause of the California constitution applied only to the state government, and did not provide for any separation of powers in the local governments.[1]

The confinement of the application of the principle of the separation of powers to the central government has for its result :

1. That the legislature may constitutionally confer powers local in their application whatever may be the theoretical nature of such powers upon (*a*) organs of the central government or (*b*) upon any local authority, and that in case it does so such powers do not partake of the nature of the body upon which they may be conferred.

(*a*) Thus the courts have frequently held that the legislature may vest in the courts the power to determine whether the limits of a local corporation shall be extended [2] or a proposed local improvement shall be undertaken.[3] It has also been held that acts of a local character regarded by the courts as administrative do not become judicial when performed by the courts. Thus where an appeal is allowed only from a judgment of a court, appeal will not run from a local act which is merely administrative in character.[4]

(*b*) It has also been held in numberless cases that

[1] See also State *vs.* George, 22 Oregon, 142 ; and Fox *vs.* McDonald, 101 Ala., 51.

[2] Callen *vs.* Junction City, 43 Kan., 627. But see Territory *vs.* Stewart, 1 Washington, 98, which takes the opposite view.

[3] Bryant *vs.* Robbins, 70 Wis., 258.

[4] Auditor General *vs.* Pullman Co., 34 Mich., 59.

the legislature may authorize local corporations both
to pass ordinances of a local police character[1] and to
put into effect in the territory of the local corporation
acts passed by the legislature of the state.[2]

2. The legislature may authorize local officers to
exercise certain powers belonging to the state regardless of the fact that the character of the authority
to which the exercise of the power is given is not the
same as that of the power granted. This is, however,
true only of certain powers, and the principle has
been upheld only on the ground that historically local
authorities have always exercised such powers and
that the principle of the separation of powers was
adopted subject to historical practice. Thus it is
very generally held that the legislature may give to
the mayors of cities, who are not a part of the judicial
department, jurisdiction over cases arising under the
laws of the state, even of crimes, notwithstanding the
fact that the constitution may vest the judicial power
in the judicial department.[3]

Third. Each of the departments of government
may exercise all those powers whose exercise is necessary to its independence. There is a certain class
of powers which must of necessity be exercised by
every one of the departments, such, for example, as
the power of appointment. If any one of the departments is to be expected to be independent of the

[1] Mayor of Mobile *vs.* Yuille, 3 Ala., 137.

[2] See Oberholtzer, *The Referendum in America*, chapter xiii. ; Wales *vs.*
Belcher, 3 Pickering, Mass., 508 ; Burgess *vs.* Pue, 2 Gill, Md., 11; Bancroft
vs. Dumas, 21 Vt., 456.

[3] *Ex parte* Slattery, 3 Ark., 485 ; Danbury *vs.* Bird, 34 Iowa, 524 ; Baton
Rouge *vs.* Dearing, 15 La. An., 208 ; but see Hagerstown *vs.* Dechert, 32 Md.,
369.

others, it must have the power to appoint its subordi-nates. The legislature may thus appoint all its sub-ordinate officers, while courts may appoint such officers as criers and others who are necessary in order that the courts may perform their duties properly. This is so notwithstanding the fact that the power of appoint-ment may be regarded as more properly an administra-tive or executive power than a judicial or legislative one.[1] In case the courts or the legislature exercise such a power of appointment, it has been held that the act of appointment does not lose its distinctively execu-tive character.[2] In case an appointment is made by a local legislative body, such appointment does not be-come a legislative act, and therefore may not be reconsidered.[3]

The question has in some cases arisen as to whether the power to appoint other officers than those neces-sary to the independence of a department can be given to a department other than the executive. This question has come up particularly in regard to the power of the legislature to make appointments of other than its subordinate officers. The question is some-what complicated by the fact that there has been quite universally inserted into the commonwealth constitu-tions a provision which declares that the governor shall nominate and by and with the consent of the senate appoint all officers whose offices are established by the constitution or shall be created by the law and whose appointment or election is not otherwise pro-

[1] State *vs.* Noble, 118 Ind., 350 ; State *vs.* Barbour, 53 Conn., 76, 85 ; Ach-ley's Case, 4 Abbott's Practice, 35 ; *In re* Janitor, 35 Wis., 410 ; State *vs.* Smith, 15 Mo., App., 412.

[2] See Auditor General *vs.* Pullman Co., 34 Mich., 59.

[3] State *vs.* Barbour, 53 Conn., 76.

vided for. The decisions of the courts as to the possession by the legislature of a power of appointment are in irreconcilable conflict. Some have held that the power of appointing officers other than the subordinates of the department making the appointment is essentially an executive power, and therefore cannot be exercised by the legislature ; that while the legislature has the right, either as a result of its general powers or as a result of the specific constitutional provision referred to, to regulate the manner in which an office is to be filled, since such regulation is a legislative act, it does not have the right to put a man into a given place, inasmuch as this is an executive act and may not therefore be performed by the legislature.[1] The majority of decided cases have adopted the view, however, that the general power of appointment may be exercised by the legislature. The logical basis for such a view would seem to be that executive power under the constitution is of an extremely limited nature, and is not intended to include all powers usually designated as executive by constitutional writers, but is to embrace only those powers which are stated in the constitution itself to belong to the executive. The enumeration of the specific powers to be exercised by the executive is by these cases regarded as a limitation and definition of the general grant to the executive of the executive power.[2] Where such an interpretation is given to the distributing clause in the constitution, a constitutional provision, which would seem to give to the governor the power of appointment and to the legislature the right to designate

[1] See State *vs.* Denny, 118 Ind., 382 ; see also State *vs.* Hyde, 121 Ind., 20.
[2] Field *vs.* People, 3 Ill., 79, 110.

the manner in which offices shall be filled, permits the legislature not only to prescribe the way in which offices shall be filled but also to designate the agent or person who shall be appointed.[1] Undoubtedly one of the reasons for such a decision is that, if the executive has only such powers as are specifically granted to him, the legislature has, as a result of its position as the one authority of general powers in our government, the power to do anything which it has not been forbidden to do, and which has not been specifically entrusted to some other authority.

The same question has also come up with regard to the courts. It has been held that the legislature may authorize the courts to appoint such officers as bridge commissioners and inspectors of elections, *i. e.,* officers having nothing whatever to do with the administration of justice.[2] On the other hand, in Massachusetts and Michigan the contrary rule has been adopted.[3]

The power of removal has also caused some trouble. It is not regarded as possessed by the executive as a result of the grant to him of the executive power by the constitution. Where it is not expressly or impliedly provided that the governor may remove an officer, such officer may be declared to have forfeited or abandoned his office only as the result of a judgment of a court.[4] This rule is not, however, applied to the

[1] See People *vs.* Freeman, 22 Pacific Reporter, 173 ; see also State *vs.* Keenan, 7 Ohio St., 546.

[2] State *vs.* George, 22 Oregon, 142 ; People *vs.* Hoffmann, 116 Ill., 587.

[3] Supervisors of Elections, 114 Mass., 249 ; Houseman *vs.* Montgomery, 58 Mich., 364.

[4] State *vs.* Pritchard, 36 N. J. L., 101 ; Page *vs.* Hardin, 8 B. Munroe, 648 ; Curry *vs.* Stewart, 8 Bush, 560 ; **Hyde** *vs.* State, 52 Miss., 665 ; Honey *vs.* Graham, 39 Texas, 1.

President of the United States, who is regarded as possessing the power of removing even officers appointed by him in conjunction with the senate and who by statute have a fixed term.[1] It is, however, not generally considered that the removal of an officer for neglect of duty is such an intrinsically judicial act, even where the removal can be made for cause only and after a hearing, that the power to remove may not be delegated to the governor or other administrative body by the legislature.[2]

Another power, which has been recognized as belonging to all the departments, which is somewhat judicial in character is the power to make investigations and incidentally to summon witnesses, who may in most cases be imprisoned for contempt for refusal to testify. There is some discussion, as will be shown later, as to the power of the legislature to act in this manner, but the better rule would seem to be that the legislatures of the various commonwealths may appoint commissions to investigate matters for the purpose of future legislation, which commissions may summon witnesses and punish them for contempt in case of their refusing to answer proper questions.[3] A power to provide for investigations has been recognized as existing also in the President.[4]

Fourth. The legislature may delegate its legislative powers. We have already considered the power

---

[1] Parsons *vs.* U. S., 167 U. S., 324; for the difference between the national and state systems, see Field *vs.* People, 3 Ill., 79.

[2] State *vs.* Prince, 45 Wis., 610; Keenan *vs.* Perry, 24 Texas, 253; *Ex parte* Wylie, 54 Ala., 226; State *vs.* Frazier, 48 Ga., 137; Donahue *vs.* County of Will, 100 Ill., 94.

[3] People *ex rel.* Keeler *vs.* McDonald, 99 N. Y., 463; see also *In re* Chapman, 166 U. S., 661.

[4] See 4 Opinions Attorneys-General, 248.

which the legislature has to authorize local corporations to exercise local police ordinance powers, and we saw that such action is perfectly proper. The question has, however, arisen as well as to the power of the legislature to delegate its powers of general legislation to executive or administrative authorities.[1]

It is difficult to state any general rule upon this point. It may be said, however, that numerous decisions have recognized the right of the legislature to authorize the executive officers of the central government both of the United States and of the separate states to regulate the administrative details of their departments, and some have gone so far as to recognize that it is proper under such an authorization for such officers to issue regulations which are binding upon not merely subordinate officers but also upon individuals, who may be punished for the violation of these regulations.[2]

It will be seen from what has been said that the principle of the separation of powers as a rule of law is not by any means so rigid as it is sometimes regarded. The courts have, in developing it in its detailed applications, been guided both by historical traditions and considerations of political expediency in the desire to adapt a doctrine of French political philosophy to the needs of a system of government which had its roots in an English past.

---

[1] It may be laid down as a general principle that the legislature may not delegate to the people its general legislative powers. Oberholtzer, *The Referendum in America*, 208, 217. Barto *vs.* Himrod, 8 N. Y., 483.

[2] This matter will be taken up later under the topics of " The Chief Executive " and " The Executive Departments," p. 138, which see.

CHAPTER V.

THE principle of the separation of powers not only involves the existence of three somewhat separate authorities, but also insists that each authority shall be independent of the other authorities, But just as it is impossible to distinguish clearly three powers and authorities of government, so it is impossible that any governmental authority shall be absolutely independent of other governmental authorities. As administrative law has to do with the position of the executive, it is necessary that we ascertain the actual relations of the executive with the other authorities in the government.

I.—Relation to the legislature.

1. *The legislature the regulator of the administration.*—In all countries the action of the executive is subject to the control of the legislature. In the first place, the legislature has power to lay down rules in accordance with which the executive and administrative authorities are to act. The legislature has been called the regulator of the administration.[1] This is true in the United States to a degree unknown

[1] Sarwey, *Allgemeines Verwaltungsreeht*, 37.

in any other country. In the United States, the legislature specifies in detail the powers to be exercised by the executive authorities, and regulates the exercise of these powers in most particulars.[1] It does so, not because minute regulation is of the essence of legislative power, but because of the position in which the executive has been placed as a result of English and American historical development. English and Americans have not recognized the executive department — notwithstanding judicial statements to the contrary — as co-ordinate with the legislative or even with the judiciary. Further, the original administrative organization in England was not, and the present administrative organization in the United States, apart from the national government, is not, hierarchical in character. That is, while the powers of the various officers differ in degree and in territorial extent, the less important administrative officers are not, in the absence of laws to that effect— and these laws are quite rare,—subjected to the control and supervision of the more important administrative officers. Each officer is within the law to act in accordance with his own views of what is right and proper. The allegiance and responsibility of each officer are to the law and not to some administrative superior. This system of administration is spoken of as a government of law and not of men. The superior or rather the more important administrative officers having little or no power of direction or control over the less important administrative officers, the legislature must necessarily determine in detail all the powers and duties of the administrative authorities.

[1] Freund, "American Administrative Law," *P. S. Q.*, vol. ix., p. 403.

The principle of specialization of powers without adminstrative or executive control imposes on the legislature functions which are really administrative in character. The restriction of specific official authority often so narrows the scope of a statute that it becomes really an administrative act. The legislature thus becomes in a certain sense the central administrative authority. The result of such a system has been to introduce politics into administration. This has been inevitable because the body, which not only theoretically has general control over administration but also actually is exercising a very minute and detailed control over it through the passage of special legislation, is of necessity dominated by political parties. The evil effect which this special legislation has had upon administrative efficiency has been so great that the attempt has been made, in a large number of state constitutions, to prohibit the passage by the legislature of special legislation with regard to a series of subjects where such legislation is seen to have bad results.[1]

Where, on the contrary, we find a hierarchical administrative organization with superior and inferior officers and a large power in the former of control and direction over the latter, we find a different relation between the administration and the legislature. The statutes of the legislature lay down general rules of conduct, leaving to the superior administrative officers to elaborate those rules in their details. In those governments where, like the United States national government, the conception of the executive power is not a broad one, these ordinances are issued by the

[1] *Infra*, p. 172.

executive as a result, not of the exercise of a supplementary ordinance power, whose possession by the
executive is recognized by the constitution, but rather
as a result of the delegation to the executive by
the legislature of a power of ordinance over specific subjects.   Such a delegation of power is not regarded as violating the principle of the separation of
powers.[1]

While in both the national and the state administrative systems the legislature is, in constitutional
theory, the regulator of the administration, still, as a
result of historical development, which has brought it
about that the administrative organization in the one
is centralized, in the other decentralized, we find the
national executive much more powerful, much more
important, and much more independent of legislative
regulation as to details than the state executive.   The
rule that the legislature is the regulator of the administration does not mean, in the case of the national
government, that the executive may act only in the
execution of the law, and that it possesses no discretion, as is largely the case with the state executives.
On the contrary, it has been held that there is a
sphere in which the administration may move without
looking to the statutes for authorization.   " Perhaps
the best general statement of the present situation in
this question is the following quotation from an attorney-general's opinion, which is paraphrased from

---

[1] A marked exception to the general principle that the President has the
power to issue only those ordinances which the Congress of the United States
has authorized him to issue, is found in the case of the Army and Navy Regulations.   These regulations, it has been held, may be issued by the President as
a result of the exercise of his constitutional powers as commander-in-chief of
the army and navy. *Infra*, p. 85.

a Supreme Court opinion in reference to the authority
of the head of a department :

> The President ' is limited in the exercise of his powers by the
> constitution and the laws, but it does not follow that he must
> show a statutory provision for everything he does. The govern-
> ment could not be administered upon such contracted principles.
> The great outlines of the movements of the executive may be
> marked out and limitations imposed upon the exercise of his
> powers. Yet there are numberless things which must be done
> which cannot be anticipated and defined, and are essential to
> useful and healthy action of government.' " [1]

Further, it is generally recognized that there is in
the President a latent power of discretionary action
which is denominated the " war power," and which is,
in times of extraordinary danger, capable of great
expansion.[2]

It is seen thus that while the legislature is the
regulator of the administration, still in the national
government of the United States there is a realm of
action in which the executive authority possesses
large discretion. In the separate states of the United
States also the constitutions often confer large discretionary powers on the governors. The mere fact
that many of the governors have the right to disapprove the resolutions of the legislature gives them an
opportunity to modify the action of the legislature as
the regulator of the administration, and to prevent its
making use of what are really administrative powers

[1] 6 Opinions Attorneys-General, pp. 10 and 365 ; 8 *ibid.*, p. 343 ; 10 *ibid.*, p.
413 ; *cf.* United States *vs.* McDaniel, 7 Peters 14 ; cited from Fairlie, " The
Administrative Powers of the President," *Michigan Law Review*, vol. ii., p.
203 : see also *Digest of Decisions of the Judge-Advocate-General of the Army*,
1901, p. 713, and *In re* Neagle, 135 U. S., i., particularly 64–68.

[2] *Cf.* Dunning, " The Constitution in Civil War," *P. S. Q.*, vol. i., p. 163.

to the disadvantage of the state. This it is prone to do, because it is not amenable to direct control, and it does not therefore feel so direct a sense of responsibility.

2. *The control of the legislature :*—Further, besides regulating the action of the administration, the legislature exercises a direct control over the administration to keep it within the law. The extent of this control depends very largely upon the degree to which the executive is dependent in tenure upon the legislature. In the United States, both in the national and the state governments, the executive is independent in tenure of the legislature, with the single exception that it may be removed as a result of impeachment for absolute corrupt and illegal action. The result is that the control of the legislature over the executive in the United States is comparatively slight. Owing to the slight control which the legislature has over the executive, the necessary harmony between the making and the execution of the law has to be secured outside of the governmental system. The attempt is made to secure it through the political party which, as a result of political necessity, has obtained during our century or more of political development great strength.[1]

II.—*Relation to the courts.*

The executive authorities are subject also to the control of the courts. The extent and character of the control which the courts may exercise over the executive authorities depend upon the character of

[1] See Ford, *The Rise and Growth of American Politics*, p. 215 ; see also Macy, *Party Organization and Machinery*, passim.

the act which it is sought to control. From the point of view of this control, the acts of the executive authorities may be classed as political and non-political acts.

1. *Political acts.*—By political acts are meant those acts, whether of general or of special application, done by the administration in the discharge of its political functions, such as the carrying on of the diplomatic relations of the country, the making of treaties, the command and disposition of the military forces, and the government and conduct of the relations of the executive with the legislature. Over such acts the courts have no powers of control. The principle of popular responsibility which has been adopted, it is believed, will be sufficient to ensure the impartial and wise performance of these political acts.[1]

2. *Non-political acts.*—The non-political acts of the executive are either general in their application when they are spoken of as legislative acts, or are special in their application when they are known by no one generic name. They may, however, be classified as contractual acts and administrative acts of special application.

1st. *Legislative acts.*—The legislative acts of the executive are to be found in the ordinances which it has the power to issue. The courts have the same power over them as they have over the statutes of the legislature—that is, they may interpret them, and in most cases declare them void or refuse to enforce them in case they are contrary to the law. Further, in the case of ordinances issued by local authorities as

[1] Luther *vs.* Borden, 7 Howard U. S., 1 ; Miss. *vs.* Johnson, 4 Wallace, 475.

a result of the exercise by such authorities of a general ordinance power, the control of the courts is somewhat greater. In such cases the courts may declare an ordinance void because they believe it to be unreasonable.[1]

2d. *Contractual acts.*—The tendency at the present time is to recognize that the courts have much the same power over the contractual acts of the executive authorities as they have over the contractual acts of individuals and private corporations. So far as these acts are the acts of the local corporations which have been established by the state governments, the control of the courts is complete. In the case, however, of the central officers of the state governments and the officers of the national government, the control of the courts is limited because of the adoption of the rule that no one can sue the government except with its consent. In some cases the national government and the states have given their consent to the bringing of suits in contract against them in the ordinary courts, while in the case of the national government and one or two states, a special court, called the Court of Claims, has been formed for the purpose of deciding certain or all such suits.[2]

3d. *Administrative acts of special application.*— We have no general term for these acts. They are called sometimes orders, sometimes decisions, precepts, or warrants. By the performance of these acts the executive authorities perform most of their duties, and in the performance of these acts they are coming continually into conflict with the individuals over whom they have jurisdiction. Some sort of a

[1] *Infra*, p. 327.   [2] *Ibid.*, p. 386.

control over these acts is therefore necessary. In the United States the rule is that when an individual act of the administration is not of a political or a contractual character, the courts have a very large control over it. In many cases they may annul it, amend it, interpret it, and prevent the administration from proceeding to execute it.[1]

III.—The position of the executive.

It is now possible, after this consideration of the relations of the executive authority with the legislature and the courts, to ascertain what its position is in the governmental system. It may be said that the executive is within the law, which may and often does descend into great detail, almost altogether independent of the legislature, and that its acts, not of a political or contractual character, are subject in many cases to the control of the courts which are to keep it within the limits of the law.

The independence of the executive over against the legislature has an important effect, both upon the position of the executive in the general political system, and on that of the political party through which the government is carried on. The independence of the executive over against the legislature makes it possible for the executive to exercise a strong personal influence, both on the making of law through the exercise of the veto power—that is, upon the expression of the state will—and upon the execution of law through his distinctly executive powers. The legislature, as legislature, can not deprive him of his

---

[1] *Infra*, p. 92.

office, and can exercise little influence over his conduct in the enforcement of the law or in the use of his
distinctly political powers.

This independent position, however, affords opportunity for conflict between the executive and the
legislature. Such opportunity for conflict is increased
by the fact that the legislature and the executive are
not commonly elected for the same term. It may
thus happen that an executive who is in accord with
the legislature at the time of his accession to office,
will be out of harmony with it at about the middle of
his term, owing to the result of the legislative elections which may take place at that time. Further,
on account of the difference in the methods of election, an executive and a legislature not in harmony
may be elected at the same election. No means is
provided in the governmental system for settling
any such conflict that may arise. The result is that
the political party which carries on the government
strives to secure the harmony necessary between the
executive and the legislature by electing a legislature
and an executive of the same political faith. To do
this the party must have not only a strong but a
permanent organization. It must have a strong organization, since it must see to it not merely that
members of the legislature of its political faith are
elected, but also that an executive in accord with the
legislature is elected. The political party must have
a permanent organization, because it must struggle
not merely at the time when a legislature is elected,
but also at the time that the executive is elected. The
relations of the national and state politics are so
close that the party must take action practically every

year, and must therefore have a permanent organization if it hopes to win.

This great strength and this permanence of the political party organization cannot fail to have great influence on the actual position of the executive in the political system. From the point of view of legal theory, independent of the legislature, the executive is, from the point of view of actual political practice, under the control of the party which has put him in office and one of whose leaders he is. The independence of the executive, which appears so great upon a consideration of the constitution, disappears when we consider his position from the point of actual political practice. The needs of practical political life take from the executive his independence and render him responsible to an extra-governmental organization.

This political dependence of the executive has its advantages and its disadvantages. Provided the political parties are reasonably responsive to the public will, responsible executive government is assured and conflicts of long standing between the executive and the legislature are prevented. The executive also is permanent enough to ensure a reasonably permanent policy. It cannot be denied, however, that the executive is liable to great temptation to use his powers in the interest of the party he represents in the hope of thereby aiding and securing a legislature which will support him and it. If, either by provision of law or as a result of public opinion, the administrative side of the executive power is not recognized as a matter which should not be subjected to the control of politics, the efficiency of the administration is liable to suffer and the attempt is likely to be made by the executive to influence improperly the expression of the state will, so that the formal expression of that will may not be in accord with the real state will.

CHAPTER VI.

*I. — Participation of local communities in adminis-
tration.*

All states of any size must be divided into districts
in order that the work of many branches of government may be satisfactorily carried on.   Thus, for the
purpose of the administration of justice there must
be districts in each of which are situated judicial officers having jurisdiction over the district.   Further,
almost all states of any size are based, from the historical point of view at least, more or less on the
federal idea.   This is as true of a number of the
states of the United States as it is of other countries.
Thus, the state of Connecticut really resulted from a
combination of the various settlements which were
made within the limits of the present state.   In many
states, however, the growth of the lowest local units,
like the towns into the counties, and that of the counties into the state, is not clear.   In some states,
indeed, the state antedates the local districts.   At
the same time, in most instances the state makes the
most important districts into which it is divided for
purposes of state government something more than

55

mere administrative districts. It endeavors to encourage within them the development of a local life of their own, separate and apart from the life of the state. It vests them with powers to satisfy local needs and not infrequently delegates to them, or to officers chosen by the inhabitants of each of the districts, the power to act in certain branches of administration which are of peculiar interest to the state as a whole, and interest only indirectly the people of such district. In so far as the state grants powers to its local divisions, or vests the officers chosen by the people of such divisions with governmental authority, the administrative system is called a decentralized one,—one of local self-government. In so far as the state does not adopt such a policy, that is, in so far as the state reserves to its own officers the power to act in the execution of the law or subjects the officers of the local communities—if such are recognized—to the supervision and control of state officers in the execution of the law, the administrative system is called a centralized one.

The establishment of the system actually adopted may be secured in one of two ways : where there is a written constitution, this may set apart to the state government on the one hand and to each of the local governments on the other hand its sphere of action ; where there is no written constitution, this apportionment of the work of government will be done by the state legislature.

Whichever method may be adopted, it may be said that the prevailing public opinion at a given time will in the end control the situation which actually exists, constitutional provisions to the contrary notwithstanding. For if the attempt is made in the constitution to insure to the state more than is its due,—that is, more than is recognized as proper by the prevailing public opinion,—extra-legal forces come into play which may really nullify the provisions of the constitution as actual rules of conduct. For example, if the state assumes to itself to provide the same regulations for the moral conduct of all of its inhabitants, regardless of the difference in the moral standards which may exist in the different parts of the state, it may find itself unable, notwithstanding the most centralized system of administration, to enforce its will in certain districts of the state. This has been the almost universal result in cities, where a state has attempted to adopt and enforce, even through state agency, a law absolutely prohibiting the sale of liquor. On the other hand, the attempt to vest the localities with powers which really interest the whole state may, indeed probably will, result in the state political parties taking control of the local governments and managing them in the interest of the state. Thus cities in the United States are made the agents of the state governments in a large variety of matters. The state political parties strive, under such conditions, to get control of the city government if the work performed by the cities is regarded by them as interesting the fortunes of the state as a whole.

If we look at this matter from the point of view of theoretical speculation, we shall find it impossible to lay down many general rules as to what subjects of government should be decentralized in the sense in which this word has already been used. At the same time there are certain kinds of governmental activity in which the local communities can, in the nature of things, not participate at all. This is true of that branch of administration which has been spoken of as the administration of foreign relations. Further, in certain other administrative branches the demand for uniformity is so imperious, the interests of the state as a whole are so vitally concerned that, if the localities are permitted to act at all, they must act subject to the control of the state government. This is true of the administration of military, judicial, and financial affairs. In these branches of administration the localities cannot be permitted to have any powers of independent action but must—where they are permitted to act at all—be regarded as agents of the central government and subject to its control.

The result of this process of exclusion is to cause us to conclude that the sphere of local administrative autonomy, if recognized at all, is to be found in that branch of administration which has been spoken of as the administration of internal affairs. Even in this branch of administration, as in the other branches mentioned, in many cases the localities must, for reasons already stated, be subjected to the control of the central government. Thus, the administration of the public health and public charity, and the preservation of the peace, cannot be left to localities acting free of all central control.

What shall be the spheres of central and local administrative action in a given state, and what shall be the kind and extent of central control exercised over the localities where they are regarded as the agents of the central government, are matters to be determined by the positive law of the state. The determinations reached by the different states differ considerably one from the other, and are based upon the different social and political conditions obtaining therein.

II.—The Anglo-American method for providing for the participation of the local communities in the work of administration.

Attention has already been called to the fact that one of the fundamental principles of the Anglo-American administrative law is the statutory enumeration in detail of the powers of administrative authorities. Inasmuch as the local communities are, from the point of view of the law, administrative authorities, it naturally follows that the powers which they may exercise—in other words, the degree of their participation in the work of government, and the ways in which they may so participate—are fixed in detail in the statutes of the legislature. The localities are, no more than any administrative authority, recognized as possessing any sphere of independent action. They may, it is true, be regarded as local corporations, with the power of owning property and of suing and being sued, but they have no sphere of action of their own, and are regarded simply as districts of the state. The officers who act for them are, in many cases, merely agents of the central government acting in local divisions. The position of the most important local corporations in the United States is well brought out in the cases of Hamilton County *vs.* Mighels,[1] and Lorillard *vs.* The Town of Monroe.[2] In the first case the court says that the

[1] 7 Ohio State, 109.   [2] 11 New York, 392.

county is merely a division of the state for the purpose of general state administration; in the latter
case the court holds that "town officers," such as
assessors and collectors, are state officers and not
officers of the town corporation for whose action the
town is pecuniarily responsible.

The cities are, from this point of view, in about the
same position as these quasi-corporations, as towns
and counties are called. Their powers are generally
enumerated, and it cannot be said that they have by
the ordinary constitutions or statutes many powers
of independent local action.[1]

Under such a system of legislative enumeration of
local powers the needs of uniform administration are,
it is thought, satisfied by the exercise by the legislature of its power to change the duties and to increase
or decrease the powers of the localities. The resulting continuing interference of the legislature with
matters which might better be attended to by the
localities, has had such evil results in the United
States that the attempt has in some cases been made
to limit, in the state constitution, the powers of special and local legislation possessed by the legislature.
This method of regarding the localities as in all cases
the agents of the central state government, and of
enumerating in detail their powers and duties, makes
it seem unnecessary to form any further central state

---

[1] See United States *vs*. B. & O. Railroad Co., 17 Wallace, 322. Here the
Supreme Court of the United States says : " A municipal corporation   .   .   .
is a representative, not only of the state, but is a portion of its governmental
power. It is one of its creatures made for a specific purpose, to exercise within
a limited sphere the powers of the state. The state   .   .   .   may govern the
local territory as it governs the state at large. It may enlarge or contract its
powers or destroy its existence."

control over the localities. The control over the localities and local officers is thus a legislative control.

While localities and local officers are thus subjected to a very extensive legislative control, they possess, however, large freedom of action from the administrative point of view; that is, if the law permits them to act they are seldom subject to the control, direction, or supervision of any state administrative officer. While this freedom from central administrative control gives them, as a matter of fact, large power in the execution of the law to modify it so as to suit local conditions, and even in some instances to nullify it where the local will differs from the state will, it does not give them any powers of a positive character. This absence of positive power is due to the fact that, while in many instances it is beyond the power of the courts to force a local officer to take action in the enforcement of a law which is unpopular in the particular locality, the courts can in a proper case declare illegal an act of a locality or of a local officer in excess of power.

The Anglo-American method of permitting the localities to participate in the work of government may be characterized, therefore, as one of legislative centralization and administrative decentralization. It is, however, to be noticed that the essential defects of such a system, which are, as has been intimated, the ineffectiveness of the state control and the narrowness of the sphere of local action, have resulted in a number of the states in quite a modification of the original system. Thus we find that constitutional provisions have been adopted which have guaranteed to certain of the localities quite a degree of local power. We also find that the tendency in almost all of the states which have reached a high degree of social development is to subject the actions of local officers more or less to central administrative control.

III.—*Sphere of central administration.*

As has been indicated, there are certain branches of administration where in the nature of things the local communities cannot act at all or cannot act to the same advantage as the central administration. For these branches the central government forms a series of offices unconnected in any way with the local corporations. The tendency in the United States has of late years been to increase the number of such administrative services attended to by the central government. Thus the customs and the indirect taxes, from the proceeds of which the expenses of the national government are largely provided, were at one time in the history of the country (that is, during the Colonial and Confederate period) often attended to by local officers,[1] but are now entrusted to officers of the national government. In the states, such matters as factory inspection, railroad supervision, and certain branches of public charity are attended to by state officers who are in no way connected with the local corporations. In other cases, while the local communities are permitted to act, they are subjected to a central administrative control.[2]

---

[1] See "History of Tariff Administration in the United States," by John D. Goss, in *Columbia College Studies in History, Economics, and Public Law,* vol. i., part 2, pp. 12 and 15.

[2] See Webster, "Recent Centralizing Tendencies in State Educational Administration," *Columbia University Studies of History, Economics, and Public*

As a result of these arrangements we conclude that not only is the function of administration largely separated from the functions of legislation and the rendering of judicial decision, and entrusted in most cases to special authorities, but also that the special authorities entrusted with the function of administration are of two kinds, namely, central and local. Of these two kinds of authorities the central authorities, *i. e.*, the national and state authorities, have to attend to those matters which, by the law of the land, have been recognized as general in character and, where the central control over the localities and local officers is an administrative one, have to exercise that control. The local authorities, on the other hand, act as agents of the central government and are at the same time local corporations. These local authorities are in all cases subject to a central control which is either a legislative or an administrative control.

Law, vol. viii., part 2; Whitten, " Public Administration in Massachusetts," *ibid.*, vol. viii., part 4; Fairlie, " The Centralization of Administration in New York State," *ibid.*, vol. ix., part 3; Sites, " Centralized Administration of Liquor Laws in American Commonwealths," *ibid.*, vol. x., part 3; Orth, " The Centralization of Administration in Ohio," *ibid.*, vol. xvi., part 3; Rawles, " Centralizing Tendencies in the Administration of Indiana," *ibid.*, vol. xvii., part 1; Bowman, " The Administration of Iowa," *ibid.*, vol. xviii., part 1.

BOOK II.

CENTRAL ADMINISTRATION.

CHAPTER I.

THE EXECUTIVE POWER AND THE CHIEF EXECUTIVE AUTHORITY.

I. — The executive power and the executive authority in general.

GREAT difficulty has been found in the determination of the extent and character of the power which shall be entrusted to the chief executive authority. Both practical men and students have always had great difficulty in obtaining a clear conception and an adequate expression in their governmental organization of their conception of the power to be given to the chief executive authority. The cause of this difficulty is twofold : The first cause of difficulty has come from the difficulty of determining the relations of the executive to the legislature. It has been pointed out that the theory of the separation of powers, which has had so much influence on all existing governments, demands that the executive shall be

largely independent of the legislature. Actual political necessity demands that there shall be harmony
between the making and the enforcement of law.
This harmony can be obtained only at the expense
either of legislative independence or executive independence. Either politics, in the sense in which that
word has been used in these pages, must be subjected
to the control of administrative authorities, or administration must be subjected to the control of political
authorities. If this is not the case governmental
paralysis is likely to ensue. The harmony between
politics and administration may be brought about
in the governmental system, or outside of it, through
the more or less voluntary political associations of
the people, or by the moral and social influence
of the executive. Whatever may be the solution of
the problem, it is clear that it is difficult, if not impossible, to define the executive power from the point of
view of theoretical speculation.

Nor is the problem much easier from the purely
legal point of view. The executive power may be
said to be legally the power which in a given state
the executive possesses by the provisions of the positive law. But it is to be remembered that where,
from the point of view of actual facts, the executive is
under the control of extra-legal political bodies, although legally independent of the legislature, the
most important political body in the government, the
powers conceded to the executive in the formal constitution may be much less independently exercised
than the constitution apparently provides. Thus, for
example, in the United States the executive is by the
constitution vested with powers which he is authorized

5

by that instrument to exercise independently of any other governmental authority. At the same time, owing his election as he does to a political party, it is almost always the case that these powers are exercised under the influence, if not the actual control, of the party to which he owes his election.

The second cause of the difficulty of determining what shall be the power entrusted to the chief executive authority is to be found in the failure which is so often made to recognize that what is called the executive power really consists of several functions which are capable of greater or less differentiation. Even if we assign what has been spoken of as the judicial power to a non-executive authority, it is still possible to differentiate two somewhat different executive functions. These are the political function and the administrative function. One of the most noted French writers on administration, M. Aucoc, has as clearly as any one brought out the distinction between these two functions. He says:[1]

When we distinguish government from administration, we mean to put in a special category the direction of all affairs which are regarded as political—that is to say, the relations of the chief executive authority with the great powers of the government: the summoning of electors, for the election of senators and representatives, the closing of the session, the convocation of the chamber of deputies and of the senate, the closing of the senate, the dissolution of the chamber of deputies, the carrying on of diplomatic relations with foreign powers, the disposition of the military forces, the exercise of the right of pardon, the granting of titles of nobility.

All of these matters are political in character in

---

[1] *Conférences sur l'Administration,* etc., i., 78.

that they reflect the general policy of the state. All the actions of the executive authority in regard to them should, if there is to be an effective popular government, be performed as a result of harmonious relations existing between the executive and the legislature as the body entrusted with the determination of state policy. It is eminently proper, indeed it is necessary, that the political party in a popular government should concern itself with these political actions of the executive, with this political or governmental executive function. We may go a step further and embrace within this political function the general supervision of the execution of the law. If the administrative system is centralized, this supervision, so far as subordinate officers are concerned, is thereby made a part of the duties of the executive. If the administrative system is not centralized, the political party will inevitably concern itself with such supervision. In either case the supervision of the execution of the law is political.

Opposed to the political executive function we find the administrative function. To quote M. Aucoc again : [1]

The administrative authority has a mission altogether different. It is charged with providing for the collective needs of the citizens, which the initiative of individuals or associations of individuals could not adequately satisfy. It must gather together the resources of society, both in men and money, in order that society may continue to exist and make progress. It must play the part of the man of business of society, in its management of the various public services, as, for example, in the matter of public works. It must take measures of supervision, and must, through the exercise of foresight, preserve the

[1] *Conférences sur l'Administration, etc.,* i., 78.

property designed for the use of the public; must maintain order and further the general prosperity.

We may add that this administrative work is almost entirely of a scientific, technical, commercial, or quasi-judicial character. Thus the construction and operation of public works require high technical and scientific skill, whether those works are constructed and maintained by governmental authorities or by private corporations or individuals. Thus, again, the maintenance and operation of such an undertaking as the post-office require skill of the same sort as is demanded for the successful conduct of a commercial enterprise. Finally, the determination of the amount of the contribution which each individual must pay to the state as a tax requires the exercise of powers similar in kind to those which are being continually exercised by judicial bodies. In all these cases it will be noticed that there is a great difference between the work which is to be done by the executive and that work which has been referred to as political. In the cases which have just been mentioned, the discharge of its functions by the executive authority should be uninfluenced by political considerations, else the work will be done inefficiently or partially, and it may be corruptly. The more politics gets into the non-political side of administration, the less effective and less impartial will the work of the executive authority be.

Some constitution makers and political scientists have regarded the executive power as composed of only the first of these two functions which it has been attempted to differentiate; others, while recognizing that the executive power is composed of both, have laid such emphasis on one side of the executive power as almost to ignore the necessity of the possession by the chief executive authority of any other power ; while, finally, others have seen that an efficient executive must be an administrator as well as a politician. The different ideas that men have had of that part of the executive power which should be given the greater prominence have thus led to great difference in the determination of the power to be given by the law to the chief executive authority. In some governments we find the executive authority is simply a political chief.[1] This is the position which was originally assigned to the executive authority by the states of the United States. In these states the administrative side of the executive power is often conferred upon a series of officers quite distinct from the chief executive authority and very largely independent of him, who are spoken of in the constitutions as administrative officers. In other governments the political power has been brought largely under the control of the legislature, and the position of the chief executive as an administrator is much more important than his position as a political authority. This is very largely true of Switzerland.[2] Finally, in other governments the chief executive authority has been recognized both as a political authority and as the head of the administration. This is the case, for example, in the United States national government.

---

[1] Even as a political chief the powers of the executive authority often vary greatly. In some the chief executive authority possesses the veto power, in others he does not ; in some he will have a large power of ordinance, in others almost none at all except such as is delegated to him by the legislature, which may be very chary of its delegations.

[2] Lowell, *Government and Parties in Continental Europe*, vol. ii., p. 197.

CHAPTER II.

THE AMERICAN CONCEPTION OF THE EXECUTIVE POWER
IN THE LATTER PART OF THE EIGHTEENTH
CENTURY.

I.—As exemplified by the early state governments.

THE American conception of the executive power
prevailing at the time of the adoption of the United
States constitution corresponded with that part of
the executive power which has been called political.
The great exception to this statement is to be found
in the fact that the carrying on of the foreign relations was not included within the powers of the state
governor. This exception does not, however, prove
that the diplomatic power was not considered a part
of the executive power. The omission of the diplomatic power from among the powers of the governor
was due entirely to the peculiar position of the colonies and later of the states. The care of the foreign relations was not in the governor's hands, simply
because during the colonial period the mother country, and during the existence of the states as sovereign states the Continental Congress, attended to
the matter.

To a similar reason is due the fact that the state
governor did not have very extensive administra-

tive powers. Administrative matters outside of those directly connected with the military powers of the governor had not been attended to by the central colonial government but, in accordance with English principles of local government, by various officers in the local districts of the state who were regarded as local in character and who often at the same time discharged judicial functions. These officers were to act in accordance with laws which descended into the most minute details. Thus executive instructions and orders were unnecessary. In the case of the administrative matters connected with justice, almost the only matters attended to by the governor were embraced in the powers of appointment and removal. The every-day matters of judicial administration were attended to either by the courts themselves or by the officers of the local communities in which the courts had jurisdiction. The facts were the same in the branch of administration known as internal affairs. Here the central colonial government had little to do except to appoint certain of the officers, namely, the justices of the peace and the sheriffs who, after their appointment, attended to these matters in accordance with their own ideas of what was proper. Further, the branch of administration known as internal affairs was really a very small one,—embracing practically only such matters as the preservation of the peace and the care of the poor and of highways. There was thus left only one branch of administration in which the central colonial government had any important powers to exercise ; this was the administration of the central finances. Here on account of the importance of the finances, the question was definitely settled before the Revolution that the legislature should exercise a very important control over the finances if it did not take them into its absolute administration. The legislature claimed and obtained the power to vote all supplies that the government could obtain, to specify in its appropriation acts for what purposes and in what amounts the money it had raised should be expended, and to designate the officer who was to have charge of its collection and disbursement. Further, the localities attended to a great many matters which were of interest to the state as a whole and paid the expenses which attention to these matters necessitated, so that even the financial administration of the central government was not, on the whole, important.

The power of appointment, which has often been regarded as distinctly an executive power, was treated differently in different states, but the conception that it belonged to the governor in the case of other than judicial and local officers was not very clear. In New York, however, the general power of appointment was regarded as one of the governor's powers, but even in New York the governor's power of appointment was subjected to a legislative control. One fact further deserves mention : that is, the governor possessed neither in the colonial nor in the original state government any general ordinance power even to supplement existing law.

The only purely administrative branch attended to by the central colonial and the state government was then the financial administration which was almost entirely within the control of the legislature. The financial administration formed the model which the framers of the new national government tried to copy when they came to build up a great administrative system, but which their successors were forced by circumstances to abandon.

II.—As exemplified by the position of the President.

1. *Original position of the President.*—The constitution of the United States provided for a President in whom the executive power was to be vested.[1] What the meaning of the words " executive power" was in 1787 has just been shown. The grant to the President of the executive power had for its effect that the President was to have military and political power rather than administrative power. The meaning of the words "executive power" is explained by the specific powers granted to the President by the constitution. These are in the main the same powers that were possessed by the state governors; they are the power of military command, the diplomatic power, the limited veto power, and the power of pardon, the power to call an extra session of Congress, to adjourn it in the case of disagreement between the houses, and the power to send a message to Congress. The general grant of the executive power to the President meant little except that the President was to be the authority in the government that was to exercise the powers[2] afterwards

---

[1] Article ii., section 1.

[2] We have few if any judicial determinations as to the meaning of the words " executive power " in the constitution of the United States. We have, however, several cases with regard to the meaning of the same words as they occur in the constitutions of the states which vest the executive power in the governor. The courts have determined that these words when used in the state constitutions mean little, if anything. For example, the Supreme Court of

enumerated as his.   The only other enumerated power of the President is the power of appointment.[1]

Finally, it is to be noted that, in accordance with the American conception of the executive power, the President did not have any general power to issue ordinances, even to supplement existing law.   As a general thing, the only ordinance power which the President may exercise is the power to issue ordinances where the legislature has specifically delegated to him the power to regulate a given subject.[2]   The great exception to the usual rule with regard to the ordinance powers of the President is, that in times of war the war power, which is generally recognized as

Vermont has said : " There are no powers incident to the executive character of a chief magistrate of this state, unless they are obviously necessary to carry into effect some of the powers expressly given." *Ex parte* Holmes, 12 Vermont 631, 635.   In the case of Field *vs.* People, 3 Illinois 79, a similar conclusion was reached.   In the first case mentioned, the court decided that the governor did not have the power to give up a fugitive from justice who had come there from a foreign state, and based its decision largely upon the theory that this power was not expressly vested in the governor and could not, in view of the interpretation which the court put upon the executive power, be regarded as having been granted to the governor as a result of the grant to him of the executive power.   In the Illinois case, the court held that where a power of removal had not been granted to the governor by the constitution, he did not have the right to remove an officer notwithstanding the fact that under the statute such officer would, in the absence of the possession by the governor of such a power of removal, have a life tenure.

[1] Article ii., section 2, paragraph 2, provides that " The President shall nominate and, by and with the advice and consent of the Senate, shall appoint ambassadors, other public ministers or consuls, judges of the Supreme Court, and all other officers of the United States whose appointments are not otherwise provided for and which shall be established by law ; but the Congress may by law vest the appointment of such inferior officers as they may think proper, in the President alone, in the courts of law, or in heads of departments." Paragraph 3 adds : " The President shall have power to fill all vacancies that may happen during the recess of the Senate by granting commissions which shall expire at the end of their next session " ; finally Section 3 gives to the President the power of commissioning all the officers of the United States.

[2] An exception to this rule is to be found in the case of the army and navy regulations, see *infra*, p. 85.

belonging to him, is susceptible of very great expansion, and may be construed, indeed in the past has
been construed, as giving to the President quite an
ordinance power, irrespective of any action taken by
Congress.[1]

It will be seen, from this enumeration of the powers
given to the President, that the conception of the
executive power held by the framers of the national
constitution was what has been spoken of as the
political power and the power of appointment. Beyond the power of appointment the President had, so
far as the express provisions of the constitution were
concerned, no control over the administration at all.

2. *Change in the position of the President.*—But
American development has completely changed this
conception of the President's position. In the first
place, the duty imposed upon the President by the
constitution to see that the laws be faithfully executed,[2] has been construed by Congress as giving it
the power of imposing duties and conferring powers
upon the President by statute, and has led to the
passage of almost innumerable laws which have
greatly increased the importance of the President's
position, and have given him authority relative to the
details of many administrative branches of the national government.[3] Powers as to administrative
details are also recognized as being vested in the
President by the constitution, even in the absence of
such statutes.[4]

[1] See Fisher, "Suspension of Habeas Corpus," *P. S. Q.*, iii., p. 463.
[2] Article ii., section 2.
[3] See Elmes, *Executive Departments*, pp. 13 and 14.
[4] *Supra*, p. 47 ; see also United States *vs.* McDaniel, 7 Peters, 1. Thus in
the case of *In re* Neagle, 135 United States 1, 64, 68, the Supreme Court has

The second cause of the change in the position of the President is to be found in the interpretation of the constitution made by the first Congress relative to the President's power of removing officers. The constitution did not give this power to any authority expressly. The question came up before the first Congress in the discussion of an act organizing the department of foreign affairs. Although there was a difference of opinion in the Congress as to who, under the constitution, possessed the power to remove officers, it was finally decided by the casting vote of the Vice-President as president of the Senate that the power of removal was a part of the executive power, and therefore belonged to the President.[1] This was the recognized construction of the constitution for more than three-quarters of a century, although it did not meet with the approval of some of the most eminent statesmen, and has finally received the approval of the United States Supreme Court.[2] In 1867, however, Congress deliberately reversed its decision, and by the tenure-of-office acts of 1867–9 decided that the constitution had not impliedly or expressly settled this point, and that Congress was therefore the body to decide who possessed the power

held that the President is not limited to the enforcement of acts of Congress, according to their express terms. His power and duty to see that the laws be faithfully executed includes rights and obligations growing out of the constitution itself. As a result of it the President may protect an officer of the United States in the discharge of his duties.

[1] See Fairlie, "The Administrative Powers of the President," *Michigan Law Review*, vol. ii., p. 195. It will be noticed that this view is quite different from that which has been held by the state courts with regard to the power of the governor.

[2] See Parsons *vs.* United States, 167 U. S., 324. Prior to this case this construction was approved by the lower courts in United States *vs.* Avery, Deady, 204.

of removal. Congress then decided that the power of removal of Senate appointees belonged to the President and the Senate. For twenty years this was the law of the land, though no one was able to say, on account of the obscurity of their wording, what was the exact meaning of the tenure-of-office acts. Finally, in 1887, Congress repealed them. The result is that the early interpretation of the constitution must be regarded as the correct one at the present time.[1] Though the tenure-of-office acts had the effect of temporarily weakening the power of the President, the complete power of removal had existed so long as to determine the position of the President in the national government, and has been of incalculable advantage in producing an efficient and harmonious national administration. The benefits which followed the determination of the first Congress on this question, now approved by the Supreme Court, were undoubtedly the reason why the tenure-of-office acts were finally repealed. From this power of removal has been evolved the President's power of direction and supervision over the entire national administration. To it is due the recognition of the possession by the President of the administrative power.

3. *Power of direction.*—The power of direction and control over the national administration, through whose exercise the President has become the chief of the national administration, is hardly recognized

[1] It is true, however, that the tenure-of-office acts were held by the lower courts of the United States to be constitutional, United States *vs.* Avery, Deady, 204, but the present view of Congress, which, since the repeal of the tenure-of-office acts, is practically the same as that which was originally taken, has been approved by the Supreme Court in the Parsons case.

in the constitution. The only provisions from which it may be derived are those which impose upon him the duty to see that the laws be faithfully executed,[1] and permit him to "require the opinion in writing of the principal officer in each of the executive departments upon any subject relating to the duties of their respective offices,"[2] but perusal of the early acts of Congress organizing the administrative system of the United States will show that the first Congress did not have the idea that the President had any power of direction over any matters not political in character. The acts of Congress organizing the departments of foreign affairs and war did, it is true, expressly give the President the power of directing the principal officers of these departments how they should perform their duties, but these were departments of a political character. The act organizing the Treasury Department[3] contains no reference to any presidential power of direction. It simply says that the secretary of the treasury shall generally perform all such services relative to the finances as he shall be directed to perform, and the context shows that reference is made to the direction of Congress and not to that of the President. The debates in Congress corroborate this view. Further, the fact that the secretary of the treasury, different from the other secretaries, is to make his annual report not to the President but to Congress, shows that Congress intended, after the manner of the states, to keep the finances under the control of the legislature.

The administration of the finances, which it has

---

[1] Article ii., section 2, paragraph 1.   [2] Article ii., section 2, paragraph 1.
[3] September 2, 1789.

been shown was really almost the only non-political branch attended to by the central government of the states, served the men of those times as a model for the purely administrative branches. Thus the post-office was organized at first in such a way as to remove it from the control of the President. The appointment of all officers in the post-office was given to the postmaster-general, while the law which finally organized the department in 1825 had nothing whatever to say about a presidential power of direction. The original absence of this power of direction is commented upon by one of the United States courts. The court says[1]:

> The legislature may prescribe the duties of the office at the time of its creation, or from time to time as circumstances may require. If those duties are absolute and specific, and not by law made subject to the control or discretion of any superior officer, they must be performed, whether forbidden or not, by any other officer. If there be no other officer who is by law specially authorized to direct how the duties are to be performed, the officer whose duties are thus prescribed by law is bound to execute them according to his own judgment. That judgment cannot lawfully be controlled by any other person. . . . As the head of an executive department he [the postmaster-general] is bound, when required by the President, to give his opinion in writing upon any subject relating to the duties of his office. The President, in the execution of his duty to see that the laws be faithfully executed, is bound to see that the postmaster-general discharges "faithfully" the duties assigned to him by law ; but this does not authorize the President to direct him how he shall discharge them.[2]

[1] United States *vs.* Kendall, 5 Cranch C. C., 163, 272,

[2] See also Kendall *vs.* United States, 12 Peters, 524, 610, where Mr. Justice Thompson says : "It by no means follows that every officer in every branch of that [the executive] department is under the exclusive direction of the

The court admits, however, that the President might remove the postmaster-general from office, and it is from this power of removal that we must derive any power that the President has to direct and control the acts of officials in those departments where the law has not expressly provided for the direction and control of the President. The influence upon the position of the President of his power of removal was made manifest at an early time in the history of the country. Notwithstanding the independent position in which Congress had attempted to place the secretary of the treasury, President Jackson was able, through his power of removal, to exercise a power of direction as effectually over the head of the treasury department as over the head of any other department of the government. The celebrated United States Bank episode is good evidence of the actual power which the President possessed. It will be remembered that when Jackson desired to weaken the position of the United States Bank he ordered the secretary of the treasury to withdraw the deposits of the government from the bank. The secretary refused to do so, was removed from office, and a secretary was appointed who was willing to obey the orders of the President. Jackson's action was regarded by many as improper and was actually censured by the Senate but afterwards this censure was expunged from the record, and the Senate at least must be regarded as having acquiesced in the view which the President

President. . . . It would be an alarming doctrine that Congress cannot impose upon any executive officer any duty they may think proper, which is not repugnant to any rights secured and protected by the constitution, and in such cases the duty and responsibility grow out of and are subject to the control of the law and not to the direction of the President."

took of his relations even to those departments which were accorded the most independent position.

Of so much force was this power of removal that in 1855, less than twenty years after the giving of the decision in United States *vs.* Kendall, to which reference has been made, we find in an opinion of Mr. Cushing, the attorney-general, the following recognition of the power of direction of the President[1]:

I think . . . the general rule to be . . . that the head of department is subject to the direction of the President [this was said in relation to duties imposed by statute upon a head of department]. I hold that no head of department can lawfully perform an official act against the will of the President and that will is, by the constitution, to govern the performance of all such acts. If it were not thus, Congress might by statute so divide and transfer the executive power as utterly to subvert the government and change it into a parliamentary despotism like that of Venice or Great Britain, with a nominal executive chief or President utterly powerless—whether under the name of Doge or King or President would then be of little account so far as regards the question of the maintenance of the constitution.[2]

This is of course an extreme view, and it is probably not meant by it that the President has any dispensing power by which he may relieve an officer from obeying a positive direction of law, since the law, when constitutional, is always above an executive order, but it indicates at any rate the drift of public opinion as to what was considered to be the position which the President occupied.[3]

The effect of recognizing that the President possesses these powers of removal and direction has

[1] 7 Opinions of the Attorneys-General, 453, 470.

[2] See also 2 Opin. Atty.-Gen., 42.

[3] For a modern illustration of the President's power of direction, see F. P. Powers, "Railroad Indemnity Lands," *P. S. Q.*, iv., pp. 452–482.

6

been, as has been said, to give him the administrative power and to make him not merely the political head of the United States national government but as well the head of its administrative system. The result of our national administrative development has been thus a great enlargement of the American conception of the executive power as exemplified in the office of the President. The executive power in the United States national government embraces both the powers of which it may in theory be composed, and the chief executive authority is at the same time the political and the administrative chief of the government and has under his direction and control the actions of all the officers of the national administration.

CHAPTER III.

I.—The President.

It may be said that the executive power possessed by the President of the United States embraces first the political power which is sometimes exercised by and with the advice and consent of the Senate, acting as an administrative council, as, for example, in the case of the making of treaties ; and second, the administrative power which is of especial interest to the student of administrative law. This administrative power consists of two classes of minor powers : first, the powers which relate to the personnel of the administration. These have been discussed in the historical treatment of the President. At the present time they are complete and the President is, therefore, the head of the national administration, with power, directly or indirectly, to appoint (with the consent of the Senate for most important offices), remove, and direct all the subordinate officers in the national administrative system.

In the second place, the President has powers relative to the administrative services themselves,—material rather than personal powers. That is, the

President has the right himself to perform a series of acts in the different branches of administration.

1. *Administrative powers.*—As has already been intimated, the President has a series of what have been called material powers; that is, powers which do not affect personally the officers of the administration. Some of these powers he has as a consequence of some specific provision of the United States constitution, in which case he may exercise these powers independently of any action on the part of Congress. In other cases he has powers as a consequence of the action of Congress, which has enacted that he may take action in certain specified cases. Where he has a power as a consequence of the action of Congress, the extent of the power is to be determined by a consideration of the act of Congress granting the power, and the continued exercise of the power by the President is dependent on the will of Congress, which may, at any time, repeal the act granting the powers. These powers of an administrative and material character may be classified as powers of ordinance and powers to perform acts of special and individual application which affect some particular point in some particular branch of the administration.

First, the ordinance power of the President.—The ordinances which the President may adopt are of two kinds: First, those which are issued simply as a result of the exercise of his power of direction over the officers of the administration and which are sanctioned merely by his power of removal; and second, those ordinances which are intended to have the force of law, which, therefore, will be enforced by the courts and which may bind not merely an officer of the government, but as well an individual who in the proper case may be punished criminally for refusal to obey them. A good instance of the first class of ordinances or general regulations issued by the President is to be found in the civil service rule promulgated in 1896, which forbids the removal for political reasons of officers in the classified civil service of the United States. Such an ordinance the courts regard as a matter of pure administration. They therefore have refused to enforce it and have declared that the only redress open to one who claims that he has been removed contrary to its provisions, is an appeal to the President to remove the offending officer.[1]

In the second place the President issues ordinances which the courts will enforce.[2] Thus the President issues army and navy regulations. The force and effect of such regulations have several times been considered by the Supreme Court, which has held that an officer may be punished even by imprisonment as the result of the adjudication of a court formed in pursuance of such regulations.[3] Regulations of this character, it has been held, also may be made to bind not only officers in the service of the United States, but also private individuals. Thus it has been held that a violation, made by act of Congress

[1] See Carr *vs.* Gordon, 82 Federal Reporter, 373; Taylor *vs.* Kercheval, *ibid.*, 497; Morgan *vs.* Nunn, 84 *ibid.*, 551; White *vs.* Berry, 171 U. S., 366.

[2] See Boske *vs.* Comingore, 177 U. S., 459. Here a collector of internal revenue of the United States was imprisoned for contempt of court by a state court for refusing to produce copies of certain official reports which the regulations of the secretary of the treasury forbade all officers to make use of for any purpose outside of the collection of the revenue. He was on habeas corpus out of the United States courts released from custody and the regulations under which he claimed to act were held to protect him.

[3] *Ex parte* Reed, 100 U. S., 13; Swaim *vs.* United States, 165 U. S., 553.

a misdemeanor, of a regulation which the secretary
of war has been authorized by Congress to make, is
properly punishable criminally.[1]   But in these cases
of the attempt to punish criminally violations of executive regulations, the rule of strict construction is
always followed.   Thus, where a manufacturer of a
taxable product is under a statute punishable for
neglecting to do "any of the things required by law
in the carrying on or conducting of his business," and
no penalty is specially imposed by statute upon him
for not keeping such books and accounts as the commissioner of internal revenue may require, such manufacturer is not liable to be punished criminally for
failure to keep the books required by the commissioner, as a failure to do a thing "required by law"
for which such punishment is generally provided in
the statute.   The court in its opinion in this case
says :

> Regulations prescribed by the President and by the heads of
> departments, under authority granted by Congress, may be regu-
> lations prescribed by law, so as lawfully to support acts done
> under them and in accordance with them, and may thus have, in a
> proper sense, the force of law, but it does not follow that a thing
> required by them is a thing so required by law as to make the
> neglect to do the thing a criminal offence in a citizen, where a
> statute does not distinctly make the neglect in question a criminal
> offence.[2]

Furthermore, such executive regulations, whether
issued by the President or by heads of departments

---

[1] United States *vs.* Breen, 40 Federal Reporter, 402.   See also Caha *vs.*
United States, 152 U. S., 211, where an individual was punished criminally for
having committed perjury before a tribunal established by executive regulation,
a statute of Congress having provided for punishing perjury "before a competent tribunal."

[2] United States *vs.* Eaton, 144 U. S., 677–688.

acting under his direction, must conform to the law, else the courts will refuse to enforce them.[1]

It has sometimes been claimed that the President has the authority to issue certain of these general regulations which bind the citizen as a result of some constitutional power which he possesses. Thus, it is said that certain of the army regulations are issued by the President, not as a result of the exercise of the power delegated by Congress, but as a result of the exercise of his powers as commander-in-chief.[2]

The extent to which the administrative law of the national government is to be found in executive regulations is not ordinarily appreciated.

There are in fact many elaborate systems of executive regulations governing the transaction of business in all the various branches of the administration. These include organized codes of regulations for the army and navy, postal service, the patent office, pension office, the land office, the Indian service, the customs, internal revenue, and revenue cutter service, the consular service, and the rules governing examinations and appointments to the whole subordinate civil service, and in addition to these systematized rules there is an enormous mass of individual regulations, knowledge of which is limited to the few persons who have to apply them and to those whom they affect.[3]

A power somewhat akin to that of ordinance is the power to determine by presidential proclamation the existence of states of fact when certain laws, up to

[1] See Morrill *vs.* Jones, 106, U. S., 466. Here Congress gave the secretary of the treasury the power to issue regulations relative to the importation free of duty of animals imported for breeding purposes. A regulation confining the importation to animals of superior stock was held to be not in conformity to law and was not enforced. See also Merritt *vs.* Welsh, 104 U. S., 694.

[2] See *In re* Smith, 23 Ct. of Cl., 452, 459, and also United States *vs.* Eliason, 16 Peters, 291, 301. See also Wyman, *Administrative Law*, p. 287 *et seq.*

[3] Fairlie, " The Administrative Power of the President," *Michigan Law Review*, vol. ii., pp. 190–205.

then held in abeyance, will at once go into effect. A marked instance of the exercise of such a power is to be found in the proclamations issued by the President as a result of the use of the power granted to him by the reciprocity clause of the tariff act of 1890. This act provided that if the President should determine that certain countries were not treating the United States fairly he should issue a proclamation to that effect, and that in that case the free list as to such countries should be suspended; and certain rates of duty provided for in the act of Congress should at once be imposed on the articles imported from such countries. The grant of such a power to the president is held constitutional by the Supreme Court.[1] The Supreme Court, by a majority vote, determined that the grant of such a power to the President was not a delegation of legislative power; for, as the court said:

> Congress itself prescribed in advance the duties to be levied . . . The words 'he may deem' . . . implied that the President would examine the commercial regulations of other countries . . . and form a judgment as to whether they were reciprocally equal and reasonable, or the contrary, in their effect upon American products. But when he ascertained the fact that duties and exactions reciprocally unequal and unreasonable were imposed . . . it became his duty to issue a proclamation, declaring the suspension as to that country which Congress had determined should occur. . . . The President was the mere agent of the law-making department to ascertain and declare the event upon which its express will was to take effect.[2]

The delegation of legislative power to the President was regarded by the whole court as unconstitutional,

[1] Field *vs.* Clark, 143 U. S., 649; see also, the Brig *Aurora*, 7 Cranch, 382.
[2] Cited from Fairlie, "The Administrative Power of the President."

—a doctrine which, to say the least, is difficult of reconciliation with the view the court has taken in other cases as to the constitutionality of executive regulations.

Second, power to perform special acts of individual application. The constitutional power of the President to see that the laws be faithfully executed has been construed, as has been pointed out, as giving the President a somewhat undefined power which may be exercised independently of any action upon the part of Congress.[1] As a result of the exercise of such a power the President may perform acts of special and individual application. Thus he may order that protection be afforded to a judge of the Supreme Court on circuit, and any one acting upon such an order will be protected from prosecution by state authority, even for so serious a charge as murder.[2]

In addition to the acts performed as a result of the exercise of his constitutional powers, the President also has, as a result of the exercise of powers vested in him by Congress by special statutory provisions, the right to do a long series of acts which affect only a single case. Thus, Congress has authorized the President to permit an advance of money to disbursing officers[3]; to reserve from settlement such portion of the public lands as in his judgment is valuable as the site of a future military post.[4] An enumeration of such cases would be both tedious and unprofitable, but a large part of the work of the national administration is performed as the result of the exercise of such powers.

[1] See *In re* Neagle, 135 U. S., 1.
[2] *Ibid.*
[3] Williams *vs.* United States, 1 Howard, 290.
[4] See Wilcox *vs.* Jackson, 13 Peters, 498.

In the exercise of the powers granted to, and the performance of the duties imposed upon, the President by the constitution or statutes of Congress, it is not necessary that the President act personally. Performance by the head of an executive department is regarded as performance by the President, who is considered as acting through the heads of departments and as responsible for what they do.[1] The only exceptions to this statement are to be found in the case of acts of vast political importance, such as the suspension of the privilege of the writ of habeas corpus, and acts of a judicial character. In the case of the first class of acts it has been intimated that the President must act by proclamation and that a general order of the war department may not be regarded by the courts as the act of the President where such order purports to suspend the privilege of the writ of habeas corpus.[2] In the case of judicial acts it has been held that if the performance of the act is by the statute entrusted to the President he must act personally,[3] but where the record of a court-martial shows that the sentence of the court has been approved by the President as provided in the statute, such a statement shows sufficient compliance with the statute, although the record does not show that the President actually affixed his signature to the approval of the sentence.[4]

---

[1] Wilcox *vs.* Jackson, 13 Peters, 498, 513; United States *vs.* Eliason, 16 Peters, 291; Confiscation Cases, 20 Wallace, 92, 109.

[2] *Ex parte* Field, 5 Blatchford, 63.

[3] Runkle *vs.* United States, 122 U. S., 543, 556.

[4] United States *vs.* Page, 137 U. S., 673–678. See on the general subject of the delegation of powers by the President and heads of departments, Wyman, *Administrative Law*, p. 204 *et seq.*

It has been held that the power of direction and supervision is always accompanied by the correlative right of appeal.[1] The doctrine which has just been laid down as to the relations of the President and the heads of departments prevents, however, the application of this rule to the President. Notwithstanding the President has the power of direction, no right of appeal to the President from the decision of the head of a department is recognized, for the President is regarded as having acted through the head of a department.[2] But it is held that where a head of a department attempts to decide a matter not within his jurisdiction an appeal may be taken to the President on the question of jurisdiction.[3]

2. *Remedies against the action of the President.*— The position of the President is one of such dignity and importance that it has been considered improper to offer to an individual the same remedies against the action of the President which are offered against the action of an ordinary public official. In the first place, the President is not regarded as subject to the process of the courts. Thus the courts have no power to subpœna the President. This was held in the famous trial of Aaron Burr :

Chief Justice Marshall, who presided at this trial and issued the subpœna, is reported to have said: " I suppose it will not be alleged in this case that the President ought to be considered as having offered a contempt to the court in consequence of his not having attended, notwithstanding the subpœna was worded

[1] Butterworth *vs.* United States, 112 U. S., 50, 57; see also Bell *vs.* Hearne, 19 Howard, 252.

[2] 9 Opinions of the Attorneys-General, 462 ; 10 *ibid.*, 526.

[3] 15 *ibid.*, 94, 100, which collects and reviews all the opinions of the attorneys-general on this point.

agreeably to the demand of the defendant. The court would indeed not be asked to proceed as in the case of an ordinary individual." Again, he is reported as saying: " In no case of this kind would the court be required to proceed against the President as against an ordinary individual. The objections to such a course are so strong and obvious that all must acknowledge them. In this case, however, the President has assigned no reason whatever for withholding the paper called for. The propriety of withholding it must be decided by himself, not by another for him; of the weight of the reasons for and against producing it he himself is judge." [1]

Furthermore the courts will never attempt to exercise such a control over the acts of the President as will bring them in direct conflict with him.[2]

The only cases where the courts can exercise any control over the President are those in which a regulation or order of the President comes up before them for execution when, if they regard it as an act in excess of the President's powers, they may refuse to enforce it, and declare it null and void.[3] Even in these cases where the acts of the President

[1] *American and English Encyclopædia of Law*, 2d ed., vol. vi., p. 1019, note 10 ; see Hartranft's " Appeal," 85 Pennsylvania State, 433 ; see also Durand *vs.* Hollins, 4 Blatchford, 451, which claims that the President is neither civilly nor criminally responsible to the courts.

[2] Mississippi *vs.* Johnson, 4 Wallace, 475. In this case the attempt was made to get an injunction from the United States courts to restrain the President from executing a law which it was claimed was unconstitutional. The court, however, refused to take jurisdiction and to issue the writ and intimated that in no case would the courts take action of this character.

[3] Little *vs.* Barreme, 2 Cranch, 170. In this case the attempt was made to hold an officer of the navy responsible in damages for having carried out a proclamation of the President, which, it was claimed, was contrary to the law. The officer attempted to plead his instructions, but the court held that he was responsible, and in this collateral way determined that the proclamation of the President, which was being considered in the suit, was illegal. See also the Schooner *Orono*, 1 Gallison C. C., 137 ; *Ex parte* Merriman ; Taney's Reports, 246.

come up collaterally for consideration, and where the courts are, on that account, in no danger of being brought into personal conflict with the President, they will refuse to interfere if the act complained of has been done by the President in the exercise of a power regarded by the courts as political in character. One of the best cases upon this point is one rising out of the trouble in Rhode Island known as Dorr's Rebellion.[1]   The circuit court in a trespass case refused to admit evidence as to the formation of Dorr's government, and as to its representative character.   On appeal to the Supreme Court, its decision was upheld on the ground that Congress had vested the power of determining the validity of the state government in the President by vesting in him the power to call out the militia in case of insurrection in any state.   Chief Justice Taney, who delivered the opinion of the court, says (page 43) :

By this act the power of deciding whether the exigency had arisen upon which the government of the United States is bound to interfere, is given to the President .   .   .   and the President must, of necessity, decide which government and which party is unlawfully arrayed against it before he can perform the duty imposed upon him by the act of Congress.   After the President has acted and called out the militia, is the circuit court of the United States authorized to inquire whether he is right ? .   .   .   If the judicial power extends so far, the guarantee contained in the constitution of the United States is a guarantee of anarchy and not of order. .   .   .   It is true that in this case the militia were not called out by the President, but upon the application of the governor under the charter government, the President recognized him as the executive power of the state, and took measures to call out the militia to support his authority, if it should be found necessary for the general government to interfere, and it is

[1] Luther *vs.* Borden, 7 Howard, U. S. 1.

admitted in the argument that it was the knowledge of this decision that put an end to the armed opposition to the charter government, and prevented any further efforts to establish by force the proposed constitution.   The interference of the President, therefore, by announcing his determination, was as effectual as if the militia had been assembled under his orders.   And it should be equally authoritative. . . .   At all events it [this power] is conferred [upon the President] by the constitution and laws of the United States, and must therefore be respected and enforced in its judicial tribunals.

The Supreme Court of the United States has also held that the courts may not review collaterally the decisions of the President as to the boundaries of foreign states,[1] as to the recognition of belligerency,[2] and as to the payment of claims based upon international awards.[3]

II.—*The state governor.*

1. *The governor a political officer.*—The constitutions of most of the states of the American Union, like the constitution of the United States, vest the executive power in a chief executive, who, in the case of the states, is now universally called the governor.[4] The meaning of the words " executive power" in

[1] Foster *vs.* Neilson, 2 Peters, 253 ; Williams *vs.* Suffolk Ins. Co., 13 Peters, 415.

[2] U. S. *vs.* Palmer, 3 Wheaton, 610.

[3] U. S. *vs.* Blaine, 139 U. S., 306.   See also *In re* Cooper, 143 U. S., 472 ; Georgia *vs.* Stanton, 6 Wall 50 ; Martin *vs.* Mott, 12 Wheaton, 19.

For a good description of the position and power of the President, see Baldwin, *Modern Political Institutions*, chap. iv., entitled " Absolute Power, an American Institution" ; see also, Woodburn, *The American Republic and its Government*, chapter on "The Presidency," which gives a very good exposition of the distinctly political powers of the President.   See also Fairlie, " The Administrative Powers of the President," *Michigan Law Review*, vol. ii., p. 190.

[4] In former times the officer we now know as governor was sometimes called President.

this connection is the same as is that of the same words used in the constitution of the United States with reference to the President. That is, little if any power is to be regarded as vested in the governor as a result of the grant to him of the executive power.[1] In order to find out exactly what is the position of the governor in the system of government adopted in any one of the states of the American Union, we have to look through the constitution of that state for the powers which are specifically and expressly granted to him. Indeed, a consideration of these enumerated powers, as they are called, is even more necessary in the case of the governor than in the case of the President of the United States. For the state courts have not derived, as has the Supreme Court of the United States, any very large powers from such a general power or duty as the duty to see that the laws be faithfully executed. In other words, the principle of narrow construction is more commonly adopted with regard to the powers of the governor than with regard to those of the President.[2]

It has been already shown that the original American conception of the governor was that of a political rather than an administrative officer The original political character of the governor has been more and more emphasized, first, because of the grant to him in the course of our constitutional history of rather larger political powers than he originally possessed; and second, because the legislatures of the states, different from the Congress of the United States, have not seen fit to confer upon him powers

---

[1] See *Ex parte* Holmes, 12 Vermont, 631 ; Field *vs.* People, 3 Illinois, 79 ; Fox *vs.* McDonald, 101 Alabama, 51 ; French *vs.* State, 141 Indiana, 618, *supra* p, 73.   [2] *E. g.* see *In re* Fire, *etc.*, Commissioners, 19 Col., 482, 503.

of an administrative character, while the constitutions of the states have very commonly assigned expressly to other officers in the state government many of the administrative powers which it is now recognized that the President possesses.

The political powers of the governor consist, in the first place, of military powers which are always exercised subject to the limitations contained in the United States constitution. This provides that the militia of the several states shall be under the command of the President when in the actual service of the United States.[1] These military powers consist both of the power of command and that of military administration. We find very seldom, if ever, a state secretary of war.[2] The absence of such an officer is due probably to the fact that the English crown possessed, at the time the office of state governor was established, the military administration which was regarded as a part of the royal prerogative. In several of the states the governor may not act personally in the field unless advised so to do by a resolution of the legislature.[3] As commander in chief, the governor has very commonly power to call out the militia in the case of insurrection, invasion, or resistance to the execution of the laws.[4] In some cases here again the exercise of his power by the governor is conditioned upon the passage of a resolution by the legislature.[5]

[1] Constitution, art. ii., sec. 2, par. 1.

[2] Stimson, *American Statute Law*, p. 41, sec. 202.

[3] This is so in Alabama and Kentucky, Maryland and Missouri ; Stimson, *op. cit.*, sec. 297.

[4] Stimson, *op. cit.*, sec. 298.

[5] This is the case in New Hampshire, Massachusetts, and Tennessee, in the case of insurrection ; and in Texas in the case of invasion. *Ibid.*

The second class of political powers possessed by the state governor are to be found in the powers he possesses over the action of the legislature. Thus, the governor very generally has what has come to be known as the veto power. The veto power includes in many cases the power to veto items in appropriation bills, and usually consists in the power to demand from the legislature a reconsideration of a bill objectionable to him. On reconsideration the bill may be passed usually by a two-thirds vote, in some cases a three-fifths, and finally in some cases by a simple majority.[1]

The governor also has the power to adjourn the legislature in case the two houses disagree as to the time of adjournment,[2] the power to call extra sessions of the legislature[3] and the power and duty to send to the legislature messages in which he is to give to that body such information as to the condition of the state and to recommend such measures as he deems proper.[4]

In the third place, the governor has very generally the power to grant pardons, reprieves, and commutations of sentence and may remit fines and forfeitures.[5] In some instances treason and conviction on impeachment are excepted from his pardoning power.[6] In certain of the states the power in all cases is conditioned upon obtaining the consent of the council,[7] or the senate,[8] or that of the judges of the supreme court, and the attorney-general or a majority of them,[9] or of a board of pardons consisting of "state officers."[1]

---

[1] Stimson, section 305 C.
[2] *Ibid.*, section 278.
[3] *Ibid.*, section 277.
[4] *Ibid.*, section 280.

[5] *Ibid.*, sections 160, 163, 164.
[6] *Ibid.*, section 161.
[7] Massachusetts, Maine, and New Hampshire.
[8] Rhode Island.
[9] Nevada and Florida.

7

Finally the governor has in some cases the power to proclaim, in accordance with the law, the time of general elections. This power is sometimes possessed by the secretary of state.

2. *Administrative powers.*—While the political powers of the governor have increased, he has not been able to increase the administrative powers which he may have possessed at the beginning of our history as an independent community. Indeed he has lost some of the most important administrative powers which he then possessed. The first among these powers to be considered is the power of appointment.

First, power of appointment.—It may be laid down as a general rule of the constitutional law of the states that the grant to the governor of the executive power does not in and of itself carry with it any power of appointment. In order that the governor may possess the power of appointment, it must be expressly granted to him by the state constitution or by an act of the state legislature. This rule is true both as to officers of the central state government [2] and as to local officers. [3] In some of the early state constitutions, particularly in the first constitution of the state of New York, the governor had large powers of appointment, both of the officers of the central state government and of the local officers. As a general thing, however, he was subject in the exercise of this power to the necessity of obtaining the consent of some body representative of the legislature. In the case of the state of New York, this body

[1] Pennsylvania. *Ibid.*, section 160.
[2] French *vs.* State, 141 Indiana, 618.
[3] Fox *vs.* McDonald, 101 Alabama, 51 ; State *vs.* George, 22 Oregon, 142.

was known as the council of appointment and was formed of members of the Senate elected by the assembly.[1] In 1801, however, the power was given to each member of the council of appointment of the state of New York to nominate for appointment.[2] The division of responsibility for appointments resulting from this amendment resulted in great evil. The patronage of the central government of the state was very large.[3] The only way in which it appeared to the people of that day that this evil could be remedied was the diminution of the patronage of the governor. This was secured by the constitution of 1821 by abolishing the council of appointment and providing that the heads of the executive departments of the central state government should be appointed by the legislature, as had been the rule from the beginning in both Massachusetts and Virginia. In the case of the local officers, the patronage of the governor was diminished by the adoption of the elective principle. The elective principle was extended by the constitution of 1846 to many of the officers of the central state government. The change from the appointive to the elective system, while due in large degree to the belief that the evils which had accompanied the appointive system could thus be remedied, was due also to the great democratic movement which is visible in almost all parts of the civilized world about the middle of the nineteenth century.

The change from the appointive to the elective system, whose introduction in the state of New York

[1] First Constitution of New York, art. xxiii.

[2] Amendment v. to the First Constitution.

[3] In 1821, the number of civil appointees was 7000; that of military appointees, 8000; see schedule in Clarke's *Debates of the Convention of 1821.*

has been noticed, was made in most of the states of
the American Union, so that soon after the middle
of the nineteenth century the governor's powers of
appointment had been almost entirely destroyed.
Since that time, however, there has been somewhat
of a reaction.   Amendments to the state constitution
and statutes of the legislature have provided new
officers unknown to the original constitutions, and
these officers are frequently to be appointed by the
governor subject to confirmation by the senate.
Finally, the general power has been given to the
governor quite commonly of appointing to any position for which no other method of appointment or
election has been provided,[1] and to fill vacancies except in the principal state offices which are filled by
the legislature.[2]   The result is that at the present
time the state governor ordinarily has the power with
the consent of a council or senate to appoint certain
of the less important "state officers," but seldom appoints any of the local officers with the exception
of the police commissioners of certain of the larger
cities.   The movement towards the appointment by
the governor of city police commissioners, which is,
although an exception to the general rule, quite an
important one,[3] has been very largely due to the
failure of the local police to enforce prohibition and
other liquor laws.   In addition to the power of
original appointment in the cases specified in the
constitutional statutes, which are not numerous, the
governor has also the power to fill many vacancies un-

---

[1] *E. g.*, see New York Law, 1892, chapter 681, section 6.
[2] *Ibid.*, sections 30 and 31.
[3] See Fairlie, *Municipal Administration*, p. 133.

til the expiration of the term or the next election, and also the power to fill all offices by appointment for which some other method has not been provided. The power of appointment possessed by the governor is generally based on the statutes, and therefore may be decreased at any time by the legislature, but in some cases it is based on the constitution,[1] when of course the legislature has no such power.

In a few states it is provided that the terms of the officers to be appointed by the governor and of those to be elected by the people shall begin and expire at the same time that the term of the governor begins and ends, so that the new governor may fill the offices to his satisfaction at the beginning of the term, and so that there will be harmony in the general policy between the governor and the elected officers, who it is supposed will belong to the same party as the governor.[2]

Second. Power of removal.—The same rule is true with regard to the power of removal as with regard to the power of appointment—*i. e.*, the grant of the executive power to the governor does not give him, in and of itself, any power of removal. Such a power must be conferred by expressed provision of the constitution or statutes. It has thus been held that, in the absence of such a constitutional or statutory provision, the governor has no power of removal, even if the term of the officer in question is not fixed by the legislature and will therefore, if there is no power of removal, be a term for life.[3]

[1] Stimson, *op. cit.*, section 202 B.

[2] See Kentucky Const., sec. 91; Nebraska Const., art. v., sec. 1; Florida Constitution, 1886, iv., sec. 20; New York Constitution, 1894, art. v., sec. 1.

[3] See Field *vs.* People, 3 Illinois, pp. 79, 84.

In New York, where the administrative powers of the governor are rather greater than elsewhere, it was provided by the first constitution that the governor had, subject to the necessity of obtaining the consent of the council of appointment, the power to remove almost every important officer in the state government not judicial in character and not purely local. This power resulted from the power of appointment which was granted to him by the first constitution, for the appointment of a new incumbent to an office was regarded as the removal of the existing incumbent. It is said that use was made of this power to produce " an entire change of officers throughout the state from the highest to the lowest ; at any rate in all those cases where the immediate predecessors of the council had made appointments."[1] The change which was made in the powers of the members of the council of appointment by the constitutional amendment of 1801, had a worse effect, if possible, upon the power of removal than it had upon the power of appointment. The powers of the council were so grossly abused that they brought about, as has been said, the abolition of the council in 1821. With the abolition of the council of appointment, the governor's power of removal was greatly diminished. At first the governor lost practically all power of removal, but later a limited power was restored to him.

At the present time it may be said that the power of removal of the ordinary state governor is as follows :

[1] Hammond, *History of Political Parties in the State of New York*, vol. i. p. 289.

The power of removal is confined, as a general thing, to the officers whom the governor appoints, though in some instances, as, for example, in New York, the governor is permitted with the approval of the senate to remove all important state officers.[1] Local officers are seldom removable by the governor. The state of New York is the most important exception to this rule. Here, either as a result of the constitution or of the statutes, the governor has quite a large power of removing such officers as the sheriff, district attorney, and mayors of important cities. In almost all cases, however, the exercise of the power of removal by the governor is conditioned upon obtaining the consent of the council or senate, and upon the existence of some cause which is usually either malfeasance in office or neglect of duty, but in a few cases may consist of incompetency.[2] Where removal may be made for cause only, in accordance with the general principles of the administrative law of the United States, the person to be removed must be given a hearing.[3] Sometimes pending the removal proceedings the governor has the right to suspend the officer to be removed.[4] As in the case of the power of appointment, the power of removal is based sometimes on the constitution, indeed generally so; but also in some cases on the statutes, when the legislature may take it away.

[1] Public Officers Law, sec. 24. Stimson, sec. 266.

[2] Stimson, sec. 266.

[3] Dullam *vs.* Wilson, 53 Michigan, 392. The decision of the governor on the merits may not, however, be reviewed by the courts, even in a collateral proceeding to which the governor is not a party, certainly where all the statute requires is that the person to be removed is to be given a hearing. *In re* Guden, 171 N. Y., 529.

[4] See Florida Const., art. 4, sec. 15.

Third. Power of direction.—The governor's powers of direction over the administrative officers are very small and must of necessity be of little importance so long as the power of removal is as weak as it is. For the statutes seldom expressly give him any power of direction. The only general exception to this rule seems to be in the case of the attorney-general who is regarded as the legal adviser of the governor and as such subject to his direction.[1]

Fourth. The governor's power over administrative services.—In addition to these rather limited powers over the personnel of the state administration, the governor has also a few but rather unimportant powers relative to the administrative services. As a general thing there is no provision in the state constitutions similar to that to be found in the United States constitution, which makes it the duty of the chief executive to see that the laws be faithfully executed. Indeed, in some instances, where such a power is recognized in the constitution of the state, it has been held by the state courts that it will not justify the governor, for example, in employing the militia of the state to put his appointees into offices to which he has the right of appointment.[2] This decision is not in and of itself important, but it is significant as showing, when compared with the decision of the Supreme Court of the United States in the Neagle case, to which reference has already been made, the difference in the attitude of the state courts from that of the United States courts in construing the powers of the chief executive of the government.

---

[1] See, for example, California Political Code, sec. 380, paragraphs 5, 6, and 7 ; Indiana Revised Statutes, 1881, 5659.

[2] *In re* Fire, *etc.*, Commissioners, 19 Colorado, 482, 503.

Furthermore, the state legislatures, different from the Congress of the United States, have not vested in the chief executives of the state governments very many specific powers with regard to the various administrative services. The legislatures have not done so because the state constitutions very commonly provide that the detailed work of administration which, under the United States constitution is under the supervision of the President, shall in the states be vested in a series of officers often spoken of as administrative officers, who are elected quite frequently by the people and are to perform their duties very largely independently of any gubernatorial supervision.

Finally, the state legislatures have not in many instances granted large powers of ordinance to the governor. There are cases which seem to hold that the legislature may vest the governor with a power of issuing regulations,[1] but the legislature has ordinarily preferred, in accordance with the general American system, to regulate in detail all matters which need regulation. An instance of a legislative delegation of the power of regulation to the governor may be found in a few of the states in the power which is granted to him to issue civil-service rules providing for appointments to the subordinate positions in the state civil service.

The governor has, however, in some states comparatively extended financial powers. Thus in several of the states[2] he is to draw up estimates of the

---

[1] See Martin *vs.* Witherspoon, 135 Massachusetts, 175, which holds that the governor may be authorized to make pilotage regulations.

[2] Alabama, Colorado, Illinois, Missouri, Nebraska, and West Virginia, Stimson, sec. 280.

amount of money to be raised by taxation for the purposes of the government. In several states also all money is to be paid out of the treasury on his order,[1] and finally in a number he has the right to examine the accounts of financial officers at stated times and sometimes unexpectedly.[2]

3. *General position of the governor.*—It will be noticed from this description of the governor's powers how different his position in the state administration is from that of the President in the national administration. Originally occupying about the same relative position, the governor has been stripped of his administrative powers and has been more and more confined to the exercise of political powers, while the President has been gaining more and more administrative power until at the present time he makes or unmakes the administration of the United States. One of the reasons for this difference in the development of the two offices is to be found in the fact that the constitution of the United States has practically made it impossible for any administrative officers in the United States system to be elected by the people or appointed by the legislature, in that it has specifically stated that officers are to be appointed by the President and Senate, by the President alone, by the heads of departments, or by the courts. In the case of the state constitutions, amendments have been so easy, as compared with the amendment of the United States constitution, that the powers of the governor have been changed as a result of con-

[1] See Code of Georgia, 1882, 76.

[2] See Virginia Code, sec. 238 ; Colorado General Statutes, 1883, sec. 1361 ; Iowa, McLane's Annotated Statutes, 1882, secs. 759, 763 ; Kansas, Dassler's General Statutes, 1901, sec. 7259.

stitutional amendment. Furthermore, the state legislature, occupying the position which it does in the state government, has had the right in the absence of a specific restriction in the state constitution, which is hardly ever to be found, to provide methods for filling offices in which the governor is denied all participation.

What has been said with regard to the power of appointment may practically be repeated with regard to the power of removal. It is true, of course, in the case of the United States government that Congress did at one time attempt to deprive the President of what had been regarded as the constitutional power of removal, but it soon saw the error of its ways and returned to the original system. Such has not been the history of the legislatures of the states of the United States which, following the example of the state constitutions, have deprived the governor of whatever power of removal he may have originally possessed, with as little compunction as they have deprived him of the power of appointment. It has been impossible for the governor to become the head of the state administration, because the people of the state have practically decided that the governor shall be in the main a political officer.[1]

The governor's office has thus been deprived of all means of administrative development. The governor is now, more than he ever was, a political officer, his political powers having tended to increase. This is especially true of the veto power, which now extends so frequently to items of bills appropriating money.

[1] For a good comparison of the positions of the President and the governor see Field *vs.* People, 3 Illinois, 79.

But, because the governor has thus been confined to the exercise of political powers, his influence upon the welfare of the state must not be underestimated. He is still a very important officer. His veto power gives him a vast power over legislation, while the little power of removal which he possesses often enables him to punish summarily any gross misconduct on the part of administrative officers, both those of the central state government and those in the localities.

4. *Remedies against the action of the governor.*— What has been said with regard to the remedies against the action of the President may be repeated with regard to the remedies against the action of the governor. The governor is held, for example, not to be subject to the process of the courts,[1] but he may be personally liable after the expiration of his term of office for acts done in office.[2] The state courts also are almost as careful not to come into personal conflict with the governor as the United States courts are not to come into personal conflict with the President. The better rule is that they will not attempt to exercise a control over him personally.[3] The only exception to this rule is in the case of the *quo warranto.* There are several cases where the *quo warranto* has been issued to the governor.[4] The courts have, however, very little hesitation about declaring an act of the governor, in which it would

[1] Hartranft's Appeal, 85 Pa. St., 433.

[2] See Druecker *vs.* Salomon, 21 Wisconsin, 621, where the court took jurisdiction of a case against an ex-governor.

[3] See People *vs.* Morton, 156 N. Y., 136; Dennett Petitioner, 32 Maine, 508. In both these cases the court refused to issue a *mandamus* to a board, of which the governor was a member.

[4] See the case of Attorney-General *vs.* Barstow, 4 Wis., 567; Morris *vs.* Bulkley, 61 Conn., 287.

appear that he exercises considerable discretion, null and void.[1]

The courts will not, however, interfere with acts of the governor which they regard as political in character. Thus they have held that the governor is the judge as to the advisability of holding an extra session of the legislature, and that his determination is not reviewable by the courts.[2] In the same way they have held that where the constitution vests in the governor the power to prorogue the legislature when a disagreement exists as to the time of adjournment, he is the exclusive judge as to the existence of the contingency provided for by the constitution, and his decision may not be reviewed by the courts.[3]

[1] See People *vs.* Curtis, 50 N. Y., 321, where it was decided that a warrant of extradition, made by the governor in pursuance of an unconstitutional law, was void; People *vs.* Brady, 56 N. Y., 182, where the court went back of a warrant of extradition issued by the governor, and decided that the evidence on which the warrant was issued was not sufficient to justify the inference that a legal crime had been committed; Dullam *vs.* Wilson, 53 Mich., 392; People *vs.* Platt, 50 Hun, 454, where the court decided that the act of the governor appointing an officer was void, on the ground that the person appointed was not qualified for the office.

[2] See Farrelly *vs.* Cole, 60 Kan., 356; see also People *vs.* Rice, 65 Hun, N. Y., 236.

[3] *In re The Legislative Adjournment*, 18 R. I., 824.

CHAPTER IV.

THE SENATE AS AN EXECUTIVE COUNCIL.

IN almost every one of the American colonies there was placed by the side of the governor a council, the members of which were appointed by the crown. The consent of this council was necessary in order that certain of the acts of the governor should be valid. In addition to acting as a council of advice to the governor and a means of control over him, the colonial council was also a part of the colonial legislature, and in some instances acted as a court of appeals in civil cases. It occupied this position in New York.[1]

When the colonies became independent states, in several of them this institution was retained and exists at the present time. Thus in the states of Maine, Massachusetts, and New Hampshire, we find even now a governor's council, whose consent is necessary to the governor's appointments.[2] In others the council as such has disappeared and the powers which it possessed have been transferred to the upper house of the legislature.[3] This is the general rule at the present time and is true of the national

[1] See Governor's Commission in *Documents Relating to the History of New York*, iii., 377.

[2] Stimson, *American Statute Law*, sec. 210 B.

[3] *Ibid.*, sec. 210 C.

government and of the state of New York. The powers which these councils, or senates as executive councils, possess at the present time are somewhat different in the national and state governments.

I.—In the national government.

The powers of the United States Senate as an executive council are stated in the constitution to be, first, to give its advice and consent to the appointment by the President of certain classes of officers,[1] and, second, to prevent the making by the President of a valid treaty, by refusing its approval thereto. Such approval must by the constitution be made by a two-thirds vote.[2]

These powers which the senate possesses over the acts of the President must not be classed among its legislative powers, for though the senate is an important legislative body it is at the same time an executive council and the only executive council in the national government. When acting as an executive council, it acts separately and apart from the other legislative body — the house of representatives. When so acting, the senate is said to be in executive session, and may sit at a time when the house of representatives is not in session, which may not be the case when the senate is acting as a part of the Congress.[3]

[1] Art. ii., sec. 2, par. 2.
[2] *Ibid.*
[3] See as to the distinction between both the United States Senate and the state senates as executive councils and as parts of the legislature, State *vs.* Knight, 63 Cal. 333 ; Atty.-Gen. *vs.* Oakman, 126 Mich. 717 ; Com. *vs.* Waller, 145 Pa. St. 235.

Further, the senate, as an executive council, may be distinguished from the senate as a part of the Congress by the difference in procedure which is followed in the two cases. When the senate acts as an executive council its sessions are, as a rule, secret, while its sessions as a part of the Congress are open to the public. The reason for the adoption of secret sessions, when the senate is acting as an executive council, is to be found in the delicate character of the business which comes before it. The same is true of the state senates when they act as executive councils.

The extent of the power which the senate, as an executive council, possesses over the acts of the President is not clearly defined in the constitution. The power of the senate as to treaties is, of course, absolute, and nothing that can be done by Congress can change or in any way affect it. The same is true as to the power of the senate to refuse its advice and consent to the appointment by the President of ambassadors, other public ministers, and consuls, and judges of the supreme court, but with the exception of these officers the power of the senate is dependent on the action of Congress ; that is, Congress is permitted by the constitution to " vest the appointment of such inferior officers as they may think proper in the President alone, in the courts of law, or in the heads of departments."

The power of Congress thus to define the extent of the participation of the senate in the appointment of officers is not, however, so great as it would at first sight appear to be. For the constitution adds to the list of those officers who are to be appointed with the consent of the senate " all other officers of the United

States whose appointments are not herein otherwise provided for and which shall be established by law." It therefore necessarily follows that, if an office is established by a law which says nothing as to the power of the senate to confirm appointments to it, the confirmation of the senate will, as a matter of law, be necessary to the validity of the appointment.[1] Of course Congress, acting with the consent of the senate, may, in the case of all officers not specifically made subject to the power of the senate, provide for a presidential appointment or an appointment by the head of the department. As a matter of fact, however, most of the important inferior administrative offices, both at Washington and through the country as a whole, are filled by and with the advice and consent of the senate, because either that method is provided by law, or because the law has established the office without stating explicitly that it is to be filled by the appointment either of the President alone or of the head of a department.

The practical result is then that the senate as an executive council has actually a very important control, the extent of which it may itself very largely determine, over two of the most important powers of the President. Further, the actual way in which this control has been exercised, and is now being exercised is such that a very serious modification has practically been made of the general position assigned by our constitutional law to the President. Thus, although in theory the President is to represent the country in diplomatic matters, it is practically impossible for him to conclude, in many instances, a treaty

[1] See 6 Opins. Attorneys-General, v., 1.

with a foreign country. Treaty after treaty negotia-
ted by the President has failed to receive the confirmation of the senate. The failure has of course in
large measure been due to the extraordinary majority
of two-thirds required for approval by the constitution. If the constitution were amended so as to permit a treaty to be approved by a majority, the
diplomatic power of the President would be vastly
increased.

Again, although the constitution vests the power
of nomination in the President, the practice of the
senate, which has come to be known as "senatorial
courtesy," has brought it about that the senators representing the state in which an appointment is to be
made, particularly if they are of the same political
party as the President, have practically the power of
nomination. Almost all that the President can do is
to insist that a certain standard of excellence accepta-
ble to himself shall be maintained by the senators
concerned in the nominations for office which they
are thus practically permitted to make.[1] The actual
transfer of the power of nomination[2] from the President to the individual senators or other members of
Congress, has caused modifications to be made in the
administrative position of the President which have
two most important effects on our political system.
They have, in the first place, lessened the responsibility of the President and diminished his power to
conduct the administration according to his ideas

[1] See Fairlie, "The Administrative Powers of the President," *Michigan Law Review*, vol. ii., p. 193.

[2] It will be remembered that such a power of nomination was finally recognized by law as belonging to each member of the famous New York council of appointment, *supra* 99.

of what is fit and proper. They have, in the second place, given to the senate a position in the government which it can hardly be believed was intended by the framers of the constitution, or is thought by most persons at the present day to be one which the senate should occupy.

The evils due to this exaggerated control of the senate over the President have been aggravated by the fact that the terms of most of the officers of the United States have, for the last half century or more, been only four years. If their terms were at the pleasure of the President, the power of the President would be much increased, and that of the senate would be much decreased, for the President would under such conditions be compelled to go seldom, as compared with present conditions, to the senate to have his appointments confirmed. The repeal of the present term-of-office acts, which could be done by an act of Congress without any change in the constitution would do much to remedy one of the most conspicuous defects in the present national administrative system.[1]

While the senate has been exceedingly jealous of its prerogative so far as concerns the appointment of inferior officers whose appointment is conditioned upon its affirmative action, it has fortunately acted much more wisely and much more in accord with the general principles underlying our national administrative system, where the appointment of heads of departments is concerned. The senate has followed the practice of according to the President almost complete freedom in filling these positions, confirming almost

[1] *Cf. ibid.*

as a matter of course any appointments the President may make for positions in what has come to be known as his cabinet. Almost the only case in our history where the senate has attempted to exercise a control over these appointments is to be found in connection with the tenure-of-office acts passed in 1867 as a result of the unfortunate struggle between Congress and President Johnson.

II.—*In the state government.*

While the United States Senate has a control over certain of both the political and administrative acts of the President, the state senate, acting as an executive council, or the governor's council, which is elected by the legislature in Maine[1] but elsewhere elected by the people,[2] has control only over certain administrative acts of the governor. Its control over these administrative acts is, however, more extended than the similar control of the United States Senate over the acts of the President, for the general rule of the states is that the consent of the executive council (senate) is necessary not only for appointments but also for removals.[3]

Furthermore the power of the senate in the state governments is absolutely fixed in the constitution. The state constitutions do not leave to the legislature, as it has been shown the United States constitution leaves in large part to Congress, the determination as to the extent of the control which the senate shall

[1] Constitution, art. 522.

[2] Stimson, *American Statute Law*, sec. 202 B.

[3] For New York, see *supra*, p. 103; see also Maine Constitution, art. ix., sec. 6 ; Stimson, sec. 210.

exercise over the governor's appointments. As a matter of fact most of the appointments made by the governor are, in accordance with the provisions of the constitution, to be made by and with the advice and consent of the senate.

The attitude of the state senate towards the governor has been very similar to that of the United States Senate towards the President, but because of the totally different kind of administrative system which has been adopted for the state, we find no such custom as was seen to exist in the United States Senate in the case of cabinet appointments, of giving the governor free hand in the appointment of officers corresponding to the cabinet officers of the United States government.

The state senate not only exercises a wide control over the governor's appointments, it exercises also almost as extensive a control over his exercise of such power of removal as he possesses. Nothing is more common in the state than to see the senate reject the governor's recommendations either for appointment or removal, for no other reason, apparently, than that they do not appear to the senate to be conducive to the interests of the political party in control thereof. This immoderate exercise of the senate's power of control over the governor has largely been accountable for the result that the governor's responsibility for the state administration has been all but destroyed.

While in the case of the national government considerable amelioration of the present conditions, it has been shown, could be secured by the passage of acts of Congress, in the state governments, owing to the fact that the relations of the governor and the senate are fixed in the constitution, and to the further fact that many of the subordinate officers of the state government are provided for and their terms fixed in the constitution, no hope can be entertained of changing for the better the relations of the governor and the senate except through constitutional amendment.

CHAPTER V.

I—Methods of distributing business.

No matter how centralized the administrative system may be, it is absolutely necessary in a state of any size that there should exist departments or offices among which the detailed work of administration shall be distributed. In many governments where the executive has not been clearly separated from the legislature, there must also be officers whose duty it is either to assume the responsibility to the legislature or to the courts for the acts of the executive. In such governments the heads of these departments combine the functions both of administrative and of political officers. In the United States, however, where the executive is pretty clearly separated from the legislature, we have no need of such political officers, and have assigned to the different departments among which administrative business is distributed, officers whose duties are not political but merely administrative. In those countries where this political and administrative business is combined, it is the habit to denominate the persons to whom these two kinds of business are entrusted, as ministers. In the

United States, however, the immediate subordinates of the executive have to be content with the more modest title of heads of departments.

It has been shown that all administration may be differentiated into five well defined branches—namely, those of foreign, military, judicial, financial, and internal affairs. All the different administrative matters requiring attention from the administration will fall under one of these five branches. It has come to be well recognized at the present time that the best arrangement of administrative business is to place some one authority at the head of each of these branches, and where it is found by experience to be necessary to make a further specialization, to take out of one of the five departments thus formed some particular matter or matters and form a separate department for its or their management.

In the United States national system of administration, we find that the military department is thus divided into two departments, — one of which has charge of the army and is known as the War Department; the other of which has charge of naval affairs, and is known as the Navy Department.[1] Again we find the care of public works is often given to a separate executive department; often also the question of education becomes so important as to de-

[1] In the United States, naval affairs were originally in charge of the War Department but were soon put in the hands of a special department where they have ever since remained, see Guggenheimer on "The Development of Executive Departments" in Jameson, *Essays in the Constitutional History of the United States*, p. 179. This gives a brief but excellent historical sketch of the development of the executive departments of the United States government. A more detailed history of the development of the United States departments will be found in the Report of the Dockery Commission 53d Congress, Second Session, House Report, 49, 1893.

mand a separate authority for its management. The same is true of agriculture and commerce.

In all these cases it will be noticed that the principle at the bottom of the distribution of administrative business among the various executive departments is the division of the work according to its nature, and to us of the present age any other method of distribution seems preposterous. But this method has not always been followed. In most of the European states, all administrative matters were originally attended to by one organ — generally a board or council of some sort. In this body the distribution of business was made according to geographical lines rather than according to the nature of the business to be transacted. Indeed such a system of geographical division was in force in England during our colonial period. The secretariat of state had two principal secretaries of state

but their duties were determined arbitrarily and geographically instead of rationally and scientifically. One secretary had charge of what was called the northern department . . . and the other of what was called the southern department, which included . . . the American and West Indian colonies . . . The secretary of state for the southern department was the secretary of state for home and imperial affairs and in part for foreign affairs, and the secretary for the northern department, the secretary in part for foreign affairs.[1]

Indeed at the present time we have in our national system of administration one or two instances of adherence to the old geographical system ; thus there is in the War Department a bureau known as the Bureau of Insular Affairs, which attends to the affairs of the insular possessions of the United States.

[1] Snow, *The Administration of Dependencies*, p. 209.

II.—*Power of organization.*

An important question connected with the subject of the executive departments is who shall organize them? Shall it be the executive or the legislative authority? The United States constitution does not contain anything very explicit upon this subject. Indeed it does not expressly provide for the organization of executive departments, although it impliedly recognizes their existence in two places.[1] It permits the President to " require the opinion in writing of the principal officer in each of the executive departments on any subject relating to the duties of their respective offices," and allows Congress to vest the power of appointing inferior officers " in the heads of departments." The last clause referred to furthermore speaks of " offices established by law." We may gather from these clauses that the constitution intended that there should be executive departments and that the power to organize these executive departments was to be vested in Congress. It is not, however, absolutely certain that the constitution, as it has been interpreted, deprives the executive of all power to establish offices. Indeed it has sometimes happened that the President has appointed agents or commissioners for particular purposes. Such agents, however, must be regarded as his mere personal representatives. It is very doubtful whether in the absence of congressional authority the President could appoint an agent who could perform an act which would in any way affect the rights of private individuals, and it is certainly regarded, even by the

[1] Art. ii., sec. 2, paragraphs 1 and 2.

administration, that the President could not grant to such officers any compensation where no provision for it had been made by act of Congress.[1]

It has also been held by the attorney-general, who would probably not be inclined to underrate the power of the President, that the establishment, in one of the executive departments, provided for by statute, of a bureau for which no provision has been made by a statute, is improper.[2] No case has arisen of an attempt upon the part of the President to establish an executive department, and there seems to be no doubt entertained by any of the writers on this subject as to the impropriety of such action.[3]

The practice of Congress furthermore has been not only to establish all the executive departments that have been established in the history of the government, but also to regulate in considerable detail their internal arrangements, fixing, for example, the bureaus into which such departments shall be divided, and determining the powers and duties not only of the heads of departments but also of the heads of the bureaus among which the work of the department is distributed.[4] In some cases it is true Congress will entrust to the head of a department the performance of certain duties and will leave to him the organization of the force which it is necessary that he shall

[1] See 4 Opinions of the Attorneys-General, p. 248 ; see also United States *vs.* Maurice, 2 Brockenbrough, U. S., 96.

[2] See 10, Opins. Attys.-Gen., 11.

[3] See Benton, *Thirty Years' View*, ii., 678 ; see also Wyman, *Administrative Law*, sections 58 and 59.

[4] It is probably true, however, that, unless Congress has acted with regard to the divisions into which the bureaus of a department may be divided, the head of the department has large discretion in the organization of the work of the bureau. See 2 Comptrollers' Decisions, 173.

provide in order to discharge the duties thus imposed upon him. As a general thing, however, departments whose organization has been the result of administrative action are later regulated by some statute, generally an appropriation act, which gives the sanction of law to the organization that may have been provided. In such a case, of course, the power of the head of the department or of the President to arrange the department is limited because of the fact that what is done by statute may not be changed by administrative action.

In the separate states, there are seldom to be found in the constitutions express provisions as to the organizing power, but in accordance with the general principle that the powers of the executive are enumerated while the legislature possesses all powers which have not been granted to some other authority,[1] the legislature under such conditions has the organizing power. In some instances the constitutions themselves organize the executive departments, and in rather rare instances not only organize the departments, but expressly forbid the legislature to establish any new departments or offices.[2] As a general thing, however, the departments or offices in the state government are organized by the legislature.

The practice of the state legislature is quite different from that of Congress. As a general thing, Congress attempts, so far as possible, to consolidate all the offices and bureaus under the general direction and supervision of the head of a department who is

---

[1] *Supra*, 40.

[2] See, for example, Constitution of Nebraska, article v., section 26, interpreted in *In re* Railroad Commissioners, 15 Nebraska, 679, 683.

usually, at the same time, a member of what we are accustomed to call the President's cabinet. In this way we find in the national government nine well organized executive departments divided up into bureaus and divisions, and very seldom any office which is not attached to some one of the departments.[1] In the states, however, apparently no serious attempt has been made to gather together, under the general direction and supervision of a head of a department, the various bureaus and offices, each of which has been established to attend to some detail of administration. But while the state legislatures have not attempted to follow the example of the United States government in systematizing the administrative system of the state, the state statutes do not descend, as a rule, into the same detail as the acts of Congress. They often provide merely for a certain bureau or office or department, and the legislature each year, or every two years, grants in its appropriation acts a sum of money to the head of the bureau, office, or department, leaving him very large freedom in its distribution.

These methods of organizing the executive departments agree, it will be noticed, in according to the legislature almost complete power over the administrative organization. This power, as a matter of fact, the legislature is continually exercising. It is very much to be doubted whether such a method of organizing the executive departments is a good one. In most other countries the rule is that, while the legislature unquestionably has power to organize the

[1] An important office at the present time, which is not so attached, is the Civil Service Commission. 22 Opinions of the Attorneys-General, 62.

departments, as a matter of practical policy it leaves the matter of organization, particularly as to details, in the hands of the executive, and confines its action to exercising a control over the amount of money which the executive may spend upon the departments. Such a method of regulating this matter would seem to be the better one, inasmuch as the executive is in a better position to know the needs of the administration than is the legislature, and is responsible for the actions of the administration. Further, the executive can act more quickly than can the legislature. The control which the legislature has over the finances is sufficient to prevent the administration from incurring too great an expense in any change that it may wish to make. There have been a number of instances in the history of the United States where the exercise of the organizing power by the executive would have been of the greatest advantage to the administrative system generally. A marked instance of this is to be found in the history of the War Department. As the result of the statutory organization of the department, it at one time was so organized, with military officials at the head of the various bureaus, that it was altogether too much exempted from the control of the President. Notwithstanding the defects in the organization of the department, it required a long time before the President and the secretary of war could succeed in inducing Congress to make the changes in the organization necessary to bring about a proper relation between the bureau heads and the secretary of war and the President. It is questionable, however, whether under our constitution as it now stands the power of organizing the executive departments could be vested in the executive. It certainly is true in the case of the states that the exercise of any such power by the governor would be impossible so long as our constitutions remain as they are. It is doubtful whether in the case of the national government, where the constitutional provisions with regard to the executive departments are not so explicit, the exercise of such a power by the President would not be regarded by the courts as the exercise of legislative power.

A comparison of the methods adopted by the national government and by the states with regard to this matter of organizing the executive departments will be profitable. One of the effects of the adoption of the system of unrelated and uncorrelated bureaus and offices, such as we find in the state system, is to subject the administration of state affairs to a far too extended political control. For if a head of a bureau is subject to no administrative superior, as is the case with most of the heads of the state bureaus, he can hardly fail to be regarded as a political officer who should, so far as possible, conform in political opinions with the political party in control of the state government. The result is that, although the duties of the heads of many of these bureaus are really almost exclusively administrative in character, the heads are changed, so far as the law allows, with every change in administration.

If, on the other hand, these bureaus are all subjected to the control and direction of some head of department, as is the case in the national administrative system, the tendency to frequent change in the incumbency is very much diminished, and it becomes possible to develop the idea that the head of a bureau who has satisfactorily performed his administrative duties should occupy a more or less permanent position. We can hardly expect to develop an administrative system in our state governments free from the control of politics, so long as it remains in the unconcentrated condition in which we find it at present.

CHAPTER VI.

TERM AND TENURE OF THE HEADS OF DEPARTMENTS.

THE relations of the heads of departments with the chief executive authority are of the greatest importance, for on their nature depends whether there is to be a harmonious administration following out some general plan, or whether the head of each department is to be a law unto himself and is to be able to conduct the affairs of his department in such manner as he sees fit, regardless of the needs of other departments and of the wishes of the chief executive. These relations of the heads of departments with the chief executive are governed almost entirely by two things, *viz.*, the term and the tenure of office of the heads of departments.

The constitution of the United States and the constitutions of the states differ considerably in this respect. The former instrument gives to the chief executive the power to appoint, remove, and direct all the heads of departments. The states, however, have pursued a different plan. In most of the original states the chief executive did not have the absolute power of appointing the heads of departments. The tendency was to fill these offices at first by appointment by the legislature, as was the rule originally in some of the states, then by election by the people, which is the rule at present. It is said[1] that at the present time "all the executive officers are, as a general rule in all the states, elected by the people at a general election." There are, of course, exceptions to this rule. Many of the incumbents of the newer state offices are appointed by the governor and senate. Further, there are still instances of the appointment of heads of departments by the legislature.

As far as the continuance of the term of office is concerned, the methods adopted in the states differ as much as the methods of filling the offices. But in most cases the term of office of the heads of departments is fixed either by the constitution or the statutes at a certain number of years. The term is not generally the same for all offices, nor does it always coincide with that of the governor. The result is that it is not necessarily the case that all the officers who are to conduct the state government belong to the same political party, or that they share the same views as to the way in which the state administration shall be conducted. Further, the governor cannot usually in case of conflict produce a uniformity in views by the removal of the head of a department.[2]

What now are the relations existing between the chief executive authority and the heads of departments in the American system of administration which result from this state of facts? In the national administration, the heads of the departments are completely subordinate to and dependent upon the chief executive authority as a result of the precariousness

[1] Stimson, *op. cit.*, p. 42, art. 20 B.
[2] *Supra*, p. 102.

of their tenure, and will be in harmony one with the other and with the President on account of the fact that they have been chosen by him to fill their respective positions as a result of his knowledge of their opinions. We find, therefore, in the national administration complete guaranties for an efficient and harmonious administration under the direction of the President.

In the states, however, the case is quite different. Each head of a department, or office, has, so long as he is not corrupt, the right to conduct the affairs of his department or office just about as he sees fit ; and is practically independent of the governor, who has little or no influence over affairs of administration. The constitutions of some of the states have been honest enough to recognize what is the real position of the governor and what is that of the heads of the departments, and devote an article to the consideration of the "administrative" officers of the state, among whom the governor is not included. But whether the constitution recognizes this or not, the fact is the same, *viz.*, that the governor is not the head of the administration in the states of the American Union. American state administrative law has added to the famous trinity of Montesquieu a fourth department, *viz.*, the administrative department, [1] which is almost entirely independent of the chief executive, and which, as far as the central administration is concerned, is assigned to a number of officers not only independent of the governor but also independent of each other.

[1] See Florida Constitution, 1881, art. 5, sec. 17 ; **Const. Ind., art. vi.; Oregon**, art. viii.; Wis., art. vi.

The independence which almost every head of department in the American state administrative system may claim under the law has resulted in their being little attempt made to secure uniformity in administrative action. While in the national government every President tries to surround himself with advisers who have the same general views as to the conduct of the government, and calls regular meetings of his heads of departments, popularly termed cabinet meetings, where these heads of departments may exchange opinions on the important questions which come up before them for settlement, in the states we seldom hear of any such thing as a meeting of the heads of the departments.[1] Such a meeting would be of little use, as there resides nowhere the power to compel a head of department to change his opinions or his policy so as to suit that of the governor or that of his colleagues. In a word, in the state administration there are seldom any guaranties for efficient and harmonious action on account of the independent position of the heads of departments not only over against the governor but also over against each other. This is not merely a theoretical objection to the state system of administration. For the jealousies and prejudices of the various heads of departments and their conflict with the governor do in practice not infrequently lead to an absolute cessation of the work of administration. The attempt has been made in some of the states to provide that the governor and most of the important state officers shall be elected at the same time and serve for the same terms in the hope that harmony between

[1] But see Florida Const., art. 5., sec. 17, and Iowa Code, 1888, p. 32.

them will be secured by the fact that they all belong to the same political party. This hope is not, however, always realized.

A study of the public law of different countries governing the relations of the heads of departments with the chief executive, would show that the almost universal rule is that the heads of departments are dependent upon the chief executive. The only country which does not make some such provision in its public law is the United States. Here, by the system adopted in the separate states, it does not seem to be considered necessary to have an administration so formed as either to shut out the possibility of conflict, or to settle such conflicts as may arise. The experience of the world is against the administrative arrangements of the states of the American Union, and our own experience has shown us that such an arrangement as we have leads to conflicts which not only diminish administrative efficiency, but in some cases produce a cessation of effective administrative work.

The only thing which prevents our state administrative system from breaking down altogether is the control which the political party exercises over both the governor and the state heads of departments. But this is not always effective, because the governor and all the heads of departments do not always belong to the same party, and factions arise within the party itself which lessen its power of control.

CHAPTER VII.

WHATEVER may be the subordination of the heads of departments to the chief executive authority, they still have a series of duties of an administrative character which they may perform largely independently of the action of the chief executive, in so far as they have not received positive directions from him. More than this is true of the states in the United States. Here the heads of departments often have functions to discharge with which the chief executive has little, if anything, to do. First to be mentioned among their powers are those that affect the personnel of the official service.

I.—The power of appointment.

In the United States national government the constitution provides that Congress may grant to the heads of departments the power to appoint to inferior offices.[1] Numerous laws have granted to the heads of departments such a power of appointment, so that now the great mass of the officers of the United States government are appointed by them. Several laws have, however, limited the power of

[1] Art. ii., sec. 2, par. 2.

appointment of the heads of departments by author-
izing the President to issue rules regulating the mode
of appointment. Notable among them is the Civil
Service law of 1883. The rules passed by the President, limiting the power of appointment by the heads
of departments, would appear, if reasonable, to be
binding upon them.[1] Most of the important subordinates of the heads of departments are, however,
appointed by the President or the President and
senate.[2]

In the states the heads of departments also very
generally have the power to appoint their subordinates.[3] It is expressly provided, however, by law
that many of the agents of the state government in
the localities shall be elected by the people of such
localities. In some of the states the power of appointment of the heads of departments is limited in
the same way as in the national government.[4] It has,
however, been held that if the state constitution
vests the power of appointing subordinate officers in
a state officer, that power may not be limited by an
act of the legislature.[5]

II.—The power of removal.

In the national government it was early laid down
by the courts that the power of removal was incident

[1] *Cf.* United States *vs.* Perkins 116, U. S., 483.

[2] See United States Revised Statutes, *passim.*

[3] Thus in New York, the Public Officers law, Laws of 1892, chap. 681, sec.
9, declares that all subordinate officers, whose appointment is not otherwise
provided for by law, shall be appointed by their principal officers.

[4] See *infra*, p. 268.

[5] People *vs.* Angle, 109 N. Y., 564.

to the power of appointment.[1]   Therefore, when the
heads of departments have the appointing power, they
have, in the absence of express statutory provision to
the contrary, the power of removal also.   The same
rule is true in the state governments.[2]   In not a few
instances, however, especially in the case of the representatives of the central state government in localities,
the duration of the office is fixed by statute, and
removal may be made only for cause, and then by the
governor, and not by the heads of departments.[3]

III.—The power of direction and supervision.

In the United States, the original conception of the
head of department was that of an officer stationed at
the centre of the government who might have, it is
true, in many cases the power of appointment and removal, but who was not supposed to direct the actions
of the subordinates of his department.   This conception was particularly applicable to that branch of
administration which has been designated the administration of internal affairs.   In this branch of
administration almost everything was attended to by
officers either elected by the people of the local districts into which the state was divided, or appointed
by the central authority of the state government from
among the inhabitants of such district, and acting
almost entirely independently of any central supervision.   The need of central instruction and supervision was not felt, because the statutes of the

---

[1] *Ex parte* Hennen, 13 Peters, 230.

[2] People *Ex rel.* Sims *vs.* Fire Commissioners, 73 N. Y., 437 ; *cf.* Mechem,
Law of Offices, sec. 445.

[3] *E. g.*, see New York Laws, 1892, chap. 681, sec. 23.

legislature descended into the most minute details as to the duties and powers of the officers. The conception of a hierarchy of subordinate and superior officers was very dim if it existed at all.

The position originally occupied in the national administration by the collectors of the customs is a good example of the position occupied by the local representatives of the governmental departments who occupied the most dependent position. Though nominally the subordinates of the secretary of the treasury, the law never recognized that they were subject to his instructions and directions, nor was it the practice to regulate administrative action by means of such instructions.[1] No one, further, thought in our early history of appealing from the decision of a collector to the secretary of the treasury.

In the state government the system was of the same character, the heads of department occupying an even less important position than that occupied by the heads of departments in the national government. Almost all administrative matters affecting the state as a whole were attended to by officers in the localities who were really quite independent, after they had assumed office, of all central instructions, notwithstanding the fact that the most important of them were originally appointed by the central government of the state. It was not the habit of the central state government to send to these officers in the localities instructions as to how they should act in the execution of the law, whatever may have been

[1] See the Report of the Secretary of the Treasury on the Collection of Duties, 1885, p. xxxvii. ; see also Eliot *vs.* Swartout, 10 Peters, 137 ; Tracy *vs.* Swartout, 10 *id.*, 80.

the actual power of the heads of departments. The independence of the local officers was later very much increased, because of the fact that they ceased to be the appointees of the central state government, but were elected by the people of the localities over which they had jurisdiction.

This theory of local administrative independence in the discharge of functions of government affecting the interests of the state as a whole still lies at the basis of our system of state administration. Nevertheless, there is a tendency in certain branches of administration towards the development, in the hands of the state heads of departments, of powers of supervision, direction, and control. This tendency is particularly marked in the domains of education, public charities, and public health. The powers of supervision which are exercised by the heads of departments over the local representatives of the departments may be classified as follows:

First.—A power of general regulation as to the methods to be followed by local officers is sometimes accorded to a state head of department. Thus, in a number of states local accounts must be kept in accordance with rules and regulations prescribed by the chief fiscal officer of the state. The state of Ohio has probably gone as far as any state in this respect. An act of 1902[1] provides for " a bureau of inspection and supervision of public officers with the auditor of state *ex officio* at its head. . . . The auditor shall 'formulate, prescribe, and instal a system of accounting and reporting that shall be uniform for every public office and every public

[1] 95 Ohio Laws, p. 5.

account of the same class,' and shall show all the
details of all the transactions consummated in the
office. . . . Every taxing body and public institution of the state is required to report to the state
auditor such accounts and statistics as he may demand."[1] Again, a similar power of regulation is often
given to the state board of charities. New York has
probably gone as far in this direction as any state.[2]

Second.—It is sometimes provided that action taken
by the local representatives of the state administration shall, to be valid, receive the approval of the
head of a state department. Thus in New York, the
civil-service rules of the cities must be approved by
the state civil-service commission before they may go
into effect.[3]

Third.—The power is sometimes granted to a state
department to issue orders to local officers to do that
which the central authority regards as necessary and
which the local authority has neglected to do. Such
a power is particularly marked in the case of the state
boards of health. Thus even in Ohio, whose central
state administration has been, and is now from many
points of view, less powerful than is the central administration of other states, the state board of health
has under the law [4] the power to " alter any regulation made by local boards and, in case of emergency
or the delinquency of local officers, it takes complete
control of local matters, making such orders as it

[1] Orth, " The Centralization of Administration in Ohio," *Columbia University Studies in History, Economics, and Public Law,* vol. xvi., p. 472.

[2] See Fairlie, " Centralization of Administration in New York State," *ibid.,*
vol. ix., p. 507.

[3] Laws of 1899, chap. 370, sec. 10.

[4] 90 Ohio Laws, p. 87.

deems fit, and enforcing the regulations established by the local boards. In such cases all the local police and health officers must enforce the orders of the state board under pain of heavy penalties." [1]

Fourth.—It is also frequently provided that the state government shall aid by grants of money the local governments in the discharge of functions of state administration imposed by law upon them. But the state aid shall not be given unless the local governments maintain a certain standard. The determination of the question whether the required standard has been maintained is to be made by some central state officer. This method of securing to the state administration a control over local officers is very common in the educational administration, and through it the localities have been forced to employ only properly certified teachers, to keep the schools open during a certain number of weeks each year, and to adopt a prescribed course of study. [2]

Fifth.—It is in some cases provided that appeals from decisions of local authorities may be made to the heads of state departments. This is more commonly provided in the educational administration than elsewhere, and is particularly marked in the state of New York, where the power is accorded to any one aggrieved of appealing from the decision of any school authority to the state superintendent of public instruction. The decision of the superintendent is final. [3] While the power to hear such appeals is

[1] Orth, *op. cit.*, p. 504.

[2] See Webster, "Recent Centralizing Tendencies in State Educational Administration," *Columbia University Studies*, etc., vol. viii., p. 156.

[3] Fairlie, "The Centralization of Administration in New York State," *ibid.*, vol. ix., p. 451..

probably greater in the case of the New York state superintendent than in the case of any other officer, this method of control is not unknown in other states.[1]

Sixth.—Finally, in a great many instances state departments are given large powers of investigation and advice although they may have no powers of actual control. This is a characteristic of the state departments in Massachusetts.[2] and of all state boards of charities.[3] Much good would seem to have been accomplished by the state departments in the dissemination of information as to conditions existing in localities in the charities administration, in securing the reformation by the localities themselves of these conditions where they were evil, and the passage of laws to remedy such conditions where the remedy could not be expected to be applied by the locality. But the tendency is for a state department, which has been formed merely with these advisory functions, to develop powers of control of one of the classes to which attention has been directed.

The tendency towards the development in the heads of departments of powers of supervision, direction, and control is much more marked in the case of the national administration than in that of the state administration. Indeed it may be said that at the present time such powers are practically complete in the former system. The result of this development

[1] Webster, *op. cit.*, p. 73 ; Bowman, " The Administration of Iowa," *Columbia University Studies*, etc., vol. xviii., p. 55.

[2] Whitten, " Public Administration in Massachusetts," *ibid.*, vol. viii., p. 395, *passim*.

[3] Barbour, " The Value of State Boards," *Conference of Charities and Correction*, 1894, p. 9.

has been the recognition of an official hierarchy in the national administration, with the power in the heads of departments to reverse or modify, on appeal of persons interested, the decisions of subordinate federal officers and to direct them how to act.[1] Here the treasury department offers a good example. At the present time the collectors of the customs would hardly think of attempting to apply a law in a doubtful case without first receiving instructions from the secretary of the treasury,[2] and the law makes an appeal from the collector of internal revenue to the treasury department necessary before the aggrieved party has any standing in court. Any one believing himself aggrieved by the decision of a collector of internal revenue must exhaust his administrative remedy before he may resort to his judicial remedy.[3] This was the case also in the customs administration until the passage of the customs administrative law of 1890, which took away the administrative remedy of appeal to the secretary of the treasury and provided an appeal to the general appraisers.[4] The same thing is true in many cases in the department of the interior.[5] Finally, it has been held that the head of a department may change the erroneous decision of a subordinate,[6] and that any person aggrieved by the refusal of a subordinate to obey the order of the

---

[1] See, for example, United States Revised Statutes, sec. 251 ; Butterworth *vs.* United States, 112 U. S., 50.

[2] *Cf.* U. S. R. S., sec. 2652.

[3] U. S. R. S., sec. 3226.

[4] See Goss, " History of Tariff Administration in the United States," *Columbia University Studies,* etc., vol. i., p. 155.

[5] U. S. R. S., sec. 2273.

[6] United States *vs.* Cobb, 11 Federal Reporter, 76 ; see Wyman, *Administrative Law,* p. 330 *et seq.*

head of department may obtain from the proper court a mandamus to force the subordinate to obey such order.[1]

IV.—The ordinance power.

What was said as to the ordinance power of the President and governor may be repeated with slight modifications here. Notice, however, must be called to the rule that the heads of departments can never be regarded as possessing any ordinance power not derived from their power of direction, except such as has been delegated to them by the legislature. In case a head of department possesses a power of direction it would seem that he may, as a result of its exercise, issue regulations with regard to the manner of carrying on the business of his office, which regulations will be binding, not only upon his subordinates acting in their official capacity,[2] but as well upon them regarded as mere citizens doing business with the department, and also on unofficial citizens carrying on such business. Indeed the Supreme Court of the United States has recognized the binding character of departmental usage, saying : " Usages have been established in each department of the government which have become a kind of common law, and regulate the rights and duties of those who act within their respective limits."[3] But while the courts will uphold all reasonable regulations of this character, it has been held that regulations which are unjust will

[1] Miller *vs.* Black, 128 U. S., 50.

[2] 21 Opinions of Attorneys-General, 318 ; see also Wyman, *Administrative Law*, p. 304.

[3] United States *vs.* McDaniel, 7 Peters, 1, 14. In the same case the court lays weight upon the long continuance of the usage of the department ; see also Merritt *vs.* Cameron, 137 U. S. 542.

not be enforced by the courts, which will interfere to protect even officers against unjust regulations.[1]

The difference in the relations of the chief executive and the heads of departments and their local agents, which has been shown to exist in the national and the state administrative systems, brings it about that the ordinance power of the head of a state department is quite different from that of the head of a department in the national administration. Thus it is a principle of the national administration that the act of a head of department is the act of the President.[2] In the states, however, a regulation of a head of department is not regarded as the act of the governor; indeed, it is quite possible that a state head of department may issue a regulation contrary to the wish of the governor. Again, the fact that the power of direction of the head of a state department is so small as compared with that of the head of a national department, brings it about that the head of a state department must look more frequently than the head of a national department to the law for his authority to issue regulations. Finally, the fact that the laws of the states descend into greater detail as to administrative matters than do the laws of Congress, brings it about that there is less need of administrative regulation in the state than in the national system. While theoretically the same general principles may apply to the two systems, the centralized character of the one and the decentralized character of the other make the actual conditions quite different.

---

[1] United States *vs.* Cadwalader ; Gilpin, 563, 577 ; United States *vs.* Mann, 2 Brock., 11.

[2] See, *e. g.*, Wilcox *vs.* Jackson, 13 Peters, 498 ; see also *supra*, 90.

Where the power of regulation has been given to a head of department, nice questions sometimes arise as to the extent and character of the power granted. Thus, it has been held that a power of regulation is distinctively a legislative one and must be distinguished from the administrative power of direction. The courts do not permit a head of department possessing a power of regulation to dispense from the regulation once issued, by ordering a subordinate not to enforce it, where such order will result in a violation of the right of a private individual[1]; nor will a change in departmental usage be permitted to have a retrospective effect where individual rights would be violated thereby.[2] But where such dispensation from the operation of the regulation does not interfere with the rights of private persons, it would seem to be proper.[3] On the other hand, it has been held that where the legislature has granted an individual a right, dependent for its complete enjoyment upon the passage of regulations by the head of department, such right may be made of no avail by the refusal or neglect of the head of department to issue the necessary regulations.[4]

V.—*Special acts of individual application.*

In addition to these general acts, the heads of departments must, in order to discharge the functions given to them, perform many special acts. They

[1] Campbell *vs.* United States, 107 U. S., 407.

[2] United States *vs.* McDaniel, 7 Peters, 1 ; see also United States *vs.* Hill, 120 U. S., 169.

[3] Bubbs's case, 4 Comptroller's Decisions, 40 ; Orne *vs.* Barstow, 175 Mass., 193.

[4] Dunlap *vs.* United States, 173 U. S., 65.

10

have to make most of the contracts which are made by the government; they must issue orders affecting only one case; they must make decisions, either of their own motion or on the appeal of interested parties. The position of the head of department is in this respect essentially the same in the national and the state governments.

The only great difference between the position of the heads of departments in the national government and that of the heads of departments in the state governments is that, inasmuch as the former have universally a power of direction over the subordinates of the departments, appeal may be taken to the heads of departments from the decisions of subordinates, even where there is no provision by law for such an appeal. For as the Supreme Court has said: "The official duty of direction and supervision . . . implies a correlative right of appeal . . . in every case of complaint, although no such appeal is expressly given."[1] Furthermore, such appeals are often expressly provided by statute of Congress.

In the states, however, where the head of department does not usually have the power of direction[2] there is no general right of appeal from the decisions of subordinates to superiors. There is no objection, however, to the grant to the individual by statute of this right of appeal, and, as has been shown, it is sometimes granted.[3]

In the case of these appeals it is often provided by statute that a person deeming himself aggrieved by the decision of an administrative authority must ap-

[1] Butterworth *vs.* United States, 112 U. S., 50, 57; see also Bell *vs.* Hearne, 19 Howard, 252.   [2] *Supra*, p. 137.   [3] *Supra*, p. 140.

peal to the superior of such authority and obtain an unfavorable decision on such appeal before he has any standing in the courts to ask for a judicial revision of the decision complained of.[1] In other cases it is provided that if an individual chooses the remedy by administrative appeal, he is excluded from resorting to the courts in case he is dissatisfied with the decision of the head of department. This rule is, however, rarely adopted, and only where the statute clearly makes the decision of the head of department final.[2]

Outside of orders to inferiors and appeals from decisions of inferiors, the powers of heads of departments in the national and state governments are, from the point of view of their special acts of individual application, about the same. In the exercise of these powers they are often called upon to make decisions. The decisions which they thus make may be said to be of two kinds. In the first place, they often have the right to make decisions of a legal character. As a general thing these decisions may be reviewed by the proper courts. The courts may practically always review their decisions on the question of their jurisdiction. This is so even where the law would seem to make their decisions final. Thus, where a law gives to the head of a department the final decision as to the deportation of an alien, inasmuch as jurisdiction exists only in the case of aliens, the decision of the head of department as to alienage in a particular case is subject to review by the

---

[1] See, *e. g.*, Nichols *vs.* United States, 7 Wallace, 122 ; Cheatham *vs.* United States, 92 U. S., 85 ; United States *vs.* Sing Tuck, 194 U. S., 161.

[2] See, *e. g.*, the decisions in New York on the power of the Superintendent of Public Instruction to entertain appeals ; People *vs.* Collins, 34 Howard's Practice, 336 ; People *vs.* Draper, 63 Hun, 389 ; People *vs.* Eckler, 19 Hun, 609 ; see also Fairlie, *The Centralization of Administration in New York State*, p. 43.

courts.[1]   But in these cases where the decisions of the heads of departments are on questions of law, the legislature sometimes make such decisions final, and there is no constitutional objection to such action on its part.   Thus Congress may provide that the decision of the secretary of the treasury as to the amount of duty to be collected on an article imported into the United States shall be final.[2]

The second class of decisions made by heads of departments are as to facts rather than law.   As a general thing such decisions are, in the absence of a provision of statute to the contrary, final.   Thus where a state board of dental examiners are authorized to license any regular graduate of a reputable dental college, the refusal of such board to issue such a license is final and may not be reviewed even in a direct proceeding by mandamus.[3]   This rule is laid down on the theory that the determination of a head of department is made in the exercise of his official discretion, and that his discretion is not, in the absence of statute to that effect, to be reviewed by the court.[4]   But the legislature may subject the discretion of the head of a department to such a control. Thus a law is constitutional which permits an appeal to a court from the decision of the commissioner of patents refusing to issue a patent.[5]

[1] Gonzales *vs.* Williams, 192 U. S., 1 ; see also *In re* Fassett, 142 U. S., 479 ; Miller *vs.* Horton, 152 Massachusetts, 540.

[2] Cary *vs.* Curtis, 3 Howard, 236 ; see also Bates & Guild Co. *vs.* Payne, 194 U. S., 106 ; Public Clearing House *vs.* Coyne, 194 U. S., 497.

[3] People *vs.* Dental Examiners, 110 Illinois, 180 ; see also United States *vs.* Commissioner, 5 Wallace, 563 ; Litchfield *vs.* The Register, etc., 9 Wallace, 575 ; Nishimura Ekiu *vs.* United States, 142 U. S., 651.

[4] See Bates & Guild Co. *vs.* Payne, 194 U. S., 106.

[5] United States *vs.* Duell, 172 U. S., 576.

VI.—Remedies.

Different from the chief executive and the governor, the heads of departments, as any administrative officers, are subject to the control of the courts. Unless their action has been made final by the constitution or a statute, which is not usually the case, all the acts of the heads of departments in both the federal and the state governments may in one way or another be reviewed by the judicial authorities, which may on such review oblige the heads of departments to keep within the law. There is generally, however, no direct remedy against their general acts. This rule is due, not to the exalted position of heads of departments, but merely to the application to them of the general rules of law relative to the control of the courts over administrative officers.[1] But if general acts of a head of a department come up before the courts collaterally, they may be declared void as done in excess of the power of the head of department.[2]

In the case of the special acts of individual application, however, the remedies are much wider. Thus there is often possible an appeal of some sort to the courts to overrule or modify the act complained of or to prevent its enforcement, or, in case the head of a department illegally refuses to act, to force his action; while the courts often have the power, in case a special act of a head of a department comes up before them in a collateral proceeding, to declare it invalid.[3]

[1] See *infra*, p. 329.   [2] *Supra*, p. 145.

[3] *Infra*, p. 432 ; see American School of Magnetic Healing *vs.* McAnnulty, 187 U. S., 94.

CHAPTER VIII.

ORGANIZATION OF THE EXECUTIVE DEPARTMENTS.

I.—National government.

In the national government there are nine well organized departments. Of these, seven, namely, the departments of State, War, the Navy, the Treasury, the Interior, Agriculture, and the recently established Department of Commerce and Labor, are presided over by a secretary. The Department of Justice, which has as its head the attorney-general, is really hardly an executive department. Its most important business is to act as legal counsel to the President and the other departments. Its only really executive business is to superintend the United States prisons and to exercise a control over the marshals of the United States and the United States district attorneys. The Post-office has as its head the postmaster-general. The heads of these nine departments, in addition to carrying on the work of the special departments which may be assigned to them, comprise what is commonly known as the President's Cabinet. This body has, however, no legal standing, and membership in it, although usually comprising the officers mentioned, is entirely dependent upon the wishes of the President. There is no department of public works in the national administrative system. Public works are attended to by the War Department whether those works be of a military character or not.

The functions of the departments are, in most cases, easily discerned from the name of the department, though each one may attend to matters not logically within its sphere. Thus the Treasury Department attends to all financial matters except postal and public-land matters, in so far as these services may be regarded as having a financial character, because of the fact that they constitute sources of public revenue. The only departments whose names are at all likely to mislead one as to the functions that they discharge are the departments of State, of the Interior, and of Commerce and Labor. The main business of the State Department is the management of the foreign relations of the country. Originally its name was the Department of Foreign Affairs, but very soon after the foundation of the national administrative system it was thought best to transfer to the department other matters such as the management of public lands, the issue of proclamations, and the preservation of archives, and to change the name of the department from that of the Department of Foreign Affairs to that of the Department of State. The main duties of the Department of State are, however, still the management of the foreign relations and the supervision of the diplomatic and consular services.

The Department of the Interior was formed about the middle of the nineteenth century to take over the administration of certain matters which, in the course

of time, had demanded attention and which had been
assigned to one or more of the existing departments.
Thus the management of the Indians had been in
the War Department, pensions to United States sol-
diers had been attended to by the departments of
War and of the Treasury, and the management of
the public lands was also vested in the Treasury.
The Department of the Interior was formed to relieve these departments, and to it were transferred
those bureaus which did not strictly belong to the
departments to which they were assigned. An idea
of the functions of the Department of the Interior
may be obtained from an enumeration of the various
bureaus under the supervision of the Secretary of the
Interior.   These are : the Indian Bureau, the Pension Bureau, the Patent Office, the General Land
Office, the Office of Education, the United States
Geological Survey, *etc.* A word or two with regard
to one of these bureaus, namely, the Office of Education, is necessary. This bureau was formed merely
for the collection and dissemination of statistics and
information relative to educational matters, both in
this country and in foreign countries. It has no
powers of supervision over educational administration in this country, because of the fact that this
matter is not within the competence of the national
government.

The Department of Commerce and Labor, which
was formed in 1903, was formed in somewhat the
same manner as the Department of the Interior. In
the years immediately preceding its formation, the
management of a long series of matters of a commercial character had been entrusted to the Treasury

Department. Furthermore, shortly before the formation of the present department, a Department of Labor had been organized, with the object of performing for industrial questions somewhat the same duties which the education office of the Department of the Interior had been performing for educational questions. The present Department of Commerce and Labor was organized to take over the work of these commercial bureaus of the Treasury Department and that of the Department of Labor. Its duty is, according to the act which established it, " to foster, promote, and develop the foreign and domestic commerce, the mining, manufacturing, shipping, and fishery industries, the labor interests and the transportation facilities of the United States." The bureaus of which it is composed are the Light-House Board, the Light-House Establishment, the Steamboat Inspection Service, the Bureau of Navigation, the United States Shipping Commissioners, the National Bureau of Standards, the Coast and Geodetic Survey, that of the Commissioner of Immigration, the Bureau of Statistics of Foreign Commerce, the Census Office, the Fish Commission, the Bureau of Manufactures, and the Bureau of Corporations. In addition to collecting and disseminating information, this department has certain functions of supervision, particularly with regard to corporations engaged in foreign and interstate commerce, with the exception of common carriers, and certain executive functions to perform, as, for example, the maintenance of the light-house service.

The Department of Agriculture has functions resembling those of some of the bureaus of the Department of the Interior—that is, the collection and dissemination of statistics and information relative to the agricultural industry. One of the most important of its divisions is the bureau of animal industry, whose duty is to prevent, so far as its limited powers allow, the exportation of diseased cattle, and, by co-operation with similar state bureaus, to provide means for the suppression and extirpation of contagious diseases of cattle. Another bureau is the Bureau of Soils. In this and other bureaus of the department, scientific work of the highest value has been done, such as the investigation of the characteristics of soils in the United States from the point of view of their adaptability to the raising of particular crops.

Besides these well recognized departments, there are a few independent boards or commissions, whose duties are more or less important. The most notable of these are the Civil Service Commission, which has charge of the administration of the civil service law and rules, and the Interstate Commerce Commission, which is vested with powers of supervision over the transportation corporations of the country engaged in interstate commerce.

II.—*The state governments.*

As a result of the democratic movements of the middle of the nineteenth century, most of the officers of the state governments corresponding to the heads of departments in the national government, became, as has been pointed out, elective. These officers were the secretary of state, whose duties, with the exception of those relating to foreign affairs, are about the same as those of the officer of the same name in the

national government; a head of the finance department, known sometimes as treasurer, sometimes as
auditor, and sometimes as comptroller; in a number
of states a further financial officer who is to receive
or disburse public moneys, and also one who is to audit
accounts against the state; and an attorney-general,
who is the legal adviser of the officers of the state
government and sometimes has powers of supervision, under the direction of the governor, of the
local prosecutors. These officers may be said to be
the normal "state officers," as they are called in all
states of the Union. There is, it will be noticed, in
this list no officer at the head of the state military administration. Military matters are, for the most part,
attended to by the governor in person, with the aid of
his military staff, particularly the adjutant general.

In addition to these "state officers," there are in
all states a series of officers who really are at the
head of state departments but who vary greatly in
different states, very largely in accordance with the industrial and other social conditions obtaining therein.
As a general thing, the higher the industrial development of the state the greater the number of
its officers. Thus in the state of New York there
were in 1901 nearly 100 different boards of commissioners and trustees, "while Massachusetts, Pennsylvania, and other public states have a like number." [1]
Further, the tendency seems to be towards an increase
in the number of these departments. [2]

[1] Blue, "Tendencies in State Administration," *Annals of the American
Academy*, vol. xviii., p. 434.

[2] Thus it is said: "The legislation of 1901 in regard to the general structure
and function of state government presents many features of interest and importance. One of the most singular is the remarkable increase in the number

These boards and officers have various duties to perform. Some have mere powers of inspection, such as factory inspectors, insurance and bank superintendents, and inspectors of mines ; some are examining bodies for different professions and occupations, such as boards of registration for medicine, dentistry, and pharmacy, civil service boards, and examining boards for barbers, plumbers, and even horse-shoers. Some have scientific or *quasi*-scientific functions to discharge, such as boards of agriculture and horticulture and statistical boards, while some have definite executive or supervisory work to do, such as the various state superintendents of schools or boards of education, state boards of charities and public health.[1]

The rapid increase of these offices and the consequent rapid increase of the expenses of state administration have resulted in an effort of late years to consolidate some of these largely independent authorities, and to adopt, to a degree at any rate, the policy of the federal government in combining the various offices established for some particular administrative purpose under the direction of a few heads of departments.   The governors of several of

of new departments, boards and commissions or commissioners, for the inspection, supervision, or regulation of various classes of activity within the state. These new governmental agencies are created for the protection of public health, of personal safety, and in the interest of agriculture or labor."—*New York State Library Bulletin*, 72, *Review of Legislation*, 1901, p. 15.   In 1902 "More than a score of these [boards, commissions, and other offices] were created, some of which amounted only to a redistribution of functions, while others involved the extension of the government's activity into new fields."—*Ibid., Bulletin*, 80, *Review of Legislation*, 1902, p. 713.

[1] See, for a classification and discussion of these boards and their work, White, "State Boards and Commissions," *Political Science Quarterly*, vol. xviii., p. 631.

the states have called attention to the defects of the existing unconcentrated system, and several state legislatures have passed laws consolidating quite a number of these offices.[1] One of the most marked instances of this tendency towards consolidation is to be found in the case of the Board of Control in Iowa, in which were consolidated all the powers formerly vested in the various boards having charge of special state charitable institutions.[2] The example of Iowa was followed in nine other states by 1901, and it is said : " If the movement should continue as rapidly during the next decade as it has during the last, the centralization of control over state institutions would very soon be completed."[3]

The establishment of this vast number of new state offices and departments has naturally had the effect of increasing considerably the importance of the position of the governor, since it has had the effect of vesting in him a much larger power of appointment than was accorded to him by the system of state government in force in 1860. It must not, of course, be understood that membership in all the new boards is

[1] See Blue, *loc. cit., New York State Library Bulletin*, 76, *Diegst of Governor's Messages*, p. 398 ; see also *ibid., Bulletin*, 80, *Review of Legislation*, 1902, p. 715, where it is said : " The tendency towards centralization of administrative authority is clearly evident in the legislature of 1902, particularly in Massachusetts and New York. . . . The centralizing tendencies evident in two such states as New York and Massachusetts, where the urban and industrial conditions characteristic of recent times are so highly developed, are very significant. They seem to foreshadow like changes in other states and a general movement toward greater unity in state administration."

[2] See Bowman, " The Administration of Iowa," *Columbia University Studies, etc.*, vol. xviii., p. 112.

[3] *New York State Library Bulletin,*, 72 *Review of Legislation*, 1901, p. 17. In the article on State Boards and Commissions by Mr. White, published in the *Political Science Quarterly*, vol. xviii., p. 655, is to be found a proposition

the result of a gubernatorial appointment. For the members of a large number of the boards are elected by the people or by the legislature, or elected state officers are made *ex-officio* members of boards, most of whose work is then done by a paid secretary. Further, whatever may be the method of filling these offices the governor seldom has any absolute power of removal, his power of removal, where it is recognized, being ordinarily for cause and often depending on the concurring action of the state senate.

The composition of these new offices varies. Three plans, it may be said, have been followed : *First,* we find boards whose members retire from office at such times as to make the boards reasonably permanent bodies. Such boards are quite large, when

for the grouping of these commissions into executive departments which provides for all the important boards and groups them as follows :

" Department of Education : Public Schools ; Nautical Training ; Free Public Libraries ; Normal Schools.

Department of Examinations : Civil Service ; Dentistry ; Medicine ; Pharmacy ; Pilots.

Departments of Manufactures : Labor Statistics ; Arbitration and Conciliation ; Inspection of Manufactures ; Lumber ; Liquors ; *etc.*

Department of Agriculture : Agriculture ; Cattle ; Dairy ; Horticulture ; Inland Fish and Game.

Department of Corporate Control : Railroads ; Gas ; Telephone ; Street Railways ; Banks ; Insurance.

Department of Public Works : Highways ; Parks ; Sewerage ; Buildings ; Land ; Harbor.

Departments of Charities and Corrections : Lunacy ; Feeble-minded ; Blind, *etc.,* ; Charity Work ; Prisons ; Reformatories, *etc.*

Department of Public Safety ; Health ; Fire Marshal ; Police."

Of course this classification does not pretend to embrace all of the departments of the state government. It attempts to classify merely the various bureaus and offices which have arisen since the middle of the 19th century. To get a complete view of the work done by the state government it would be necessary to add to this list the work done by the officers who have been spoken of as " state officers."

their members are unpaid and the detailed work is done by a paid secretary, or

Second, these boards are small, consisting of not more than three members. Their members are in such case usually salaried and themselves attend to the detailed work. There would seem to be a tendency towards this form of organization. This is characteristic of the Iowa Board of Control which has been so extensively copied by other states.

Third, we sometimes find the office entrusted to one officer, who is then of course, salaried.

Each of these methods of organization has its advantages. The unsalaried board form is believed to take the administration of the particular work entrusted to the board somewhat more effectually out of politics than any other form of organization, and has been most enthusiastically advocated for the administration of state charities by those interested in those matters. On the other hand, it is claimed that this method of organization produces an inefficient and expensive administration, and the tendency would seem to be away from it and towards a small paid board or a single paid commissioner.

It is probable that both freedom from politics and efficiency could be secured under the commission form of organization if the various offices could be grouped together in well defined departments according to some such plan as has been referred to. If such a plan were adopted it would be comparatively easy to bring it about in time that the only political officer in the department would be the head of department, whether appointed by the governor—which would undoubtedly be the best method—or elected by the people of the state or by the legislature. The heads of the various bureaus or offices into which the department would then be divided need not change with each state administration, but, being under the general direction and control of a head of department, might develop in time into non-political administrative officers having a reasonably permanent tenure. Under present conditions such a solution of the question is difficult if not impossible, on account of the independent position most of the heads of these offices occupy towards all other officers in the state government —even the governor.

III.—Local subordinates of the executive departments.

Certain of the executive departments have scattered about the country, in districts into which it has been divided for the purposes of administration, subordinate officers who are more or less subject to the control of the heads of departments. Thus in the national administration the treasury department has its collectors, naval officers, surveyors, inspectors, measurers, weighers, and gaugers in the customs and internal-revenue districts; the department of the interior, its land receivers and registrars and Indian agents, *etc.* The national administration is highly centralized, rarely making use of the officers of the state or of the various local corporations within the state, such as the counties and the towns. While this is true also of certain branches of state administration (as, for example in New York, the factory inspectors of the labor commissioner and the various agents of the department of public works), still in many cases the central state government makes use of officers

who are at the same time officers of the local corporations, or even imposes duties of state concern
upon such local corporations themselves. Indeed,
these local corporations are primarily administrative
districts for the purposes of the central state administration.[1] For example, in most of the states the
counties and the towns attend to the collection of
state taxes, defray most of the expenses of the judicial
administration, take care of the poor, schools, and
highways, while the county authority is not uncom-
monly made a board of canvassers for state elections.
The control which the central executive departments
have over such local corporations and their officers,
both when acting as the agents of the central administration and when acting as the agents of the local
corporations, is, as compared with the control possessed by the departments of the national administration over their subordinates, very slight. At the
same time it is increasing, particularly in the fields of
education, public health, charities, and taxation and
accounts. Most of the local corporations, however,
elect their own officers, who, when acting, as they so
often do, as the agents of the central administration,
are not infrequently quite independent of the heads
of the central executive departments.

[1] *Infra*, p. 167.

BOOK III.

LOCAL ADMINISTRATION.

CHAPTER I.

LOCAL CORPORATIONS IN THE UNITED STATES.

I.—Corporate capacity of local areas.

THE original English system of administration did not permit of the recognition of corporate capacity in the various local areas. At the time of the Norman Conquest William the Conqueror districted the kingdom of England, using, in the main, the old divisions —that is, the shires—which had come down from Anglo-Saxon times, but did not recognize that these divisions were local corporations with powers of local government. The conception that the local areas were merely administrative districts for the purpose of the administration of government was due to two things.

First, the hostile relations of the conquering Normans and the conquered Saxons made it impossible to conduct the government under any scheme granting large local powers. Little freedom could be granted to the localities if every matter in their juris-diction was to be decided from race motives. Some system of government must be devised by means of which the peace might be preserved and the king might stand as an arbiter between the conflicting race elements of the nation.[1]

In the second place, William the Conqueror had had an experience with the feudal system, based as it was on the recognition of large local powers, and was determined to do what within him lay to prevent its development in his new kingdom.

Therefore the old districts which were maintained, *i. e.*, the county or shire, the hundred, and the borough, were recognized as administrative districts, in which were placed officers appointed and dismissed at the pleasure of the crown, who were to attend to the administration of all public business needing attention in the district. The centralized character of the administrative system was later changed, as will be pointed out, but the local areas remained for a long time as they were during the Norman period—that is, non-corporate bodies.[2] It was not until 1888 that the English county, and not until 1894 that the English parish, really became corporations. By the beginning of the reign of the Tudors, however, municipal boroughs were incorporated—that is, were recognized as juristic persons with the right to hold property, to sue and be sued, and to exercise specific governmental powers such as police and judicial powers.

The rule adopted in England was applied to the local districts of the American states. They were,

[1] Gneist, *Self-government*, etc., p. 14.

[2] See Russell *vs.* The Men of Devon, 2 Durnford & East, 667, A.D. 1788. In this case it was held that an action in damages could not be maintained against a county for negligence in the care of a bridge, because, although it was the county's duty to repair the bridge, the county was not incorporated.

with the exception of the incorporated cities, not regarded as corporations, or as having services of their
own to attend to, apart from the sphere set aside to
them by the statutes of the state legislature, nor could
they even hold property or sue or be sued.[1]

One result of the original non-corporate character
of towns is to be found in the fact that, by common
law, the property of an inhabitant of a New England
town may be taken upon execution on a judgment
against the town.[2]   The first step in New York towards recognizing that the areas of administration
possessed any juristic personality was taken in the
case of North Hempstead *vs.* Hempstead,[3] which held
that a town had a certain corporate capacity, though
what that corporate capacity was was not clearly defined.   In 1801 the legislature expressly made the
county a capable grantee of lands,[4] and finally the
New York revised statutes of 1829 expressly declared
each county and town to be a body corporate with
certain specified powers, to wit, the powers to hold
property and to sue and be sued.[5]   The principle
established in Massachusetts and New York has been
adopted in most of the states of the American Union,

[1] See for New York, which may be taken as typical, the cases of Jackson *vs.* Hartwell, 8 Johnson, 422; Jackson *vs.* Cory, *ibid.*, 385; Hornbeck *vs.* West-brook, 9 Johnson, 73; and Jackson *vs.* Schoonmaker, 2 Johnson, 230.

[2] Beardsley *vs.* Smith, 16 Conn., 368; see also Bloomfield *vs.* Charter Oak Bank, 121 U. S., 121, 129; Horner *vs.* Coffey, 25 Miss., 434.

[3] 2 Wendell, New York, 109. In Massachusetts, however, towns were authorized to grant lands in 1635, to sue and be sued in 1694, and were ex-pressly incorporated in 1785. See 9 Gray, Mass., 511, note, which gives a history of the legislation as to towns.

[4] 1 Kent and Radcliff's Laws, 561.

[5] The chapter devoted to the towns is explained by the original report of the revisers to the legislature, in 1827, in which it is said that " this article is wholly new in its present form."

so that it may be said that the American county and town, where they have any administrative importance, are at the present time bodies corporate.[1]

But while the result of American development has been the recognition of the rural local areas as public corporations, the further step has not been taken of recognizing that such corporations possess any sphere of action of their own. The duties attended to by them or by the officers acting within them are regarded generally as almost exclusively of central concern, and their officers, though elected by the people of the locality, are not regarded as local officers in the sense that they are agents of the local corporations. They are simply state officers who are, in accordance with the method adopted in the United States of filling these positions, elected by the people resident in the local areas. The position of the town, or township as it is sometimes called, is well stated in the case of Lorillard *vs.* The Town of Monroe.[2]

The several towns in this state says Judge Denio, are corporations for certain special and very limited purposes, or to speak more accurately, they have a certain limited corporate capacity. They may purchase and hold lands within their own limits for the use of their inhabitants. They may, as a corporation, make such contracts and hold such personal property as may be necessary to the exercise of their corporate or administrative powers, and they may regulate and manage their corporate property, and, as a necessary incident, may, sue and be sued where the assertion of their corporate rights or the enforcement of their corporate liabilities shall require such proceedings. In all other respects—for instance, in everything which concerns the administration of civil or criminal justice, the preservation of

---

[1] See Dillon, *Municipal Corporations*, 4th ed., i., chap. 2; Levy Court *vs,* Coroner, 2 Wallace, 501, 507.

[2] 11 New York, 392, 393.

the public health and morals, the conservation of highways, roads, and bridges, the relief of the poor, and the assessment and collection of taxes—the several towns are political divisions, organized for the convenient exercise of portions of the political power of the state, and are no more corporations than the judicial or assembly districts. The functions and the duties of the several town officers respecting these subjects are judicial and administrative and not in any sense corporate functions or duties. The judge goes on to say: It is a convenient arrangement to have the assessors chosen by the electors of the towns, [but], when chosen, they are public officers, just as much as the highest official functionaries of the state. They are, therefore, not in any legal sense the servants or agents of the towns.

In New England, however, where the village organization has never flourished, towns do sometimes have local services, such as waterworks, in the management of which they are regarded as having the characteristics of municipal corporations proper and are, therefore, held liable for negligence in the performance of these local duties.[1]

The position of the county, which is quite similar to that of the town, is well stated in the case of Hamilton County *vs.* Mighels.[2] The court says here:

A county organization is created almost exclusively with a view to the policy of the state at large, for purposes of political organization and civil administration, in matters of finance, of education, of provision for the poor, of military organization, of the means of travel and transport, and especially for the general administration of justice. With scarcely an exception, all powers and functions of the county organization have a direct and exclusive reference to the general policy of the state, and are, in fact, but a branch of the general administration of that policy.[3]

[1] See Hand *vs.* Brookline, 126 Mass., 324.
[2] 7 Ohio State, 109, 119.
[3] See also Talbot County *vs.* Queen Anne's County, 50 Md., 245, 259.

Municipal corporations proper, *i. e.*, cities, villages, and incorporated towns, are regarded as organized primarily for the satisfaction of the local needs of their inhabitants. They are, therefore, not regarded as so representative of the state as are the *quasi*-municipal corporations, such as towns and counties. At the same time, no more than the *quasi*-municipal corporations are they regarded as possessing any inherent powers of local government to be derived from the fact of their corporate existence.[1]

It will be seen what a slight recognition there has been, notwithstanding the corporate capacity of the local areas, of the possession by them of any sphere of action of their own as distinguished from their sphere of action as agents of the state government. Their corporate capacity is made a mere incident to their public governmental capacity, and is of value to them only in that, through it, they may own land and property generally. The courts have, for example, held that as a result of their corporate capacity counties and towns have no power to borrow money.[2] It is true, however, that either general or special statutes have conferred upon local areas the power to borrow money for a series of specified purposes.

Thus, notwithstanding the great decentralization of the administrative system which has resulted from the development of American local institutions, and to which attention will be called in the next chapter, and notwithstanding the recognition of the juristic personality of the local areas, it cannot be said that the course of American local administrative history has given to the localities any sphere of independent local

[1] *Infra*, p. 169.   [2] Stain *vs.* Town of Genoa, 23 N. Y., 439, 447.

action. They are, as their English prototypes were
after the Norman Conquest, agents of the state with,
however, a corporate capacity, which is to be made
use of more for the benefit of the state as a whole
than for the benefit of a particular area. Our constitutional local self-government has consisted rather in
the right of the people of the localities to choose the
officers who are to execute the laws, both general and
local, than in any right of the people of the localities
to determine what branches of administrative activity
they shall take up.[1]

II.—*Subjection of the local corporations to the control of the legislature.*

1. *Local corporations are authorities of enumerated
powers.*—It has been shown that local corporations
are not recognized as having any inherent sphere of
local action. This is due to the rule of law that the
state legislature, in the absence of a constitutional
provision, is absolutely supreme, and to the practice,
which has been adopted by the legislatures of this
country, of enumerating in detail the powers of all
public authorities. Local corporations being merely
public authorities with a territorially circumscribed
jurisdiction, there is no escape from the conclusion
that their powers must be enumerated in detail by the
legislature. No better or more authoritative statement of the powers possessed by local corporations
can be found than that given by Judge Dillon in his
great work on municipal corporations, and approved

---

[1] As to the conception of local self-government in this country, see Eaton,
" Right to Local Government," *Harvard Law Review*, 13, p. 441.

by many of the later decisions of the courts themselves.[1] He says :

It is a general and undisputed proposition of law that *a municipal corporation possesses and can exercise the following powers and
no others :* First, those granted in *express* words ; second, those
necessarily or fairly implied in, or *incident* to the powers expressly
granted ; third, those *essential* to the declared objects and purposes of the corporation—not simply convenient, but indispensable. Any fair, reasonable doubt concerning the existence of
power is resolved by the courts against the corporation, and the
power is denied. Of every municipal corporation, the charter or
statute by which it is created is its organic act. Neither the corporation nor its officers can do any act, or make any contract, or
incur any liability, not authorized thereby, or by some legislative
act applicable thereto. All acts beyond the scope of the powers
granted are void. Judge Dillon adds, that while the rule of
strict construction of corporate powers is not so directly applicable to the ordinary clauses in the charter or incorporating acts
of municipalities as it is to the charters of private corporations
. . . it is equally applicable to grants of powers to municipal and public bodies which are out of the usual range, or which
may result in public burdens, or which, in their exercise, touch
the right to liberty or property, or, as it may be compendiously
expressed, any common-law right of the citizen or inhabitant.[2]

The necessary result of such a rule of law, with the
accompanying strict construction which is usual, is
that public corporations will often apply to the source
of authority—that is, the legislature—in order that
any doubt as to the existence of particular powers
which it is desirable to exercise, but which are not
clearly conferred, may be dissipated.

2. *Legislative control of local corporations.*—Further, it is to be remembered that almost all the local
corporations in the United States have, as has been

[1] Dillon, *Municipal Corporations*, 4th ed., p. 145.
[2] *Ibid.*, p. 148.

shown, to discharge functions interesting the state as a whole. They are practically agents of the central government of the state. This is true, even of the cities.[1] The fact that these local corporations are agents of the central state government must have an important influence on their relation to the legislature, for the legislature is in the American system of decentralized administration, or local self-government, as we usually call it, the only guardian of administrative harmony and uniformity. So long as a local corporation is merely an organization for local government, the legislature is not necessarily called upon to interfere with or control its actions. But just so soon as a local corporation begins to act as the agent of the state, to exercise powers which concern the people of the state as a whole, it becomes necessary for the guardian of the people of the state to see to it that these powers are exercised uniformly and efficiently throughout the state.

Unfortunately, however, for American local corporations, and particularly for American cities, which have important local functions to discharge, the American state legislature has not distinguished, so clearly as it should have done, these two kinds of activity. It has in many cases forgotten that local corporations are discharging local functions, in the discharge of which they should be largely free from central control; it has perceived merely that these local corporations are state agents, which by law are subject to its control, and it has not scrupled to exercise this control over all of their actions, local as well as general. This the state legislature has been able

[1] *Infra*, p. 209.

to do because, apart from certain rights to property which these corporations may have under general constitutional provisions protecting private property, the power of the legislature over local corporations is unlimited.[1]

The continual exercise by the legislature of its unquestioned powers resulted in the gradual assumption by the state legislatures, in parts of the country, of a long series of local powers. This centralization of local functions had a particularly disastrous effect upon the cities of the United States, causing not only great lack of local interest in the management of municipal affairs, but also an ignorant and inefficient management of these affairs, and an unwise solution of many of the problems which have to be solved by our cities.[2] The evil effects of legislative regulation of local affairs have been aggravated by the fact that this central interference has been in many instances caused, not by the desire on the part of the legislature to reform local abuses or to grant powers whose exercise is desired by the localities, but by the hope of deriving some temporary political advantage for the party in control of the legislature.

The undoubted, well recognized evils of the American system of special legislation and continual legislative interference in purely local affairs have led many of the states to insert in their constitutions

---

[1] See Commonwealth *vs.* Moir, 199 Pennsylvania State, 534, which held that the legislature might provide for the state appointment of the mayor of a city ; Laramie County *vs.* Albany County, 92 U. S., 307, which held that the legislature might divide a county and make such distribution of its property on the occasion of the division as it sees fit ; and Perkins *vs.* Slack, 86 Pennsylvania State, 270, which held that the state legislature could force a city to expend a large sum of money for the erection of a city hall.

[2] See Goodnow, *Municipal Home Rule*, pp. 23–28.

provisions intended to limit the power of the legislature to interfere with the affairs of local corporations. In all these cases, however, the framers of the constitution have borne in mind the fact that these local corporations are agents of state government. They have therefore been careful not to prohibit central legislative interference except as to purely local matters.

3. *Constitutional limitation of legislative control.* —The constitutional provisions which have been adopted with this end in view may be classed under two general heads. In the first place, they forbid absolutely interference by the legislature with particular matters. Thus, for example, many of the constitutions assure to the localities the right of the local selection of local officers.[1] Thus, also, in quite a number of states the legislature may not divide counties or change the county seats without the consent of the people.[2] Thus also in a number of states it is provided that the consent of the local authorities is necessary in order that street railway franchises may be granted.[3] In a few states, such, for example, as California, Washington, and Illinois, taxes for local purposes can be levied only by corporate authorities.[4] Probably the most radical step that has been taken is that which has been taken by the states of Missouri,

[1] Goodnow, *Municipal Home Rule*, p. 60, note 5, where it is shown that more than twenty states have adopted such a constitutional provision. Some cases have claimed the right to the local selection of local officers in the absence of a specific constitutional provision. People *vs.* Hurlbut, 24 Mich., 44 ; State *vs.* Barker, 116 Iowa, 96. This is not, however, the better rule. See Commonwealth *vs.* Moir, 199 Pennsylvania State, 534 ; State *vs.* Smith, 44 Ohio State, 348 ; Commonwealth *vs.* Plaisted, 148 Mass., 375.

[2] *Ibid.*, p. 61, note 1.

[3] *Ibid.*, p. 61, note 3.　　　　　　　　　　　　　　[4] *Ibid*, p. 60.

California, Washington, Minnesota, and Colorado.
Here the constitution provides that cities of a certain
size shall alone have the power to frame their own charters and amend them.[1] The purpose of this provision
being merely to protect the cities from legislative
interference in the management of their local affairs,
the constitution has not been considered by the courts
as affecting anything but what is purely local. Inasmuch as a large part of administrative work actually
attended to by cities is not regarded by the courts as
of a local character, it follows that much of what is
popularly termed municipal government is still under
the control of the legislature, notwithstanding the
existence of such a constitutional provision.[2] But so
far as the purely local affairs of the cities are concerned, this method of protecting them from legislative interference would seem to be on the whole
the most effective one which has as yet been adopted.

The second class of constitutional provisions
adopted to protect local corporations from legislative
interference do not absolutely prohibit action by the
legislature but prohibit action in a particular manner,
that is, prohibit a certain kind of legislative action.
In other words, inasmuch as the legislative control
productive of most evil has resulted from the passage
of special legislation, the constitution attempts to
prohibit special legislation with regard to a large
class of subjects.[3] At the same time, the indirect
effect of these constitutional provisions prohibiting

[1] See Kansas City *vs.* Scarritt, 127 Mo., 642 ; St. Louis *vs.* Dorr, 145 Mo., 466.
[2] See Dewart, '' The Municipal Condition of St. Louis '' ; Hopkins, '' The Municipal Condition of Kansas City,'' *Louisville Conference for Good City Government*, p. 218, 233. See also St. Louis *vs.* Dorr, *supra.*
[3] Goodnow, *Municipal Home Rule*, p. 56.

special legislation is to strengthen the position of local corporations over against the legislature. For the prohibition of special laws often prevents the legislature from interfering in matters of purely local concern affecting some particular municipal corporation, and really obliges the legislature to delegate greater powers than it otherwise would delegate to local bodies. The exact degree to which the power of the legislature over local corporations is limited by these constitutional provisions can be determined only as a result of answering two questions: first, What is a special act under the constitution? and second, What are local matters which may not be interfered with by special act?

First, what is a special act? The only constitution which clearly defines a special act is the constitution of the state of New York, adopted in 1894. This constitution divides the cities of the state into three classes, and provides that an act is special which affects less than all the cities of a class. The constitution of New York differs, however, from most of the constitutions in not prohibiting absolutely special legislation, but in making it more difficult of passage.[1]

In most of the states, what is a special act under the constitution is to be determined by the courts. In their decision of this question, they have held very commonly, that they may go back of an act which is general in form and see whether it is special in its application, and that, if on such examination they find it is special in its application, they will declare it to be unconstitutional.[2]

---

[1] *Infra*, page 177.   [2] See Devine *vs.* Cook County, 84 Ill., 590.

On the other hand, the courts do not generally attempt to prevent the legislature from classifying municipal corporations. Practically the only state in which the courts have decided that a constitutional provision prohibiting special legislation does not permit the legislature to classify municipal corporations, is the state of Ohio.[1] But, while permitting the legislature to classify municipal corporations, the courts insist that the classification adopted must be a reasonable one. Thus they have held very generally that a classification based merely upon geographical conditions is improper.[2] A classification, further, of cities by name has been held to be improper.[3] The courts have, however, generally regarded the classification of local corporations by population—which is to operate in the future as well as in the present—to be a reasonable classification, even if, at the time the classification is made, only one city is to be found in a class.[4]

It will be seen that the prohibition of special legislation does not, under the ordinary decisions interpreting a constitutional provision prohibiting such legislation, prevent the passage by the legislature of legislation which at the time it is passed is really special in character. The reason why the courts have adopted the view they have as to what is special legislation, is the impossibility of local development and growth under general acts affecting local corporations when such acts descend into great detail. So long as

[1] State *vs.* Cowles, 64 Ohio St., 162; State *vs.* Jones, 66 Ohio St., 453; State *vs.* Beacom, *ibid.*, 491.
[2] Commonwealth *vs.* Patten, 88 Pa. St., 258.
[3] City of Council Grove, 20 Kans., 619.
[4] See Wheeler *vs.* Philadelphia, 77 Pa St., 338.

the plan of detailed enumeration of powers is adopted, so long must we expect the courts to permit the legislature pretty free hand, notwithstanding the existence of constitutional provisions forbidding special legislation.

Second, what are local affairs?—It has been said that the constitutional provisions under consideration do not attempt to prohibit special legislative action with regard to all matters of government, but only such action with regard to the local affairs of corporations. The decisions of the courts show that in the opinion of the judges there is no very clear line of demarcation between matters of general interest and local affairs. The courts regard as unconstitutional, acts which they regard as special relative to many matters which, from the point of view of other branches of the law, are regarded as of interest to the state as a whole rather than local in character.[1] The courts have held also that the legislature may, notwithstanding the prohibition to interfere by special act or otherwise with the affairs of a particular corporation, form by special act a new corporation to which certain matters attended to by the old corporation may be transferred, and that in so doing the legislature violates no constitutional provision.[2]

At the same time, a number of cases have been

---

[1] See Commonwealth *vs.* Patten, 88 Pa. St., 258; Board of Freeholders *vs.* Buck, 51 N. J. Law, 155.

[2] See People *vs.* Draper, 15 New York, 532, which held that the legislature might provide for the state appointment of police commissioners who were to have jurisdiction over a new district to which the police powers of the city were to be transferred ; see also Wilson *vs.* Board of Trustees, 133 Ill., 443, which held that the legislature might, notwithstanding the prohibition of special legislation contained in the constitution, provide by special act for the new Chicago drainage district.

decided with regard to these constitutional provisions which indicate that the courts have attempted, at any rate, to distinguish between local affairs and state affairs. Thus, for example, a number of cases have come up relative to what are corporate officers and corporate powers, where the constitution has provided that the legislature shall not grant the power to levy taxes for corporate purposes to other than corporate officers. Here the courts have held that the attempt to give powers of taxation for levee and drainage purposes to private corporations is a violation of the constitution.[1] In the same way, it has been held that parks, from this and also other points of view, are to be regarded as local affairs.[2]

The question has also arisen as to whether police matters are local matters, and it has generally been held, though not without conflict, that they are to be regarded as state rather than local matters.[3] Even where the constitution provides that local officers shall be locally selected, the legislature is permitted to provide for a central appointment of municipal police commissioners.[4]

A word perhaps ought to be said with regard to the method of limiting the power of the legislature to pass special legislation relative to the local affairs of cities provided by the constitution of New York.

[1] Harward *vs*. St. Clair and Monroe Levee *etc*. Company, 51 Ill., 130.

[2] See People *vs*. The Mayor, 51 Ill., 17 ; People *vs*. Detroit Common Council, 28 Mich., 228 ; see also People *vs*. Hurlbut, 24 Mich., 44.

[3] People *vs*. Kolsem, 130 Ind., 434 ; Commonwealth *vs*. Plaisted, 148 Mass., 375 ; State *vs*. Hunter, 38 Kan., 578 ; Mayor *vs*. State, 15 Md., 376 ; State *vs*. Leavey, 22 Neb., 454 ; Recell *vs*. Moores, 63 Neb., 219 ; Newport *vs*. Horton, 22 R. I., 196.

[4] See People *vs*. Mahaney, 13 Mich., 481 ; but see People *vs*. Albertson, 55 N. Y., 50.

This constitution provides that a special act, which is an act that affects less than all of the cities of one of the three classes of the cities in the state, must be submitted to the authorities of the cities which it affects, and if it does not receive their approval, shall be passed over again by the legislature before it is submitted to the governor. This method of limiting the control of the legislature over local corporations has been successful in preventing a great deal of the most objectionable kind of special legislation. It has not, however, prevented the passage by the legislature of special acts which have been regarded as of great importance by the party in control of the legislature.

CHAPTER II.

*I.—History of rural administration in England to
the 18th century.*

1. *The sheriff.*—The character of the English system of local government was fixed by the Norman kings. The absolutism of the Norman government reduced all classes of the inhabitants to complete submission to the crown.[1] In each of the districts into which the kingdom was divided, namely, the counties or shires, were placed officers originally known as *vice comites* and later as sheriffs, who were appointed and removable by the crown, and who were to attend to all administrative business to be transacted within the district over which they had jurisdiction.[2] The sheriffs were always unpopular officers; they were therefore gradually stripped of their powers and a system of administration established, which was more popular in character. But before this was done, the strong centralized administration of the Normans

---

[1] Stubbs, *Constitutional History of England*, i., pp. 257-259; note 1, 260; 338, *Cf.* Goodnow, "Local Government in England" in *Political Science Quarterly*, ii., 638.

[2] Stubbs, *op. cit.*, i., 276; *cf.*, *P. S. Q.*, ii., 639.

had consolidated the people of England into a nation. This was accomplished in England much sooner than on the Continent. As a result of this centralization, autonomous communities had no opportunity to develop, and though the administrative system later became really quite decentralized, the local areas remained simply administrative districts without juristic personality and with no affairs of their own to attend to,—districts in which royal officers attended to all administrative business. This prefectoral administration of the sheriffs lasted from the time of the Conquest to about the reign of Richard II., when changes were made which reduced the sheriff to the position of a ministerial officer of the royal courts, which had sprung up in the meantime, a returning officer for elections, and a conservator of the peace.[1] These changes are to be found in the establishment of the office of the justice of the peace.[2]

2. *The justice of the peace.*—To the justice of the peace were given most of the powers of the sheriff. The justices further gained control of the parish administration, which sprang up in the times of the Tudors in connection with the ecclesiastical organization, and in their courts of quarter sessions acted as the county administrative authority. They were finally by far the most important officers in the localities, discharging both administrative and judicial functions and having under their direction almost all the other officers in the localities.

The system, whose whole tone was given by the justice of the peace, was eventually much more de-

[1] See Anson, *The Law of the Constitution*, vol. ii., p. 236.
[2] 34 Edward III., chap. i., *cf.*, *P. S. Q.* ii., 644, and authorities cited.

centralized than the prefectoral system of the sheriffs.[1] All the officers were resident in the localities in which they acted. Most of them, it is true, were appointed directly or indirectly by the central government and could be removed by it. But the facts that they received no salary, though service, as a rule, was often obligatory and always arduous, and that they were chosen from the well-to-do classes, made the personnel of the service ultimately very independent and kept it from falling into bureaucratic ways. For the threat of dismissal from office had little terror for a justice of the peace. Dismissal meant relief from arduous service and not the loss of the means of livelihood. The system thus in the end secured a high degree of local self-government. The independence of the justices brought it about that the control over their actions which could be exercised by the central administration amounted finally to nothing. To provide for some sort of central control, the statutes of parliament regulating the powers and duties of the justices had to descend into the most minute details. That the justices acted in accordance with these detailed statutes was insured by the control given to the royal courts over their action, by means of which the courts might, on an application of any person aggrieved by the action of justices, force them to act as the law required or else quash their illegal action.

[1] In the earlier periods of the history of the office, the office of justice of the peace was a part of a highly centralized administrative system. Beard, "The Office of Justice of the Peace," *etc., Col. Univ. Studies, etc.,* vol. **xx**, p. 1.

II.—The development of the system in the United States.

1. *The three original forms of local administration.*—The justice of the peace system was in full force at the time of the British colonization of North America. It is only natural that its main features should characterize the original system of American local administration. We find, however, three pretty distinct forms of local administration in the different colonies: one in the New England colonies, one in the middle colonies, and a third in the southern colonies. The main distinction between these three forms is to be found in the relative position which was assigned to the areas adopted for the purposes of administration, namely, the town and the county. In New England, while the county was recognized,[1] it was not nearly so important as the town. There are several reasons why such an important position was given to the town in the New England colonies. These colonies were settled mainly by persons who had left England for the purpose of enjoying freedom of religious worship. They came over here in many instances in religious congregations, and when they settled, settled in the neighborhood of the church which they established. Furthermore the, relations of the settlers with the Indians were quite commonly hostile, and it became necessary for them to group themselves rather closely together for purposes of defence.[2]

---

[1] Howard in his *Local Constitutional History of the United States*, vol. i., 320, says that the county was formed in Rhode Island in 1703, but was comparatively unimportant. In Massachusetts, however, it is found as early as 1635. See 9 Gray, Mass., 512, note.

[2] For example, the Massachusetts legislature forbade at one time the building of dwellings distant more than half a mile from the meeting-house in any new "plantation." See 9 Gray, Mass., 511, citing Colonial Records, vol. i., p. 157.

In the middle colonies, also, we find both the town and the county. The functions of administration were quite equally distributed between them, or else the town was less important than the county. The latter was especially true of Pennsylvania, where the town was not established until the latter part of the 18th century, and after its establishment was much less important than the New England town.[1] The existence of the town in one of the middle colonies at any rate, *viz.*, New York, is due partly to New England influences, which were very marked, for example, in the eastern part of the colony; partly also to the fact that the attempt was made during the Dutch period to establish under the control of the Patroons, as they were called, colonies which, under the English occupation, developed into manors, and which played somewhat the same rôle in administration as the New England town.

In the south, social and geographical conditions were such as to discourage the development of the town during the colonial period, and to encourage the system of county administration. Thus the south was in large part settled by persons who had received large grants of land from the crown of England, and who came over here with the idea of bettering their economic condition. This resulted in the establishment of large plantations. The development of such plantations was favored by the geographical character of the country in which there were many navigable rivers entering quite far into the interior. Furthermore, the relations with the Indians were not as hostile as in New England, and therefore did not

[1] Howard, *op. cit.*, i., 385.

necessitate the gathering together in small districts of the settlers.

2. The early American county.—The county was found in all the American colonies with the exception perhaps of some of the New England colonies, where, if it existed at all, it existed in a very rudimentary form. Wherever the county did exist as an administrative district, the county authority was, as in England, the court of sessions of the justices of the peace who were appointed by the governor of the colony.[1] By the side of the justices of the peace was the sheriff, occupying a position similar to that of the English sheriff of the same period. That is, the sheriff was, in our colonial period, a conservator of the peace, the returning officer for elections, and the ministerial officer of the courts. He was appointed also by the governor.[2] In the court of sessions were centred about all the administrative duties relating to the county. In this court the justices appointed some person to be county treasurer, attended to the county finances and supervised the administration of, the poor-law. Acting separately, they had charge of police and highway matters, and directed the acts of a great number of subordinate officers who had duties relative to these matters.

The first change to be noticed in the county organization is the substitution of officers elected by the people of the county for the appointed justices. This movement began in New York certainly as early as 1691, probably as early as 1683.[3] In 1691 an officer,

[1] For New York, see *Documents Relating to the Colonial History of New York*, iv. 25; *cf.*, Howard, i., 406.

[2] See Brodhead, *History of New York*, vol. i., 63, and authorities cited.

[3] See Laws of 1691, chapter vi. On November 2, 1683, a law was passed

called a " supervisor," was to be elected in each town.
His name comes from the fact that when these officers from each of the towns in the county were assembled together, they formed the county board, and
were "to supervise and examine the publick and
necessary charge of each county."[1] The motive for
this change was probably to provide for the coexist-
ence of local representation with local taxation, since
the main duties of the first board of supervisors were
relative to the fiscal administration of the county.[2]
The justices still retained important functions in other
administrative branches, such as highways.[3]

A little later the elective system was introduced
into Pennsylvania, but in a somewhat different form,
there being no town representation on the county
board.   In 1724 provision was made for the election
by the people of the county of three commissioners
who were to manage the fiscal affairs of the county.[4]
Sheriffs were also elected by the people in Pennsylvania from an early time.[5] This change in the
county organization was destined to have a profound

providing that there should be elected in each town persons " for the supervise-
ing of the publique affaires and charge of each respective towne and county,"
see *Colonial Laws*, vol. i., p. 131. But as the assembly in New York previous
to 1691 was an almost extra-legal body, it is safer to place the introduction of
the elective principle in county organization at 1691.

[1] This system was abolished ten years later by the Laws of 1701, chapter 96,
but was reëstablished by a law of June 19, 1703.   This accounts for the mistake which is so commonly made of assigning 1703 as the date of the introduction of the supervisor system in New York.

[2] See New York Law of November 1, 1722, where it is said : " Whereas by that
means," *i. e.*, the method of voting provided by the act of 1703, " the inhabitants of several manors, liberties, and precincts, which bear a considerable
share of the county rate, have not the liberty of chusing their own supervisors,
be it enacted " that they may vote in the town adjoining the manor, *etc.*

[3] *Cf.* Howard, i., 352.

[4] *Ibid.*, i., 382.   [5] *Ibid.*, i., 382, and authorities cited.

influence on the subsequent development of local administration in the United States.   As Howard well says [1] :

> To New York first and next to Pennsylvania belongs the honor of predetermining the character of local government in the West.   But if New York was first to return to the ancient practice of township representation in the county court, it was in Pennsylvania that the capabilities of the independent county were first tested.   Here the principle of election to county offices was carried farther than it was ever carried in England.[2]   New York is the parent of the supervisor system, Pennsylvania is the originator of the commissioner system.

The elective system thus introduced into New York and Pennsylvania has been adopted in almost every state, and has been extended to almost all the county offices, not only the original county offices, but also those which the increase of the work of administration has caused to be provided.

3. *The early American town.*—While we find in the early American county an organization similar to that of the English county of the seventeenth and eighteenth centuries, in the early American town we do not find an organization which resembles very closely the English parish of the same period.   The town is not regarded as the legal successor of the English parish but is an American creation,[3] and its development has been quite different in different sections. In New England it is older than the county,[4] in the middle colonies it seems to be a later creation.

[1] *Cf.* Howard, i., 387.

[2] It is, however, to be noted that the New York Law of 1683, above referred to, provided that the county treasurer should be elected by the voters of the county.

[3] Morey *vs.* Town of Newfane, 8 Barbour, N. Y., 645, 648.

[4] We find it in this section as early as 1630; see 9 Gray, Mass., 511.

From the very beginning, the principle of election
by the voters of the town seems to have been the
method of filling all town offices, and in the adoption
of this principle is to be found the great point of
difference between American town organization and
the English parish organization, and between the
position of the American and that of the English
justices of the peace. For in the English parish the
justice of the peace ultimately appointed almost all
of the parish officers and directed them how to act.
The powers of the American justice of the peace over
the officers of the town were also much less extensive
than were those of the English justices over parish
officers.

In the New England town the principal town
officers were elected by the town meeting, *i. e.*, the
assembly of the political people of the town, which
determined also what the town should do. The
resolutions of the town meeting were executed by the
town officers. There were also almost innumerable
town officers, each one of whom attended to some
particular matter affecting the welfare of the town.
Some of these officers were elected at the town meeting ; some were appointed by the selectmen,—the
principal town officers.[1] The existence of such a
number of officers was necessary because salaries
were not paid and because service was, as a rule,
obligatory. For no man could be expected without
compensation to give up a large share of his time to
the performance of public duties. In New York the
principal officers of the town in 1691 were the supervisor, two assessors, a constable, a collector, a clerk,

[1] Howard, i., pp 78, 88, 96.

highway commissioners or surveyors, and overseers
of the poor. These officers were, for the most part,
elected as in Massachusetts by the town meeting.
This body in New York had functions to discharge
similar to those discharged by the Massachusetts
town meeting, with the difference that its sphere of
action was not so extended. For the county did a
great deal of the work in New York that was attended
to by the town in New England.[1] In Pennsylvania,
we find in the town after its establishment two overseers of the poor, appointed by the justices, and two
supervisors of highways elected by the people of the
town. As the county was much more important in
Pennsylvania even than in New York, there was very
little for the town to do. It was more in the nature
of an administrative division of the county than a
local organization with its own duties to perform;
therefore the town meeting was not present in the
original Pennsylvania plan of local administration.[2]

[1] See N. Y. L., June 19, 1703.   [2] Howard, i., 385.

CHAPTER III.

I.—The county.

1. *The position of the county.*—The present position of the county depends on the general character of the system of local government adopted in the particular state. Thus, in New England,[1] where the town is practically supreme, the county has very little importance. It is generally little more than an administrative district for the purposes particularly of judicial administration, although it would seem to be increasing in importance. In a number of the states it has none of the characteristics of a corporation, and therefore may not either sue or be sued.[2] It has not, further, as yet obtained a county authority of any independence which is separate from other departments of the state government. Thus, in Connecticut and New Hampshire the county is under the control of the representatives to the legislature of the towns in the county,[3] while in Vermont the most important

---

[1] Except Massachusetts, which does not belong to New England from this point of view.

[2] See Ward *vs.* Hartford County, 12 Conn., 404.

[3] See General Statutes of Connecticut, 1902, sections 1742–1756; General Statutes of New Hampshire, 1901, p. 123. On the general subject of the county administration in New England, see Howard, i., pp. 459, 464. See also Goodnow's *Comparative Administrative Law*, i., p. 185.

administrative functions in the county are discharged by the assistant judges of the ordinary county court.[1] Insofar as a separate county authority has developed in New England, as, for example, the commissioners who are found in Connecticut and New Hampshire, the Pennsylvania rather than the New York form is the model that is being copied. The rule as to the filling of the other officers in the New England county is not at all uniform; in some cases the people of the county electing such officers, in others some other, sometimes a state authority, having the right to appoint them. In all other sections of the United States, however, not only is the county important, but there is also a county authority of large powers.

2. *The county authority.* — As a general thing, the county authority is elected by the people of the county; the only exception is that in some of the southern states, within recent years, the legislature, on account of the fear of negro domination, has provided that the members of the county authority shall be appointed by the central government of the state.[2] Where the principle of election has been adopted, it is usually extended to most county officers. Thus, the sheriff, the county clerk, the county treasurer, the register or recorder of deeds, the district attorney, and the county superintendent of the poor—where that officer is to be found—are generally elected by the people and not appointed by the central administration of the state or by the county authority, as was the case in the original English and American system. In many cases the election of these officers by

[1] See Vermont Statutes, 1894, section 2881, *et seq.*
[2] See "Local Self-Government in the Southwest," *J. H. U. S.*, xi., p. 473.

the people is prescribed by the constitution of the state.[1]

The elective county authority is of two types, namely, the commissioner type and the supervisor type. The former provides for three commissioners generally elected by the people of the county at large. Sometimes we find the county divided into three districts, each one of which elects a commissioner.[2] This type, which it will be remembered originated in Pennsylvania, prevails in the south, where the appointed justice of the peace has not been provided, and in most of the western states.[3] The supervisor type, which provides for a representative on the county board of each of the towns into which the county is divided, originated, it will be remembered, in New York, and is to be found in several of the northwestern states, such as Michigan and Wisconsin.[4]

The supervisor type while not by any means so widely distributed as the commissioner type, has the advantage of securing local representation, and is believed by many to assure a greater sense of popular responsibility, on the part of members of the county authority. It is significant that one of the most recent laws relative to the government of counties, namely, the Indiana law of March 3, 1899, changed the commissioner system, by placing by the side of the county commissioners a county council of seven members, four of whom are elected by separate council districts.[5] The Indiana law, to which attention

---

[1] See Stimson, *op. cit.*, p. 47, section 210 B.
[2] Howard, i., pp. 439, 442.
[3] *Ibid*, i., 439, 443, 465, and 468.
[4] *Ibid*.
[5] Sparling, " Responsible County Government," *P. S. Q.*, xvi., p. 437.

has just been called, is interesting also as indicating a tendency towards a further modification of the general scheme of county government, which has existed for so long a time in this country with so little change.   It is an instance of the application to county government of the principle of the separation of powers which has had such an influence on the organization of the state and city governments.   To the new county authority, the county council, in Indiana have been given most of the financial powers, while the county commissioners are confined to the exercise of executive powers.   While the Indiana law of 1899 is an exceptional instance of the application to distinctly rural county government of the principle of the separation of powers, there are a number of instances of such application by special legislation to counties which embrace within their limits large cities.[1]

But apart from these exceptional instances of the attempt to disintegrate the county authority, what are known as county affairs are, regardless of their character, entrusted to a single county authority.   Under the head of county affairs are to be included the county finances,—including public buildings and the care of the expenditures for services attended to by other county officers, such as superintendents of the poor, county clerks, *etc.*,—and the care of bridges and roads.

In addition to attending to county affairs, the county authority has powers which only indirectly affect the county but are of interest to the state as a whole.

[1] See, for example, the County President of Cook County, Illinois, *ibid.* In the county of Kings, in the state of New York, there was formerly a supervisor-at-large who presided over the board of supervisors, and discharged a number of executive functions.

Thus the county authority has often to publish the laws and election notices for state elections, acts as the county board of canvassers for state elections, draws up in some cases the lists of grand jurors, and discharges duties mainly of a financial character in relation to the state military affairs.[1]

But the characteristic and most important powers of the county authority are those relating to the county finances. For the expenses of many matters affecting the state as a whole and not the county, are devolved by law upon the county. Such, for example, are many expenses connected with the administration of justice which, though the courts are recognized now as state rather than local agencies, are generally borne by the county. This is in accordance with the old English idea of devolving the expense of almost every administrative service upon the counties or the parishes. Such expenses are not optional with the county authority but are what are known as county charges, and may be enforced in the proper way by the courts.

We do, however, find certain differences in the different states as to the powers of the county authority relative to other county officers acting within the county. The usual rule would appear to be that the county authority may not be regarded as responsible for the actions of the other officers in the county who are elected by the people. At the same time we do find instances of an attempt to concentrate the whole responsibility for county administration in the county authority.[2]

[1] For example, see Morehouse's *Supervisor's Manual* (N. Y.), 115, 347, 352, 355, 363.

[2] Thus, for example, in Nebraska the county authority may hear complaints against any county officer and may remove him for official misdemeanors which

Again, there is a difference in the relations of the county authority to the lesser areas of administration—namely, the towns or townships. The usual rule would seem to be that the county authority has no control over the town administration. In some of the states, however, as, for example, New York, the county authority has considerable supervisory power over the town administration. Thus, in this state, the towns do not possess the taxing power, but all the town taxes are to be voted by the county authority.[1]

3. State control over counties.—In few, if any, instances, are acts of the county authority subjected to a central administrative control. Such control as is exercised over them by the central state government is exercised by the state legislature, which, through its power of detailed legislation sometimes special in character, may seriously interfere with the freedom of action of the county authority. A good example of such legislative control is to be found in the case of the borrowing power. In our early history, the ordinary rule being that a county authority might not, as the result of the exercise of its ordinary powers, borrow money, resort to the legislature was always necessary in case it was desirable for the county to pay for an extraordinary expenditure from the proceeds of bonds.

The very general adoption of constitutional provisions prohibiting the passage of special legislation, and limiting the debt-making capacity of counties,

are defined in the statutes. It may remove for this cause the county officer, whether he has been elected by the people or appointed by the county authority. Compiled Statutes of Nebraska, 1889, 369; compare Howard, i., 445.

[1] *E.g.*, N. Y. L., 1892, chapter 682, section 12, p. 569; L., 1890, chapter 568, section 139.

has, however, brought it about that the control of the legislature over the acts of county authorities has been seriously diminished. The former legislative control has been, particularly in the case of the exercise of the power to borrow money, sometimes replaced by a popular control. Debts may often be incurred only as the result of a popular vote, sometimes a vote of the taxpayers. Further, there is a tendency to provide a central administrative control over county accounts.[1]

In the case of particular county officers, there is, in a number of instances, a central administrative control. This is particularly marked in the case of the educational administration, and the administration of public charities and highways.[2] Finally, the governor has sometimes the right, either for cause or after a hearing, to remove most of the county officers.[3]

II.—The town.

1. *The position of the town.*—What has been said relative to the county may be repeated here; that is, the town's importance in a given state depends on the kind of local government we find within that state. Just as the county's importance is greatest in the south where the town does not exist, so the town's importance is greatest in New England where the county has no administrative importance. Whereever the town has any importance, it is, as has been shown, a corporation, but as a corporation it exhibits

---

[1] *Supra*, p. 138.

[2] See Fairlie, " State Administration in New York," *P. S. Q.*, xv., p. 50; see, also, *supra*, p. 140.

[3] *Supra*, p. 103.

two pretty distinct forms. The New England town often approaches in character the municipal corporation proper on account of the fact that it often discharges the functions in other parts of the country discharged by the city, incorporated town, or village. Outside of New England, the town or township, as it is sometimes called, is but a *quasi*-corporation with the limited powers and liabilities possessed by such an organization.

2. *The town meeting.*—The organization of the town differs in about the same way as its corporate capacity. Thus we find in the New England town a town meeting, consisting of the voters of the town, which both elects the town officers and determines, by its deliberations, the policy of the town, voting appropriations and levying taxes. Such an institution is also found in some of the states like New York, which have adopted the supervisor type of county authority. The sphere of action of the town meeting differs considerably in different states. Everywhere it has jurisdiction of the roads, in many cases of the town poor, and in some cases of the schools.

3. *The town officers.*—By the side of the town meeting we find a series of town officers. These are, in the first place, officers who represent the peculiar corporate interests of the town. In New England they are the selectmen ; in New York, the supervisor ; and outside of these districts, usually the town trustee. In the second place, there is a series of officers attending to the particular branches of administration, sometimes state administration, carried on in the town. Thus we find assessors and collectors for

the assessment and collection of both the state tax on property, where that exists, and the town taxes ; the town clerk, who keeps the records of the town including sometimes, as in New England, the records of the transfer of real property ; constables and justices of the peace for the preservation of the peace and the commitment of persons charged with crime ; commissioners of highways, overseers of the poor, and school and health officers. In New England, the tendency is to combine in the hands of the selectmen some of the functions discharged by a number of these officers in other sections of the country.

Outside of New England and the states following the New York plan, we do not find a town meeting. In the states not making provision for a town meeting, the officers specially charged with the corporate affairs of the town attend to the work, other than the election of officers, attended to by the town meeting in New England. There is, however, a tendency, even in the town-meeting states, to subject the actions of such officers to the control of some sort of a town council. This town council is the real town authority in a number of states,[1] and often has to audit the accounts of other town officers.[2] In some cases this town board consists of town officers, as, for example, in New York, or of persons elected for this purpose alone, as in Indiana.

What has been said with regard to the central state control over the county, may *mutatis mutandis* be repeated here as to the town, with the exception that

---

[1] Howard, i., 168, 169. The new Indiana Law of 1899 provided such a body to exercise a control over the town trustees.   [2] *Ibid.*, 172.

the governor does not possess the right to remove town officers.

In New England very generally the town is the school district and the officers who attend to the schools, sometimes known as the school committee, are elected at the town meeting and occupy towards it about the same position occupied by other town officers. In some parts of the south, on the other hand, the schools are managed by the county authority as a part of its general functions of administration. Generally, however, we find a special administrative organization for the schools based upon the special school district,[1] which sometimes not only manages the schools, but has its own financial system for the purpose of raising the funds necessary to carry on the schools.   This is the rule in New York.[2]   The tendency at the present time is said to be away from the district system and towards vesting the control of educational matters in the hands of a higher body, "sometimes the town, sometimes the county, sometimes the state."[3]

[1] Howard, i., 235.

[2] Fairlie, *The Centralization of Administration in New York State*, p. 34; see also Orth, *Centralization of Administration in Ohio*, p. 34.

[3] Webster, *Centralizing Tendencies in State Educational Administration*, 173; see also Rawles, *Centralizing Tendencies in Administration of Indiana*, 115.

CHAPTER IV.

I.—History of the English municipality to the seventeenth and eighteenth centuries.[1]

1. *Origin of the borough.*—According to the English method of permitting the localities to participate in the work of administration, the more thickly populated districts have always had a somewhat peculiar organization. The origin of this peculiar organization is to be found in the grant to districts with a greater than average population of a series of privileges for the exercise of which there was gradually formed a series of authorities differing in many respects from the authorities in the rural districts. These privileges were known as the *firma burgi* and the court leet.

The *firma burgi* was the lease of the urban district by the Crown to the inhabitants. From the very beginning of the Norman period, the inhabitants of the urban as well as of the rural districts owed certain payments or services to the Crown. As a rule, these payments were to be collected by the sheriff, as the fiscal representative of the Crown in the localities.

[1] See Gneist, *Self-Government*, etc., 580–592.

199

In order to permit of the more easy collection of such payments, the Crown made contracts with the inhabitants of the urban districts.   In accordance with such contracts, the inhabitants of the urban districts having the *firma burgi* paid the Crown a fixed sum, which they were permitted to raise among themselves in such manner as they saw fit.   For the collection of this quota there was provided an officer called the fermor or provost or mayor, who was to be selected, as a rule, by the urban inhabitants, their selection being subject to the approval of the Norman exchequer, and who was to act under its supervision.

The court leet was the privilege, granted to the inhabitants of special districts or to the lord of a given manor, to hold a special police and judicial court when the inhabitants of the district were exempted from the jurisdiction of the ordinary court, to wit, the sheriff's tourn.   This privilege was granted by the Crown, generally in the case of the urban districts, in return for a sum of money.   Like the *firma burgi*, it soon came to be regarded as a right. The union of these two privileges constituted a municipal borough.   The burgesses, meeting in court leet, found it a natural and easy matter to assume such other functions as were necessitated by the presence of a large number of persons in a small district.   They established rules as to participation in the court leet and as to the election of the mayor or provost. The general rule was that no one should participate in the court leet who did not pay taxes, was not a householder, and was not in the eyes of the law capable of participating in the administration of justice.   In the quaint language of the period, only those could be members of the court leet who were freemen householders, paying scot and bearing lot; and the formal criterion of the existence of these qualities in a given person was the fact that he had been sworn and enrolled in the court leet. This body had thus the ultimate decision as to the qualifications of municipal citizenship.

2. *Development of the borough council.*—The originally simple and representative organization of the borough was later completely changed through the acquisition by a large number of the boroughs of the right of representation in Parliament, which was formed in the time of Edward I. (1295). The *quota* of the borough was, after the formation of Parliament, fixed by that body, so that all that remained to be done by the borough in the financial administration was to assess the quota assigned to it by Parliament. This business could be transacted better by a small committee of the burgesses than by the entire court leet or municipal assembly. At the same time that this influence was at work, the whole judicial system was being completely changed by the introduction of judges learned in the law, who held the new royal courts, and by the establishment of the office of justice of the peace, which was introduced into the urban as well as the rural districts. Through the formation of these authorities the court leet lost almost all its judicial functions. The result was the formation of a committee of the original court leet or assembly of the municipal citizens for the transaction of borough business. This committee gradually assumed the performance of all municipal business which had sprung up, such as the management of the

property of the municipality, and finally was composed of the larger taxpayers—the most important men of the town, who often at the same time were granted by the Crown a commission of the peace, as a result of which they became justices of the peace with the usual powers. The larger boroughs had not only a commission of the peace but also the right to a court of quarter sessions for the borough, with the usual powers.

The larger taxpayers got these extensive powers as a result of the fact that the smaller taxpayers did not avail themselves of their rights. The old basis of municipal rights *i. e.*, the paying scot and bearing lot, was undermined, and was replaced by different principles, varying in accordance with the social and economic conditions of the various boroughs. In those boroughs which, like London, had great commercial and manufacturing interests, membership in one of the guilds or mercantile companies became the basis of the right to discharge municipal functions. Thus was formed the borough council or leet jury or capital burgesses, as the new municipal authority composed of the important men of the borough was called, which, whatever the name that was given to it, was generally renewed by co-optation. The result was that in the fifteenth century in the boroughs as well as in the open country the government was administered by the well-to-do classes, the nobility and gentry in the rural districts, and those who had become rich through commerce and trade in the urban districts.

3. *Period of incorporation.*—Soon after this definite form of municipal organization was reached, in ac-

cordance with which the borough was controlled by a council of rich men chosen by co-optation, the period of municipal charters began. The charters of incorporation which were granted incorporated not the inhabitants of the borough, but the council which controlled the affairs of the borough. The only purpose of these charters was to give to these districts the right to hold property and to sue and be sued. The charters had no special political significance, they did not grant any new governmental powers to the borough authorities.

The desire of the Crown to control, through the representation in Parliament granted to the municipal boroughs, the composition of Parliament, led the Crown to make most improvident grants of municipal charters carrying with them parliamentary representation, with the result that the municipal population had for a long time more than its fair share of representation in Parliament. As the grant of such charters would not have served the purpose of the Crown if it were not able to control the municipal elections, the Crown strove so far as it could to put all municipal powers into a few hands. The courts, therefore, which were dependent upon the Crown, held that any custom which provided for the control of the municipal administration by the narrow borough council was in accordance with public policy and valid.[1] Further, in the early part of the reigns of the Stuarts, *quo warranto* was issued in many cases to municipal corporations in order to forfeit their charters for irregularities and illegal actions, and on

---

[1] See the case of corporations decided in the time of Elizabeth, Dillon, *op. cit.*, i, 18 ; and Ireland and Free Borough, 12 Coke, 120.

the decision of the courts against the corporations
new and less liberal charters were granted.   Many
corporations, alarmed at the action of the Crown and
the courts, surrendered their charters and received
new charters of a much less liberal character.   All
this was done to enable the Crown to control the
action of the boroughs in their election of members
of Parliament.[1]   The result was that the municipal
organization was so formed and its powers so prosti-
tuted as almost entirely to destroy its usefulness for
administrative purposes.   When, after the revolution
of 1688, the nobles and gentry got the control of the
government, the case was the same, the only difference
being that the nobles instead of the Crown made use
of the municipal organization in order to control the
composition of Parliament.   Not only was the condition of the municipalities an extremely bad one,
but all hopes of reform were vain so long as either
the Crown or the nobles controlled the government.
For the control of Parliament was too valuable to be
given up voluntarily by its holders.

So long as the municipal organization was so defective, it was useless to expect that the new functions
of municipal administration, the adoption of which
was necessitated by the increase of urban population,
would be put into the hands of the municipal authorities.   When the parish administration grew up in the
time of the Tudors, it was therefore extended into
the urban as well as into the rural districts.   In this
way the poor-law was administered, not by the borough council, but by the parish authorities, which

---

[1] See Dillon, *op. cit.*, i., 18 ; Allinson and Penrose, *Philadelphia*, 10 ; Rex
vs. London, 8 How. St. Tr., 1039, 1340.

acted under the continual supervision of the justices of the peace. As it became necessary to make some provision for the lighting and paving of the streets, the course adopted for the satisfaction of these needs was the same. Either these matters were entrusted to the parishes or special trusts, or commissions were formed for their care by local and special legislation in particular boroughs, and the inhabitants were forced to contribute to the expenses of these branches of administration.[1]

Such was the condition of the English municipality at the time that America was colonized. The strictly municipal affairs, which were mainly such matters as the care of the city property, the issue of local police ordinances, and a certain power in the administration of justice,[2] were attended to by the borough council, or by its members in their capacity as justices of the peace; and this council was chosen generally by co-optation. This body did not attend to all matters affecting the welfare of the borough, since many of these matters were entrusted to the parishes and other special authorities, and had almost no functions to discharge which related to the general administration of the country. The form of the borough council was the same as it had been during the middle ages. It was composed generally of the mayor, recorder, aldermen, and councilmen.

II.—History of the American municipality.

1. *The original American municipality.*—Just as the English system of rural local government was

---

[1] Gneist, *Self-Government, etc.,* 595.

[2] On account of the fact that a special commission of the peace was often issued to the boroughs.

made the model on which the original system of American rural local administration was formed, so the form of the municipal administration, as it existed in England in the seventeenth century, was made the model of the original system of American municipal administration.

In the first place, a special organization was provided from the beginning for most of the cities in the colonies. Only one city, to wit, Boston, was ever governed in the same way as the rural towns.[1] New York and Philadelphia have, from the beginning of their history as English municipalities, had charters or forms of organization which differed considerably from the organization of the surrounding rural districts. The original form granted by these charters also resembled very closely the English municipal organization of the same period.[2] The city authority was the council, composed of the mayor, recorder, aldermen, and assistants or councilmen. In this body was centred the entire municipal corporate business. The administrative powers were not, however, so large as they are now. Like the English municipal corporation, the original American municipal corporation was mainly an organization for the satisfaction of purely local needs, *i. e.*, for the management of the local property and finances, and the issue of local police ordinances. Certain of the officers of the corporation, however, discharged a series of judicial and police

[1] *Johns Hopkins University Studies in Historical and Political Science*, v., 79.

[2] For New York see the Dongan Charter of 1686 and the Montgomerie Charter of 1730, to be found in Kent's *Commentary on the City Charter*, and Ash, *Charter of the City of New York ;* for Philadelphia, see Penn's Charter *J. H. U. S.*, v., 15.

functions, as was the case in the English municipality. Thus, in both New York and Philadelphia, the mayor, recorder, and aldermen were the municipal justices of the peace and judges.[1] The affairs of the general administration of the colony were attended to in the municipality by officers similar to the regular officers in the counties and rural districts.[2] One of the results of this purely local character of the American municipality was that the council had no power to tax in order to provide for the expense of the municipal services. It was not regarded as a sufficiently governmental authority to be endowed with this attribute of sovereignty.[3] A New York law of 1787 provided that the mayor, recorder, and aldermen, as the board of supervisors of the county of New York, were to levy the taxes demanded by the central state government of the inhabitants of the city as inhabitants of the state, the principle of the *firma burgi* having long ago been forgotten.

The city council in New York, with the exception of the mayor and recorder, who were appointed by the governor and council, were by the charter to be elected by the freemen of the city, being inhabitants,

---

[1] For New York, *Charter of 1730*, secs. 23, 26, 27, and 31. All the present local courts in New York City, with the exception, of course, of the supreme court, are simply outgrowths of the original judicial powers of the mayor, recorder, and aldermen. The recorder has also become an almost exclusively judicial officer. For Philadelphia, see *J. H. U. S.*, v., 19 and 29.

[2] *E. g.*, for the administration of the poor-law there were the regular overseers of the poor, elected in the wards of the city, and the expenses of this branch of administration were defrayed by the church parishes. See Black, *The History of the Municipal Ownership of Land on Manhattan Island*, in *Columbia College Studies in History, etc,.* i., 182; also *J. H. U. S.*, v., 27. For the collection of the central colonial tax, the New York Charter provided for the election of assessors and collectors similar to the town officers of the same name. See *Charter of 1730*, sec. 3.

[3] See Black, *op. cit.*, 181; *J. H. U. S.*, v., 22.

and the freeholders of each of the wards into which the city for the purposes of administration was divided. The freedom of the city was given by the mayor and four or more aldermen in common council, generally in return for the payment of money; and, besides giving in the proper cases the right to vote, was the only authorization to pursue certain trades within the confines of the city.[1] In Philadelphia the council was, as was so common in England at the time, elected by co-optation.[2] Finally, the city corporation was, as in England, regarded as consisting of the city officers, *i. e.*, the council, or the council and the freemen.[3]

Such was the original position and such was the original organization of the American city. Since the beginning of its history the American city has developed in two directions. In the first place, the position of the city and the duties to be attended to by its officers have greatly changed.

2. *Change in the position of the city.*—The state legislature has, to a large extent, lost sight of the original purpose of the city, and has come to regard it as an organ of the central government for the purposes of the general state administration. One result of the more public character which has been assigned to the city by the American law and development is that the corporation is not regarded as consisting of the officers, but consists of all the people residing within the municipal district, while municipal suffrage is in most cases the same as state suffrage.[4] Further,

[1] See Kent's *Charter*, note 35.
[2] See Allinson and Penrose, *op. cit.*, 9.
[3] So in Philadelphia. See Allinson and Penrose, *loc. cit.*
[4] Dillon, *op. cit.*, i., p. 70.

the state makes use very frequently of the city or its officers as agents for the purposes of state administration. Thus, in financial matters, the city, when of large size, is often made the agent of the state administration for the assessment and collection of taxes; indeed, the city itself is often practically the taxpayer of certain of the state taxes, *e. g.*, the general property tax,[1] which it is then to collect of the owners of property.

Further, in many cases, where the city has not been made directly the agent of the central state administration, in that it itself, or through its officers, is to attend to certain matters of general interest, the expense of a long series of matters is often devolved upon the city. This is particularly true of the matter of education.[2] The board of education, which has control of the educational administration within the limits of the city, and which is often regarded as a separate municipal corporation, is usually elected by the people residing within the district. In some cases, however, this body is appointed by the municipal authorities, as, *e. g.*, in New York;[3] in others, it is appointed by the legislature, as in Baltimore.[4] Finally, municipal officers are often made use of for the purposes of general state administration. Thus, in most of the large cities, municipal officers, either elected by the people of the city, or appointed by the

---

[1] It is to be noted, however, that the city has very generally been granted the local taxing power. *Ibid.*, 6ç. It is no longer compelled to defray its municipal expenses from the revenue of its property. See Ould *vs.* Richmond, 23 Grattan, Va., 464 ; 14 Amer. Rep., 139, for an example of the general grant of taxing power to cities.

[2] *Cf.* Bryce, *American Commonwealth*, first American edition, i., 599.

[3] Rollin, *School Administration, etc.*, and table, p. 24.

[4] *Ibid.*

14

municipal authorities, are entrusted with the care of
the public health and the support of the poor, attend
to election matters, and have a series of duties to perform relative to the administration of judicial affairs,
such as the making up of the jury lists.

In certain cases duties, which were in the old times
entrusted to the municipalities or their officers, have
been assumed by the central state administration.
Thus the preservation of the peace has in several of
the large cities been put into the hands of a commission appointed by the central government of the state.[1]
Further the courts of several of the states have held
that the preservation of the peace is not a municipal
function.[2]

What is true in exceptional cases of the preservation of the peace is almost universally true of the administration of justice, which is no longer regarded
as merely of local concern, but as a matter which should
be attended to in accordance with a uniform system
throughout the state.   The courts which act at the
present time in the various cities are not municipal
but state courts.   Their expenses may, it is true, be
paid in large part by the cities in which they act, but
the judges and their subordinate officers are not
regarded as municipal officers.[3]   An exception to this

[1] This is so in Boston, where the care of the police is given to a board of
police, appointed by the governor and council of the commonwealth, Mass. L.
of 1885, c. 323. In Nebraska the boards of police and fire commissioners in
cities of over 80,000 inhabitants are appointed by the governor. Compiled
Statutes 1889, pp. 147, 148. See for St. Louis, *J. H. U. S.*, v., 166. In
Baltimore the board of police is appointed by the legislature of the commonwealth.   See Allinson and Penrose, *Philadelphia*, 329 ; Fairlie, *Municipal
Administration*, 142.

[2] People vs. Mahaney, 13 Mich., 481 ; Redell vs. Moore, 63 Neb., 219 ;
State vs. Hunter, 38 Kan., 578.   But see People vs. Albertson, 55 N. Y., 50.

[3] Dillon, *op. cit.*, i., 99, and cases cited.

rule may be found in the case of the local tribunals called by different names, such as the mayor's court, the recorder's court, and the like.[1] These may be regarded as municipal courts when the judges who form them are elected by municipal electors or appointed by the municipal authorities, and when they have jurisdiction over municipal police ordinances only. In some cities the mayor and aldermen still discharge judicial functions.

But, although the state agency of cities has been made much more prominent than it once was, the work which the city does of a character which affects the interests of its own inhabitants has also greatly increased. This increase is in large part due to the attention which has been devoted by the cities to the matter of public works. Most of the important cities of the country have caused themselves to be supplied with water, with means of intra-urban transportation, and with some system of public lighting. In some cases this has been done by means of direct municipal administration; in other cases resort has been had to private corporations, which conduct these services under municipal or state supervision. Further, most cities have provided themselves with sewerage systems, parks and playgrounds, and in many places public libraries, and have everywhere provided paved streets and boulevards which afford a great contrast with the streets as they existed at the beginning of the nineteenth century.[2]

The fact that cities have become such important

[1] Dillon, *op. cit.*, i., 492.

[2] For a description of what American cities have done along these lines, see Zeublin, *Municipal Progress;* Fairlie, *Municipal Administration;* Wilcox, *The American City.*

agents of the state government in their management of taxes, education, care for the poor and the public health, and the preservation of the public peace and safety, has, however, brought it about that the state government has very generally changed its attitude toward them. While in the early period of our municipal history the cities, very largely, attended to the affairs whose management was entrusted to them quite free from central control,[1] the enlargement of their functions has been followed by the attempt on the part of the state to regulate their acts. This attempt upon the part of the state has, in many cases, had a disastrous effect upon the welfare of cities, and the tendency of the legislature thus to interfere has been checked through the adoption of constitutional provisions limiting the power of the state legislatures.[2]

III.—*Change in municipal organization.*

1. The application to municipal organization of the principle of the separation of powers.[3]—The original system of city government in the United States was, it has been shown, a council system; that is, there was practically only one municipal authority, the council, in whose hands were centred all municipal powers. Very early in the nineteenth century, however, the attempt was made to apply to the city organization the principle of the separation of powers which

[1] See Mayor vs. Ordrenan, 12 Johnson, N. Y., 125, where it is said that it was the almost universal course of proceeding for the legislature not to pass an act relative to the city of New York without first obtaining the city's consent.

[2] *Supra*, p. 172.

[3] See Fairlie, *Municipal Administration*, chap. v.

lies at the basis of the state governments. The application of the principle of the separation of powers to the city governments resulted, in the first place in the differentiation of the mayor from the council. The mayor, who had been the presiding officer of the council, sometimes appointed by it, sometimes appointed by the governor of the state, became elective by the people of the city. Since 1830, most city charters have provided for a mayor elected by the people of the city.

The next change in the city organization consisted in emphasizing the separation of the executive from the legislative part of the system. The attempt was made to form by the side of the mayor what were called executive departments, the heads of which were to be selected in various ways. Prior to the establishment of such departments, the detailed organization of the city government was fixed by ordinances of the city council. These usually provided for council committees which under the general direction of the council attended to the various branches of activity assumed by the city. Inasmuch as the new executive departments were commonly provided for by the charter and not by municipal ordinance, the council lost the power to regulate the detailed organization of the city government. For what was fixed by the charter could not be changed by ordinance. Furthermore, largely as a part of the great democratic movement of the middle of the nineteenth century, the officers at the head of these departments were frequently made elective by the people of the city. The elective method did not, however, work satisfactorily, and soon popular election was replaced by appointment by the mayor, subject to confirmation by the council.

By 1860, the executive departments were made even more independent of the council, and even independent of the mayor, by the provision for the appointment of the heads of these departments by the state government. Such central appointment was particularly common in the case of the head of the police department. This department was established in somewhat its present form about 1840, when the present professional, disciplined, semi-military police force, modelled after the London metropolitan force,[1] was formed.

2. *The board system.*—The system of city government composed of the council, mayor, and independent city departments may be called the board system. It lasted from about 1860 to about 1880, when it showed a tendency to be replaced by the present mayor system. During the latter part of the existence of the board system, the method of state appointment of municipal department heads was, apart from the police department, generally abandoned, but the terms of the heads of departments were generally longer than that of the mayor, who had no power to remove them from office. A given mayor under these conditions had practically only the power to appoint to vacancies occurring during his term.[2] The mayor could not, therefore, be said to be responsible for the administration of city government during his term of office, but his position resembled

[1] Organized by Sir Robert Peel in 1829.

[2] The charter of the city of New York, provided by the consolidation act of 1882, is a good example of the board system.

very closely that of the governor of one of the states.

3. *The mayor system.*—By 1880, however, the belief began to be held that the board system of city government was unfortunate in that it split up the city organization too much and made no provision for the concentration of responsibility. Therefore the charter amendments that were commonly made after that date increased the powers of appointment and removal of the mayor, so that in the latest form of city government which we have, and which may be called the mayor system, we find a mayor who often has the powers to appoint absolutely the heads of the departments when he comes into office, and to remove them from office whenever he sees fit and for whatever reason he may allege.

4. *Loss of power by council.*—While the council was thus losing in power to the mayor and executive departments, it was also losing in power to the state legislature, which passed charters more and more detailed in their character. The council lost in this way a large part of its financial power in that the charters or special acts relative to the city government fixed in detail many of the municipal expenses. The council lost also a large part of its ordinance power in that matters formerly regulated by ordinance were regulated by some provision of the charter, or their regulation was vested in some one of the executive authorities of the city government. The very general adoption of constitutional amendments limiting the power of the state legislature has had, however, the effect of restoring to the council some of the former powers of which it had been deprived.

IV.—The present organization.

The changes in municipal organization which have been outlined have not all been made in all cities, nor have they received the same degree of approval in all parts of the country. The result is that we find at the present time three pretty distinct types of municipal government: the first resembles most closely the original type and may, therefore, be called the council type.

1. *The council type of city government.*—The characteristic of the council type of city government is that, although the mayor may be elected by the people of the city and not by the council, he has few powers except to preside over the council, to cast a deciding vote in the case of a tie vote, or to disapprove the council's resolutions, which, in such cases, must be passed again by that body by an extraordinary majority. In this type of city government, the council is, as it originally was, the prominent factor. It discharges both legislative and executive functions, and attends, through committees or through officers whom it appoints, to the detailed administration of the city services. This type of city government is to be found in most of the smaller cities, particularly in the west and south, and is found only now and then in the larger cities.

2. *The board type.*—The second type of city government resembles more closely the board system as it has been described. We find not only a council and a mayor, but also a number of independent officers or boards whose members, once in office, are largely independent of any other city authority. The members

of these boards and these officers are sometimes elected by the people of the city, sometimes appointed by the central state government, but most commonly appointed by the mayor with the confirmation of the council. They serve for comparatively long terms, often for as long as six years, and may be removed before the expiration of their term only for cause and usually by the mayor, but sometimes by the governor of the state. Where the board system has been adopted in this extreme form, the powers of the council are apt to be small, most of the financial powers being exercised by the boards and officers independently of the council, and in accordance with the provisions of state laws. Frequently the entire local policy of the city in this form of city government is determined by the state legislature and carried out by these independent boards and officers. One of the most important of these boards in the board system is a financial board, often called the board of estimate or revenue, which either exercises almost all the important financial powers of the city or shares their exercise with the council. The new municipal code of the state of Ohio offers a good example of the board system.

3. *The mayor type.*—The third type of city government to be found in the United States is what has been called the mayor system. Under this system, the mayor appoints all the heads of city departments or all, with perhaps the exception of the chief financial officer who is elected. He likewise has the power to remove his appointees from office whenever he sees fit and may therefore be regarded as absolutely responsible for the administration of the city

government. This system of city government has been very commonly adopted in the larger cities of the country. The present city of New York offers a good example of the mayor system. The council or board of aldermen, as it is called in New York, is, however, less important than in most other large cities which have adopted the system, though it has greater powers than it had prior to the adoption of the present charter.

4. *Terms of city officers.*—The terms of office of city officers under these various systems differ greatly without having any very close relation to the type of city government adopted. As a general thing, the term of both council and mayor is two years, though it varies between one and four years. Often the term of the mayor is a short one as in New York, where it is two years, although New York has adopted the mayor system of city government. On the other hand, it is often a long one—four years—as in St. Louis, where the board system is the type adopted.

The council further is organized quite differently in different states, and also apparently without any regard to the character of the system adopted. Sometimes, it is renewed entirely at the same time ; at other times it is renewed in such a way as to make it more or less of a permanent authority. As a rule, however, it is entirely renewed at the same time. Again, sometimes certain of its members are elected at large and certain, by single districts, though, in most cases, all the members would seem to be elected on the single-district plan.[1]

[1] For the details of the organization of the city council, see Fairlie, " American Municipal Councils," *P. S. Q.*, June, 1904

5. *City schools.*—The relation of the city to the school system differs considerably in the various cities of the United States. It may be said, however, that, as a rule, the territorial district of the city is the district for the purposes of school administration, but it is usually organized separately for this purpose. It is true that in certain instances the authority in charge of the schools occupies a position very similar to that which is occupied by the other city departments, but even in this case it is often organized somewhat differently, consisting of a reasonably large and representative body of municipal citizens. In a great many instances, however, the school board is regarded not as a municipal department but as a corporation which, while having jurisdiction over the same territorial district as the city, is a corporation separate and apart from it. In such cases it has a power to levy taxes and to determine the amount of money which shall be spent within the city for the purposes of education.[1]

V.—Villages.

1. *General position.*—The city is not, however, the only municipality known to the American law. In many cases the needs of a locality, which may be a portion of one town or township or may lie in two towns, demand a different form of government from that offered in the ordinary town organization, while

[1] For the details of municipal school administration, see Rollins, "School Administration in Municipal Government," submitted in part fulfilment of the requirements for the degree of Ph.D. in the Faculty of Philosophy, Columbia University, New York, June, 1902; see also Young, "Administration of City Schools," *Annals of the American Academy of Political and Social Science,* xv., p. 171; Rowe, "The Financial Relation of the Department of Education to the City Government," *ibid,* p. 186..

at the same time they do not demand, so compact an
organization as that to be found in a city.   For the
purpose of satisfying these demands, the village, borough, or incorporated town organization has been
provided.   In New England, where the people have
been able to satisfy the demands made by thickly
populated districts through the ordinary instrumen-
talities of the town, this form of municipal organization is comparatively rare, though it is still to be
found, as *e. g.* in Connecticut and Vermont, which
have probably been influenced by their nearness to
New York.   But in the middle commonwealths, and
in the west and northwest, the village organization is
very common, so common indeed as very seriously
to encroach upon the sphere of town government.
For in almost all cases where the social conditions
are such as to permit the adoption of the village
organization (*i. e.*, where a comparatively large number of people live within a small area), we find that it
is as a matter of fact adopted.   Thus in New York
the general law for the incorporation of villages provides that the village organization may be adopted
where three hundred resident inhabitants are to be
found in a district of less than one square mile in extent.[1]   The main difference between the town and
the village is that, while the town is sometimes governed by the town meeting, *i. e.* the meeting of the
political people of the town, the village is always
governed by a select body, to wit, the board of
trustees or burgesses.   Further, while the town is a
quasi municipal corporation, the village is a municipal
corporation proper,[2] since it is formed primarily for

---

[1] See N. Y. L., 1870, c. 291, sec. 1.   [2] Dillon, *op. cit.*, i., 45.

the satisfaction of local needs. But, like the city, the village, though formed primarily for local needs, may be made use of by the commonwealth for the purposes of general administration. On the other hand, the village may practically be distinguished from the city from the fact that, on account of its small size, it is seldom as a matter of fact made an agent of general administration. About the only branch of general administration which is entrusted to the village is the preservation of the peace.

2. *The village organization.*—The ordinary village organization provided by the states of this country is a very simple one. It consists either of a board of trustees or burgesses elected by the voters resident in the village, which has control of village affairs, appointing and removing most of the village officers, and themselves serving for a short term. The term of office is usually arranged so that only a portion of the members of the board retire each year. In many instances the village board cannot incur indebtedness without the approval of the voters expressed at a general or special election.[1]

[1] An example of the village organization is to be found in the New York Law of 1870, c. 291. For an analysis of this law together with its amendments, see Goodnow—*Comparative Administrative Law*, vol. i., p. 220; see also the village laws of Indiana, Burns's *Annotated Indiana Statutes*, 1894, secs. 4333, 4357, *et seq.*

BOOK IV.

THE OFFICIAL RELATION.

___

CHAPTER I.

OFFICES AND OFFICERS.

I.—Definition.

BY an office is understood a right or duty conferred or imposed by law on a person or several persons to act in the execution and application of the law.[1]   By officers are meant those persons on whom an office has been conferred or imposed.   The conceptions of office and officer are conceptions of the public law. The government may, however, either in its central or local organizations enter into private legal relations and as a consequence may have employees. Inasmuch as its employees are regarded as having entered into contract with the government, no state may, under the constitution of the United States, pass any law which impairs the obligation of a contract of employment made by such state.[2]   But since the official relation is not regarded as a contractual

___

[1] *Cf.* Mechem, *Law of Public Offices and Officers*, i.
[2] Hall *vs.* Wisconsin, 103 U. S., 5.

relation but as a relation of the public law, a state is
not regarded by the courts as prevented from changing the terms of the official relation even after it has
been entered into by the officer.[1] Furthermore, inasmuch as the official relation is a public legal relation
and the relation of employer and employee is a private legal relation, the rules of the public law apply
to the official relation, while the rules of the private
law apply to all government employments.[2]

The difference between the legal aspects of the
contractual relation of employer and employee and
those of the official relation makes it necessary to
distinguish between the contract of employment and
the official relation. While there are other criteria
which may be of use in distinguishing an office from
an employment, the most important means of distinction is that, while an employment is created by contract, an office finds its source and its limitations in
some act of governmental power. Thus where
the legislature creates by an act of legislation the
position of public printer, such a position is regarded
as an office, its incumbent is an officer and therefore
may not assign the position, inasmuch as an office is
not by law capable of assignment.[3] On the other
hand, where the legislature provides that the public
printing is to be contracted for, the public printer is
regarded as a contractor or an employee and not as
an officer.[4] In other words, if a provision of law—
namely, the constitution, a statute of the legislature,

[1] Butler *vs.* Pennsylvania, 10 Howard, 402.
[2] *Cf.* Fitzsimmons *vs.* Brooklyn, 102 N. Y., 536.
[3] Ellis *vs.* State, 4 Indiana, 1.
[4] Brown *vs.* Turner, 70 N. Car., 93; see also Detroit Free Press Company *vs.* State Auditors, 47 Mich., 135.

or an ordinance of an administrative authority or a municipal corporation—provides for a definite position in the public service, fixing the duties to be discharged by the incumbent, his term of office, and the method by which the position is obtained, such position is to be regarded—in the absence of some peculiar statute —as an office and not as an employment. If, on the other hand, the position finds no basis in the law as above defined, but is founded upon an agreement made between the person holding such position and some authority in the government, which agreement determines the compensation, the duration of the employment, and the duties to be discharged by the person with whom such agreement is made, such a position is regarded as an employment and not as an office.[1]

It will be noticed from what has been said that the conception of an office does not depend upon the character of the duties to be performed. These duties may be similar to, or even identical in character with, the duties discharged by private persons, but if the right to discharge them is dependent upon some provision of law as above set forth, and not upon an agreement or a contract, the right to discharge them is regarded as an office and not as an employment. Thus, a clerk in an executive department of the United States, or one of the states, may be an officer.[2]

While the rule, that a position established by law, and not by contract, is an office, is a safe rule to follow under ordinary conditions, at the same time peculiar

---

[1] Olmstead *vs.* The Mayor, 42 Superior Court Reports, N. Y., 481.

[2] *Ex parte* Smith, 2 Cranch C. C., 693 ; United States *vs.* Hartwell, 6 Wallace, 385 ; Vaughan *vs.* English, 8 Cal., 39.

statutes may result in the adoption of a different method of determining whether a given position is an office or an employment. Thus, for example, the United States Supreme Court has held that no one can be an officer of the United States government unless he be appointed as the constitution provides, *viz.*, by the President and Senate, the President alone, one of the United States courts, or the head of an executive department.[1] Furthermore, particular statutes are sometimes so framed as to indicate that the legislative intention is to confine or to extend the conception of officers contrary to the general rule which has been set forth.[2]

II.—*Methods of organizing offices.*

Official authorities differ in the way in which they are organized. Thus, an official authority may consist of one person or of more than one person. In the first instance, while one person may not do all the work of the office, while he may be assisted in the performance of his duties by many subordinates or deputies, who in their turn may be officers, still all the acts of the office which such person holds are done under his direction and on his responsibility. The

[1] United States *vs.* Germaine, 99 U. S., 508. In the case of the United States *vs.* Hartwell, 6 Wall, 385, however, it was held that one appointed with the approval of the head of an executive department was an officer under the United States constitution.

[2] See for an example of the influence which such statutes have upon the decisions of the courts as to whether given positions are or are not offices, the case of United States *vs.* Mouat, 124 U. S., 303, and United States *vs.* Hendee, *ibid.*, 309, which hold, respectively, that a paymaster's clerk, who was not appointed by the head of a department, and whose position was not provided for by law, is not an officer for the purpose of mileage, but is one for the purpose of longevity pay. See also *Ex parte* Reed, 100 U. S., 13.

15

system of offices founded on this principle is some-times called the single-headed system.

Where an office is held by several persons, they exercise their powers and perform their duties by means of resolutions of the entire body. In the making of these resolutions each one of the holders of the office has legally as much influence as any of the others, with perhaps the exception of the president of the board, who may have the right to give the casting vote in case of a tie.[1] A system in which the official authorities are organized as boards is called the board system.

Each of these plans of organizing offices has its advantages and disadvantages. The single-headed system is well fitted for the discharge of duties which require energy and rapidity of action, and for which it is advisable to have a fixed and well-defined responsibility; while the board system may be adopted with advantage in all those branches of administration in which carefulness of deliberation, regard for all sides of the case, and impartial decisions are particularly desired. Boards are therefore often provided for the consideration of those matters in which a controversy between individuals is to be decided, that is, for judicial authorities; while the single-headed system is often adopted for purely executive and administrative authorities. It is, however, to be noticed that for many administrative matters, the board system is to be preferred, for the reasons which make the adoption of the board system desirable for judicial authorities. This is particularly true in the

[1] See for the rules of law relative to the action of boards, Mechem, *op. cit.*, secs. 571–581.

case of the assessment of property for the purpose of taxation. For these reasons, we find that seldom does any system of administration adopt either one of the two methods of official constitution to the exclusion of the other, but that the attempt is usually made to combine the two forms in such a way as to produce the best results.

III.—*Honorary and professional offices.*

In the United States we have no very clear conception of a professional office, that is, an office the incumbent of which devotes his entire time to the discharge of public functions, who has no other occupation, and who receives a sufficiently large compensation to enable him to live without resorting to other means. The nearest approach to such an office made by the American law is what is sometimes known as a lucrative office. Opposed to the professional office, as above defined, we find the honorary office. The incumbent of an honorary office does not devote his entire time to his public duties, but is, at the same time that he is holding public office, permitted to carry on some other regular business, and as a matter of fact finds his main means of support in such business or in his private means since he receives from his office a compensation insufficient to support him.

From the incumbent of a professional or lucrative office, knowledge of the affairs to which his official duties relate is often required by law. In some cases this requirement is carried so far as to necessitate the pursuit, by the candidates for such a position, of a regular course of professional instruction. In the case of honorary officers no such requirements are made. The duties which are imposed upon such officers are not regarded as requiring any special knowledge on their part.

A system of administration which relies mainly upon professional officers is termed a bureaucratic system ; a system of administration which relies mainly upon honorary, non-professional officers, is sometimes called a self-government system, because government in it is administered by members of society who temporarily or occasionally discharge public functions. In the United States our system of administration is formed by a combination of professional and honorary officers, the latter predominating.

Each of these two systems, the bureaucratic and the self-government system, has its advantages. The special knowledge and training possessed by professional officers, their generally long terms of office, and the fact that they are occupied exclusively in the management of public business, make it almost certain that they will act more wisely and efficiently than officers who have no special knowledge of their duties, who serve for short terms, and are expected to devote only a part of their time to the public service, and make it extremely probable that the cost of such a system will in conditions at all complex, notwithstanding the fact that salaries are paid, be less than the cost of self-government administration. If wise, efficient, and economical administration were the only or even the main end sought in the organization of an administrative system, it must be admitted that the bureaucratic system is often preferable to the self-government system.

It must not be lost sight of, however, that good administration is only one, and that a minor, end of an administrative system. It must always be kept in mind that an important end of all governmental systems and particularly of systems of popular government should be the cultivation in the people of political capacity. History shows that this end is only imperfectly attained by a thoroughly bureaucratic system. The experience of almost every state which, to carry forward pressing reforms or to secure administrative efficiency, has adopted a bureaucratic system of administration, goes to prove that bureaucracy is unfavorable to the development of political capacity.

What the bureaucratic system tends to destroy, the self-government system tends to foster. The participation of numerous citizens in the work of administering government tends to increase, by the sure method of practice, the political capacity of the people. There are, however, some branches of administration in which the inherent defects of the system of popular, non-professional officers are very marked. These defects—*viz.*, extravagance, inefficiency, and unwise action—become so serious as to force the conclusion that in some branches the self-government system is impossible of application. There are many positions, for example, in the municipal administrative services—positions which are increasing in number with the enlargement of the city's sphere of activity—which require great technical knowledge, and whose duties are so arduous as to occupy the entire time of the incumbents. Here it seems necessary to demand of the incumbents a professional training and to pay them salaries.[1] Bureaucracy is made necessary by the conditions of the case. The question is not whether we shall have a bureaucracy —for we must in the nature of things have it,—but how we shall organize it so as to give it the best proportions possible and avoid the evil results by which it is so generally attended. Especially must care be taken not to organize the bureaucracy on principles which are applicable to the self-government system. If salaries are to be paid, professional knowledge and the devotion of the entire time of the officer to the work of the office should be required. Further, since the impossibility of such an officer's earning his living in any other way is the only reason why a salary should be paid, long terms of office should take the place of the short terms of the self-government system. What should be a profession should not be allowed to degenerate into a trade.

[1] *Cf.* President Eliot in *The Forum*, October, 1891, on "One Remedy for Municipal Misgovernment."

CHAPTER II.

I.—*Appointment or election.*

THE two most important methods of forming the official relation are appointment and election. Originally the common method of filling offices in the United States was by executive appointment. The only exception to this rule was to be found in the case of the town officers. Partisan use was early made of the power of appointment in the state of New York. Each new party that came into power felt that it was its right if not its duty to fill all the offices to which appointment might be made with its own adherents and to make places for them by the discharge of existing officers.[1] This habit was not confined to the state of New York, but afterwards made its way into the national administration, and thus spread to every one of the states. The evils resulting from such a practice led the people very generally to change the method of forming the official relation in the state governments. Many of the offices were made elective. The movement continued from 1825 to 1850, with the final result that almost all the important offices, both in the central state government and in the localities, were filled by popular election.

[1] Gitterman, "New York Council of Appointment," *P. S. Q.*, vii., 80.

Since 1850, however, there has been somewhat of a reaction in favor of the former method of executive appointment, the reason being found in the fact that the method of election did not have the beneficial results which were expected of it.   No change in the original method of forming the official relation was made in the national administration, not because the same evils were not present here as were present in the states, but because the method of appointment, being provided by the national constitution, could be changed only with great difficulty.   Where the method of appointment has been adopted, the appointment is not in all cases to be made necessarily by the chief executive, but in many cases may be made by the heads of the executive departments and in the localities by the chief local authorities.

The aims of these two methods of forming the official relation are quite different.   The method of appointment aims at administrative harmony and efficiency.   The method of election endeavors to insure that popular control over the administration which is one of the fundamental principles of popular government.   In order, however, that such a popular control may be exercised, the people must be in a position to judge intelligently of the merits of the respective candidates for office.   The people are undoubtedly in such a position in the rural districts, where the feeling of neighborhood is strong.   Here they know the merits of the candidates who present themselves for office and are able to make a wise choice.   When we come, however, to more complex conditions, such as exist, for example, in the central state administration and in the municipalities, where the feeling of neighborhood is not strong, and where it will be difficult, if not impossible, for the people to know much about the merits of the different candidates, it is useless to adopt the elective method in the hope that the people will by this means be able to exercise any effective permanent control over the administration. The only way in which the people may exercise such a control over the administration is for them to elect only the most prominent officers of the government, who are then to appoint to the subordinate offices. If a long list of candidates is presented to the elector for his choice, if many of the offices to be filled by election are of a subordinate or unimportant character, even the most intelligent voter is apt to become confused. Other reasons than the merits of the candidates are apt to influence his choice, and the result of the election is apt to be in accordance with the wishes of those few persons who have the time and the inclination to busy themselves with the conduct of public affairs, rather than in accordance with the real wishes of the people.

The elective method of forming the official relation thus in many cases does not secure the popular control, which is the purpose of its adoption. It not only fails of its purpose in these cases, but also has one or two serious positive defects. Through its means it is often the case that men of totally opposed views on vital questions are put into office where, in order that the administration may be efficient, it is necessary that it be harmonious. The necessity for harmony in such matters is so great that as a matter of fact the attempt is made to attain it through recourse to the political party, which here, as in so many other instances in our system, affords the only means by which our lack of governmental concentration may be remedied.

For the central state administration and the municipal administration, the method of forming the official relation should be by appointment, if an efficient, harmonious, and responsible administration, subject to popular control, is desired. This is the method which has been so successfully adopted in the national administration. This is also the method which has been adopted by most of the recent municipal charters for the larger cities in the United States.

Further, the elective method of filling offices is, in all instances, unfitted for offices, the efficient performance of whose duties requires the possession by the incumbents of large professional or technical knowledge. Such offices are those of judge, law officer, civil engineer, *etc.* The requirement of the possession by the incumbents of these positions of certain degrees or certificates, which are supposed to evidence the necessary qualifications, is not really sufficient. For the people, even if their choice is thus confined, are here again not in a position to choose wisely. Public inclination is too apt to be swayed by other than scientific reasons. Such a method may shut out absolute ignorance from the office ; it will not, however, usually result in the choice of the best man for the office.

II.—*The law of elections.*

1. *Right of legislature to regulate elections.*—Subject to the limitations contained in the fifteenth amendment of the United States constitution, which pro-

vides that the right of citizens of the United States
to vote shall not be denied or abridged on account of
race, color, or previous condition of servitude, the
right to vote in both national and state elections is to
be determined by the states.[1] As a general thing, the
right to vote is determined by the state constitution.
Where the state constitution has defined who shall
have the right to vote, the state legislature may not
add to or diminish the qualifications thus provided.[2]
Where, however, it is clearly the intention of the constitution to confine the effect of its provisions to state
elections, the legislature may, under the ordinary
state constitution, provide qualifications, such as
property qualifications, for elections for local and
municipal offices, and for elections to determine what
action shall be taken by a given municipal corporation, as, for example, elections to determine whether
bond issues shall be made.[3]

The legislature may, however, provide reasonable
regulations regarding the exercise of the right to
vote. Thus, the legislature may provide for the
registration of voters where such registration is not
required by the constitution.[4] But registration laws
are not generally regarded as constitutional where
they absolutely deprive an elector of the right to

[1] Kinneen *vs.* Wells, 144 Mass., 497.

[2] Rison *vs.* Farr, 24 Ark., 161 ; 87 American Decisions, 53 ; Coffin *vs.* Commissioners, 97 Mich., 188. Thus, if the constitution requires thirty days' residence, a statute which prescribes as a qualification for voting a residence of
ninety days is unconstitutional. People *vs.* Canaday, 73 N. C., 198 ; 21 American Reports, 465.

[3] Hanna *vs.* Young, 84 Md., 179 ; 57 American State Reports, 396 ; Spitzger
vs. Village of Fulton, 172 N. Y., 285 ; Mayor *vs.* Shattuck, 19 Colo., 104 ; 41
American State Reports, 208.

[4] Capen *vs.* Foster, 12 Pickering, 485 ; 23 American Decisions, 632.

vote, unless registered on one of three or four days, the last one being ten days or thereabouts prior to the election.[1] Where registration laws are regarded as constitutional, it is held that they may be adopted for portions of the state, and need not necessarily be made to operate through the entire state.[2]

2. *Method of voting.*—The original method of voting at elections was *viva voce.* This was the rule in England at the time the North American colonies were established, and remained the rule in England up to the passage of the ballot act of 1872. There were, it is said, however, even in England, cases where voting papers or ballots, as they came to be called, were used at a very early time.[3] Similar instances of voting by ballot are to be found in the colonies, but, as a general thing, these methods were adopted, not so much to secure a secret vote, as to further the convenience of the inhabitants, who were thus permitted to vote by proxy.

The use of the ballot, as a means of securing a secret vote, seems to have originated in the state of New York.[4] For quite a time, however, after the adoption of the ballot, the ballot was simply a paper drawn up in such form as the individual voter desired, and contained the names of the candidates for whom the voter, casting such ballot, desired to vote.[5] The desire which was at the bottom of the adoption of the

[1] See Attorney-General *vs.* Common Council of Detroit, 78 Mich., 545 ; 18 American State Reports, 458 ; *contra* People *vs.* Hoffman, 116 Ill., 587.

[2] See Patterson *vs.* Barlow, 60 Pa. State, 54.

[3] Ford, *The Rise and Growth of American Politics*, p. 6.

[4] See Constitution of 1777, art. 6.

[5] "The ballot, in the modern sense of a party ticket put into the hands of voters, is a comparatively late development. In 1794, John Adams extenuated a 'very unwarranted and indecent attempt . . . upon the freedom of

system of voting by ballot, namely, to secure secrecy in voting, was not, however, realized by the mere provision that election should be by ballot. This was so, because it was possible, after the ballot became an instrument in the hands of the party, to provide a ballot which had distinctive marks upon it, and at the time of the count of the votes to ascertain the way in which the voters voted. The legislatures of many of the states, therefore, passed laws regulating the form, color, size, and general characteristics of the ballot, and prohibiting the counting for any candidate of ballots cast for him which did not comply with the law. Such statutes at once gave rise to judicial decisions as to the power of the legislature in this respect. It has been almost universally held by the courts in interpreting such statutes, that it is within the power of the legislature, in the exercise of its right reasonably to regulate the franchise, to designate in great detail, where such designation is necessary to secure a secret ballot, the characteristics of a legal ballot.[1]

The method of voting, in accordance with which ballots were provided by private initiative and put into the hands of the voter by the agents of the parties, was not, however, satisfactory in producing the desired secret vote, notwithstanding all of the provisions of the statutes, and the rather strict interpretation put upon them by the courts in order to

election' committed by his own party, on the ground that 'the opposite party . . . practise arts nearly as unwarrantable in secret, and by sending agents with printed votes.'" Adams's *Works*, vol. i., p. 474; quoted from Ford, *The Rise and Growth of American Politics*, p. 7.

[1] State *vs.* Phillips, 63 Texas, 390; 51 American Reports, 646; People *vs.* Board of Canvassers, 129 N. Y., 395.

secure the desired secrecy. Because of this fact, as well as because of the great expense to which the parties were put in order to pay for the ballots used, the system of voting known as the Australian system was adopted. The characteristics of this system were that the ballot to be used was to be an official ballot, printed by the state, and distributed by state officers. The voter was required to mark upon the ballot so as to indicate the name of the candidate for whom he desired to vote, a cross which, in accordance with the provisions of the law, was to be made either by a stamp, a pencil, or a pen. Several interesting questions have arisen in connection with this system, as to how far the legislature may limit the freedom of the voter in marking the ballot. In their decisions of the questions arising under these statutes the courts have naturally been very largely governed by the wording of the statute which was being considered. On this account there appears at first blush to be considerable conflict in their decisions as to what marks are to be regarded as distinguishing marks, and thereby as invalidating the ballot upon which they may appear. But in general it may be said that, where it is the evident intention of the legislature to declare invalid any ballot which is marked contrary to its provisions, and where such marking will result in making possible the identification of the ballot, the ballot containing such improper marks will be regarded as illegal, and will not be counted.[1]

---

[1] See People *vs.* Board of Canvassers, 129 N. Y., 395 ; Taylor *vs.* Bleakley, 55 Kansas, 1 ; 49 American State Reports, 233 ; State *vs.* McElroy, 44 La. Annual, 796 ; 32 American State Reports, 355 ; see also monographic note upon the distinguishing marks which will invalidate a ballot under the ordinary Australian ballot law in 49 American State Reports, 240. It has,

3. *Election regulations directory.*—As a general thing, it is held that election regulations made by the legislature, which do not attempt to secure the secrecy of the ballot, are to be regarded as directory rather than mandatory—that is, their violation, provided the will of the voter is clearly expressed, will not invalidate the election. Thus, it has been held that, where the law provides that the ballot shall be of plain white paper, through which the printing or writing cannot be read, ballots printed on colored paper, given by mistake to all of the electors of a given district, are not illegal ballots, because the secrecy of the ballot is not interfered with by the use of such ballots.[1]

The general rules with regard to elections are that the election must be regular—that is, must be held at the time and place appointed by the proper authority. This authority may be the constitution, the statute, or an administrative act done in pursuance of the statute.[2] In the second place, notice of the time of election does not seem to be necessary, even when expressly required by statute, except where such notice is, in the nature of things, necessary, in order that the voter may know that an election is to take place. Thus, the failure to give notice of a general election, though required by law, will not invalidate the election.[3]

however, been held that the legislature, in its desire to secure secrecy, may not provide a system of voting by which it is impossible for an illiterate person to vote, where the constitution makes no provision for an educational qualification for voting. Rogers *vs.* Jacobs, 88 Kentucky, 502.

[1] Boyd *vs.* Mills, 53 Kansas, 594 ; 42 American State Reports, 306 ; see also De Berry *vs.* Nicholson, 102 N. C., 465 ; 11 American State Reports, 767.

[2] Brewer *vs.* Davis, 9 Humphrey, Tenn., 208 ; Stephens *vs.* People, 89 Ill., 337.

[3] People *vs.* Hartwell, 12 Mich., 508.

But a special election would not be regarded as valid in case no notice of it was given.[1] While notice of the time of election is not always necessary, notice of the place of holding the election seems to be absolutely necessary. Indeed, statutory provisions as to the place of elections are regarded as mandatory rather than directory. Failure to observe them will generally invalidate an election.[2]

4. *Duties of election officers ministerial.*—At every election officers are provided, generally known as inspectors of elections, whose duty it is to receive all legal votes. The duties of these officers are prescribed in detail in the election laws, but under the election laws which have generally been passed the duties of such officers are ministerial and their performance of them is subject to the review of the courts.[3] Notwithstanding the fact, however, that the duties of such officers are thus ministerial, it has been almost universally held that the reception of illegal votes will not void the election, unless it is shown that their reception affected the result.[4]

After the votes have been received they are counted ; sometimes by the officers who have received them, but commonly by officers known as judges of elections, and frequently chosen from the parties which have candidates for election in the field.[5] In counting the ballots the judges of elections have, of

---

[1] Secord *vs.* Foutch, 44 Mich., 89 ; State *vs.* Gloucester, 44 New Jersey Law, 137.

[2] Melvin's Case, 68 Pa. State, 333.

[3] People *vs.* Pease, 27 N. Y., 45 ; 84 American Decisions, 242.

[4] People *vs.* Cicott, 16 Mich., 243 ; 97 American Decisions, 141.

[5] The selection of the judges of elections from the two principal parties is made obligatory in New York by the constitution ; see Constitution, 1894, art. ii., sec. 6.

course, to judge in the first instance of their legality, but their decision, as that of the inspector in receiving the vote, is not conclusive.[1] After the returns have been made out by the judges of elections in election districts, they are sent to the boards of canvassers acting for districts larger than those in which the vote was taken. These officers examine the returns in order to determine which of the candidates has the greatest number of votes. There are thus boards of town and city canvassers who canvass all the returns for town and city officers, boards of county officers who canvass all returns for county and state officers, and boards of state officers who canvass all returns for state officers. It is universally held that the powers of such boards, acting merely as boards of canvassers, are ministerial—that is, their powers consist in adding up the returns as sent in by the judges of elections of the various election districts, or those of the lower canvassing bodies. While the inspectors of elections have of necessity the duty of determining, subject to the review of the courts, the question whether a given vote is a legal vote or not, boards of canvassers are not usually permitted by the statutes, as interpreted by the courts, to go back of the returns as sent to them by the judges of elections.[2] It has even been held that where a board of canvassers has adjourned *sine die*, the court has the right to require it to reassemble and correct the canvass.[3] But in the absence of such a direction from the court the canvassing board is held to be

[1] People *vs.* Van Cleve, 1 Mich., 362.
[2] Lewis *vs.* The Commissioners of Marshall County, 16 Kansas, 102 ; 22 American Reports, 275.
[3] Florida *vs.* Gibbs, 13 Fla., 55 ; 7 American Reports, 233.
16

functus officio after it has made its canvass, and
has no right to reconvene and correct errors in its
decisions.[1]

This rule as to the ministerial character of their
duties is true with regard to state canvassing boards.[2]
If, however, the governor of the state is a member of
the board of state canvassers, its determination is
beyond judicial review by means of a direct action
against the board to compel them to correct any
return that they have made.[3]

5. *Methods of representation.*—The difficulty under the ordinary methods of representation of securing adequate representation of the voters has led to
various attempts to secure the representation of
minorities. Only two such methods appear to have
been adopted in this country. They are known as
limited voting and cumulative voting. Limited voting consists in confining the elector, in casting his
vote, where several officers are being voted for, to a
number less than the whole number of persons to be
elected. Such a method of representation is regarded
under the ordinary constitutional provisions as unconstitutional, inasmuch as it deprives the voter of
his right under the constitution to vote at all
elections.[4]

Cumulative voting provides that, where more than

[1] Hadley *vs.* Mayor, 33 N. Y., 603.

[2] People *ex rel.* Derby *vs.* Rice, 129 N. Y., 461.

[3] Dennett Petitioner, 32 Maine, 508 ; 54 American Decisions, 602. *Cf.*
People *vs.* Morton, 156 N. Y., 136.

[4] State *vs.* Constantine, 42 Ohio State, 437; 51 American Reports, 833. If,
however, the constitution expressly permits such a method of voting to be
adopted for some of the offices of the government, it is held that it may be
adopted by the legislature for others. Commonwealth *vs.* Reeder, 171 Pennsylvania State, 505.

one officer is being voted for in a district, each voter shall have as many votes as there are persons to be elected and may distribute his votes as he sees fit. Thus if there are three officers to be elected, he has three votes which he may distribute in one of three ways : he may cast his three votes for one candidate, or he may cast one vote for three candidates, or he may cast one and a half votes for two candidates. This is the method which has been adopted by the constitution of Illinois for elections to the lower house of the state legislature. Where the constitution has not made specific provision for it, it has, however, been held to be unconstitutional.[1]

Another method of securing minority representation is the method known as proportional representation. This has, however, never been put in practice within the United States though it has been made use of in elections in Switzerland.[2]

III.—The law of nominations.

1. *Parties originally voluntary organizations.*—It has already been shown that originally the preparation and distribution of the ballots were left in the hands of the citizens, who organized into voluntary political associations known as political parties. These voluntary associations not merely provided and distributed the ballots, but also attended to the preliminary operations necessary to the nomination of

---

[1] Maynard *vs.* Board, 84 Mich., 228. But where the constitution has provided cumulative voting for some offices of the government, it has been held that the legislature may provide it for others. People *vs.* Nelson, 133 Ill., 565.

[2] For a general discussion of the various plans of proportional representation, see Maynard *vs.* Board, *supra*, and Commons, *Proportional Representation*.

candidates for office. All the necessary preliminary proceedings were attended to by these parties originally and for quite a time after the formation of the government, without being subjected, in any way, to the supervision of any governmental organs.[1]

From the very beginning of the history of parties in this country, however, partly it is believed because of their voluntary character and of their not being subject in any way to governmental control, their operations necessary for the nomination of candidates and their conduct generally have been characterized by both violence and disorder and chicanery and fraud.[2] The frequent and long-continued recurrence of fraud and violence at primary meetings has resulted in the abstention of the majority of party members from participation in its deliberations. This is particularly true of the cities.[3] If, as the result of extraordinary

---

[1] It is said in the case of Stephenson *vs.* The Board of Election Commissioners, 118 Mich., 396, 399 : "From our earliest recollection, party politics has always been a matter of shrewdness and management, not always defensible ; yet the people have been left to deal with the difficulties as they arise. It is not to be supposed that committees on credentials, however fairly selected, have always dealt justly ; and, no doubt, expediency or political exigency has governed their actions to the exclusion of abstract justice. The remedy has been either a bolt on the part of the dissatisfied, and the selection of an opposition candidate within the party, or a refusal by the electors to support the nominee ; and the courts have been careful not to interfere with the application of these remedies which have usually been found adequate." See also *In re* Redmond, 25 N. Y., Supplement, p. 381 ; Attorney-General *vs.* Drohan, 169 Mass., 534 ; 61 American State Reports, 301. In this case it was held that the writ of *quo warranto* could not be made use of to try title to party office. See also People *ex rel.* Trayer *vs.* Lauterbach, 7 Appellate Division, N. Y., 293, which held that the determination of the party authority could not be reviewed on *certiorari.*

[2] Dallinger, *Nominations for Elective Offices in the United States*, p. 97.

[3] See Bernheim, "Party Organizations and their Nominations to Public Office in New York City," *P. S. Q.*, iii., 99.

exertions, the elements in the party opposed to those in its control, secure possession of any primary and are thus enabled to elect delegates to the party convention, it is frequently the case that the regular faction, as it is apt to call itself, will nominate a contesting delegation. This contesting delegation often receives recognition at the hands of the highest party authority, which is in the control of the regular party organization. The acts of the highest party authority, as has been shown, have not been in the past subject to the control of the courts ; therefore, there has been no appeal from their determination.

In many instances the parties themselves have recognized the evils by which their system of nomination and their conduct have been attended, and rules and regulations have been adopted by them whose intention is to prevent both violence and fraud. These rules and regulations have, however, had practically no sanction and have been enforced or not as suited the desires of those in control of the party organization.

2. *Governmental control of parties.*—Because of the evils attending particularly the party system of nominations and because of the apparent inability of the parties themselves to remedy them, many of the states of the American Union have attempted to regulate by legislation the nomination operations of political parties. The attempts which have thus been made to remedy the evils complained of may be classified under two heads : In the first place, the attempt has been made to recognize by legislation the rules and regulations adopted by the parties and to give to the courts the authority to enforce them.

Such a method of regulating the subject would appear to be proper.[1]

The laws which were thus passed in order to give the courts jurisdiction to enforce the rules and regulations of party authorities were not successful in remedying the existing evils. Many of the states, therefore, decided to pass legislation directly regulating the operations of the political parties. The statutes passed with this end in view are of two kinds : They either recognize the convention system which has become the most commonly adopted system for nominating candidates, or else they attempt to establish what has come to be known as the system of direct nomination, which has also been adopted voluntarily in several parts of the country by the action of the political parties.[2]

Whether the states which have attempted to regulate this matter have chosen the convention system, or the direct nomination system, they have in either case found it advisable, if not necessary, to provide some means by which membership in the party, which carries with it the right to vote at the party elections, shall be determined. They have therefore either attempted to provide a test of party membership, in which case the system of direct nomination, if adopted, will be found in connection with what is

---

[1] See *In re* Guess, 38 N. Y. Supplement, 91, where it was held that the courts would compel a political association to place upon its rolls one who swore that he was an adherent of the party and its principles, that he supported its ticket at the last election and intended to support its principles and candidates in the future. See also People *ex rel.* Spire *vs.* General Committee, 49 N. Y. Sup., 723. In this case it was held that where an enrolment of the registered voters in the city, made for the benefit of the party, is by the party rules open to inspection to any member of the party, the right to inspect may be enforced by the courts. [2] See Meyer, *Nominating Systems*, chap. v.

known as a closed primary ; or they have adopted a system of primary known as an open primary, in which any citizen, regardless of his previous party affiliations, is permitted to vote for party nominations. The constitutionality of the first method, namely, that of providing a test of party membership, has been several times attacked, and has in some instances been denied where there is in the state constitution a provision which, as interpreted by the courts, limits the powers of the legislature relative to primary elections, in that it prevents the legislature from tak_ing certain action with regard to all elections. While there is considerable conflict among the authorities, quite a number of them regard primary elections as within the term " all elections," particularly where the expense of the primary election is to be defrayed by the state.[1] If the courts regard primary elections as subject to the limitations of the constitution, they have sometimes held that a statute of the legislature which, for the purposes of primary elections, either enlarges or contracts the right of suffrage, as given by the constitution, is not constitutional.[2] The reasoning of some of the opinions which have thus declared legislation providing a test for party membership to be unconstitutional, would seem to indicate that, in the absence of such a constitutional provision, the court would declare such legislation to be improper. Thus, in the last case cited, the court says : " If such a power may be sustained under the constitution, then the life and death of political parties are held in the hollow of the hand by a state legislature." [3]

---

[1] See Marsh *vs*. Hanley, 111 Cal , 368.   [2] Spier *vs*. Baker, 120 Cal., 370.
[3] But see Ladd *vs*. Holmes, 40 Oregon, 167.

On the other hand, the courts have sometimes considered that an act of the legislature providing for
what has been spoken of as an open primary is unconstitutional, because it is "an unwarrantable invasion
of the rights of political parties and an innovation of
the rights reserved to the people by the constitution,
.   .   .   providing that the rights enumerated in
the constitution shall not be construed to impair or
deny others retained by the people." [1]   Both of the
cases which have thus denied the power of the legislature either to determine the test of party membership
or to authorize any one, irrespective of his past political conduct, to vote at primary elections of the party,
are California cases, and it is not believed as a general
thing that the rule laid down in these cases would be
adopted generally by the courts.   At any rate, in New
York there has been a primary law upon the statute
book for a number of years which authorizes an individual to place his name upon the roll of the party,
and to vote at the primaries of that party, if he has
not participated in any other party primary election
within a year.   This law has never been directly contested, and, as will be shown, the highest court of the
state would appear, indirectly, to have held it to be
constitutional.

In case the legislature adopts the first method of
regulation to which reference has been made, namely,
the maintenance in practically its present condition of
the convention system of nomination, and recognizes
a nomination made by the convention of one of the
parties which have received recognition by the state
government, the question has sometimes been raised

---

[1] Meyer, *op. cit.*, p. 361 ; see also Britton *vs.* Board, 129 Cal., 337.

as to whether such action is unconstitutional as a dis-
crimination against the rights of smaller parties—
parties, for example, which have cast a percentage of
the vote at the last election too small to bring about
their recognition as parties whose convention nominations will be recognized. Generally the question
has been decided in favor of the power of the legislature. Thus, it has been held that a law is constitutional which subjects merely the larger parties to the
control of the primary laws and forces the smaller
parties, in making a nomination, to resort to the circulation of a nomination petition.[1]

Where the legislature has adopted the method of
nomination by convention as the formal method of
selecting candidates for office, it has sometimes felt
itself obliged to regulate, in considerable detail, the
actions of the parties and their organizations, and to
subject the determination of party authorities relative
to these matters to the control of the courts. Probably the states of New York and Massachusetts have
gone as far in this direction as any other states in the
Union.[2] The question as to the propriety of these
regulations has been settled in the affirmative by the
highest court of the state of New York.[3]

3. *Direct nomination.* — In some instances, as has
been said, the legislature has attempted to replace the

[1] See State *vs.* Black, 54 New Jersey Law, 446 ; State *vs.* Poston, 58 Ohio
State, 620 ; Miner *vs.* Olin, 159 Mass., 487 ; DeWalt *vs.* Bartley, 146 Pa.
State, 525 ; but see Britton *vs.* Board, 129 Cal., 337.

[2] An abstract of the law of New York will be found in Meyer, *op. cit.*, p.
108.

[3] See People *ex rel.* Coffey *vs.* The Democratic General Committee, 164 N.
Y., 335. In this case the county committee of a party attempted to expel a
member because he had not supported one of the party candidates, and the
court reinstated him.

former convention system by the system of direct nomination.[1] Probably the most advanced legislation which has been taken in this direction has been taken by the state of Minnesota, where the system of direct nominations, based upon an open primary, has been adopted. This system would appear to be based upon the following principles. In the first place, no one may have his name placed upon the official ballot as a candidate for office who has not been nominated either as the result of a petition signed by the requisite number of persons, or as the result of a nomination election which has taken place at a direct primary of one of the parties whose actions are, under the statute, subject to legislative regulation. In the case of these parties, the statute provides that at the time that the voter presents himself to register for the purpose of state elections, he shall be given a ballot for the purpose of the nomination elections of the party, on which he shall indicate his preference for the candidates of one of the parties. No voter at such a time is permitted to participate in the nomination elections of more than one party, but which party he shall affiliate with is a matter for him to determine. Provision is made further, by this law, that any one who desires to be a candidate at a nomination election may file a statement to that effect, accompanied by a sum of money, the amount of which varies with the importance of the office for which he desires to be a candidate. The persons who receive the greatest number of votes from the members of a particular party are declared to be the candidates of the party, and their names are then put on the official ballot at the

[1] See Meyer, *Nominating Systems*, part ii.

election. This takes place within a reasonable time after the completion of the nomination elections.[1]

These are in the main the methods which have been adopted to remedy the evils accompanying purely voluntary nominations of the political parties. It is somewhat difficult to say which has proved the more successful. It is certainly the case that in New York the action of the parties is much more considerate of the wishes of the majority of the party members than it was prior to the passage of the statute regulating primaries. At the same time it cannot be said that the control of the parties has been changed to any great extent. The same persons who were in control of the parties prior to the advent of the legislation would appear to be in control now, though it would seem that their actions are less arbitrary than they once were. In the case of the Minnesota law, greater changes in party control would appear to have been made. The system of direct nominations, however, is accompanied by the great disadvantage that in almost all cases the nomination is the result of a plurality of votes, which is not a majority of the votes of all the members of the party. Furthermore, it is said that the nomination campaign is a very expensive one, and many believe that the tendency of this method of nomination is to put into office persons who are notorious rather than famous.

4. *Effect of Australian ballot.*—Finally, the mere introduction of the Australian ballot has, in many cases, brought about the subjection of the nomination actions of the parties to the control of the courts, even

[1] For a discussion of this method of nomination see *Chicago Conference for Good City Government*, p. 321 *et seq.*

where no such control has been expressly provided for by the legislature. For example, the courts have sometimes regarded themselves as authorized, in case there is a contest between two factions of a party with regard to the nomination of a candidate, to determine which one of the factions represents the party. Thus, they have in some instances held that nominating conventions must be regularly called, and the delegates thereto must be regularly chosen[1]; that the nominating election must be fairly conducted[2]; and that a convention must meet at the place fixed by the rules of the party.[3] In some cases, however, the courts have held that if the highest authority in the party has determined which of the factions of the party is the representative of the party, they are concluded by such determination.[4] In other cases the courts have refused to go into the question at all, and have, where such a contest has sprung up, ordered the names of the candidates of both factions of the party to be placed upon the official ballot, believing that by such action they were permitting the people to decide the question.[5]

Whatever may be the method which is adopted, it will be noticed that, partly as a necessary result of the Australian ballot acts, which have been so universally passed, and partly as a result of primary or other similar legislation, the parties have, in many instances, assumed the position of organizations which are

---

[1] State *vs.* Tooker, 18 Mont., 540.

[2] Matter of County Clerk, 21 Miscellaneous Reports (N. Y.), 543.

[3] Liggett *vs.* Bates, 50 Pacific Reporter, 860.

[4] See The Matter of Fairchild, 151 N. Y., 359; see also Cain *vs.* Page, 42 Southwestern Reporter, 336.

[5] See Stephenson *vs.* Board, 118 Mich. Reports, 396.

recognized by the government. They have, therefore, to that extent ceased to be what they once were,
—merely voluntary associations, and are subject more
or less to government regulation and control.

IV.—*The law of appointment.*

As has already been indicated, there is considerable
doubt in certain states as to whether an appointment
is an executive act or not, though the better rule
would seem to be that it is not an executive act, but
an act which, so far as concerns the constitution, may
be performed for almost all classes of offices by any
of the three authorities of the government.[1] It therefore follows that no executive or administrative
authority has any inherent power of appointment in
the absence of legislation to that effect, and that, in
the absence of a constitutional provision, the legislature may take away the power of appointment from
any authority to which it has granted such power[2];
and may grant the power of appointing public officers
to any authority in the government or even to a private corporation.[3]

One of the most interesting questions connected
with the law of appointment is : In what does an appointment consist? The answer to that question is,
An appointment consists in the choice by the appointing authority of the person appointed.[4] This definition, it will be noticed, lays emphasis on two things :
first, upon the choice of the appointing authority—

---

[1] *Supra*, p. 38.
[2] Davis *vs.* The State, 7 Maryland, 151 ; 61 American Decisions, 331.
[3] Overshiner *vs.* State, 156 Ind., 187 ; Sturges *vs.* Spofford, 45 N. Y., 466.
[4] Johnston *vs.* Wilson, 2 N. H., 202.

that is, the exercise of discretion by the appointing authority ; and, second, upon the fact that, once that choice is exercised, the power of appointment is exhausted. Thus, it is held that if a power of appointment is vested in an authority by the constitution, legislation which takes away from such an authority the exercise of discretion is unconstitutional.[1]

In the second place, once the choice of the appointing authority has been exercised, the power of such authority is exhausted—that is, if the appointing authority has not the power of removal, which must be regarded as a distinct power, it has not the right to revoke an appointment which has once been made.[2] In case, however, the appointment consists in the nomination by one authority and the confirmation by another, the appointment is not complete until the confirmation by the confirming authority has been secured, and it is often provided by statute, as interpreted by the courts, that the appointment is not complete until a commission of some sort has been signed by the authority making the appointment. This is the rule in the national administrative system.[3] In such a case the appointment may not be said to have been made until the appointee has, first, been nominated by the appointing authority, second,

---

[1] See People *vs.* Mosher, 163 N. Y., 32. In this case it was held that a method of appointment which provided that the appointing officer must select some one standing highest on a list made up by another authority was unconstitutional where the power of appointment was vested in the appointing authority by the constitution. But where there is no such constitutional provision it is perfectly proper so to limit the power of appointment. People *vs.* Kipley, 171 Ill., 44.

[2] See Speed *vs.* Common Council, 97 Mich., 198 ; see also State *vs.* Barbour, 53 Conn., 76.

[3] See Marbury *vs.* Madison, 1 Cranch, 137.

confirmed by the authority authorized to confirm appointments, and, third, commissioned by the appointing authority.

But in the absence of a statutory provision the completion of the appointment is not dependent upon the issue of any commission, which is merely evidence of the appointment, and is not the appointment itself; and where, as is sometimes the case, the commissioning authority is not the same as the appointing authority, the commissioning authority may be forced to issue a commission to the person who has been selected by the appointing authority.[1]   It is not as yet settled in what form the appointment is to be made—whether it must be made in writing, or whether an oral appointment is sufficient.[2]   In accordance with the principle that the appointment consists in the choice by the appointing power of the person appointed, the appointing authority has the right to revoke a commission which has been, by mistake, issued to the wrong person.[3]

V.—*Acceptance of the office.*

By the common law the acceptance of office would appear to be obligatory.[4]   This would seem to be the case even where the statute provides a fine for the refusal to accept office.   In such a case it has been held

---

[1] See State *vs.* Crawford, 28 Florida, 441.

[2] See People *vs.* Murray, 70 N. Y., 521, which holds that the appointment must, in the absence of statutory provisions to the contrary, be in writing, and Hoke *vs.* Field, 10 Bush., Ky., 144, which holds that it may be oral.

[3] See Gulick *vs.* New, 14 Ind., 93 ; State *vs.* Capers, 37 Louisiana Annual, 747.

[4] People *vs.* Williams, 145 Ill., 573 ; 36 American State Reports, 514, and monographic note.

that payment of the fine does not excuse the acceptance of the office, which may be enforced by *mandamus*.[1] It has, however, been intimated that the acceptance of an office which will take all the time of the incumbent is not obligatory where no provision for compensation is made.[2] It has also been held that the possession of one office will justify the incumbent in refusing to accept another,[3] and that no one can be forced to accept an office, such as a judicial office, which will disqualify him for any office in the state not a judicial one.[4] It naturally follows from what has been said that there is no constitutional objection to a law which makes acceptance of office obligatory, and imposes a fine for refusal to serve.[5]

When acceptance of the office is not obligatory, some evidence of intention to accept the office is necessary.[6] Qualification for the office is regarded as the best evidence,[7] while the failure to qualify is regarded as evidence of refusal to accept.[8] Acceptance is also presumed from the exercise of the duties of the office.[9]

The old common-law rule of obligatory service has, however, been much modified in actual practice, and, while theoretically in force and capable of application by the courts, in order to prevent an interregnum by

---

[1] *Ibid.*

[2] See Hinze *vs.* People, 93 Ill., 406.

[3] Hartford *vs.* Bennett, 10 Ohio State, 441.

[4] Smith *vs.* Moore, 90 Ind., 294.

[5] Brooklyn *vs.* Scholes, 31 Hun, N. Y., 110 ; London *vs.* Headon, 76 N. C., 72.

[6] Smith *vs.* Moore, 90 Ind., 294, which holds that acceptance of a nomination for the office is not such evidence.

[7] *Ibid.*, Johnston *vs.* Wilson, 2 N. H., 202.

[8] Thompson *vs.* Holt, 52 Ala., 491.

[9] Johnston *vs.* Wilson, 2 N. H., 202.

means of which private rights may be jeopardized, is seldom applied. Much more reliance is placed upon voluntaryism than formerly. There are still instances, however, of obligatory official service, as, for example, in the town and county services, where many of the unpaid offices are obligatory.

VI.—Officers de facto.

While it is in general true that the official relation can be formed only in one of the ways recognized by the law, and that the acts of persons who without right intrude into office are absolutely void, both as against the public and third persons,[1] it is also a general principle of the common law, based upon reasons of public convenience, that persons, who though not legally officers have yet acted under color of right—that is, have been declared elected or appointed, or have held over their term of office in good faith, or whose assumption of office has been for a long time acquiesced in by the public, are regarded for many purposes as officers, and that their acts will be given the same faith and credit in proceedings to which they are not parties as the acts of officers *de jure.* Such persons are called officers *de facto.*[2] While for reasons of public convenience the acts of officers *de facto* are given in collateral proceedings to which they are not parties the same faith and credit as are given to the acts of officers *de jure*, officers *de facto* are not permitted to build up any claims for themselves from the fact that they have

[1] State *vs.* Taylor, 108 N. C., 196.
[2] See State *vs.* Carroll, 38 Conn., 449, and cases cited.

17

assumed office. Thus, they cannot recover compensation,[1] nor may they bring action in their official capacity without showing title,[2] nor may they, when sued, escape responsibility for an act which may be justified only by title to the office.[3] A third result of this position of officers *de facto* is that they are liable for damages resulting from their negligence,[4] must perform all duties connected with the office during the time they assume to hold it,[5] and may be punished criminally for the commission of official crimes.[6]

The attempt has sometimes been made to make a distinction between *de facto* officers and *de facto* offices. It has been held, for example, that there can be no such thing as a *de facto* office, and that in order that there may be a *de facto* officer there must be a *de jure* office,[7] but the rule supported by the greater weight of authority, apart from the authority of the United States Supreme Court, would seem to be that a person who holds a position which has been established by an unconstitutional law, should be regarded, until the law establishing the position has been declared unconstitutional, a *de facto* officer, inasmuch as he is holding a position under color of the title which comes from a law which has not been formally declared unconstitutional. This view of the subject may also be sustained upon the theory that the title to office may not be impeached in a col-

[1] Dolan *vs.* Mayor, 68 N. Y., 274.
[2] People *vs.* Weber, 86 Ill., 283.
[3] Green *vs.* Burke, 23 Wendell, N. Y., 490, 503.
[4] Longacre *vs.* State, 3 Miss., 637.
[5] Kelly *vs.* Wimberley, 61 Miss., 548.
[6] Diggs *vs.* State, 49 Ala., 311 ; State *vs.* Goss, 69 Me., 22 ; State *vs.* Gardner, 54 Ohio State, 24.
[7] See Norton *vs.* Shelby County, 118 U. S., 425, 442.

lateral proceeding to which the officer is not a party, even though the ground of the impeachment is the fact that the position is based upon an unconstitutional law.[1]

---

[1] See State *vs.* Gardner, 54 Ohio State, 24 ; see also Burt *vs.* Railway Company, 31 Minn., 472 ; *American Law Review*, January, 1896.

CHAPTER III.

I.—*The legislature may provide qualifications.*

THE power to hold office is not regarded as a right guaranteed by the constitution to all electors, but rather as a privilege which is given sometimes to all citizens or electors, sometimes to persons who are neither citizens nor electors, and sometimes only to certain classes of citizens, and is in all cases subject to the regulation of the legislature, in the absence of a constitutional restriction,[1]

There are quite a number of cases, however, which hold that under the ordinary constitutional provisions the legislature may not provide either political or religious qualifications. Thus statutes which have provided for commissions, the members of which are to be chosen from the two leading political parties, have usually been regarded by the courts as improper.[2] In

---

[1] State *vs.* McAllister, 38 W. Va., 485, holding that a property qualification may be provided for by statute ; see also Ohio *vs.* Covington, 29 Ohio State, 102, holding that an educational qualification is proper.

[2] People *vs.* Hurlburt, 24 Mich., 44 ; Attorney General *vs.* Board of Councilmen of Detroit, 58 Mich., 213 ; Evansville *vs.* State, 118 Ind., 426 ; see also Mayor of Baltimore *vs.* The State, 15 Md., 376, and Brown *vs.* Haywood, 4 Heiskell, Tenn., 357. It is difficult to say from these cases whether a law containing such provisions is in and of itself unconstitutional—that is, whether, where the appointing power chooses to conform to the provisions of the stat-

order to avoid the objections which the courts have to this method of organizing bi-partisan commissions, the attempt has frequently been made to provide for commissions, no more than two members of which, the commission consisting of either three or four members, may belong to the same political party. Such a method of organizing commissions is regarded as proper.[1] In some cases, however, provision is made in the constitution for political qualifications. This is the case, for example, in New York, where election officers are to be chosen from the two leading political parties.[2] In such a case, of course, no question as to the constitutionality of such qualifications could arise.

II.—Usual qualifications.

The usual qualifications provided for officers, both elective and appointive, are citizenship or the right to vote, the attainment of a certain age, the possession of good character, and, for the majority of offices, the male sex.

1. Citizenship and residence.—The possession of citizenship does not appear to be the universal rule at any rate in the United States national government.

---

ute, the appointments made by him are void. The only case when such a matter could come up squarely before the court so that the law could be the subject of judicial review, would be where the appointing power refuses to obey its provisions. In such a case these cases would seem to indicate that the courts would not enforce the statute. The courts have alleged two reasons for the impropriety of such legislation : one is that it is unconstitutional ; the other is that it would be impossible for them to determine whether a person belonged to one of two parties as provided for in the statute.

[1] Rogers *vs.* Buffalo, 123 N. Y., 173. See also State *vs.* Hoffman, 116 Ill., 587. As to the extent to which political qualifications have been provided in the state of New York, for example, see Wilcox, " Party Government in the Cities of New York," *P. S. Q.,* Dec., 1889.

[2] N. Y. Const., art. ii., sec. 6.

The United States statutes seem to contain nothing absolutely decisive on the point, although the sections of the Revised Statutes which govern the form of the official oath [1] seem to presuppose that citizenship is necessary, but nowhere is it expressly required. The civil-service law of 1883 does not require citizenship but general rule V, passed in execution of the law, would seem to require citizenship for the classified service. But, apart from these provisions, the law does not seem to be explicit on the point, and it is well known that subordinate positions in the diplomatic and consular service are sometimes filled by persons who are not citizens of the United States. In the states the qualification of citizenship or of the right to vote, which is sometimes conferred upon persons not citizens, would seem to be usually required. [2] A qualification akin to citizenship is residence. In the national service there is a peculiar rule for the classified departmental service, which provides that appointments to the classified public service at Washington shall be apportioned among the states, territories, and the District of Columbia in accordance with the population as fixed by the last census. [3] In some of the states, as, for example, New York and Massachusetts, the civil-service rules would appear to require a residence in the state of one year for positions in the classified service.

2. *Age.*—It is often provided, particularly in the services classified under the civil-service laws and

---

[1] Sections 1756-7.

[2] See State *vs.* Trumpf, 50 Wis., 103 ; but see In the matter of Ole Mosness, 39 Wis., 509, 511, where the court says that extra-territorial officers, as, for example, commissioners to take acknowledgments, need not be citizens or electors.   [3] See Laws 1883, c. 27, s. 2, third.

rules, that no one shall enter the service when he is either below or above a certain age. The purpose of these provisions is to exclude both the too young and the too old. Thus, in the national service the limits of age vary with the particular branch of the service from the minimum of fourteen for the position of page in the departmental service, to the maximum of fifty-five for the position of superintendent in the classified Indian service.[1]

3. *Character.*—The qualification of good character as a general thing means nothing more than that the candidate has not been convicted of crime.[2] In certain cases, however, the qualification of good character is more stringent. The civil-service laws very generally provide that no person shall be appointed to office who habitually uses intoxicating beverages to excess.[3] The rules also generally provide that no person shall be appointed who has beeen guilty of notoriously disgraceful or infamous conduct.[4] Finally it is often provided in the civil-service rules that certificates of good moral character shall be presented at the time the application for appointment is made.[5]

4. *Eligibility of women.*—It is difficult to say whether in the absence of legislative provision women are eligible to office. In Robinson's case[6] it is said that the male sex is required when no provision as to the eligibility of women exists, though it is admitted there is no constitutional objection to women being

---

[1] *Nineteenth Report U. S. Civil Service Com.*, p. 60.

[2] See Mechem, *op. cit.*, §§ 77–79, for the usual disqualification resulting from conviction for crime.

[3] U. S. L., 1883, c. 27, § 8.

[4] United States General Rule, v., paragraph 3.

[5] See, *e. g.*, U. S. L., 1883, c. 27, § 10.   [6] 131 Mass., 376.

made eligible by statute.[1] The contrary rule is, however, laid down in Connecticut.[2] Furthermore, it has been held or intimated that a woman may be appointed to the position of postmistress and pension agent,[3] of deputy clerk,[4] and of master in chancery.[5] Further, the United States civil-service rules seem to presuppose that women will be appointed.[6]

In some instances the possession of property, particularly real property, is required in order to be eligible for local offices. As has been shown, this qualification may constitutionally be made.

III.—*Qualification of intellectual capacity.*

In the case of offices of a technical or professional character, the law often requires that the candidate must have undergone some course of training or must possess some degree or certificate. Thus, no one but a practical civil engineer may be elected to the position of state engineer and surveyor in New York.[7] Further, where judges or prosecuting officers are elected by the people, it is usually provided that the candidates for such positions shall be a counsellor at law of a certain number of years' standing.[8] In the case of appointed officers, qualifications of intellectual capacity are much more stringent than they are in the case of elective officers.

[1] See also 115 Mass., 602, and Huff *vs.* Cook 44, Iowa, 639; see also Ostrogorski, " Woman Suffrage," *etc.*, *P. S. Q.*, vi., 677, 707.

[2] *In re* Hall, 50 Conn., 131.

[3] *Ibid.*

[4] Jeffries *vs.* Harrington, 17 Pacific Reporter, 505.

[5] Schuchardt *vs.* The People, 99 Ill., 501.

[6] See Rule VIII.

[7] Constitution, art v., § 1.

[8] See People *vs.* May, 3 Mich., 598.

1. *Original discretion of appointing officers.*—Originally there seem to have been no legal requirements as to intellectual capacity in the United States civil service. The whole matter was left to the discretion of the appointing officers. No difficulty seems to have resulted from the exercise of this discretion until about the middle of the nineteenth century. The introduction into the national service of what came to be known as the spoils system led, however, to frequent removals of the incumbents of public offices and to the insistance by the appointing officers upon political qualifications on the part of candidates for office.[1]

The idea of frequent changes in the official service seems to be traceable to President Jackson, who says in his message of December 8, 1829:

> There are, perhaps, few men who can for any great length of time enjoy office and power without being more or less under the influence of feelings unfavorable to the faithful discharge of their public duties. . . . The duties of all public officers are, or at least admit of being made so plain and simple that men of intelligence may readily qualify themselves for their performance; and I cannot but believe that more is lost by the long continuance of men in office than is generally to be gained by their experience. I submit, therefore, to your consideration whether the efficiency of the government would not be promoted and official honesty and integrity better secured by the general extension of the law which limits appointments to four years.[2]

The law to which President Jackson here alluded was passed in 1820 during the administration of

[1] A good history of this whole subject will be found in the *Fifteenth Report of the United States Civil Service Commission*, No. vi., p. 443, entitled "Practice of the Presidents in Appointments and Removals in the Executive Service, from 1789 to 1883."

[2] *Messages and Papers of the Presidents*, vol. ii., p. 448.

President Monroe. It provided that certain officers should be appointed for a term of four years but should be removed from office at pleasure. Jackson's suggestion was adopted with the result that almost all officers in the United States service were given a term of four years.

2. *Civil-service laws.*—Notwithstanding the opposition to this method of filling offices which immediately arose, the method was adopted. It was immediately followed by bad results, and there is hardly a year from the time of Jackson's administration until the passage of the civil-service law when attempts were not made to remedy the evils due to the adoption of the spoils system in the United States administration. Thus in 1841 a committee was appointed by the House of Representatives to examine into the conditions of the civil service, and reported in favor of a board of examinations which should examine the candidates for appointment designated by the heads of departments as to their character, moral habits, and intellectual capacity. In 1853, Congress passed acts relative to appointments which provided for a classification of the clerks in the various departments at Washington, and for a pass examination for entrance into the service. In 1864, Mr. Sumner introduced a bill to provide for competitive examinations. This bill failed of passage and little was done except to rouse public opinion until the administration of President Grant. In his annual message of 1870 the President said:

I respectfully call your attention to one abuse of long standing which I would like to see remedied by this Congress. It is a reform in the civil service of the country. . . . The present system does not secure the best men and often not even fit men for public place. The elevation and purification of the government civil service will be hailed with approval by the whole people of the United States.[1]

In response to this urgent appeal, Congress passed the act of March 3, 1871, which gave the President power " to prescribe such regulations for the admission of persons into the civil service of the United States as may best promote the efficiency thereof."[2] The attempt was made under this statute to provide competitive examinations for practically all subordinate positions in the service. In 1874, however, Congress refused to make an appropriation for the work of the commission. The commission practically disbanded, but competitive examinations were continued in certain branches of the service, particularly in the New York customs-house and post-office. In the meantime a number of Presidents urged upon Congress the necessity of civil-service legislation, and finally in 1883 the present civil-service act was passed. Since 1883 there has been practically no legislation upon the subject, but the Presidents have gradually subjected more and more branches of the service to the operation of the rules, so that at the present time there are over 120,000 positions subject thereto, appointment to most of which is made as a result of examinations.[3]

Since the passage of the United States civil-service law several states have adopted the system either for the state service, or for the service of all or particular

[1] *Messages*, vol. vii., p. 109, December 5, 1870.
[2] This act was afterward incorporated into section 1753 of the Revised Statutes.
[3] *Nineteenth Report of the Civil Service Commission*, p. 22.

cities within the state or for both.   Thus in New
York an act similar to the United States law was
passed on May 4, 1883.   In 1894, an amendment of
the constitution was adopted which provided a system
of examinations for appointed positions in the civil
service of the state and all its civil divisions.   Subsequent to the adoption of the constitutional amendment, the present act of 1899 was passed.   This act
follows in the main the principles of the national law
of 1883.   In 1884, an act was passed in Massachusetts
similar to the United States law and the New York
law.   Statutes have been passed in other states also
adopting the method of appointment as a result of
examination for all or particular cities in the state.
This has been done, for example, in Illinois for the
city of Chicago, and in Ohio for all of the cities.

As a general thing at the present time the civil-
service law is regarded as mandatory and appointments made in conflict with its provisions are void.[1]
In the United States national system, however, the
law is not regarded as mandatory but merely authorizes the President to adopt such rules as he sees fit for
the regulation of appointments in the civil service.
The rules which he adopts are, however, regarded as
binding on the heads of departments in whom the
power of appointment is vested.[2]

The laws and rules of the United States do not
pretend to prescribe intellectual qualifications for all
positions in the service but specifically exempt certain

[1] See People vs. Roberts, 148 N. Y., 360.
[2] See United States vs. Perkins, 116 U. S., 483.   As to the constitutionality
of civil-service legislation, see Rogers vs. Buffalo, 123 N. Y., 173 ; People vs.
Kipley, 171 Ill., 44, which uphold this legislation provided it does not interfere with any power vested in an appointing officer by the constitution.

positions from the operations of the rules. Thus section 7 of the law provides that none of the senate appointments shall be classified for examination except with the consent of the senate, which, up to the present time, has neither been asked for nor given, and that laborers shall not be compelled to pass an examination in order to be appointed to positions in the service. The rest of the national executive service is at the disposal of the President, who may require such intellectual and other tests for entrance into the service as he deems best.

3. *Classification of civil service.*—The present classification of the civil service is to be found in Rule III. In this it is provided that the civil service of the United States shall be arranged in branches as follows: First the Departmental Service; second, the Custom-House Service; third, the Post-Office Service; fourth, the Government Printing Service; and fifth, the Internal Revenue Service.

The Departmental Service, which is the only branch of the service requiring explanation, includes practically all officers and employees except those in the other branches, embracing thus such services, in addition to those in the executive departments at Washington, as the Railway Mail Service, the Indian Service, the Marine Hospital Service, Steamboat Inspection Service, Pension Agencies, Lighthouse Service, Life-saving Service, Mints and Assay Offices, Revenue Cutter Service, the force employed under Custodians of Public Buildings, the several Sub-Treasuries, the Engineer and Ordnance Departments at large, as well as all executive officers and employees outside of the District of Columbia, of whatever designation, who are serving in a subordinate capacity in the various government offices, except persons merely employed as laborers and those whose appointment is subject to confirmation by the Senate.

4. *Exempted positions.* — The rules provide that a long list of positions shall not be subject to any of the rules, with the exception of those which forbid the collection of political assessments, the use of official influence in obtaining appointment, and the dismissal of officers or change in their rank of compensation because of their political or religious opinions or affiliations. It is difficult, from a consideration of the rules affecting these excepted positions, to find any general principle upon which they have been based.[1]

[1] Among the positions so excepted may be mentioned, however, the following : Persons who do not devote their entire time to government business, and at the same time do not receive more than $300 per annum from the government. All persons in the military or naval service of the United States detailed for the performance of civil duties ; persons employed in a confidential capacity under any executive department or other office ; persons of a *quasi*-military or naval character, or local physicians employed as Acting Assistant Surgeons in the Marine Hospital Service ; all quarantine attendants. Finally, there is a series of positions in the Quarter-Master's Department at Large, the Medical Department at Large, the Ordnance Department at Large, the Engineer Department at Large, whose incumbents are in the nature of laborers, appointments to which positions it is specifically provided shall be made on registration lists of fitness to be prescribed in regulations to be issued by the Secretary of War, with the approval of the President.

Further, Rule VI. provides for the exception from the requirements of an examination of all private secretaries, not exceeding two in number, for the President and the various heads of department, and one in number for the assistant heads of department and heads of bureaus and the heads of the various local offices of the United States Government, such as Collectors of Customs, Collectors of Internal Revenue, District Attorneys, Postmasters of the more important Post-Offices ; Deputies, not exceeding one in number, provided that they are not employed in ordinary clerical duties, of Customs and Internal Revenue Collectors and similar officers ; Auditors, not exceeding

The various state and municipal civil-service laws and rules make quite similar provisions, although, of course, the classification is quite different in each instance on account of the needs of the particular service. The exemptions from examination made in these laws are based upon the same principles which have governed the national administration in its action.

5. *Laborers.*—It has been said that the laws and rules specifically except laborers from examination. This exception was made because of the belief that competitive examinations were an improper means of ascertaining the qualifications of a laborer. In Boston, however, soon after the civil-service act was passed, provision was made for the registration of laborers and for obliging the heads of departments which employed laborers to select those whom they were to employ from a registration list. This scheme worked quite successfully there, and in 1891 was adopted by the Secretary of the Navy of the United States for workmen employed at navy yards.[1]

one in number, in the important post-offices; Paymasters, not exceeding one in number, in the New York Customs District; certain other specified officers, in certain of the other branches of the government, such as a Mint and Assay Officer; Storekeepers and Gaugers in the Internal Revenue Department whose compensation does not exceed three dollars per day when actually employed, and whose aggregate compensation shall not exceed $500 per annum; and a series of other officers whom it is extremely difficult to classify, but whose exemption from an examination or registration is thought to be required by the necessities of the service.

[1] The regulations for the registration of laborers in the navy yards may be taken as an example of the methods adopted (see *Fifteenth Rep. U. S. Civ. Serv. Com.*, p. 94). By them the applicants are obliged to furnish certain certificates with regard to their character, no one not having a good character, as defined in the regulations, being permitted to register. They are registered in schedules of trades provided by a board of labor employment which is established among the officers at the different navy yards. No applicant can remain on

6. *Civil-service examinations.* — The examinations of candidates for the positions under the act are competitive except, first, where competent persons cannot be found who are willing to compete; second, to test fitness for transfer or for promotion in a part of the service to which promotion regulations have not been applied; third, to test fitness for appointment of Indians as superintendents of teachers, teachers of industries, kindergartners, and positions in the Indian service generally; fourth, to test the fitness of any person to fill a position which requires certain peculiar qualifications in respect to knowledge and ability, or such scientific or special attainments wholly or in part professional or technical, not ordinarily required in the executive service of the United States, where the head of the department desiring the appointment of such persons shall so certify to the President and he shall approve the certification. But no person so nominated or appointed shall be transferred to any other position in the classified service except the one that may be filled under the provisions of this clause. In all cases these examinations shall be of a practical and suitable character, involving such tests as the commission may direct. On page 75 of the *Fourteenth Report of the Civil Service Commission* the

the list longer than a year unless one month prior to the expiration of the year he requests that his term of eligibility be extended, when it may be extended to another year. Those whose names are on the labor list in this way are to be certified in a prescribed order. Where work requires a high degree of skill, heads of departments are authorized to make a special requisition, and provision is made for a test by the head of the department of the qualifications of candidates, so as to enable him to grade the candidates provisionally and to ascertain if they are suitable for the work. No person certified on a special requisition shall be taken except as a first-class workman, and then only when the test made by the head of the department shows him to be entitled to be graded provisionally as first class.

following statement is made with reference to the different kinds of examinations :

From a careful review of the conditions prevailing in the public service, it appears that three general classes of examinations are required to properly meet the demands upon the Commission. The first general class embraces those designed to test merely the general intelligence and adaptability of the competitors. These examinations are used to test the qualifications for positions where a greater or less amount of intelligence is necessary as a measure of ability, but where there are no special duties to be performed which require a special character of qualifications, as for ordinary clerks, messengers, *etc.* For such positions a series of examinations has been arranged, graduated in character from a mere educational test of the most simple kind, to an examination requiring scholastic ability about equal to that obtained in the ordinary common or graded schools. They are known as the first grade, the second grade, and the third grade basis examinations. The third grade requires merely the ability to read, write, add, subtract, multiply, and divide whole numbers and a knowledge of United States money. The second grade requires in addition to these a knowledge of simple operations in common and decimal fractions, while the first grade requires a knowledge of the use of the English language in business correspondence and of such arithmetical operations, including interest and discount, as embrace those principles necessary to solve ordinary business problems.

The examinations of the second general class contain appropriate tests of general intelligence, combined with those specially designed to bring out the particular information needed to satisfactorily perform the duties of technical positions in the service. These positions require scholastic ability usually of a high order in connection with some special or unusual training or experience. In this class are the examinations for bookkeeper, stenographers, and typewriters, examiners of patents, weather observers, the various kinds of draftsmen, civil engineers, *etc.*

The third general class of examinations are those where no educational qualifications are necessary to satisfy the requirements of the service, but where some peculiar experience or skill

18

is demanded, either in a mechanical or other special line. In these examinations occasionally applicants have been accepted as competent, although unable to read or write, the Commission having been satisfied that they were fully qualified to perform the duties required. The specific name applied to this class of examinations is the fourth grade or trades examinations. They are employed to test applicants as skilled mechanics, *etc.*

During the past five years it has seemed wise to include in many of the examinations an investigation into the business experience as well as capacity of the competitors. It is the purpose of the commission to fill many of the technical positions in the government service as the result of such investigations. In certain examinations the attempt is made to secure the full industrial history of each competitor for the purpose of affording as complete information as possible to the commission and to the appointing officers. In illustration of this sort of examination the following extract from the notice of an examination to secure a person qualified to assist in the preparation of opinions on questions arising under the administration of the public-land laws is pertinent :

The department asks for lawyers not over fifty-five years of age who have had (1) an actual practice of not less than five continuous years in the highest court of their state ; and (2) an active practice of not less than five years (either during the same five years above required or otherwise) either before public-land tribunals or before the courts in a state where the application of public-land laws constitutes a material part of the work. . . . Service on the bench will be counted as practice in these requirements. No application for this examination can be accepted unless the applicant is shown to be possessed of these preliminary qualifications. The examination will consist of : (1) 10 questions in general law ; (2) 30 questions in public-land laws, including homestead, desert, mining, pre-emption, timber-culture, town-site, swamp-land, school-land, and railroad-grant laws ; and (3) questions calculated to call forth the competitor's experience in the application and administration especially of public-land laws. The relative weights of the subjects will be (1) general law, 20 per cent.; (2) public-land law, 60 per cent., and (3) experience, 20 per cent.

It is said in the report of the Chief Examiner for the year ending June 30, 1902,[1] that during the year five hundred and forty-seven different kinds of examinations had been held.

Before presenting himself for examination, every person must make an application under oath upon a form prescribed by the commission and accompanied by certain certificates. Neither the application nor the certificates shall contain any information with regard to the applicant's religious or political affiliation. With the exception of persons who have been honorably discharged from the military or naval services of the United States, no applicant shall be examined who is not within the age limitations which are fixed for entrance for the position to which he seeks to be appointed, and no application shall be accepted for examination for a position which belongs to one of the recognized mechanical trades, unless it shall be shown that the applicant has served as apprentice or as journeyman at such trade for such period as the commission may prescribe. Further, the regulations with regard to the specific kinds of examinations require certain special qualifications from the applicants. Finally, the commission may, in its discretion, refuse to examine an applicant or to certify an eligible who is physically so disabled as to

[1] *Nineteenth Report of the Civil Service Commission*, p. 37.

be rendered unfit for the performance of the duties of the position to which he seeks appointment, or who has been guilty of a crime or infamous or notorious and disgraceful conduct, or who has been dismissed from the service for delinquency or misconduct within one year preceding the date of his application, or who has intentionally made a false statement in any material fact, or practised or attempted to practise any deception or fraud in securing his registration or appointment. The result of the stringent qualifications required for the applications is that many applicants for positions in the service who are not competent are excluded by the application alone, regardless of the result of the examination which is to follow the acceptance of the application.

Examinations are marked on the scale of 100, the subjects upon which they are held being given different weight. Every competitor who obtains an average percentage of seventy or over is eligible to appointment to the position for which he was examined. The names of eligibles are entered in the order of their average percentages on the proper register of eligibles, with the exception that persons who have been honorably discharged from the military and naval services of the United States and who have obtained an average percentage of sixty-five or over are placed in the order of their average percentages at the head of the proper register of eligibles. In certain cases where extremely technical and special qualifications are required, no eligible list is kept; but examinations are held as the vacancies occur. Further, in the case of vacancies in positions for which competitive tests are not practicable, the registration of applicants shall be in the order in which they fulfil the requirements prescribed therefor by the regulations of the commission, except that here also persons honorably discharged from the military and naval services of the United States, and also those who have been separated from these competitive positions through no delinquency or misconduct, are placed at the head of the proper register in the order of their fulfilment of such requirements. The term of eligibility is one year from the date on which the name of the eligible is entered on the register, and no one shall remain there after he has received three certifications to an appointing officer and has not been appointed.

Whenever a vacancy occurs not in an excepted position, the filling of such vacancy, unless filled through non-competitive examination, or by reinstatement, transfer, promotion, or reduction, takes place as follows : The appointing or nominating officer requests certification to him of the names of eligibles for the position vacant, and the commission certifies to such officer from the proper register the three names at the head thereof which have not been three times certified to the department or office in which the vacancy exists. But if the appointing or nominating officer, after submitting his evidence to the commission and receiving its approval, objects to an eligible named in the certificate because of some physical defect, mental unsoundness, or moral disqualification, the commission certifies the eligible on the register who is in average percentage next below those already certified, in place of the one to whom objection is made and sustained. The certification is made regardless of sex where the law does not confine the office to a particular sex, or where in the request for certification the sex of the person to be appointed is not specified.

From the three so certified the appointing officer selects one. This person receives an appointment on probation for six months, at the end of which, if his conduct and capacity are satisfactory, his retention in the service is equivalent to absolute appointment. If, however, his conduct or proficiency is deemed unsatisfactory, he is notified by the appointing officer that he will not receive absolute appointment, and such notification discharges him from the service.

The rules contain careful provisions with regard to the employment of substitutes, temporary appointments, and transfers whose purpose is to prevent appointment in this manner from being made so as to violate the spirit of the law and the rules.

The civil-service laws of the various states are founded upon the same principles. It must be remembered, however, that the constitutions of the states contain peculiar provisions which result in making the law somewhat different from that of the United States government, and in making the law of some particular state different from that of some other state. The attempt has been made in some states to extend much more than is done in the United States law the preference which is accorded to veterans of the military and naval services of the United States. Thus in Massachusetts, in 1895, the attempt was made to exempt veterans entirely from examination, and to give them preference in appointment to positions in the civil service of the state. The constitutionality of the law was questioned[1] and it was held that the act, so far as it purported absolutely to give to veterans particular and exclusive privileges distinct from those of the community in obtaining public office could not be upheld as within the constitutional power of the legislature. The state laws and rules relative to veterans would appear to give to such persons rights to a place on the eligible list which may be enforced by mandamus proceedings. Finally in some cities the commission is to certify only the one standing highest on this list. This is perfectly proper if the constitution does not give a power of appointment to the appointing officer.[2]

7. *The civil-service commission.*—For the purpose of attending to the examinations provided for by the law and rules, and of generally enforcing the provisions of the civil-service act, there has been established both in the national and the state services a commission of a non-partisan character. In the national and state governments this commission is appointed by the chief executive, with the consent of the senate or council, and generally removable by him alone. The non-partisan character of the commission consists in the provision that not all of its members shall belong to the same political party.[3] In the case of the cities, with the exception of those of Massachusetts, where the state commission attends to the municipal exami-

---

[1] Brown *vs.* Russell, 166 Mass., 14 ; 55 A. S. R., 357.

[2] People *vs.* Kipley, 171 Ill., 44.

[3] This has been held to be a perfectly constitutional qualification for the office in the case of Roger *vs.* Buffalo, 123 N. Y., 173 ; People *vs.* Kipley, 171 Ill., 44.

nations as well as the state examinations, the mayor appoints and removes the civil-service commissions, which are, as in the case of the state civil-service commissions, of a non-partisan character. In New York, however, the rules of the municipal commissions must, to be valid, be approved by the state commission. Under the commission is a chief examiner whose duty is, under the direction of the commission, to secure uniformity and justice in the action of the various examining boards. These examining boards are in the national service to be designated from among persons in the public service after consultation with the heads of departments by the civil-service commission. They may hold their examinations at the capital or elsewhere ; any fraud on their part or on the part of any person in the public service concerning the examination is to be punished. The composition and the duties of these boards are defined in the regulations of the commission and the commission will consider complaints as to the unfairness of any board, and will revise the marking or grading, or will order a new examination if it thinks best.

In addition to the powers which the civil-service commissions have over examinations, some of the civil-service acts grant to these commissions very large powers of investigation and examination into the general observance by appointing officers of these civil-service acts and the rules. These acts sometimes give the civil-service commissioners the power to issue, or to apply to some court for the issue of subpœnas which require both the attendance and testimony of witnesses, and the production of books and papers relative to certain investigations, and the power to administer oaths to such witnesses.[1]

[1] It has been objected to these laws on this account that they are unconstitutional because of vesting the civil-service commissioners with judicial powers. This objection was raised in the case of People *vs.* Kipley, 171 Ill., 44, and was overruled. See also on the general subject the case of the Inter-State Commerce Commission *vs.* Brimson, 154 U. S., 447, in which it was held that it was constitutional to vest similar powers in the Inter-State Commerce Commission.

CHAPTER IV.

I.—Right to the office.

THE first right to be noticed is the right of the officer to exercise the powers and perform the duties connected with his office. A continuing right to the office can be spoken of only in the case of an officer whose tenure of office is independent of any administrative superior, so far as the length of term is concerned. Only those officers have a permanent right to exercise the powers and perform the duties of the office who may not be arbitrarily discharged by an administrative superior.[1]

The question of the right of an officer to his office is one, however, which may come up at the beginning of the official relation. It will naturally come up more frequently in the case of elected than in the case of appointed officers, but it may come up in the case of appointed officers where their term is fixed by law. Thus, for instance, the appointing

---

[1] Thus the remedies by means of which the right may be enforced, namely. the *mandamus* and *quo warranto*, may not be made use of in the case of offices of no certain duration. State *vs*. Champlin, 2 Bailey, S. C., 220. Nor may the injunction be used to protect the incumbent of an office from removal. Thus the United States Supreme Court in the case of White *vs*. Berry, 171 U. S., 366, has held that the injunction may not be made use of to prevent the exercise of a power of removal contrary to the civil-service rules passed by the President. See also *In re* Sawyer, 124 U. S., 200, 212.

authority may make an appointment to an office when he believes that the term of the incumbent has expired, while the incumbent may claim that his term has not expired and that he has therefore a right to hold the office until the expiration of the term. In the case of an elective office, the question as to the right to the office may come up as the result of a dispute as to who has been elected. The title to such an office is to be tried by the *quo warranto* or its statutory substitute, by means of which the courts will decide who is the rightful incumbent of the office in question, and as such entitled to exercise its powers and receive its emoluments. Further, one who is clearly entitled to an office may by *mandamus* force the delivery to him of the insignia of office, and may in like manner obtain possession of public buildings and records.[1] In some of the states special tribunals have been established to try election cases. If this is the case, resort must be had to such tribunals and use may not be made of the *quo warranto*.[2] The appeal to the courts in these cases is generally open to any candidate for the office, to the people as represented by the attorney general, and in many cases to any elector of responsibility.[3]

II.—*Special protection.*

The second right of officers is the right to special protection offered by the criminal law. This protec-

[1] People *vs.* Kelduff, 15 Ill., 492 ; Walter *vs.* Belding, 24 Vt., 658 ; Hooten *vs.* McKinney, 5 Nev., 194.

[2] State *vs.* Marlow, 15 Ohio State, 114 ; see also People *vs.* Hall, 80 N. Y., 117, and Mechem, *op. cit.*, § 214.

[3] See Commonwealth *vs.* Meeser, 44 Penna. State, 341 ; Commonwealth *vs.* Swank, 79 Penna. State, 154 ; see Mechem, *op. cit.*, § 213.

tion is, as a rule, extended only to certain classes of officers, namely, those who come in contact with the people as the bearers of a direct command from a competent authority. Where, for the purpose of executing such commands, it is necessary for such officers to use force, they may do so, and, not only are they relieved from responsibility for the damage which they may cause, but the law has declared it to be a crime to resist them, and where an armed resistance is offered it becomes a very serious matter for the persons who offer such resistance. These officers are generally to be found among those who have to do with the administration of justice, the collection of revenue, and the exercise of the police power.[1]

The offence of offering resistance to officers in the performance of their duties, it will be noticed, is a distinct offence separate and apart from the simple offence of violating the law which the officer is attempting to enforce at the time when the resistance is offered. The latter offence is an offence against the law itself, while resistance to an officer in the performance of his duty is more in the nature of a personal matter, and the provisions of law in regard to it are intended to protect administrative officers in the discharge of their duties. This protection is accorded to them only during the discharge of their duties.[2]

---

[1] See, for example, United States Revised Statutes, section 5447 ; New York Penal Code, sections 46, 47.

[2] As to when officers are to be regarded as acting in the discharge of their duties and thus protected by the criminal law, see *In re* Neagle, 135 U. S., 56, and cases cited in the opinion. In this case it is held that the President of the United States may provide special protection for officers in the discharge of their duties.

III.—*Promotions.*

It is difficult to speak of the officer as having a right to promotion except in the sense that he has, so far as it is so provided by law, a right to an increment of salary at the expiration of some specified period. Nevertheless some of the civil-service laws make provision for promotion regardless of this matter of the increment of salary. Thus, United States Civil-Service Rule XI, makes provision for promotion, which, it says, shall be adopted as the method of filling certain offices so long as it is practicable and useful. Provision is made for the appointment of a board of promotion in each department.

The regulations for promotion which are made by the commission are, however, made in consultation with the heads of the various departments, and when once made they cannot be amended or revoked without the consent of the commission. The regulations are different in different departments, the difference being caused by the difference in the needs of the particular departments. They are, however, very largely based upon the same general principles. In the first place, the attempt is made to prevent promotion being made use of to fill places, entrance to which is dependent upon examination, by promotion of persons who have not been examined. In the second place, certain places, such as higher clerical positions, it is provided, shall be filled, as a general rule, only by promotion, and the promotion examination upon which the promotion is dependent consists very largely of an examination into the efficiency of officers as shown by the efficiency record which the

chief clerk of each bureau has to keep under the
direction of the head of such bureau. Provision is
made for an appeal from the efficiency rating to the
board of promotion. If the board does not sustain
the chief clerk, the question is to be referred to the
head of the department and a full report of the case
is to be filed by the board of promotion with the civil-
service commission.[1]

Somewhat similar regulations are adopted in the
civil service of the states and the municipalities, which
have adopted the merit system of appointment. It
must be said, however, that at the present time the
promotion regulations which have been adopted are
not altogether satisfactory.[2]

IV.—*Compensation.*

1. *Not a contractual right.*—The fourth right of
importance possessed by the official is the right
to compensation. This right is not, however, a contractual right, since the official relation is not a contractual relation. If the right to compensation exists
at all, it exists as the result, not of any contract or by
virtue of any service rendered to the government, but
because the law has attached a compensation to the
office.[3] Therefore one who accepts an office to which
no compensation is attached by law is presumed to
assume the office as an honorary office, and cannot
recover anything for his services.[4] But where one
undertakes work for a public corporation at its re-

[1] A list of the various regulations in force relative to promotions will be found
in the *Fifteenth Report of the United States Civil Service Commission,* p. 107.
[2] See *Nineteenth Report of the U. S. Civ. Ser. Com.,* p. 22.
[3] Fitzsimmons *vs.* Brooklyn, 102 N. Y., 536.
[4] White *vs.* Levant, 78 Maine, 568.

quest, he may recover either on an express or an implied contract. It has been held that such a recovery may be had by a public officer provided the service he renders is absolutely foreign to the office which he holds.[1]

The official relation not being a contractual relation, and the existence of the right to compensation being dependent upon the law, we must go to the law to find if there is a compensation attached to any given office. The compensation, however it may be fixed, may be changed by the authority fixing it, provided no higher law, such as the constitution when it is fixed by statute, or a statute when it is fixed by the administration, prevents.[2] The compensation may be altered, diminished, or altogether terminated during the term of office of the incumbent, and such change will not be regarded as impairing the obligation of a contract, since the official relation is not a contractual relation[3]; but the act changing the compensation must be clear and specific.[4] It is, however, a very common provision in the state constitutions and statutes, that the salary or compensation shall not be increased or diminished during the term of office of the incumbent. Where such a provision is made, it is absolutely mandatory upon the authorities having the right to fix the compensation, and any attempt to change the compensation contrary to the rule laid down either in the constitution or the statutes is void.[5] Where, however,

---

[1] Evans *vs*. Trenton, 24 N. J. L., 764 ; see also Converse *vs*. U. S., 21 Howard, U. S., 463.

[2] Kehn *vs*. State, 93 N. Y., 291.

[3] Butler *vs*. Pa., 10 Howard, U. S., 402 ; Conner *vs*. Mayor, 5 N. Y., 285.

[4] United States *vs*. Langston, 118 U. S., 389.

[5] Evans *vs*. Trenton, 24 N. J. L., 764 ; Converse *vs*. U. S., 21 Howard, U. S., 463.

official services have been rendered, a contract to pay for them at the rate fixed by law is implied which cannot be impaired even by the legislature.[1]

A further result of the fact that the official relation is not a contractual relation is that the incumbent does not lose his right to his compensation by reason of his inability, as, for example, from sickness, to discharge the duties of the office. So long as he holds the office he has the right to his compensation.[2] Finally, if an officer is illegally prevented by his superiors from discharging his duties, as by an unauthorized removal, he does not lose his claim to his compensation.[3] The only apparent exception to this rule results from the application of the rule as to *de facto* officers. The application of the latter rule brings it about that if the salary has been paid to a *de facto* officer, the *de jure* officer has no claim for the salary against the officer or corporation paying the *de facto* officer,[4] but may sue the *de facto* officer who has received the salary.[5]

Finally, it is to be noticed that the salary or compensation of public officers is, from motives of public policy, not subject to garnishment or attachment,[6]

---

[1] Fiske *vs.* Police Jury, 116 U. S., 131 ; Stewart *vs.* Police Jury, *ibid.*, 135.

[2] O'Leary *vs.* Board of Education, 93 N. Y., 1.

[3] Fitzsimmons *vs.* Brooklyn, 102 N. Y., 536 ; which holds further that in such a case the officer is not obliged to deduct from his claim for salary what money he earns during the period of his absence from duty.

[4] Dolan *vs.* Mayor, 68 N. Y., 274. If an officer is prevented, however, by injunction from taking possession of his office, he has, it has been held, the right to his salary for the time during which he has been excluded. Memphis *vs.* Woodward, 12 Heiskell, Tenn., 499.

[5] Nichols *vs.* McLean, 101 N. Y., 526. There is some conflict on this particular point, see Stuhr *vs.* Curran, 15 Vroom, 181.

[6] Buchanan *vs.* Alexander, 4 Howard, U. S., 20

and that unearned salary may not according to the better rule be assigned.[1]

2. *How enforced.*—The claim for compensation has been spoken of as a right on the part of officers. This description of it is not in all cases correct, since where the officer's compensation consists of a salary which is to be paid by the government, it would seem that, if there is no special law permitting him to sue the government and if he cannot put his claim into such a shape as to make some municipal corporation responsible for it, he has in many cases no claim which is enforceable in a court of law. This rule is due to the application of the principle that the government may not be sued without its consent.[2] In the national government, however, as the result of special statute, officers may sue the government for their compensation.[3] In the states as yet, the general rule is that officers may not sue the central government for their salaries. It is to be remembered, however, that many of the officers who are discharging duties which affect the state as a whole are still paid by some one of the various local corporations which are liable to suit. Furthermore, where an officer may not sue the state government, if the duty is imposed upon some disbursing officer of paying the legal compensations of other officers, and he should refuse to do so, he may be forced to act by means of the writ of *mandamus.*[4]

---

[1] Bliss *vs.* Lawrence, 58 N. Y., 442 ; but see State Bank *vs.* Hastings, 15 Wis., 78, which holds the contrary, applying to this public legal relation the rules of purely private law.

[2] See *infra*, p. 387.

[3] United States *vs.* Langston, 118 U. S., 389.

[4] See Nichols *vs.* Comptroller, 2 Stew. and Port., Ala., 154 ; Turner *vs.* Meloney, 13 Cal., 621.

19

Finally, where the compensation of an officer consists of fees to be paid by third persons employing such officer, the officer has a right to the payment of the fees as fixed by law, and may retain until such fees are paid any documents in his possession upon which he has expended labor.[1]

Somewhat akin to the right to recover compensation is the right which all officers possess to force the payment to them of all the expenses which they have been obliged to incur in order to discharge their duties. This is true whether the expense has been incurred for the government or for an individual.[2]

3. *Civil pensions.*—In a number of instances officers are guaranteed by the law pensions or superannuation allowances, which they are to receive, after a certain number of years' service, on the occasion of their retirement from office. There is apparently nothing in the constitution of the United States which causes any doubt to arise as to the constitutionality of such pension legislation. There are, however, a number of provisions in the state constitutions which have been so interpreted by the courts as to make the question of the constitutionality of these civil pensions one of considerable difficulty. Many of the constitutions of the states contain a provision which prohibits the grant of public money as a gratuity to any individual. Others contain provisions which require uniformity in taxation. Under either one of these provisions pretty nearly every method of raising money for the payment of civil

[1] People *vs.* Harlow, 29 Ill., 43 ; see also Baldwin *vs.* Kouns, 81 Ala., 272.
[2] Powell *vs.* Newburgh, 19 Johnson, N. Y., 284; United States *vs.* Flanders, 112 U. S., 88.

pensions has been contested, and has in some states been declared unconstitutional.

The first civil-service pensions which it was attempted to provide in this country were apparently pensions to members of the fire departments of the cities. Originally these pensions were granted out of a pension fund which was not dependent upon the public treasury for its resources, but usually such pension funds were found to be insufficient to pay all the pensions which it was necessary to pay, and recourse was had to the good offices of the government. Thus it was provided by law that foreign fire-insurance companies should pay to the pension fund a certain percentage of their premiums received from business done within the state. Such exactions have usually been upheld upon the theory that they were not taxes imposed upon the insurance companies, but merely one of the conditions which the state imposes on the right of the foreign corporation to do business within its limits.[1] Inasmuch as such a payment is not a tax, it is held not to be in violation of the provision of the constitution prohibiting the grant of gratuities to individuals, and pensions thus established are upheld notwithstanding the fact that they are given to persons who at the time that they receive them are not officers of the city government. In a recent case the highest court in New York has held, however, that public monies may not be made use of to pay pensions to persons not in the service at the time of the grant of the pension.[2]

[1] See, *e. g.*, Firemen's Fund *vs.* Roome, 93 N. Y., 313.

[2] In the matter of Mahon, 171 N. Y., 263. A somewhat similar result was reached in the case of the State *vs.* Ziegenhein, 144 Mo., 283, which held that pensions from public monies were improper except as an inducement to future

These cases would seem to indicate that while pensions payable out of public funds may be offered as an inducement to persons to enter the service, it is very doubtful whether a pension can be added to the compensation which persons once in the service are receiving for the work they are doing. It is certainly true that once officers have severed their connection with the service the pension may not be granted to them if such pension is to be paid out of public monies.

Another source of pension funds is to be found in deductions made from the salaries of officers. There is considerable doubt whether it is proper to impose such a deduction upon an officer against his will after he has once entered the service.[1]

Whatever may be the rule as to the constitutionality of pensions which are paid out of public monies or out of deductions of salary, it is unquestionably the rule that the claim to a pension, like the claim to an official compensation, is not of a contractual character. Therefore, a pension may be changed at any time, even after the right to it has vested, where authority to make the change has been granted by the legislature.[2]

services ; but see on this point Commonwealth *vs.* Walton, 182 Penna. State, 373, which would seem to take the opposite view.

[1] Thus it has been held that such deductions may not be imposed as the result of a rule or regulation of an administrative authority which has not been authorized by the legislature to adopt such a regulation; State *vs.* Rogers (Minn.), 58 Lawyers Reports Annotated, 663. In Hubbard *vs.* State (Ohio), *ibid.*, 654, it was held that a deduction from an officer's salary, provided by statute even, is improper under a constitution providing for uniformity of taxation, since such deduction is really the imposition of a tax upon a class in the community.

[2] See United States *vs.* Kellar, 107 U. S., 64 ; and Pennie *vs.* Reis, 132 U. S., 464, affirming 80 Cal., 266. See also People *ex rel* Devery *vs.* Coler, 71

Within the last few years there has been considerable agitation for the establishment of civil pensions
in the civil service of the United States, and one or
two investigations of the subject have been made.
At present the plan which seems to receive the greatest favor is to impose upon all candidates for office
the obligation of securing annuity insurance.[1]

The whole matter of civil pensions in this country
is in a very unsatisfactory state. No systematic attempt has apparently been made, outside of the attempt
which is now being made at Washington, to investigate the matter of civil pensions, and the result has
been that in the same city, as, for example, in the city
of New York, various pension plans have been
adopted for the different branches in the service.
Apparently, also, no attempt has been made to prevent one who has served the period necessary to ac-
quire a pension, from holding a salaried office in the
government of the same city from which he receives
a pension.[2] In Europe, however, where civil-service
pensions have been established for a long time, there
is practical uniformity as to the general requirements
of pension legislation. Most of the pension laws that
have been adopted have been based upon the French
law of June 8, 1853. By this law the right to the
pension is acquired by the attainment of sixty years

App. Div. (N. Y.), 584, affirmed in same *vs.* same, 173 N. Y., 103. In
the former case it is stated that a claim to a pension is not a contract even
where the funds from which the pension is paid are derived from deductions
from the officer's salary. In the latter case it is held that, whatever may be
the character of a claim to a pension, the claim to an office to which a pension
is attached is not in the nature of a contract.

[1] A discussion of this subject will be found in the *Nineteenth Report of the
Civil Service Commission*, p. 24.

[2] See, for example, People *ex rel* Mulvey *vs.* York, 41 App. Div., 419.

of age after thirty years of service. The amount of the pension is based on the average salary for the last six years of service, one-sixtieth of such average salary being granted for each year of service up to a maximum of forty-five sixtieths. The fund from which these pensions are paid is obtained partly out of deductions made from the salaries of officers and partly from appropriations made by the government. The deduction that is made is five per cent. of the salary.

CHAPTER V.

I.—Ministerial and discretionary duties.

THE duties of officers may be classified from several points of view. From one point of view they are either mandatory and ministerial, or discretionary and judicial. Mandatory duties are those which are imposed upon officers by provision of statute, which is interpreted as making the discharge of such duties by such officers absolutely imperative. Thus, the courts may be called upon by individuals to force officers to discharge their duties which are regarded as mandatory. Again, the failure to observe a mandatory provision of statute imposing a duty has the effect of making the action taken in non-observance of such a provision absolutely void.[1]

From another point of view, duties are spoken of rather as ministerial than as mandatory. In case duties are regarded as ministerial, any individual who has suffered damage as a result of the failure of the

---

[1] See French *vs.* Edwards, 13 Wall (U. S.), 506. In this case the statute authorized the sheriff to sell property in order to compel the payment of taxes, but provided that he should sell only the smallest quantity which any purchaser would take, and pay the judgment and costs. It was held that the action of the sheriff in selling the entire parcel in order to enforce the payment of taxes was a violation of this mandatory provision, and that the deed given by the sheriff to the purchaser at the tax sale was on that account void.

officer to perform such duties, or of his negligence in the performance of such duties, may, in an action brought in the proper way, recover from such officer the damages suffered.[1]

While, as a general thing, the character of an officer's duties is to be determined by the wording of the statute which confers the duty upon him, the word "may" is often construed as meaning "must" or "shall."[2] Furthermore, it is usually held that even where the law imposing a duty upon an officer is not mandatory in form, it will be regarded by the courts as mandatory where it has been adopted with the idea of affording protection to the individual.[3]

As opposed to the ministerial or mandatory duties are the discretionary or judicial duties. Statutes imposing such duties are sometimes referred to as directory. The general rule with regard to discretionary duties and directory statutes is, that the officer who executes them is not liable for the way in which he executes them, nor may he be forced by the courts to execute them in any particular manner. From this latter point of view, all the control of a direct character that the courts can exercise over the discharge of discretionary duties is to be found in their right to insist that the officer shall exercise his discretion.[4]

[1] These matters will be treated more in detail when we come to consider the control which the courts have over the actions of administrative officers.

[2] The rule as to the construction of these words has been well stated in the case of Mayor *vs.* Furze, 3 Hill (N. Y.), 612, where the court says: "Where a public officer has been clothed by statute with power to do an act which concerns the public interest or the rights of third persons, the execution of the power may be insisted on as a duty, though the phraseology of the statute be permissive merely and not peremptory." See also Supervisors *vs.* United States, 4 Wall. (U. S.), 435.

[3] French *vs.* Edwards, 13 Wall. (U. S.), 506.

[4] People *vs.* Com. Council, 29 Mich., 108. The one exception to this rule

From another point of view we may classify the duties of officers as those to which is attached a criminal sanction and those to which no such sanction is attached, and which are more of a moral character. In the first place, the law states positively certain things which all officers must or must not do, and provides penalties of a criminal character for disobedience of its provisions. In the second place, the very existence of the official relation makes it necessary that the officer shall or shall not do certain things or shall behave towards the public in a certain way. The duties of the first class are generally negative in character, and the rules of law in which they are to be found form a sort of special criminal law for officers. The duties of the second class are more positive in character, and form a sort of official code of ethics, which can be maintained, where an official *esprit du corps* has not been developed, only through the existence and exercise of a strong disciplinary power. Where great reliance has been placed upon *esprit du corps*, or where the disciplinary power is large, it will not be necessary to form an extensive official criminal code. Where, however, this official *esprit du corps* is not to be found, or where the disciplinary power is slight, we find such an extensive official criminal code.

is to be found in the case of a serious abuse of discretion which is practically equivalent to fraud, bad faith, or corruption. In such instances there are a number of cases which hold that the officer who has been guilty of such abuse of discretion both is liable to any individual who is injured by his action, Pike *vs.* Megoun, 44 Mo., 491, and may be forced by the courts to exercise his powers in the proper manner, State *vs.* Board, 134 Mo., 296. This exception to the general rule as to discretionary duties is usually made with regard to actions of officers impairing the right of suffrage. Mechem, *op. cit.*, § 640.

II.—Duties with a penal sanction.

1. *Common-law crimes of officers.*—In the first place, it may be laid down that officers, even more than ordinary persons, are bound to obey the law. The criminal law regards as a crime almost every act of an officer which, if committed by an individual, would be a crime.[1] Further, the law of the United States declares "any act or omission, in disobedience of official duty, by one who has accepted office, when of public concern," to be a crime.[2] The endeavor is, however, made to distinguish between discretionary and ministerial officers. The general rule is "particularly applicable," says Mr. Bishop, "where the thing required to be done is of a ministerial or other like nature and there is reposed in the officer no discretion." In the case of officers acting with discretion, the act, to be punished criminally, must be wilful and corrupt.[3] But it is to be noticed that the law excepts the highest officers of state from this criminal common-law liability for misfeasance or nonfeasance in office.[4] In these cases the control of the legislature[5] is regarded as sufficient. In some of the states this common-law liability of officers is increased by statute so as to make the mere wilful violation of official duty without corrupt motives punishable criminally.[6]

[1] See Bishop, *Criminal Law*, ii., § 982.

[2] *Ibid.*, i., § 459. See also Commonwealth *vs.* Coyle, 160 Pa. St., 36.

[3] People *vs.* Coon, 15 Wend. (N. Y.), 277; People *vs.* Norton, 7 Barb. (N. Y.), 477.

[4] Bishop, *op. cit.*, i., § 462.

[5] For which see *infra*, p. 422.

[6] See in New York, People *vs.* Brooks, 1 Denio, 457, construing the provisions of the Revised Statutes.

2. *Statutory official crimes.*—Further, certain specific acts of certain specific officers, or of officers generally, are, by statute, expressly made punishable criminally.[1] Thus, the civil-service law of the United States provides that it shall be a crime for any officer to solicit or receive assessments for the payment of party expenses from any one in the service.[2] It would, of course, be impossible to enumerate these criminal provisions imposing punishment upon officers for the doing of illegal acts. All that need be said about the system in the United States is, that this method of enforcing the performance by officers of their duties has been carried further than in almost any other country, simply for the reason that the general disciplinary powers of the higher administrative officers are rather weaker in the United States than elsewhere.[3]

III.—*Duties of a moral character.*

The second class of duties to which allusion has been made are more moral than legal in character, are largely based on executive usage, and owe their force almost entirely to the existence in the executive of a disciplinary power.[4] Although they may, in some instances, be sanctioned by criminal penalties as is the class of duties which has been considered, still, they will never be well performed unless, as a

---

[1] See United States *vs.* Germaine, 99 U. S., 508.

[2] U. S. L. 1883, c. 27, §§ 11–15.

[3] M. La Férrière in his work on *La Juridiction Administrative* has called attention to this peculiarity of the American law. See vol. i., p. 101.

[4] For instance, take the duty not to exercise the power of removal for political reasons. This duty, which is based on civil-service rules, the courts have held they will not enforce, but will leave it to the executive authority to enforce. White *vs.* Berry, 171 U. S., 366.

result of the long-continued exercise of a disciplinary power, there has grown up in the civil service an *esprit du corps* similar to that which is found in the military service, and which forbids an officer to be guilty of conduct which is regarded as unbecoming an officer. These duties of a moral character, so far as they may be classified at all, may be classified under the following heads ;

1. *Obedience to orders.* — The general duty of obedience to the orders of superior officers is to be found in all hierarchically organized administrative systems, and can, in the nature of things, exist only in such systems. In the United States, however, no officer, except a ministerial officer in certain cases,[1] is relieved from responsibility over against third persons for violating the law or the constitution because he has obeyed the orders of his superior. In case he disobeys orders, he may be subjected to the exercise of the disciplinary power of his superior where no limit has been placed upon such power, but even in the national system of administration, which is almost the only instance of a completely hierarchical administrative system in this country, such liability to punishment for disobedience of orders does not relieve officers from civil liability for the execution of such orders in case they are illegal.[2]

2. *Prompt performance of the duties connected with the office.*—This duty consists in the uninterrupted performance of the duties of the office, except when leave of absence has been granted by a superior, as in the case of legal vacations and sickness. In some cases the performance of this duty involves also

---

[1] See *infra*, p. 401.   [2] *Infra*, p. 401.

residence at the place where the office is situated, but this would not seem to be the universal rule. In some cases also it means the devotion of the entire time of the officer to the duties of the office. This does not seem, however, to be the common rule. Of course there are a number of offices whose duties will, in the nature of things, be so absorbing that the incumbents of such offices will have no time to devote to any other occupation, but when this is the case it is the practical outcome of the position rather than the result of a legal rule. Seldom is it the law that an officer has not the right to engage in other occupations if he can, in the nature of things, do so. Many of the higher officers in the United States who receive large salaries and have very responsible duties to perform are, at the same time that they are holding office, engaged in some other occupation, such, for example, as the practice of the legal profession. In such case they simply superintend the performance of the work of their offices, leaving most of the routine work to be attended to by deputies. Our political system makes it necessary to permit the higher officers, at any rate, to engage in other occupations, because, on account of the legal precariousness of the official tenure and of the actually frequent changes made in the offices, it is almost impossible to demand of any man that he shall give up his entire time to his official work.

3. *Good conduct.*—The duty of good conduct—that is, courteous behavior to the public and orderly behavior generally, is a duty almost altogether of a moral character, and is hardly susceptible of legal definition. Further, it is dependent for its enforce-

ment almost entirely upon the existence and exercise of the disciplinary power. In some cases, however, it is explicitly recognized in the law. Thus, the civil-service law of the United States provides that no person shall be retained in the service who habitually indulges to excess in intoxicating liquors.[1]

This duty of orderly conduct has of late years come, in the United States, to mean that the officer must not be guilty of offensive partisanship against the ruling party in the executive office or take active part in political contests.[2] A good example of what the duty of courteous behavior to the public means and how it may be enforced may be found in an incident which occurred at Washington a number of years ago. An individual who had business with one of the departments was treated with incivility by one of the clerks. Complaint was made to the superior officer and the clerk was dismissed from the service by the head of the department with the remark that "every man who had business with the treasury was entitled to civil treatment, and that no employee who was unable to remember that he was a servant of the public and bound to be courteous to those whom he served, need expect to be retained."[3]

IV.—Responsibility of officers for violation of duty.

The violation of the duties which have been so briefly outlined may result in a three-fold responsibility. In the first place, if an individual is damaged

[1] U. S. L. 1883, c. 27, § 8. See also the various provisions of city charters relative to the members of the police, fire, and similar departments.
[2] See Powers, " The Reform of the Federal Service," *P. S. Q.*, iii., 247, 252.
[3] See *New York Times*, Nov. 24, 1885.

by the violation of his duty by an official, the official
may in some cases be held liable to reimburse the
injured individual to the extent of the damage suffered.[1]   In the second place, if the law has attached
a criminal penalty to the violation of official duty, the
officer may be punished criminally.   Finally, if the
administration is at all centralized, and if the disciplinary power is strong, as it generally is in all centralized systems of administration, the violation of
official duty may lead to an administrative responsibility.   In some cases, the disciplinary power, where
it exists, consists merely of the power of removal.
Where this is unconditional it would seem that the
power to inflict lighter disciplinary penalties than
removal would practically though perhaps not legally
be derived from it, as the offending officer would
prefer to submit, for example, to the imposition of a
fine, rather than lose his place altogether.   A disciplinary power may, however, exist where there is no
absolute power of removal, or where the power of removal is conditioned upon the finding of some cause
when the decision of the disciplinary power as to
what is cause is sometimes reviewable by the courts.
For the power may be given to a disciplinary authority to impose fines, to decree the loss of promotion,
where that is provided as a claim in the nature of
a right, to degrade the officer by placing him in a
lower rank than that which he occupies at the time
he violates his duty, to suspend him from the service,
and even in extreme cases to order his arrest.   Although such a disciplinary power does not as a rule
exist in the American administrative system, still we

---

[1] See, for a further development of this subject, *infra*, p. 000.

do find instances of it in the case of the purely professional services which have been established in some
of the cities, *e.g.*, the fire and police forces.   Thus
the present New York charter[1] provides that the
commissioner of police

shall have power, in his discretion, on conviction, by him or by
any court or officer of competent jurisdiction, of a member of
the force of any criminal offence or neglect of duty, or violation
of the rules, or neglect or disobedience of orders, or absence
without leave, or any conduct injurious to the public peace or
welfare, or immoral conduct, or conduct unbecoming an officer,
or any breach of discipline, to punish the offending party by
reprimand, forfeiting and withholding pay for a specified time,
suspension without pay during such suspension

not exceeding thirty days, or dismissal from the force.
Each of these three kinds of responsibility, *i.e.*, the
civil, criminal, and administrative, reinforces and sup-
plements the others.   Therefore, as might be expected, the extent of each kind of responsibility is
not the same in different states.   Where the disciplinary power is small, the criminal responsibility is
very large, as is usually the case in the United States.
Where the civil responsibility is small, as is also
usually the case in the United States, again we find
a large criminal responsibility.   Finally, if the administrative responsibility is extensive it may be unnecessary to develop the other kinds of responsibility to
any great extent.   No hasty judgment should be
drawn regarding the responsibility of officers in any
one state from a consideration of only one of these
various kinds of responsibility as all reinforce and
supplement each other.

[1] N. Y. L. 1901, c.   466, § 302.

CHAPTER VI.

TERMINATION OF THE OFFICIAL RELATION.

THE official relation is terminated in various ways. The first to be mentioned is by death. This is so simple that it hardly needs any discussion. All that need be said in regard to it is that an office held by several is not usually terminated or made vacant by the death of one of the incumbents.[1] In some cases the widow or the family of the deceased officer has a claim to a pension and the estate of the deceased officer may be made responsible for claims made against him by the government. The official relation is thus not in all cases absolutely terminated by the death of the incumbent of an office. A more important way of terminating the official relation is the expiration of the term of office.

I.—*Expiration of the term.*

The general rule would seem to be that the expiration of the term of an office causes the official relation to cease so far as the future is concerned.[2] An officer has, after the expiration of his term, no duties and no authority to act except to complete

[1] People *vs.* Palmer, 52 N. Y., 83.

[2] Romero *vs.* United States, 24 Court of Claims, 331. In some cases, however, it is held that in the absence of a specific provision of statute an officer holds over after the expiration of his term until his successor has duly qualified. Stratton *vs.* Oulton, 28 Cal., 44.

unfinished business and except in so far as the principles of law with regard to officers *de facto* may come in to modify this rule.[1] In order to overcome the inconveniences of such a rule, it is often provided by statute that the officer shall hold over until his successor enters upon the performance of his duties. In such a case the hold-over holds the office, not as a *de facto*, but as a *de jure*, officer.[2] Where such a provision exists, it is held that so far as it is necessary to the protection of the public the officer will be deemed to be in office even if he has resigned and his resignation has been accepted.[3]

The subject of the term of office has become very important on account of the practice of fixing a specified term of office for almost every position. This principle was introduced into the United States national government about 1820, when a term of four years was provided for most officers in the government. It has had the effect of encouraging changes in the incumbency of offices through the exercise of the power of appointment by the President, which must of necessity be exercised at the expiration of the terms of officers. There has been a great deal of opposition to this practice, and the attempt has been made a number of times to repeal the term of office laws, as they are called, but up to the present time the opponents of the law have failed in securing what they desire.[4]

[1] People *vs.* Tieman, 30 Barb. (N. Y.), 193 ; Newman *vs.* Beckwith, 61 N. Y., 205.

[2] State *vs.* Bulkeley, 61 Conn., 287 ; State *vs.* Howe, 25 Ohio State, 588.

[3] Badger *vs.* United States, 93 U. S., 599, 603 ; Jones *vs.* Jefferson, 66 Tex., 576.

[4] See vol. 15 of the *United States Civil Service Commission*, p. 453 *et seq.*

II.—*Resignation.*

The official relation may be terminated by resignation on the part of the incumbent. While all the cases agree upon the principle that a completed resignation terminates the official relation, there seems to be a difference of opinion as to the right an officer has to resign, and, where that right is admitted, as to the necessity of the acceptance of the resignation. Some of the courts, basing themselves on the old English rule that governmental offices are obligatory, and seeing that the recognition of an absolute right in the officer to resign, regardless of the wishes of his superiors, would result in the destruction of the obligation to assume office, have held that a resignation is not effective until it has been accepted.[1] Other cases have added to the old English rule the corollary that resignation has, at common law, absolutely no effect; that unless the statute gives the power to some one to accept a resignation, acceptance of a resignation, even by an authority which is the recognized superior of the officer resigning, does not have the effect of terminating the official relation.[2] Other cases still, losing sight of the fact that at common law acceptance of a long series of offices was obligatory, have laid down the general rule that acceptance of a resignation is never necessary.[3] If, however, the general rules laid down in these cases are not considered but only the actual decisions rendered, it will be found that the contradiction is not

[1] Van Orsdell *vs.* Hazard, 3 Hill, N. Y., 243.

[2] See State *vs.* Ferguson, 31 N. J. L., 107.

[3] See People *vs.* Porter, 6 Cal. 26 ; State *vs.* Clarke, 3 Nev., 566 ; Wright *vs.* U. S., 1 McLean, 509, 512 ; 14 Opinions Atty.-Gen., 259.

really so great as it seems. For almost all the cases holding that acceptance of the resignation is necessary were decided with regard to local offices which were obligatory offices in the local self-government system of administration, while those cases which have held the acceptance to be unnecessary have been decided with regard to offices of the general government or the central state government, which take up most, if not all, the time and attention of the incumbent, and are, therefore, more or less professional in character.[1]

Where resignation is permitted, it consists in the intention to relinquish the office accompanied by an absolute relinquishment.[2] Provided these conditions are present it makes no difference how the resignation is made. It may be and usually is in writing, but it also may be made by parol.[3] Where the acceptance of the resignation is not regarded as necessary, it has been held that the resignation is complete as soon as it is out of the power of the officer resigning to recall it. Thus the resignation has been held to be complete after it has been mailed.[4] Where, however, acceptance of the resignation is necessary, the resignation is not complete until it has been received by the authority that has the right to accept it and may be withdrawn by the officer resigning at any time with the consent of the officer who has the power to accept it.[5] Finally, where it is

[1] See Edwards *vs.* United States, 103 U. S., 471.

[2] Biddle *vs.* Willard, 10 Ind., 62; but see Blake *vs.* U. S., 14 Ct. Cl., 462, holding that the resignation of an officer while temporarily insane is invalid.

[3] Barbour *vs.* U. S., 17 Ct. Cl., 149.

[4] State *vs.* Clarke, 3 Nev., 566.

[5] Biddle *vs.* Willard, 10 Ind., 62 ; but see State *vs.* Hauss, 43 Ind., 105.

provided that an officer shall hold over until his successor enters upon the duties of the office, it has been held that resignation has no effect, even if it has been accepted, as the purpose of the law is to prevent an official *interregnum.*[1] As there is no formal method prescribed for the making of a resignation, so there is no formal method prescribed for its acceptance. Thus the filing, without objection, of the resignation in the proper office has been held to be an acceptance.[2] The appointment of a successor is also regarded as an acceptance of a resignation.[3] The resignation may never, however, be retrospective, since that would permit an officer to escape official responsibilities.[4]

III.—Loss of qualifications.

Loss of qualifications generally entails loss of office. Thus the attainment of an age which by law disqualifies for the office, will terminate the official relation, except so far as the doctrine of *de facto* officers comes in to modify the rule. Conviction for a crime which results in the loss of the qualification of good character, where that is provided for by statute, will also terminate the official relation. One of the most common methods of losing the necessary qualifications is the acceptance of an incompatible office. This is regarded as *ipso facto* a vacation of the first office, even

---

[1] Badger *vs.* United States, 93 U. S., 599 ; see also Edwards *vs.* United States, 103 U. S., 475 ; Thompson *vs.* United States, 103 U. S., 480.

[2] Pace *vs.* People, 50 Ill., 432 ; see also Gates *vs.* Delaware Co., 12 Iowa, 405.

[3] Edwards *vs.* United States, 103 U. S., 471.

[4] 1 First Comptroller's Decisions, 325.

if the second office is inferior to the first.[1] Even though the title to the second office is defective, the first office cannot be claimed if, in the meantime, it has been filled.[2] The only exception to this rule is that where the incumbent of the first office has not the right to resign, or where, when he has the right to resign, his resignation is not complete, *e. g.*, where it has not been accepted, where acceptance is necessary. In such a case the attempted acceptance of the second office has no effect.[3]

The incompatibility which is necessary to vacate an office may result from common law or from statute. The common law holds that an "inconsistency in functions of the two offices, and not a mere lack of time or inability properly to perform the duties of the two offices, is an incompatibility."[4] Sometimes the statutes merely declare that two offices are incompatible when the rule, as stated, would apply. Sometimes they declare that no person shall hold, at the same time, two lucrative offices. Where the two offices are found in the same government, as in the state, or where the second office is held in another government (as *e. g.* the national government) over which the government laying down the rule (as *e. g.* the state government) has no jurisdiction, the rule is that the second office is to be deemed an incompatible office and that, therefore, the first office is vacated.[5]

---

[1] Milward *vs.* Thatcher, 2 T. R., 81 ; 1 First Comptroller's Decisions, 324 ; Mechem, *op. cit.*, § 420; Oliver *vs.* Mayor, 63 N. J. L., 634.

[2] The King *vs.* Hughes, 5 B. and C., 886.

[3] The King *vs.* Patteson, 4 B. and Ad., 9.

[4] People *vs.* Green, 58 N. Y., 295 ; Mechem, *op. cit.*, § 423, and cases cited.

[5] Dailey *vs.* State, 8 Blackford, Ind., 329 ; Dickson *vs.* People, 17 Ill., 191; State *vs.* Buttz, 9 S. C., 156.

But incompatible offices must be clearly distinguished from forbidden offices. In the case of forbidden offices the rule is not that the first office is vacated, but that it is absolutely impossible for a person to accept the second office for which he is made ineligible by the fact of his holding the first office.[1] When the law provides that no person shall hold two lucrative offices, and the person holding an office over which the government laying down the prohibition has no control (as, for example, a United States post-office) accepts an office over which such government has control (as, for example, a state office), then the second office is regarded as a forbidden office. The first office, therefore, is not vacated as in the case of incompatible offices, but the individual is deemed ineligible to the second office.[2]

Finally, persistent neglect to perform the duties of the office is regarded as an abandonment of the office.[3] All cases of resignation, disqualification, or abandonment of office are decided finally by the courts.[4]

IV.—*Removal from office.*

Except in the case of the President of the United States,[5] the power of removal is not regarded as being vested in the chief executive as a result of the grant to him of the executive power.[6] The power is often,

---

[1] People *vs.* Clute, 50 N. Y., 451 ; Attorney-General *vs.* Marston, 66 N. H., 485.

[2] State *vs.* De Gress, 53 Tex., 387 ; Bishop *vs.* State, 149 Ind., 223.

[3] Wardlaw *vs.* Mayor, 137 N. Y., 194.

[4] Van Orsdell *vs.* Hazard, 3 Hill, N. Y., 243 ; Mechem, *op. cit.*, sections 435 *et seq.*, 478, and cases cited.

[5] Parsons *vs.* United States, 167 U. S., 324.

[6] State *vs.* Field, 3 Ill., 79.

however, vested by statute in either the chief executive or other executive officer to remove officers whom he does not appoint. Thus the power may be given to the chief executive to remove officers who obtained their offices by popular election. But where no such power has been expressly granted, the rule which is applicable to the executive of the state is applicable to all executive officers—that is, no executive officer possesses the power of removal where the officer to be removed owes his office to an election or has a term of office fixed by statute.[1]

If, however, the officer is appointed by another, it would seem to be the rule, in the absence of any statute fixing the term or tenure, that the power of removal is incident to the power of appointment.[2]

The power of removal may be either absolute or conditional. It is usually absolute when incident to the power of appointment. It is also absolute in the case of the President, since it is regarded as vested in the President as part of the executive power.[3] In the states it is also usually absolute for the subordinates in the central departmental services and also for the clerical services in the local governments. In case the power of removal is absolute, it may be exercised in the discretion of the removing authority, and no hearing need be given the officer removed.[4]

Where conditions are imposed, they consist sometimes in the necessity of obtaining the consent of an

[1] Speed *vs.* Common Council, 97 Mich., 198; State *vs.* Chatburn, 63 Ia., 659; Speed *vs.* Common Council, 98 Mich., 360.

[2] *Ex parte* Hennen, 13 Peters, U. S., 230; People *ex rel.* Sims *vs.* Fire Commissioners, 73 N. Y., 437.

[3] Parsons *vs.* United States, 167 U. S., 324.

[4] Trainor *vs.* Board, 89 Mich., 162.

executive council. This is frequently true of the power of the governor to remove the important "state officers."[1] In other cases, which are very frequent in the states, the condition consists in the fact that the removal may be for cause only. Where the removal may be for cause only, a hearing must be given the officer to be removed,[2] except perhaps in the case of officers removed by the President.[3] In other cases, while the removal is not conditioned upon the existence of cause, the statute provides that the individual to be removed must be given a hearing. The control which the courts possess over the exercise of the power of removal differs considerably in these two cases. In the first case—that is, where removal may be for cause only, it would appear to be the rule that the courts have, except in the case of officers removed by the President, the right to review the determination of the removing officer as to what is cause.[4] Where, however, the statute does not limit removal to cases where cause is present, but merely provides that a hearing shall be given, the tendency of the courts is to insist merely that the hearing shall be given, and to refuse to go into the question of the existence of cause.[5] Where the cause is not particularly specified, the courts then have the right, except in the case of removals by the President, to review the determination of the removing officer as to what is cause. In

---

[1] *Supra*, p. 103.

[2] Dullam *vs.* Willson, 53 Mich., 392.

[3] Shurtleff *vs.* United States, 189 U. S., 311.

[4] Nichols *vs.* Mayor, 79 N. Y., 582; see also People *ex rel.* Munday *vs.* Fire Commissioners, 72 N. Y., 445; Shurtleff *vs.* United States, 189 U. S., 311. But see Dullam *vs.* Willson, 53 Mich., 392.

[5] People *vs.* Brady, 166 N. Y., 44; In the Matter of Guden, 171 N. Y., 529.

the exercise of this power the courts have said that the cause sufficient to justify a removal for cause must be some dereliction of duty, or incapacity, or delinquency, and that the mere fact that another person might perform the duties of the officer better than the incumbent is not sufficient cause.[1]

Sometimes the statutes granting the power of removal or fixing the term of office specify definitely the causes for removal. If such is the case, the removing officer may remove only for the causes specified in the law.[2] The causes which are thus specified are usually official misconduct, maladministration in office, breach of good behavior, wilful neglect of duty, extortion, and habitual drunkenness. The legislature may, in the absence of constitutional provision, determine what shall be sufficient to justify the exercise of the power of removal, but where the constitution provides that certain causes will justify the exercise of the power, the legislature may not add new causes.[3] Where the law provides for removal for official misconduct, it is necessary to separate the character of the officer from the character of the man who holds the office—that is, the misconduct must be official misconduct.[4]

As a general thing, the power of removal does not include the power to suspend,[5] though it may be expressly so provided by statute. The exercise of the power of removal may be express or implied. Where the power of removal is absolute, the appoint-

[1] People *vs.* Fire Commissioners, 72 N. Y., 445.
[2] Mechem, *op. cit.*, § 450, with cases cited.
[3] Commonwealth *vs.* Williams, 79 Ky., 42.
[4] Commonwealth *vs.* Barry, Hardin, Ky., 229, 231.
[5] Gregory *vs.* New York, 113 N. Y., 416.

ment of another person to an office with the intention of superseding the incumbent is regarded as a
removal.[1]

V.—*Legislative action.*

It has already been pointed out that an office is not
a contract. It is, therefore, perfectly within the
power of the legislature, in the absence of some special constitutional limitation, to terminate the official
relation, either by abolishing the office, shortening
the term, declaring the office to be vacant, or trans-
ferring the duties of one officer to another.[2] Furthermore, where the legislature has no power of removal,
it has been held that it still may abolish the office
with the incidental result of terminating the official
relation of the incumbent.[3] The same rules are true
with regard to municipal officers. The municipal
authority having the power to create offices has the
right to abolish them.[4] Finally, the legislature often
has, by constitutional provision, the right to terminate
the official relation through the process of impeachment.[5]

[1] See Mechem, *op. cit.*, § 459.

[2] Butler *vs.* Pennsylvania, 10 How., U. S., 402 ; State *vs.* Douglas, 26 Wis.,
428 ; Attorney-General *vs.* Squires, 14 Cal., 12 ; Bunting *vs.* Gales, 77 N. C.,
283.

[3] Koch *vs.* Mayor, 152 N. Y., 72.

[4] Augusta *vs.* Sweeny. 44 Ga., 463 ; Ford *vs.* Commissioners, 22 Pacific
(Cal.), 278.

[5] *Infra*, p. 458.

BOOK V.

METHODS AND FORMS OF ADMINISTRATIVE ACTION.

CHAPTER I.

THE administration has, up to this point, been considered at rest; its organization, both at the centre and in the localities, the relations of the officers and authorities with each other, and the rules in regard to the official service have, it is hoped, been treated with sufficient fulness, to give an adequate idea of the administrative machinery and the character of the official system of the United States. It now becomes necessary to consider the methods and forms of the action for the purpose of which the administrative system is formed.

Care must be taken to distinguish the methods and forms of administrative action from its directions—that is, the various services which the administration may attend to in the interest of the community. While these latter vary greatly in different states, while in some the directions of administrative action may be much more numerous than in others, the forms and methods of administrative action are everywhere essentially the same. Thus the administration may or may not attend to the telegraphic or railway service of the country. Whether it does or does not, it must, in all cases, make some contracts if the government is to be conducted at all. Again, the administration may or may not exercise a supervision over the press ; whether it does or does not, it must in all cases exercise a certain amount of police power.

The forms and methods of administrative action, being everywhere essentially the same, can be classified under essentially the same categories. We may go a step further ; we may classify also the directions of administrative action in essentially the same general categories. This is so, notwithstanding the fact that in some states the directions of administrative action are much more numerous, and the extent of administrative activity is much wider than in others. In all states, on account of the uniformity of modern civilization, we may classify these directions of administrative action under the same general heads.

In the first place, we find everywhere that the administration, acting as the delegate of the sovereign, exercises powers of compulsion over those persons who are in obedience to the state. Thus everywhere the government must provide for the levying of taxes in order to carry on the various services which it undertakes. Thus again, the government has to exercise what are called police powers, over the persons in its obedience. It has thus to maintain the public health and security, it has to regulate trades and occupations where the regulation of such trades and occupations is necessary for the public good, and in such cases has seriously to curtail the freedom of individual action. The government has further to provide means for the administration of justice, both to determine the rights of its citizens where contest has arisen with regard to them, and to preserve the peace. The government must also provide means for supporting its dependent classes and for giving to the youth of the community means to educate themselves. Finally, in all popular governments, provision must be made for the selection of the various officers whose action is necessary, in order that any part of the work of the government may be performed.

In all these cases the administration is called upon to do a large part of the work demanded of the government. Thus, in the case of elections, the administration has to provide for the necessary means by which elections shall be carried on, it has to supervise the registration of voters, the counting of the votes, and the announcement of the result.

In the second place, the government acts, not so much as a delegate of the sovereign, but, so to speak, rather as the man of business of society, carrying on commercial and similar undertakings, which are too vast to be well managed by individual or corporate effort, or of such a nature that better results to the community as a whole may be expected to follow governmental than private management and control. It is in this particular that the states of the world differ the most, the one from the other. In those states which have adopted, as it may be said the United States has adopted, what is known as the *laisser-faire* policy, the action of the government will not be nearly so extensive as it is in those states which have adopted the system of government which we are accustomed to denominate paternal. But wherever the government has determined to enter upon any one of these directions of governmental activity, it is the administration that is called upon to attend to the detailed work of the government. If the government determines itself to attend to the postal service, it is the administration which must attend to the details of receiving and forwarding postal matter from one part of the country to another.

Thirdly and finally, the government, under almost all systems, in addition to acting as the sovereign, demanding sacrifices of individual freedom from the citizens of the state, and in addition to entering upon undertakings of a commercial character, does certain things which do not curtail individual freedom, but which, on the contrary, further directly the welfare of the individual, things which the individual cannot, under any circumstances, do for himself. Thus we find the government collects a vast amount of information, which is kept on record, and is made use of by both the officers of the government and by students who are investigating social problems. The census is the most prominent example of this kind of action. The government also makes provision for the filing and authenticating of documents and records; and issues patents which give the individual certain rights under the private law. It issues charters of incorporation which permit individuals to act in a particular manner that without such charters of incorporation would be improper. In all these cases, as in the cases already mentioned, just so soon as the government, through its legislative department, determines to enter upon one of the directions of activity, the administration is at once called upon to take action.

We may say, therefore, that the directions of administrative action are, in the first place, authoritative or governmental; in the second place, commercial, and, in the third place, directly in furtherance of the public welfare. Any detailed account of these directions of administrative action would necessitate the systematic treatment of the whole field of administrative action : of the five great administrative branches which have already been distinguished, namely, foreign, military, judicial, financial, and internal affairs. Such a treatment will not be undertaken here, as it is not within the scope of the present work, which must, on account of lack of space, be confined to the presentation of the main principles lying at the basis of the administrative system of the United States.[1]

It is, however, necessary for us to enter upon a somewhat detailed consideration of the forms and methods of administrative action if we are to hope to obtain an adequate idea of the way in which the administration performs the work which is entrusted to it. Such a consideration is necessary, not only from the point of view of administrative activity, but

[1] For an interesting discussion of this subject from the point of view of the activity of municipalities, see Wilcox, *The Study of City Government*, chapter ii. Dr. Wilcox's classification is made from the economic and social rather than the legal point of view.

also from the point of view of the rights of the individual. The remedies of the individual over against the administration practically determine his rights, and these remedies are governed almost entirely by the character of the acts which the administration is permitted to perform.

The methods and forms of the action of the administration are largely dependent upon the character of the duties which the administration is called upon to perform. The character of these duties is in turn dependent upon the nature of the rules of administrative law which the administration has to apply. These rules are of two kinds, they either contain a complete expression of the will of the state, or so incompletely express the will of the state that some further action is necessary in order that this will may be capable of execution.

21

CHAPTER II.

I.—*Unconditional statutes.*

THOSE rules of administrative law which completely express the will of the state are found in statutes which are put into the form of unconditional commands to the people to do or to refrain from doing some particular thing, and which threaten the violation of their provisions with the imposition of a penalty, in the nature of a fine or of imprisonment. Such rules of law naturally bear a strong resemblance to criminal laws; but in no ordinary classification of the law would they be included within the criminal law, nor would they ordinarily be inserted in the penal code. The penal code contains, as a general thing, those penal provisions of law which are intended to protect from invasion the rights of persons and of property.

The laws to which penalties are attached, which at the same time are laws laying down general rules of conduct with regard to administrative matters, are to be found scattered through the statute books generally in connection with that part of the administrative law which they are intended to protect. For example, take what is known as the customs administrative law. The endeavor has been made to put this law into the form of absolute unconditional commands to the officers of the customs and to individuals, violation of which commands is punishable under penal provisions inserted in the laws themselves. Thus the customs administrative law says to importers and shipmasters that they must transact their business in a certain way; that they must do given things, as, for example, enter their ships and their invoices of merchandise in a certain way and at certain times. They must also refrain from doing certain things, as, for example, they must not unload their ships at certain times of the day without a permit from the customs officers. To the violation of these provisions is attached, in the law itself, a penalty. The mere fact that such provisions of administrative law have penalties attached to their violation does not make them any the less administrative in character.[1] The legislature has by this means endeavored to insure that the business of importing merchandise shall be transacted in a certain way. If it is transacted in this way the duties upon imported merchandise will be easily assessed and collected. A similar example might be drawn from the law relative to the collection of the internal revenue and from police laws generally.

Every country strives to put its administrative law into the form of absolute, unconditional commands, since no rule of law is so easy of enforcement by the administration as a direct command whose violation is criminally punishable. There is little chance of conflict between the administration and the individuals to whom the law is to be applied, since in applying

[1] Taylor *et. al. vs.* United States, 3 How., U. S., 197, 210.

this class of the rules of administrative law the action of the administration is confined to hunting up all violations of them and to seeing that the penalties for such violations are enforced. The administration has little or no discretion to exercise, since the will of the state has been completely expressed in the law, and since, therefore, the administration has only to execute the will of the state—that is, the law, and is not called upon to aid in any way in its expression.

Not only is the attempt always made to put all the administrative law possible into the form of such unconditional commands, but it may also be said that the first step in the regulation by the government of any particular matter consists in the passage of a law which forbids the doing of certain things or commands that they shall be done. Take, for example, the early highway law of England. This imposed upon the parish the duty of maintaining the highways and subjected all the inhabitants of the parish to the liability of criminal prosecution for failure to perform their duty.

As civilization becomes more complex, such a method of regulation in many instances becomes ineffective. There are many duties which the government is called upon to perform in a complex civilization which cannot be performed under a system of unconditional commands. No legislature has such insight or so extended a vision as to be able to regulate all the details in the administrative law, or to put in the form of unconditional commands rules which will in all cases completely or adequately express the will of the state. It must abandon the system of unconditional commands and resort to conditional commands which vest in the administrative officers large powers of a discretionary character. The legislature, therefore, enacts a series of general rules of administrative law which in distinction from those we have just considered, may be called relative or conditional statutes.

II.—Conditional statutes.

These conditional statutes lay down the conditions and circumstances in which it will be lawful for the administration to act, and the action of the administration in enforcing them does not consist merely in seeing that the laws as passed by the legislature are executed, but rather in elaborating the details as to points which the legislature is unable to foresee, or which, if it can foresee, it is unable to regulate. While the absolute unconditional statutes are, as a general thing, addressed to the persons subject to the obedience of the state, these conditional statutes are rather addressed to the administrative authorities and are in the nature of instructions to them how to act in the general classes of cases for which provision has been made. The action of the administration in the case of the unconditional statute is confined simply to the execution of the state will. In the case of the conditional statute, the administration has not merely to execute the state will, but has as well to participate in its expression as to the details which have not been regulated by the legislature.

As a natural result, the forms and methods of administrative action are quite different in the case of these conditional statutes from what they are in the case of the unconditional statutes.   In enforcing these conditional statutes, the administration acts in one of two ways : In the first place it either issues ordinances or general rules which regulate the details not regulated in the statutes, and not possible of regulation by the legislature, or it issues special orders, not of general but of individual application, which apply to concrete cases either the statute law alone or the statute law supplemented by administrative ordinance.

1. *Administrative ordinances.* — The ordinances which are issued by the administrative authorities are issued under an ordinance power which is either independent or delegated.   By an independent ordinance power we mean a power which by the constitution is recognized as vested in the administration regardless of the action of the legislature.   This independent ordinance power may give the right to issue ordinances which govern matters that have not been at all the subject of legislative regulation or such ordinances as are merely supplementary to a statute already passed by the legislature.   The independent ordinance power is not recognized as being vested in the President, except perhaps in military matters[1] or the governor or other administrative authorities in our system of government, except in the case of municipal corporations.   These bodies have from time immemorial been recognized as having, in the absence of statutory provision, the right, as a result of their incorporation, to issue local police ordinances.[2]

Apart, however, from the case of the President, and the municipal corporations, the general rule in

---

[1] *Supra*, p. 87.   [2] See City of Crawfordsville *vs.* Braden, 130 Ind., 149.

this country is that the administrative authorities possess only the delegated ordinance power—that is, they may issue ordinances only where the power to issue such ordinances has been expressly given to them by the legislature. As a general thing, the legislature does vest in the chief executive, the heads of executive departments, or other specified executive officers, as well as in the governing bodies of the various local corporations, the power to issue ordinances with regard to specific subjects. In the case of municipal corporations, it is quite commonly the fact that a general power of ordinance is granted. It has already been shown that the grant of such legislative or *quasi* legislative powers to administrative and executive authorities and officers is not regarded as a violation of the principle of the separation of powers.[1]

The difference between an independent power of ordinance and the general ordinance power due to a general grant by the legislature on the one hand, and a delegated power of ordinance with regard to specific subjects on the other hand, is quite important. The independent ordinance power or the general ordinance power, standing alone, is much greater than the power to pass ordinances in specific cases. Indeed, it has been held that a general grant appended to a special grant does not abrogate the limitation which may be contained in the special provision— that is, it will not enlarge the powers granted by special provision as to the specific matter, but simply gives the power to pass ordinances upon other matters within the general scope of the delegation.[2]

---

[1] *Supra*, p. 84 *et seq.*　　　[2] See State *vs.* Ferguson, 33 N. H., 424.

Inasmuch as the legislature cannot delegate more power than it itself possesses, the authorities to which ordinance powers are given are subject to the constitutional limitations upon the power of the legislature.[1]

In order to prevent the various administrative authorities from abusing their power of ordinance, it is generally the case that their exercise of it is subject to some sort of control. The control which is exercised over the ordinances of the administrative authorities varies. It is in the first place sometimes exercised by the legislative authority. That is, the legislature provides in the statute vesting the administrative authorities with ordinance power that the ordinances issued by such authority as a result of the exercise of the power shall, before they may go into execution, be submitted to the legislature and be approved by it.[2] This method of control is practically unknown in the United States.

The second way in which a control is exercised over the ordinance power is by requiring the necessity of the approval of some higher administrative authority before the ordinance shall go into effect. This may be spoken of as an administrative control. In this country, however, the ordinance power of administrative authorities is seldom subjected to an administrative control.[3] Where authorities are vested with

[1] Sayre Borough *vs.* Phillips, 148 Pa. St., 482.

[2] An example of this kind of control over the ordinance power of the administration is to be found in the relations of the English Local Government Board, and the Board of Trade with Parliament. It is frequently the case that the power to issue provisional orders, as they are called, has been conferred upon these administrative authorities, but these provisional orders, before taking effect, must always be confirmed by Parliament. See Maltbie, *English Local Government of To-day*, page 250.

[3] An instance of such an administrative control over ordinances may be found in the power the State Civil Service Commission in New York has to

the ordinance power, it is almost never the case that, before the ordinances issued as a result of its exercise are valid, they must be approved by any other authority.

The common control over ordinances in this country is the judicial control This judicial control consists, in the first place, in the power which the courts have, when individuals are brought up before them charged with having violated an ordinance of the administration, to examine into the ordinance for the purpose of determining whether the authority which issued it was under the law competent to issue it. In acting thus, the courts are merely exercising over the legislative power of the administrative officers the same control which it is recognized they may exercise over the legislature with the view of ascertaining whether the statutes of the legislature are in accord with the constitution. In the second place, the courts have the right, in the case of local ordinances, issued as a result of the exercise of the independent ordinance power, or of the general ordinance power, to declare as void and illegal all ordinances which are unreasonable.[1] In case, however, an administrative authority disapprove the civil-service rules of cities within the state. See Rogers *vs.* Common Council, 123 N. Y., 173.

[1] Thus it has been held that ordinances requiring druggists to furnish a quarterly certified statement of the amount and quantity of intoxicating liquors sold by them, and when and to whom they were sold, are unreasonable and oppressive. See Clinton *vs.* Phillips, 58 Ill., 102 ; 11 Am. Dec., 52. Similarly, an ordinance which required cotton merchants to keep the names of the sellers of loose cotton and the quantity of each purchase was held to be against the principles of personal liberty and the common right. Long *vs.* Taxing Districts, 7 Lea, Tenn., 134. The courts have also declared municipal ordinances which were in restraint of trade to be illegal. See the case of Sayre Borough *vs.* Phillips, 143 Pa. St., 482 ; 33 Amer. St. Rep., 842. In this case the courts declared illegal an ordinance which provided that all peddlers not residents of the town must take out a license.

has been given express power by the legislature to pass an ordinance of a specified and defined character, the courts will not interfere on the ground of its unreasonableness, its reasonableness being regarded as a matter settled by the granting of the power to the corporation.[1] In such a case all that the courts will do will be to construe the extent of the grant of power to the ordinance-making authority and the constitutionality of the grant.[2]

All ordinances must, as a general rule, in order that they shall have force, be brought by some means to the notice of those persons whom they will affect. If no particular method is provided by statute for giving such notice it is held that the notice need not be given by publication in a newspaper, but posting copies of the ordinance in public places within the limits of the district which it affects is a sufficient publication. The method of giving such notice is, however, generally determined in the statutes, and since the object of publishing police ordinances is to give notice to all who must obey them, and since this class of regulations operates to restrict the exercise of the personal rights of the citizens, the courts often insist upon a strict and literal compliance with the terms of the statute.[3] The ordinary method of giving the necessary notice of these ordinances is, how-

---

[1] See Haynes *vs.* Cape May, 50 N. J. L., 55.

[2] District of Columbia *vs.* Weyman, 4 Mackey, 328. See also as to the ordinance power of administrative authorities *infra*, p. 337, on power to declare things to be nuisances.

[3] Thus where alternate methods of publication are allowed by statute and a board of health or other designated authority is required to direct which mode shall be adopted, a publication ordered by a clerk of his own motion is not valid. The authority named in the statute must point out in which one of the permitted ways the publication shall be made. Higley *vs.* Bunce, 10 Conn., 435.

ever, by publication in a newspaper of general circulation within the district affected.[1]

2. *Special administrative acts.*—But just as the legislature cannot put into the form of a general command all of the duties of the individual and express in all its details the will of the state, so the administration cannot accomplish this purpose by means of general orders. Thus no general rule, whether passed by the legislature or adopted by the administration can declare by name what persons shall pursue those trades which require a license, or what persons or property shall pay direct taxes or the amount in money of these taxes. All that can be done by general rule is to determine what requirements those persons who desire to pursue licensed trades shall fulfil, and under what conditions and at what rates taxes shall be levied on persons and property. The general rules of law of this character require in order that they may be executed the further action of some administrative authority in order to bring the concrete case within the operation of the general rule. This action necessitates upon the part of the administration the performance of a great many acts which affect merely one particular concrete case.

Thus where a general rule of law states, for example, that particular classes of persons shall pay taxes or that a tax shall be determined in amount either by the extent of the business or by the amount of the property of the taxpayer, before it can be ascertained

---

[1] In such case, it has been held that such paper need not be a local paper, but any paper circulating generally in the community will suffice. Tisdale *vs.* Minouk, 46 Ill., 9 ; and when no particular paper is designated by the authorities, the clerk may lawfully make publication in any paper in the place. *In re* Durkin, 10 Hun., 269.

what amount of tax a given individual shall pay, it is
necessary that it be determined in the first place,
whether he is one of the class which is liable to pay
the tax ; and, in the second place, what is the amount
of his business or what is the value of his property.
This determination must be made by an administrative authority.   In the particular case this administrative authority is called an assessor and the special
act which he performs in order to enforce the law is
known as an assessment.   There are a great variety
of these special acts of individual application in all
the various branches of the administration.   There
is, however, no generic name which is applied to
them.   Some thus are called orders, others precepts,
others warrants, and others decisions.   Some are in
the form of commands to subordinate officers or to
individuals to do or to refrain from doing some particular thing, as tax warrants, orders of payment,
nuisance-removal and sanitary orders ; some are per-
missions to individuals to carry on a given business, as,
for example, licenses and authorizations ; some are
prohibitions to carry on a business, as, for example, re-
vocations of licenses or authorizations.   Some are
acts which create new legal persons, as, for example,
charters of corporations.   Some are contracts, made
by the administration for the government, acting as a
subject of private law.   Some are decisions as to the
existence of certain facts, as, for example, assessments, appraisements, classifications of articles for
duty in the customs administration ; and, finally, some
are appointments to office or orders to individuals to
serve the government in some capacity, as notice to
serve as jurors or in the military service.

The action necessitated on the part of the administration in order to perform these acts is action which often closely resembles what we are accustomed to call judicial action. Take, for example, the case of the assessment of property for the purpose of taxation. It is necessary, in order that the value of property liable to taxation be determined, that the assessors receive evidence and come to a determination both as to the legal liability of the owner and of the particular piece of property to taxation, and as to its value. In the same way in the case of election officers, it is necessary that they determine, for example, when a man presents himself to vote, whether he is legally qualified. Indeed, under the original English system of administration, as well as under that which obtained generally in this country during the colonial period, and which obtains even now in certain of the states which have not had the greatest administrative development, many of these duties were and are entrusted to officers discharging at the same time judicial functions. The most marked instance of such an officer is the English justice of the peace. As, however, our administration has developed, the tendency has been towards differentiation—towards confining the action of judicial officers to the decision of conflicts arising between either individuals or between individuals and the government, and towards assigning all this class of work, notwithstanding its similarity to judicial action, to special officers who are in no way connected with the administration of justice.

The grant of these powers to administrative officers is regarded as perfectly constitutional and proper, notwithstanding the fact that the result of the exercise

of the powers granted will often be a serious encroachment upon the rights of private property and
personal liberty guaranteed by the constitution.   It
has been held, thus, that the determination by an administrative officer of the amount of tax that an
individual is to pay, or the determination by an
administrative officer that given conditions are un-
sanitary, the result of the determination being the
necessity of the expenditure upon the part of the
owner of a large amount of money, either to discharge his tax liability or to bring his property into a
sanitary condition, is not in violation of the constitutional provisions requiring due process of law in
order that any citizen may be deprived of his
property.[1]

An interesting question in connection with these
administrative determinations is whether they may
constitutionally be made final by statute.   There are
very few cases upon this point, although there are
numerous *dicta* which are absolutely conflicting. Let
us consider the question, first, from the point of view
of the constitution of the United States; in other
words, let us see what is the due process of law called
for by the Fourteenth Amendment.   For the main,
if not the only, objection to vesting this power of final
determination in administrative bodies is that an administrative proceeding which finally determines is
not due process of law.

The United States Supreme Court has refused to
give us a definition of due process of law, preferring
to decide, as concrete cases come before it, whether

---

[1] See the case of McMillen *vs.* Anderson, 95 U. S., 37 ; and Department of
Health &c. *vs.* The Rector &c. of Trinity Church, 145 N. Y., 32.

the methods followed in such cases are consistent with the constitution.[1] The court has, however, indicated, first, that due process of law is to be determined by the state legislature,[2] and, second, that any judicial proceeding is due process of law where the tribunal, before which the proceeding is had, has by the law of the state jurisdiction of the subject matter, and, in case of a determination resulting in a personal liability, where the defendant has notice and an opportunity to be heard.[3]

The Supreme Court has not, however, decided whether, if these conditions are observed, all final determinations by administrative authorities are due process of law, but several decisions of the court have settled the question that in the classes of cases to which they refer final administrative determinations are due process of law.

In the first place, it has been held that, if the statute so provides, the ascertainment by the administrative officers of the government of the amount of indebtedness due the government from one of its officers who is a receiver of public moneys is due process of law, even if the law provides that the indebtedness so determined is to be collected summarily without resort to the courts ; in other words, that it is due process of law to provide that the determination of administrative officers shall in such cases have the force and effect of the judgment of a court, and may not, therefore, be attacked in a collateral proceeding, except as to the jurisdiction of

[1] See Davidson *vs.* New Orleans, 96 U. S., 97.
[2] Walker *vs.* Sauvinet, 92 U. S., 90.
[3] Pennoyer *vs.* Neff, 95 U. S., 714.

the officer making the determination.[1] Such is the general rule with regard to assessments of property for taxation.[2]

In the second place, the determination by administrative officers of the amount of tax a given individual shall pay is held, in the case of a license tax, to be due process of law, even if such individual has had no opportunity to be heard before the authority assessing the tax. In this case, however, the law gave the individual the power to sue out an injunction to restrain the collection of the tax.[3]

Finally, it is held that it is due process of law to vest in administrative officers the final determination as to the right of an alien to land in the United States under a statute excluding certain classes of aliens from admission into the United States.[4]

On their face these decisions, or rather the opinions in which they are given, would seem to go a long way toward laying down the rule that it is perfectly consistent with due process of law to vest in administrative officers the final determination, after a hearing of the persons concerned, of facts upon which the

[1] Murray's Lessee *vs.* Hoboken Land and improvement Co., 18 How., 272.

[2] Barhyte *vs.* Sheperd, 35 N. Y., 238 ; Mygatt *vs.* Washburn, 15 N. Y., 316.

[3] McMillen *vs.* Anderson, 95 U. S., 37 ; see also Cary *vs.* Curtis, 3 Howard, 236.

[4] Nishimura Ekiu *vs.* United States, 142 U. S., 651, where Mr. Justice Gray, who delivered the opinion of the court, said : "The final determination of these facts [that is the facts on which the right of an alien to land depends] may be entrusted by Congress to executive officers, and in such a case, as in all others in which a statute gives a discretionary power to an officer, to be exercised by him upon his own opinion of certain facts, he is made the sole and exclusive judge of the existence of those facts, and no other tribunal, unless expressly authorized by law to do so, is at liberty to re-examine or controvert the sufficiency of the evidence on which he acted." See also Buttfield *vs.* Stranahan, 192 U. S., 470.

right to property or liberty depends. It is, however, to be remembered that these cases—that is, cases of government officials tax and importation cases, and cases of the admission of aliens—were decided largely in view either of historical considerations or of the plenary power of the government to regulate foreign commerce and to expel aliens.[1] It cannot, therefore, be said that under the decisions of the United States Supreme Court it is absolutely certain that the power of final determination may constitutionally be vested, in all cases, in an administrative authority where such determination seriously infringes upon private rights.

When we come to the consideration of the rule, as it has been laid down by the courts of the various states, we cannot be much more certain than we are in the case of the decisions of the United States Supreme Court, for, while there are a number of cases which would seem to indicate that this power of final determination may constitutionally be vested in administrative authorities, these cases are, as a rule, pretty early in point of time, and the later *dicta* of the courts would seem to indicate a tendency to depart from the early rule.

The decisions of the state courts which have been made upon this subject may be put into two classes : In the first class are those which recognize that a determination of a board of health with regard to the existence of a nuisance is, provided a hearing is given

[1] One noticeable reason for the decision both in the case of Murray's Lessee *vs.* The Hoboken Land and Improvement Co., and in that of McMillen *vs.* Anderson was the historical usage of the English Crown and the American governments, while the fact that Ekiu was an alien who never had a domicile in the United States had just as much effect on the decision in her case.

22

to the party affected, final, so far as any collateral
proceeding is concerned. But a condition of the
finality of such a determination of an administrative
authority is, in some of the cases, the possibility of
reviewing it by some direct judicial proceeding like
certiorari. When it is remembered that at the time
these decisions were made *certiorari* was made use
of merely to review questions of jurisdiction and regularity of proceedings, it will be seen that the finality
of the determination upon the question of fact was not
really much encroached upon by this limitation.   It
may therefore be said that this first class of decisions
goes a long way towards supporting the proposition
that the determination of a board of health as to the
existence of a nuisance may constitutionally be made
final.[1]

[1] The first class of decisions are illustrated by the case of Van Wormer *vs.*
The Mayor &c. of Albany, 15 Wend., 262.   In this case it was held that a determination, made after a hearing, that a thing was a nuisance, not overruled by
direct proceedings, such as *certiorari*, could not be reviewed in an action for
trespass brought against a health officer, and that it was not error in such an
action to refuse evidence that the thing complained of was not actually a
nuisance. Some of the cases, however, make the constitutionality of the law providing for such final determination dependent on the right, accorded by statute
to the individual concerned, of a hearing before the administrative authority
making the determination. Cases of this character are Kennedy *vs.* The
Board of Health, 2 Pa. St., 366, and Metropolitan Board of Health *vs.*
Heister, 37 N. Y., 661.   The first case holds that a determination of a board
of health that a thing is a nuisance is final under the Pennsylvania statute, and
that on a suit to collect expenses or abate the nuisance the defendants could not
offer evidence to show that there was no nuisance. In the second case the
court says : " Before leaving the consideration of this constitutional objection
[namely, that one is being deprived of property without due process of law
and without trial by jury], it ought, perhaps, to be observed that the act provides for notice to the party affected, before the judgment finally passes
against him. In substance the board upon the evidence before it determine
that a *prima-facie* case exists requiring their action. In the present instance,
after such preliminary determination made, notice was given to Heister of
what had been done, and that he could be heard upon the subject, with his

It may be said therefore that both the decisions of the state courts and those of the Supreme Court of the United States would seem to indicate that it is constitutional from the point of view both of the United States Constitution and of the state constitutions to vest in administrative authorities the power, after a hearing, of making a final determination, as to matters within their jurisdiction, even though the determination may seriously affect rights of property.

Special orders, like ordinances, must generally be brought to the notice of the persons whom they affect.

witnesses, at a time designated. This gave the same protection to all his rights as if notice had been served upon him before any preliminary proceedings had been taken. He refuses to litigate before the board the question whether his pursuit is dangerous to the public health. . . . He cannot complain now that their judgment upon the facts is to be held conclusive upon him." As a result the court refused to issue an injunction to prevent the enforcement of the order of the board of health to abate the nuisance. See also Green *vs*. Mayor of Savannah, 6 Ga., 1. In support of the rule thus laid down are to be found a number of *dicta* in the state courts. The strongest of these are to be found in Salem *vs*. The Eastern R. R. Co., 98 Mass., 431, and People *ex rel* Copcutt *vs*. Board of Health, 140 N. Y., 1. See also Bates & Guild Co. *vs*. Payne, 194 U. S., 106 ; Public Clearing House *vs*. Coyne, 194 U. S., 497, *supra* p. 147. Opposed to the rule laid down in these decisions is a *dictum* in a recent case in the New York Court of Appeals, Department of Health &c. *vs*. The Rector &c. of Trinity Church, 145 N. Y., 32. This case decided that a penalty might be recovered for violation of an order of the Health Department to comply with the law requiring water to be furnished "in sufficient quantity at one or more places in each floor" of any house occupied by one or more families, although such order was given without notice. In the course of the opinion Judge Peckham says : " Where property of an individual is to be condemned and abated as a nuisance, it must be that somewhere between the institution of the proceedings and the final result the owner shall be heard in the courts upon that question, or else he shall have an opportunity when calling upon those persons who destroyed his property to account for the same, to show that the alleged nuisance was not one in fact. No decision of a board of health, even if made on a hearing, can conclude the owner upon the question of nuisance."

The manner of giving such notice is usually prescribed by statute, and in such cases the terms of the statute must be literally and precisely complied with. In the absence of explicit directions in the statute, the orders must be served by delivering copies to the persons to whom they are directed personally, or by leaving copies at the last known place of abode of such persons, if they are known and reside within the state,[1] or if personal service cannot be made, or if the premises to which the order refers are unoccupied, and the residence of the owners or agents is unknown, by posting them in a conspicuous place on the premises and advertising in one or more public newspapers in such manner or for such length of time as the . . . [authority issuing the order] may direct. In the absence of any prescribed length of time it must be such as to afford reasonable opportunity for compliance or for demanding a hearing or a reconsideration of the matters to which the order relates.[2]

In the case of a great many of the orders notice is not, however, absolutely essential.

3. *Procedure to be followed.*—In the performance of these acts, both of a general and a special character, the administrative authorities must follow a certain procedure which is laid down in the law granting the power to act. The law thus says in the first place that certain acts shall be performed only by certain authorities. The authority before acting in any of these cases must assure itself that it has jurisdiction, for its acts will be void if it exceeds its jurisdiction.

The jurisdiction of an administrative authority is dependent, in the first place, on territorial limitations. "The authority of public officers being derived from the law, it necessarily follows that the authority cannot

[1] See Mason *vs.* Bibby, 2 H. & C., 881 ; Gould *vs.* The City of Rochester, 105 N. Y., 46.

[2] Parker and Worthington, *op. cit.*, § 89. See also Metropolitan Board of Health *vs.* Heister, 37 N. Y., 661.

exist in places where that law has no effect. The authority of all public officers is therefore limited and confined to that territory over which the law, by virtue of which they claim, has sovereign force. . . Thus a state officer can exercise no official authority beyond the confines of the state."[1] This is not only true of public officers in general, it is also particularly true of those having jurisdiction within the lesser municipal subdivisions, such as counties, towns, and cities. A sheriff, for example, cannot execute civil process outside of his county[2]; nor can a United States marshal execute a process outside of his district.[3]

The jurisdiction of officers depends, in the second place, upon whether the law has given them the power to act in the specific case. For the right to exercise the powers of a public office must find its source in some provision of law.[4] This law may, however, be the common law. There are a series of officers, such as the sheriff, who are known as common-law officers, and whose powers are thus not determined by any statute, but by the decisions of the courts. As a general thing, however, the jurisdiction of officers is determined by the provisions of the statute law. Where the legislature has thus conferred powers upon officers by statute, the statute is usually subjected to a strict interpretation.[5] Therefore "when officers undertake by virtue of the

[1] Mechem *op. cit.*, § 508. See also Jackson *vs.* Humphrey, 1 Johnson, N. Y., 498.

[2] See Page *vs.* Staples, 13 R. I., 306.

[3] Carr *vs.* Phillips, 39 Mich., 319.

[4] See Attorney General *vs.* Detroit Common Council, 58 Mich., 213-219; also reported in 55 Am. Rep., 675.

[5] See Mayor of Baltimore *vs.* Reynolds, 20 Md., 1; 83 Am. Dec., 535.

authority conferred upon them to build up rights against third persons, especially where their acts may result in penalties or forfeitures against such persons, the limits and conditions imposed upon their authority must be rigidly observed or their acts will be unavailing."[1] All administrative officers are regarded as tribunals of special jurisdiction. The effect of this treatment of administrative officers is that their power to do a particular thing is never presumed. Any one who claims any rights under their actions must show affirmatively that they had power to do the thing whose validity is in question.[2] Exception to this rule is sometimes made by statute, as, for example, in the case of tax officers.

Finally, it is to be noted that, although the general rule is that officers may exercise discretionary powers as best suits them, at the same time the discretion which is given to them is not an arbitrary one, but is what is understood as legal discretion, and will not permit them to take any arbitrary, capricious, inquisitorial, or oppressive proceedings.[3]

Not only must the administrative authority have jurisdiction to act in the particular district, and the power to do the particular act in question, but also the act in question must be performed in the way

[1] Mechem, *op. cit.*, § 511.

[2] See Lowry *vs.* Erwin, 6 Robinson, La., 192 ; 39 Am. Dec., 556.

[3] Thus in the case of State *vs.* Board of President and Directors, 134 Mo., 296, also reported in 56 Am. St. Rep., 503, it was held that a board of school directors is guilty of gross abuse of discretion in selecting, for purely partisan purposes, judges and clerks of election of the same political party for election of members of such board, and arbitrarily refusing to select election officers from different political parties, and that the supreme court may, by *mandamus*, compel such board to rescind the selection of election officers so made, and to select them from the different political parties. *Cf.* Mechem, *op. cit.*, sec. 513.

provided for in the law. This is particularly true if the way provided for by law has been provided in order to protect individual rights.[1] This rule is particularly applicable to all cases of the assessment of property for taxation,[2] and to cases where the action of the officer will result in depriving the individual of his property, as in the case of the sale of land for the non-payment of taxes, or the exercise of the right of eminent domain.[3] The rule is applicable also to the method of procedure prescribed for the making of contracts upon the part of governmental officers. Thus, it has been held that, if a municipal corporation may by law contract only in a prescribed way, as after publishing specifications and inviting bids and awarding the contracts to the lowest bidder, no contract which is attempted to be made in any other than the prescribed way will be legal.[4]

It is very commonly provided, in the case of administrative decisions whose effect is to deprive the individual of his property rights, that opportunity must be given to all persons who are interested in the decision to make any objections which they may desire to make to the proposed action. Where such provisions of law are made they are regarded as absolutely mandatory, and failure to give notice of the proposed action, or an opportunity for a hearing, will result in the invalidity of such proceedings.[5] Indeed, the courts have held that the " due process of law "

---

[1] See French *vs.* Edwards, 13 Wall., 506.

[2] See Cooley, *Law of Taxation*, 2d ed., 280 *et seq.*

[3] See Dillon, *Municipal Corporations*, vol. ii., 706 ; Mechem, *op. cit.*, sec. 581.

[4] McDonald *vs.* New York, 68 N. Y., 23.

[5] See Cooley, *Law of Taxation*, p. 483.

required by the fourteenth amendment to the United States Constitution for the taking of private property makes the opportunity to be heard at some stage of the proceeding a necessary formality in property tax assessments.[1]

Offices, as we have seen, are often organized as boards, and the statute frequently prescribes the method by which these boards shall act. Any other method of action than the one prescribed will make the act so performed absolutely void and of no effect.[2] Thus, if the law clearly provides for the joint act of all, a majority cannot take valid action.[3] In the absence, however, of such a provision, the general rule is that a majority of the entire membership of the board will constitute a quorum, which may act also by a majority vote.[4] But "the rule permitting a majority to act implies that a full board, as required by law, is actually in existence. Thus, where by law a board cannot consist of less than three members, and only two qualify, the two cannot act, for there is then no board of which the two would constitute a majority."[5] The act of a majority can be upheld, however, only when the conditions provided, either by statute or by the

---

[1] See San Mateo County *vs.* Railroad Co., 13 Fed. Rep., 722 ; Stuart *vs.* Palmer, 74 N. Y., 183.

[2] McCortle *vs.* Bates, 29 Ohio St., 419 ; 23 Am. Repts., 758. Here individual members of a school board had, in writing, agreed to a contract to purchase supplies for the district, and had, in the same document, requested a special meeting of the board to be called, and they agreed with each other that they would ratify the contract at such meeting. The court held the contract so agreed upon to be void.

[3] See First Nat'l Bank *vs.* Mt. Tabor, 52 Vt., 87 ; 36 Am. Rep., 734.

[4] *Ibid.*, Williams *vs.* School District, 21 Pickering, Mass., 75 ; 32 Am. Dec., 243 ; Rushville Gas Co. *vs.* Rushville, 121 Ind., 206.

[5] Mechem *op. cit.*, sec. 575 ; see also Williamsburg *vs.* Lord, 51 Maine, 599 ; Downing *vs.* Rugar, 21 Wendell, N. Y., 178.

general rule of law, requiring notice and so on, exist, for if, *e. g.*, one member of a board of three " took no part in the transaction, and was ignorant of what was done, gave no implied consent to the action of the others, and was neither consulted by them nor had any opportunity to exert his legitimate influence in the determination of the course to be pursued," the action of the majority would be void.[1] " It will be presumed," however, " in the absence of anything to the contrary, that all members of a board met and deliberated, or were duly notified,[2] unless the statute requires an express statement of that fact in the record. If that be required, parol evidence of the fact is inadmissible."[3]

[1] Schenck *vs.* Peay, 1 Woolworth, C. C. Rep., 175.
[2] McCoy *vs.* Curtice, 9 Wend., 17 ; 24 Am. Dec., 113.
[3] Mechem, *op. cit.*, sec. 573 ; People *vs.* Williams, 36 N. Y., 441.

CHAPTER III.

I.—*Means of execution.*

THE will of the state, whether expressed in **statute,** ordinance, or special act of individual application, always contains either expressly or impliedly the command that it shall be executed. Various means are adopted to insure its execution. The first to be mentioned is :

1. *Imposition of penalties.*—These penalties may consist of : First, fines; second, forfeiture of property and privileges; and third, arrest and imprisonment. They are usually provided for by legislation, but it is competent for the legislature to vest the power of sanction, *i. e.*, the provision of penalty, in the officers of the administration. It is often the case that municipal corporations and boards, such as boards of health, have the right to impose penalties for the violation of their ordinances or orders. The rules with regard to the imposition of the various kinds of penalties are somewhat different in accordance with the character of the particular penalty which it is desired to impose. It is thus recognized as within the power of an authority, which has the right to issue ordinances or special orders, to sanction

346

such orders and ordinances by reasonable penalties in the nature of fines. But in the absence of specific legislative authorization it is held that this penalty may not consist of anything but a fine.[1] The reasonableness of the fine imposed is, in the absence of a statute, subject to the control of the courts.[2] Generally, however, the law fixes a maximum fine which may be imposed. Where this has been fixed by statute, it may not be exceeded directly or indirectly— that is, by multiplying the offence or by making it several.[3]

Penalties in the nature of fines for the violation of ordinances are ordinarily to be collected by an action for debt, which insures the control of the courts over the exercise of the ordinance power. Thus it has been held that the non-payment of these fines may not, in the absence of a statute to that effect, be punished by imprisonment to be provided by the sanctioning authority[4]; nor under similar conditions may such fines be collected by distress and sale.[5]

It is, however, frequently the case that the legislature declares that the violation of the ordinances of administrative authorities shall be a misdemeanor which shall be punished by arrest and imprisonment. This it is perfectly competent for the legislature to do. Further, it is also competent for the legislature to " declare the possession of certain articles of property,

---

[1] See Mayor of Mobile *vs.* Yuille, 3 Ala., 137 ; 36 Am. Dec., 441. Breiswick *vs.* Brunswick, 51 Ga., 639 ; 21 Am. Rep., 240. Thus the right to impose fines does not include the right to decree a forfeiture of property. White *vs.* Tallman, 2 Dutcher, N. J. L., 67.

[2] In the Matter of Ah You, 88 Cal., 99.

[3] Chicago *vs.* Quimby, 38 Ill., 274.

[4] See Breiswick *vs.* Brunswick, 51 Ga., 639 ; 21 Am. Rep., 240.

[5] See White *vs.* Tallman, 2 Dutcher, N. J. L., 67.

either absolutely or when held in particular places or under particular circumstances, to be unlawful, because they would be injurious, dangerous, or noxious," and to provide through proceedings *in rem* for the seizure, confiscation, removal, or destruction of the noxious articles.[1] "This right has been exercised by the legislature in respect of the places where intoxicating liquors are manufactured or sold in violation of law, and of all the articles and appliances used in or about the manufacture or sale of such liquors, and in respect of adulterated or unwholesome articles of food and impure and adulterated milk and dairy products, and in respect of various other kinds of personal property in possession or use in violation of quarantine or health laws or of a character likely to prove noxious to the public."[2]

This power of the legislature is, however, subject to the same limitations which limit the right of the legislature in respect to all legislation affecting the liberty or property of the citizens. It must not be exercised arbitrarily, *i. e.*, without reasonable relation to the accomplishment of a lawful purpose. Thus it would be beyond the legitimate scope of legislative authority to declare that to be a nuisance which is clearly not a nuisance.[3]

2. *Enforced performance of the act ordered.*—Some times the execution of the will of the state will not be effected by the imposition of a penalty. The individual upon whom the penalty is imposed may prefer to suffer the penalty and continue in his oppo-

[1] See Fisher *vs.* McGirr, 1 Gray, 1.

[2] Parker and Huntington, *The Law of Public Health and Safety*, 271 ; see also Mugler *vs.* Kansas, 123 U. S., 623 ; Shivers *vs.* Newton, 45 N. J. L., 469.

[3] *In re* Jacobs, 98 N. Y., 98 ; see also Wynehamer *vs.* People, 13 N. Y., 378.

sition to the expressed will of the state. Therefore
it becomes necessary in these cases, if the will of the
state shall be executed, that it be executed by the
doing of a definite thing. This definite thing may
often consist in the payment of a sum of money, or
it may be absolutely necessary that a thing be done
which does not consist in the payment of a sum of
money.

*First, Execution of the law by the payment of a
sum of money.*—A great many of the orders of the
administration and of the laws which completely express the will of the state may be executed by insuring the payment of a sum of money. Thus the
orders of the administration to individuals to pay
taxes and the like will naturally be executed by the
payment of a sum of money, and be executed, also
naturally, only in this way. Further, it may be possible that the act demanded of the individual may be
done by the administration itself, whose expenses in
the doing of the act may, like taxes, be made an obligation of the person disobeying the administrative
order. For example, if a board of health should order
a landlord to make repairs which are necessary from
a sanitary point of view, and he refuses, it is perfectly
easy for the administration to step in and do the work
itself and thus found an obligation, which is binding
upon the individual, to repay the expenses which it has
been obliged to incur in order to do the work.[1]

The methods adopted to insure the payment of
such an obligation are usually the same as those adopted to insure the payment of judgments of courts—

---

[1] Salem *vs.* The Eastern Railroad Co., 98 Mass., 431, also reported in 96
Am. Dec., 650.

that is, the amount due is either made a lien upon the real property in relation to which the obligation was incurred and is to be collected by the sale of such property, or it is to be collected by the sale of the personal property of the individual upon whom the obligation is imposed.

But the will of the state cannot always be executed by the payment of a sum of money, any more than it can be executed by the imposition of a penalty. In many cases it can be executed only by the direct application of physical force to either a person or some article.

Second, Application of physical force.—It becomes necessary frequently in the sanitary administration that certain articles which are noxious to the public health, safety, or morals shall be actually destroyed. The destruction of such articles differs somewhat from the legal point of view from their forfeiture as a penalty for the violation of the statute. Thus the courts have said :

Where a public nuisance consists in the location or use of tangible personal property so as to interfere with or obstruct a public right or regulation, the legislature may authorize its summary abatement by executive agencies without resort to judicial proceedings, and any injury or destruction of the property necessarily incident to the exercise of the summary jurisdiction interferes with no legal right of the owner, but the legislature can go no further; it cannot decree the forfeiture of property used so as to constitute a nuisance as a punishment of the wrong, nor even to prevent a future illegal use of the property, it not being a nuisance *per se*, and appoint officers to execute its mandates. The plain reason is that due process of law requires a hearing and trial before punishment or before forfeiture of property can be adjudged for the owner's misconduct. Such legislation would be a plain usurpation by the legislature of judicial powers, and under the guise of exercising the power of summary abatement of nuisances, the legislature cannot take into its own hands the enforcement of the criminal or quasi criminal law.[1]

The United States Supreme Court, to which this case went on appeal, said in its opinion[2]:

The extent and limit to what is known as the police power have been a fruitful subject of discussion in the appellate courts of nearly every state in the Union. It is universally conceded to include everything essential to the public safety, health, and morals, and to justify the destruction or abatement by summary proceedings of whatever may be regarded as a public nuisance. Under this power it has been held that the state may order the destruction of a house falling to decay or otherwise endangering the lives of passers-by, the demolition of such as are in the path of a conflagration, the slaughter of diseased cattle, the destruction of decayed or unwholesome food, the prohibition of wooden buildings in cities, . . . the suppression of obscene publications and houses of ill fame, the prohibition of gambling houses and places where intoxicating liquors are sold.[3]

This distinction between the forfeiture of articles decreed as a penalty for violation of the law, which can result only from judicial proceedings, and a summary destruction by administrative officers of articles which are in and of themselves public nuisances, brings us to the consideration of the different methods provided by law for the execution of the will of the state, as distinguished from the means adopted for the execution of the will of the state which have been under consideration.

II.—*Methods of execution.*

While the means of execution which have just been considered are quite numerous and varied in character,

---

[1] See Lawton *vs.* Steele, 119 N. Y., 226.

[2] Lawton *vs.* Steele, 152 U. S., 133, on page 136.

[3] See also Buttfield *vs.* Stranahan, 192 U. S., 470.

the methods of executing the will of the state, although quite different in character, are only two in
number : They consist, in the first place, of judicial
process ; in the second place, of summary administrative proceedings.

1. *Judicial process.*—The method of executing the
will of the state by judicial process is the result of an
attempt to introduce into administrative matters the
controversial system of procedure, which has been so
universally adopted in other civil and criminal proceedings. Its main characteristic consists in the fact
that the administration and administrative officers are
regarded as acting for one party in the controversy,
and the courts occupy the position of an impartial
arbiter between the administration on the one side
and the individual upon the other, who, it is claimed
by the administration, has violated the constitutionally
expressed will of the state. A good example of this
method of executing the will of the state is to be found
in the case of those rules of administrative law which
have been put into the form of unconditional commands. In these cases, as it has been pointed out,
the rôle of the administration is to call the attention
of the courts to an alleged violation of the law.
When the administration takes such action, it is for
the courts to determine, as we have seen, whether the
law is constitutional, in case the rule of administrative
law is contained in a statute, or, where it is contained
in an administrative ordinance, whether the ordinance
has been passed as the result of the exercise of an
ordinance power possessed by the ordinance-making
authority. Where the ordinance has been passed as
the result of the exercise of an independent ordinance

power, the court is called upon to consider not merely the question of the legality of the ordinance—that is, the question of whether the ordinance is among those which it is recognized the possession of the independent ordinance power by the authority permits it to pass, but as well the question of the reasonableness of the ordinance. Finally, where the ordinance-making authority has been recognized as possessing the power to impose penalties for the violation of its ordinances, the court is also called upon to determine whether the penalties provided are reasonable; or, where the penalty has been imposed as a result of the exercise of a power to impose penalties delegated by the legislature, whether the penalty actually imposed is within the limits of the delegation which has been made.

This method of executing the will of the state through judicial process is not, however, confined to the enforcement of ordinances or general orders. It is also frequently adopted in the case of special orders of individual application. Thus, it is not unfrequently provided in the American law that, before such an order of special and individual application may actually be enforced, resort must be had, by the administrative authorities making the order, to a court of competent jurisdiction for the issue of its warrant, which will be the only justification under the law for the officer who attempts to enforce such order. This is very commonly provided in the case of the forfeiture of articles as a penalty for the violation of the law. Indeed, as has been shown, it has been held[1] that administrative officers may not be

---

[1] Lawton *vs.* Steele, 119 N. Y., 226.

authorized by the legislature, to forfeit articles or destroy them by summary proceedings without judicial process, where the forfeiture is made in order to impose a penalty upon the individual for the violation of a rule of administrative law. The doctrine of the United States Supreme Court would seem to carry this principle still further, inasmuch as it holds that forfeitures of articles of substantial value can never be constitutionally made except by judicial process.[1]

While judicial process would seem to be the only method of executing the will of the state, which may be constitutionally adopted in the case of the forfeiture of articles as a penalty for violation of the law, it would not seem to be required by the constitution in all cases of executing these orders of individual and special application. The law of the United States, however, very commonly makes provision for such a method of execution, as, for example, in the case of nuisance-removal orders in the sanitary administration and in the police administration, such as the building police and police regarding the public safety. Indeed, it may be said that, with few exceptions, in the absence of a statute providing for summary methods of procedure, resort must be had to the courts by the administration in order to enforce the will of the state as expressed in the administrative law. Thus, in the case of the collection of taxes, it is held that resort may not be made to summary methods, unless specifically authorized by law.[2]

An important exception to the rule that judicial process must, in the absence of statutory provision to

[1] Lawton *vs.* Steele, 152 U. S., 133.
[2] See Bergen *vs.* Clarkson, 6 N. J. L., 352.

the contrary, be resorted to in order to enforce the administrative law, is made in the case of nuisances. This exception, it will at once be recognized, is a pretty large one on account of the very wide meaning that is given to the term "nuisance." The consideration of this question will be taken up in the next division of the subject.

The last instance of the method of judicial process for the enforcement of the rules of administrative law to which attention need be called, is to be found in the case of the attempt upon the part of administrative officers to impose an obligation upon a person or a lien upon property for work done upon it by the administration, where the owner has refused to do such work when ordered to do it by the proper authorities. In these cases it is commonly provided that in order to enforce the payment of the obligation or to enforce the lien upon the property, resort shall be had to the courts.[1]

The purpose of the adoption of the method of judicial process for executing the will of the state is to subject the action of administrative authorities to a judicial control. Its very common adoption in the English and the American law is undoubtedly due, in large part, to the desire which is noticeable in all parts of the law to prevent, so far as possible, arbitrary action upon the part of the administration. Certainly the retention of such a method of executing the rules of administrative law is due to this desire. At the same time the English and American law has always recognized that it was

[1] See Salem *vs.* The Eastern Railroad Co., 98 Mass., 431 ; 96 Am. Dec., 650. But see Kennedy *vs.* Board of Health, 2 Pa. St., 366.

both necessary and proper in certain cases to enforce the administrative law by summary administrative proceedings.

2. *Summary administrative proceedings.* — The principle of the English law, that in certain cases summary proceedings for the execution of the administrative law are proper, was adopted in this country by the courts, notwithstanding the existence of constitutional provisions which required due process of law in order that property might be taken from individuals. The leading case upon this point in the Supreme Court of the United States is Murray's Lessee *vs.* The Hoboken Land and Improvement Company.[1] This was an action of ejectment in which both parties claimed title, the plaintiffs under the levy of an execution, and the defendants under a sale made by the marshal of the United States for the district of New Jersey, by virtue of what was denominated a distress warrant issued by the Solicitor of the Treasury under an act of Congress. This act provided, by its first section, that a lien for the amount due the government from a government officer should exist on the lands of the debtor from the time of the levy and record of the warrant in the office of the district court of the United States for the proper district, and the date of that levy in this case being prior to the date of the judgment upon which the plaintiff's title was based, the question was raised in the circuit court whether the warrant of distress previously mentioned, under which the defendants claimed title, was sufficient under the constitution of the United States and the law of

[1] 18 How., U. S., 272.

the land to pass the title and estate of the premises in question as against the lessor, the plaintiff. In the opinion of the supreme court, the questions which arose in this case were whether under the constitution of the United States a collector of the customs from whom a balance of account has been found to be due by accounting officers of the treasury designated for that purpose by law could be deprived of his property in order to enforce payment of that balance, without the exercise of the judicial power of the United States and yet by due process of law within the meaning of those terms in the constitution; and if so, then, second, whether the warrant in question was such due process of law. The court said in giving its opinion:

That the warrant now in question is legal process is not denied. It was issued in conformity with an act of Congress; but is it due process of law? The Constitution contains no description of those processes which it was intended to allow or forbid. It does not even declare what principles are to be applied to ascertain whether it be due process. It is manifest that it was not left to the legislative power to enact any process which might be devised. The article [1] is a restraint on the legislative as well as on the executive and judicial powers of the government and cannot be so construed as to leave Congress free to make any process " due process of law " by its mere will.

Further along in the opinion the court says:

We apprehend there has been no period since the establishment of the English monarchy when there has not been by the law of the land a summary method for the recovery of debts due to the Crown, and especially those due from receivers of the revenue. It is difficult at this day to trace with precision all the proceedings had for these purposes in the earlier stages of the common law.

---

[1] Art. V. of Amendments: " No person . . . shall be deprived of life, liberty, or property without due process of law."

That they were summary and severe and have been used for purposes of oppression is inferable from the fact that one chapter of
Magna Charta treats of their restraint.

It was therefore decided that the sale of the property
under the distress warrant was good.   The case we
have just been considering applies specifically merely
to the power of the United States government to
provide such summary methods with regard to the receivers of public revenue.   The principle, however,
which lies at the bottom of the case was applied to
the summary sale of property, even real property,
for non-payment of taxes,[1] and to the destruction of
property by administrative order, where such property
had been imported contrary to the mandate of an act
of Congress.[2]

The same principle is applied in the construction
of similar provisions in the state constitutions.   Thus
Judge Cooley says[3]:

A distress warrant is in the nature of an execution, and therefore
seems, at first blush, a very arbitrary process, since it issues under
most of our tax laws, without any previous judicial determination
of liability.   But . . .   this does not deprive a party aggrieved
of his remedy ; it only makes his remedy wait the superior ur-
gency of government necessities.   It has been well said of col-
lections by distress : " This method of collecting taxes is as well
established by custom and usage as any principle of the common
law.   A similar practice prevailed in all the colonies from the
first dawn of their existence.   It has been continued by all the
states since their independence and had existed in England from
time immemorial.   Indeed, it is necessary to the existence of

[1] McMillen *vs.* Anderson, 95 U. S., 37, and Springer *vs.* United States, 102
U. S., 586.

[2] Buttfield *vs.* Stranahan, 192 U. S., 470.

[3] *Law of Taxation*, second edition, page 438.

every government and is based upon the principle of self-preservation. This is conclusive of the right to provide for it." [1]

In the second place, summary administrative proceedings may be resorted to in order to abate public nuisances. [2]

[1] State *vs.* Allen, 2 McCord, 55 . see also Commonwealth *vs.* Byrne, 20 Grattan, Va., 165, where it was held that arrest decreed by an administrative officer, as provided by law for non-payment of taxes, was not a deprivation of liberty without due process of law, under the constitution of Virginia.

[2] The opinion of the Supreme Court of the United States has already been referred to. This is to be found in the case of Lawton *vs.* Steele, 152 U. S., 133. Here, however, the decision of the court limits the right of summary abatement, where such summary abatement involves the destruction of property, to articles of small value. In explaining its position on this point the court says: "It is not easy to draw the line between cases where property illegally used may be destroyed summarily and where judicial proceedings are necessary for its condemnation. If the property were of great value as, for instance, if it were a vessel employed for smuggling or other illegal purposes, it would be putting a dangerous power in the hands of a custom officer to permit him to sell or destroy it as a public nuisance, and the owner would have good reason to complain of such acts as depriving him of his property without due process of law. But where the property is of trifling value and its destruction is necessary to effect the object of a certain statute, we think it is within the power of the legislature to order its summary abatement. For instance, if the legislature should prohibit the killing of fish by explosive shells and should order the cartridges so used to be destroyed, it would seem like belittling the dignity of the judiciary to require such destruction to be preceded by a solemn condemnation in a court of justice. The same remark might be made of cards, chips, and dice in a gambling room. The value of the nets in question was but $15 apiece. The cost of condemning one (and the use of one is as illegal as the use of a dozen), by judicial proceedings, would largely exceed the value of the nets, and doubtless the state would, in many cases, be deterred from executing the law by the expense. They could only be removed from the water with difficulty and were liable to injury in the process of removal. The object of the law is undoubtedly a beneficent one, and the state ought not to be hampered in its enforcement by the application of constitutional provisions which are intended for the protection of substantial rights of property. It is evident that the efficacy of this statute would be very seriously impaired by requiring every net illegally used to be carefully taken from the water, carried before a court or magistrate, notice of the seizure to be given by publication, and regular judicial proceedings to be instituted for its condemnation.

" There is not a state in the Union which has not a constitutional provision entitling persons charged with crime to a trial by jury, and yet from time immemorial the practice has been to try persons charged with petty offences before

The rule is stated by Messrs. Parker and Worthington, in *The Law of Public Health and Safety*,[1] as follows :

> The right of summary abatement of nuisances existed at common law. It has never anywhere been abrogated. There is nothing . . . in the constitution of any state that takes away or impairs this remedy. Indeed, all constitutions presuppose the existence of this right ; their provisions for the protection of liberty and property from arbitrary invasion were framed with reference to the right and are to be construed accordingly.[2] The private rights secured by constitutional guaranties are such as existed at common law. They have always been held and exercised in subordination to the general law that the public health, the public morals, and the public safety are of paramount importance, according to the maxim " *salus populi suprema est lex.*" The objection, therefore, that, by this summary proceeding, a person may be deprived of liberty or property without due process of law or trial by jury, has no force nor application. Formal legal proceedings and trial by jury are not appropriate to and have never been used in such cases.[3]

Public nuisances are classified as common-law and statutory nuisances. That is, the courts have in the course of time determined that certain things are nuisances, and the legislature has the right also to determine by statute that certain other things are

a police magistrate, who not only passes upon the question of guilt, but metes out the proper punishment. This has never been treated as an infraction of the Constitution, though technically a person may in this way be deprived of his liberty without the intervention of a jury. (Callan *vs.* Wilson, 127 U. S., 540, and the cases cited.) So the summary abatement of nuisances without judicial process or proceeding was well known to the common law long prior to the adoption of the Constitution, and it has never been supposed that the constitutional provision in question in this case was intended to interfere with the established principles in that regard."

[1] P. 268.

[2] Village of Carthage *vs.* Frederick, 122 N. Y., 268.

[3] See also the cases already referred to, Salem *vs.* The Eastern R. R. Co., 98 Mass., 431 ; 96 Am. Dec., 650 ; see also Fields *vs.* Stokley, 99 Pa. St., 306.

nuisances,[1] subject, however, to the review of the courts, which may hold that the action of the legislature in decreeing a given thing a nuisance is such a violation of private rights as to result in depriving one of his liberty or property without due process of law.[2]

Further, the legislature may, subject to the same limitations, delegate the power to declare classes of things to be nuisances to local bodies and local boards of health.[3] It has also been held that the legislature may delegate to the council of a municipal corporation the right to pass ordinances providing for the compulsory vaccination of all inhabitants of the city and preventing children from going to school who have not been vaccinated.[4]

[1] Mugler *vs.* Kansas, 123 U. S., 623 ; Beer Co. *vs.* Mass., 97 U. S., 25 ; Lawton *vs.* Steele, 119 N. Y., 226.

[2] In the Matter of Jacobs, 98 N. Y., 98. In this case the New York Court of Appeals held that the legislature might not prohibit the making of cigars in tenement houses in cities of over five hundred thousand inhabitants. In the course of the opinion it said : " Generally it is for the legislature to determine what laws and regulations are needed to protect the public health and secure the public comfort and safety, and while its measures are calculated, intended, convenient, and appropriate to accomplish these ends, the exercise of its discretion is not subject to review by the courts. But they must have some relation to these ends. Under the mere guise of police regulations, personal rights and private property cannot be arbitrarily invaded and the determination of the legislature is not final or conclusive. If it passes an act ostensibly for public health and thereby destroys or takes away the property of a citizen or interferes with his personal liberty, then it is for the courts to scrutinize the act and see whether it relates to and is convenient and appropriate to promote the public health. It matters not that the legislature may in the title of the act or in its body declare that it is intended for the improvement of the public health. Such a declaration does not preclude the courts and they must yet determine the fact declared and enforce the supreme law."

[3] People *vs.* Polinsky, 73 N. Y., 65 ; Metropolitan Board of Health *vs.* Heister, 37 N. Y., 661.

[4] Morris *vs.* Columbus, 102 Ga., 792 ; Duffield *vs.* School District, 162 Pa. St., 476 ; see also Abeel *vs.* Clark, 84 Cal., 226. It has, however, been held that a general power to supervise the public health and to pass regulations whose purpose is to prevent the spread of contagious diseases will not justify

The legislature may not only delegate to administrative authorities the power to declare that certain things are nuisances; it may also, in the same way, provide for their summary abatement by the proper officers of the government, and without notice or hearing.[1]

In the case of the abatement of a nuisance which has not been declared by some due process of law to be a nuisance, officers of the government act in its abatement at their peril.[2] Courts of equity will often issue an injunction to restrain attempts to abate what is claimed to be a nuisance, and an action will lie against administrative officers for unlawful invasion of private property for the purpose of abating nuisances before proceedings have been had in which the conditions complained of have been determined to be a nuisance.[3]

Proof of a nuisance which has been declared so by statute is naturally much easier than the proof of a common-law nuisance. That which the legislature has declared to be a nuisance is a nuisance, provided the law declaring it so is constitutional, and evidence that the thing is not a nuisance is, subject to this limitation, inadmissible. The only question which can be considered is whether the statute is constitu-

the passage by a state board of health of an order that all children must be vaccinated before they are permitted to attend the public schools, where there is no immediate danger of an epidemic of smallpox in the particular locality to which the order may refer. See Potts *vs.* Green, 167 Ill., 67. It has even been intimated that the legislature may not under any conditions vest such a legislative power in a board of health. See State *vs.* Burdge, 95 Wis., 390.

[1] New York Department of Health *vs.* Rector of Trinity Church, 145 N. Y., 32.

[2] People *ex rel.* Copcutt *vs.* Board, 140 N. Y., 1.

[3] Bristol Door and Lumber Co. *vs.* City of Bristol, 97 Va., 304; Fields *vs.* Stokley, 99 Pa. St., 306; 44 Am. Reps., 109.

tional.[1] In the case of the abatement of statutory nuisances, however, administrative officers must show that they acted strictly within the authority given by the statute, and that the character of the thing acted against was that specified in the statute. The determination of an administrative authority will be no protection if made without notice—and opportunity to be heard—to the party charged with the nuisance.[2]

In these cases of summary destruction of property, health officers and other public officers are not, however, regarded as liable for damages if they have acted in good faith and with reasonable cause to believe that the thing proceeded against was actually a nuisance, even if, upon all the evidence, there is a doubt as to the necessity and propriety of their action.[3] Notwithstanding the presumption which is made in favor of the legality of the action of officers in suppressing nuisances, the liability to be held for damages in an action brought against them subsequently for trespass is regarded as a serious hindrance to the efficient administration of the law as to nuisances. On that account quite a number of the laws, particularly with regard to the preservation of the public health, provide that a board of health or similar authority shall, prior to the determination that a

[1] Powell *vs.* Pennsylvania, 127 U. S., 678 ; Mugler *vs.* Kansas, 123 U. S., 623.

[2] People *vs.* Board, 140 N. Y., 1.

[3] " There is a strong presumption favored by the law that what has been done under the sanction of official duty in the discharge of public functions, in good faith for the public benefit, and without private advantage, has been rightly done. Any doubt as to the necessity or propriety of the official action, provided it be within the general scope of the official authority, must be resolved against him who impeaches it and in favor of the public officer." Parker and Worthington, *op. cit.*, p. 192, citing Rudolphe *vs.* New Orleans, 11 La. Ann., 242.

thing is a nuisance, give the individual who, it is alleged, is maintaining it, an opportunity to be heard before the board as to the existence of the particular conditions complained of as being a nuisance, in which case it is probably the law that the propriety of their action cannot be questioned except in a direct suit to review it.[1]

In the abatement of nuisances public officers may not destroy articles where their destruction is not necessary in order to abate the nuisance.

In many cases a nuisance can be abated only by the destruction of the property in which it consists. The cases of infected cargo or clothing or of impure and unwholesome food are plainly of this description. They are nuisances *per se*, and their abatement is their destruction. So, also, implements and articles of personal property capable only of illegal use may be destroyed as a part of the process of abating the nuisance they create, if this be directed by statute. In short, in every case, the thing itself, or the condition of things constituting or creating the nuisance, whatever the nature or description of the property, whether a building or other structure, growing crops, deleterious articles of food or drink, things infected with germs of disease, or things applied to illegal use and incapable of lawful use, may be seized and destroyed, or so dealt with, according to the nature of the case, as to do away with their injurious effects.[2]

Thus, take the case of Fields *vs.* Stokley, already referred to.[3] In this case it was held proper for the mayor of a city to abate a nuisance by the demolition of a wooden house which was dangerous to the safety of the community. In connection with this power of summary destruction of property should be mentioned the common-law right of local bodies to demolish property in order to prevent the spread of a conflagration. The first reference to this rule would seem to have been made by Lord Coke in "The Case of the King's Prerogative in Salpetre,"[1] where he says: "For the commonwealth a man shall suffer damage; as, for saving a city or town a house shall be plucked down if the next be on fire . . . and a thing for the commonwealth every man may do without being liable to an action.' This rule has been adopted in the law of the United States, by both the state and the national courts.[2]

" But where the nuisance arises from unlawful acts or the use of things innocent in themselves, the case does not call for their destruction in order to effect an abatement, but for the discontinuance of the objectionable method of using them and for the suppression of the unlawful acts. This would be the only mode of abatement in such cases known to the common law, and any other mode would have no sanction in that law."[3]   Thus in the case of Barclay *vs.* Commonwealth[4] the nuisance consisted in the fact that hay, straw, and other products were put in a barn in which also horses, mules, cattle, and other animals were kept, and the barn being near certain springs, the offence consisted in the use made of the barn and yard in close proximity to the springs.   The order of the authorities was the removal of the barn.   The court, in reversing the order, said: "Where an erection or structure itself constitutes the nuisance, as

---

[1] 12 Coke, 12.

[2] See Bowditch *vs.* Boston, 101 U. S., 16; New York *vs.* Lord, 18 Wendell, 126.

[3] Parker and Worthington, *op. cit.*, p. 277.

[4] 25 Pa. St., 503; 64 Am. Dec., 715.

where it is put up in a public street, its demolition or removal is necessary to the abatement of the nuisance ; but where the offence consists in a wrongful use of a building, harmless in itself, the remedy is to stop such use and not to tear down or remove the building it-self." Thus again, where the nuisance arose from a pond of water, it was held improper to abate it by filling up the pond. The cause which rendered the water impure could have been removed without so doing.[1]

[1] Finley *vs*. Hershey, 41 Ia., 389.

BOOK VI.

CONTROL OVER THE ADMINISTRATION.

DIVISION I.—METHODS OF CONTROL.

CHAPTER I.

NECESSITY OF CONTROL.

THE action of the administration, whose forms and methods have just been described, is so important that it is impossible in any country possessing constitutional government to allow every administrative officer a perfectly free hand in the discharge of his duties. The public is so dependent upon the action of administrative officers that it is of the utmost importance that their action shall be efficient and harmonious. The officers of the administration attend to many things which it is impossible for individuals to attend to at all. If they do not perform their duties, or perform them unwisely or inefficiently, it will necessarily follow that these things will not be done at all or will be done in such a way that the result of administrative action will be of little value. Some means must be provided also which shall insure harmony in administrative action where uniformity of treatment of a given subject throughout the state is necessary.

Individuals further are so at the mercy of administrative officers, who have behind them the entire power of the state, that some protection must be offered against the violation of private rights. The administration is often thrown into relations with individual citizens which must necessarily be hostile. It demands of them sacrifices which they regard as unreasonable or as not justified by the law of the land. Nearly all the expressions of the will of the state which are to be carried out in their details and executed by the administration cause a conflict at times between the conception by the administration of what the public welfare demands and the conception by the individual of the sphere of private rights guaranteed to him by the law. If the officers of the administration had, in all such cases, uncontrolled discretion, it is to be feared that individual rights would be violated. Of course it is the purpose of all administrative legislation to lessen as far as possible the realm of administrative discretion and to fix limits within which the administration must move. But it is impossible to do this with such precision as effectively to protect private rights. The discretion of administrative officers cannot be taken away by legislation without causing their usefulness seriously to be impaired. Large discretion must be given to administrative officers by the legislative authority, so large that some means of controlling the administration must be devised if private rights are to be guaranteed inviolate.

Finally, the action of the administration should be as far as possible in harmony with the state will as expressed in the law, for an unexecuted law is, from the point of view of actual conduct, no law at all. The action of the administration should also conform, not merely to the letter of the law, but also to its spirit, should promote the public welfare as that is conceived of by the body representative of the public. But the discretion of the administration relative to concrete cases cannot be controlled by the statutes of the legislature without seriously impairing administrative efficiency. As before, some means must be devised of controlling the action of the administration, more concrete in character, more adaptable to particular cases.

For all these reasons, then, it is desirable, indeed necessary, that there be formed methods of control over the action of the administration by means of which it will be possible to render that action efficient, and to force the administration to consider private rights to conform to the state will as that has been expressed by the legislature.

24

CHAPTER II.

THE formation of a system of control over the administration, which shall secure all that is desired, is as difficult as it is necessary, partly on account of the variety of the interests to be regarded, partly on account of the variety and continual recurrence of the administrative acts to be controlled. Analogies from other branches of the law must be followed with caution, because each of these other branches of the law has, as a rule, regard for only one interest, and because the acts to be controlled in the other branches of the law are less varied in character. Thus the private law aims merely at the maintenance of private rights and at the observance of the law as laid down in the books. It has little, if any, regard for public policy. Thus again, the criminal law aims merely at the attainment of good social conditions, while constitutional and international law aim primarily, if not exclusively, at the efficiency of governmental organization and the maintenance of state integrity and power. Constitutional law, it is true, endeavors to secure the protection of private rights in so far as it formulates a bill of such rights, but the remedies for their violation, and without which they are themselves valueless, are to be found very largely in the control over administrative action provided by the administrative law.

Administrative law, however, endeavors to attain all these three ends, *viz.*, state integrity and power, governmental efficiency, the maintenance of private rights, and the attainment of good social conditions. Therefore, we cannot rely, as in these other branches of the law, on any one kind of control. No system of private or even public actions will suffice to control the application of the administrative law or the action of the administration made necessary thereby, as it undoubtedly does suffice for the control of the application of private and criminal law. No system of administrative centralization or legislative control will suffice, as in the case of international and constitutional law. On the contrary, a well-organized control over the application of the administrative law and over administrative action must make use of all these methods of control, since the administrative law aims at governmental efficiency, individual liberty, and social well-being, as interpreted by the body representative of public opinion.[1]

In the formation of the control over the administration, regard must be had, then, for the interests to be furthered by the administrative law. The first of these interests is that of governmental efficiency. Some method of control must be devised by which harmony and uniformity of administrative action and administrative efficiency may be secured, as many cases may arise where the neglect of officials will not cause a serious violation of private rights, but will simply tend to impair governmental efficiency. This method of

---

[1] *Cf.* Gneist, *Das Englische Verwaltungsrecht*, 1884, bk. ii., p. 321.

control should be so framed that it may be exercised by the organs of the government of their own motion and not simply at the instance of private persons.

The second interest to be regarded is the preservation of individual rights, the maintenance in its entirety of the sphere of freedom of individual action guaranteed by the law of the land. Some method of control must be devised by which the officers of the government may be prevented from encroaching upon this sphere. As this method of control is framed in the interest of the individual, it should be possible for the individual to set it in motion by appealing to impartial tribunals from those administrative acts which he believes violate the rights assured to him by the law. Such impartial tribunals are found in the courts which in various ways may be entrusted with the power to prevent encroachment by the administration on the domain of private rights.

The third interest to be regarded by the administrative law is the social well-being. There must be some method of control devised which will force the administration in its action to keep before it always the fact that it is not a law unto itself ; that one of the great reasons of its existence is the promotion of the social well-being as expressed in the law. Such a method of control should be so organized as to allow that body which is most thoroughly representative of public opinion—that is, the legislature—to step in and compel the administration to obey the law.[1]

[1] *Ibid.*, p. 320 *et seq.*

CHAPTER III.

THERE are three distinct interests which are sought
to be subserved by the administrative law. There
are therefore three methods of control, each of which
aims primarily at the protection of one of these
interests and is to be exercised by a special governmental authority. These three methods of control
may be called respectively the administrative, the
judicial, and the parliamentary or legislative control,
their names being derived from the authority which
exercises them.[1]

I.—The administrative control.

We have in the first place the administrative control. This is exercised primarily in the interest of
governmental efficiency, though it may be used subsidiarily in the interest of the protection of private
rights and the promotion of the social well-being.
Its main endeavor is to obtain harmony and uniformity in administrative action, efficiency in the administrative services, and uprightness and competency in
administrative officers. It is exercised, as its name

---

[1] Gneist, *Das Englische Verwaltungsrecht*, 1884, bk., ii., p. 320 *et seq.*

implies, by the higher officers of the administration over the actions of their subordinates, and its extent and effectiveness depend almost entirely upon the degree of administrative centralization present in the administrative system. Where the administration is not somewhat centralized, the administrative control is naturally undeveloped. Where the administrative control is undeveloped, it will be almost useless to expect any great efficiency. Administrative efficiency may, of course, be sought in some other way, but the main means of obtaining it is through centralization and the administrative control.

When analyzed, this administrative control will be found to consist, first, of a disciplinary power, second, of a power of direction, and third, of a power of supervision, possessed by higher administrative officers over lower administrative officers.

1. *The disciplinary power.*—Higher administrative officers have often the right to remove inferior officers. This power of removal, as has been shown, may be arbitrary or subject to conditions. Where it is subject to conditions, the fulfilment of which may be determined by the courts, as is frequently the case in the United States, the disciplinary power due to the existence of the power of removal is very largely destroyed. Besides the power of removal, higher officers may have the right to impose a disciplinary punishment less severe than removal, such as fines, suspension, and loss of pay. Such a disciplinary power is not commonly found in the United States, except in certain permanent services organized in a semi-military fashion, like city police forces. It is very doubtful whether such a disciplinary power is

possessed by administrative officers in this country in the absence of statutory provision to that effect.

2. *Power of direction.*—The existence of a power of direction is an indispensable element of a highly centralized administrative system. Reference to what has been said with regard to the administrative organization of the national and state governments will show that, as a general thing, the power of direction, in the absence of statutory provision, is possessed only by the higher officers of the national administration. The tendency, however, in the United States, at the present time, is towards the extension of this power of direction in the administrative systems both of the states and of the cities. The loosely organized system which at one time existed in the United States, in which each officer was practically a law unto himself, is giving way to a system in which many officers are regarded as subject to the direction of superiors.

3. *Power of supervision.*—Higher administrative officers are often given the power to revise the action of lower administrative officers. This power of revision may be exercised either on their own motion or on the appeal of some individual who deems himself aggrieved by the decision of the inferior. Instances of its exercise on the motion of the higher administrative officers are to be found for the most part in the national administration.[1] A common instance of its exercise in the case of the state administration is to be found in the power which is often given to either state or county boards of equalization to change the

---

[1] See, *e. g.*, United States *vs.* Cobb, 11 Fed., 76, where it was held that the secretary of the treasury had the right of his own motion to change the erroneous decision of a collector of the customs.

valuation of property for the purposes of taxation, fixed for specific taxing districts by the assessing authorities of such districts. The power of revising the decisions of inferior officers on the appeal of persons deeming themselves aggrieved thereby is more commonly vested in the higher administrative officers of the national government than in similar officers in the state governments.[1] A common instance of such a power in the state administrative systems is to be found in the appellate jurisdiction which is given in the state of New York, as well as in some other states, to the state superintendent of public instruction or similar officer, through the exercise of which he has the right, upon appeal by any one interested, to quash or amend the determination of any inferior educational authority.

While the administrative control in its various forms is peculiarly adapted to secure administrative efficiency, it is also made use of for the protection of private rights. This is particularly true of the appeals which private individuals are permitted to take to higher administrative officers from the decisions of lower administrative officers, by which they deem themselves aggrieved.

II.—*The judicial control.*

We have, in the second place, the judicial control. This is exercised by the courts on the application of individuals. Its primary purpose is the protection of individual rights, but it may be made use of subsidiarily in the interest of administrative efficiency, when

[1] See, *e. g.*, United States *vs.* Butterworth, 112 U. S., 50, where it was said by the Supreme Court of the United States that a power to hear appeals is implied in the power of direction given to the heads of departments in the United States government.

it is frequently exercised on the application of higher administrative officers.

III.—Legislative control.

We have, in the third place, the legislative control. This is exercised primarily, and it may be said almost exclusively, in the interest of the general social welfare and is exercised, on its own motion, by the legislature or one of its committees.

Every constitutional state has formed a control over its administration out of these three elements, but the strength of each of these elements in different states varies largely in accordance with the relative prominence of the end sought in the formation of the general system of control, and indeed in the whole body of the administrative law. In the United States, for example, where the end most prominently sought is the maintenance in its integrity of the sphere of individual rights, the judicial control is very great, while the administrative control is comparatively slight. As the administrative control has been sufficiently considered in what has already been said, particularly with regard to the organization of the administration, we shall proceed at once to the discussion of the judicial control.

DIVISION II.—THE JUDICIAL CONTROL.

CHAPTER I.

ANALYSIS OF THE JUDICIAL CONTROL.

I.—Use of ordinary judicial institutions.

THE judicial control may be secured in many instances by the use of the ordinary judicial machinery and by the application of the ordinary rules of law to the officers of the administration who are to be controlled. Thus the government may be regarded as a juristic person when it enters into contracts or violates the rights of individuals, and as such juristic person may be treated as the subject of private rather than public law. If the government is so regarded, the ordinary means of enforcing contracts and redressing wrongs which are applicable to private persons may be adopted in the case of the government. Again, the administration may be put in the position of an ordinary suitor, and may be obliged to apply to the courts before it may enforce the law. Such is the case where the law provides for what has been spoken of as judicial process in the execution of the state will. Finally, the officers of the government may be treated as private persons without regard to their official capacity, and their acts done under color of office but not in accordance with the law may then be treated like the acts of private persons and subjected to the control of the ordinary courts. If, without jurisdiction, such officers have injured private individuals, they may be made responsible to such individuals in damages.

Analogies may also be drawn from the criminal law. Many of the rules of administrative law may be put into the form of absolute, unconditional commands to the persons in the obedience of the state to do or refrain from doing particular things, and the violation of such rules of law may be punishable criminally. The application of the penalties may be entrusted to the ordinary criminal courts which, before taking action, will have to decide as to the criminality of the act complained of by the administration, and will thus exercise a control over the action of the administration when it endeavors to impose penalties for the violation of the law. Again, the ordinary misdemeanors of officers, as well as the violation by them of their administrative duties, may be made punishable by the criminal courts.

In all of these cases the law, in order to provide a judicial control over administrative action, makes use of ordinary judicial machinery, and applies to the administration and its officers the ordinary rules of the private and criminal law. For many of the rules of administrative law such methods of control will be sufficient, since the action of the administration in applying them will be of such a character that it can in this way be subjected to judicial supervision. Thus, the wrongful use of governmental power by officials to the detriment of individuals will, in many cases, be prevented by the fear of incurring a liability for damages or criminal punishment. Especially will this method of judicial control be sufficient in the case of all rules of administrative law which are put into the form of absolute, unconditional commands. The power which the courts have to refuse to enforce the penalties for the alleged violation of the law in case the administration has endeavored to act illegally, will make practically impossible permanent illegal administrative action.

But in a large class of cases the action of the administration is not of such a character as to permit of its being brought under the control of the courts by the use of ordinary judicial institutions and by the application to the administration of the ordinary rules of private or criminal law. In others, the rule as to the conclusiveness of administrative action in collateral proceedings makes it necessary to provide peculiar judicial remedies against such action. In these cases it becomes necessary, in order that the judicial control shall have any value, that special remedies against administrative action shall be provided.

II.—*Special judicial remedies.*

It has been shown that it is impossible in all instances to resort to the method of putting the rules of administrative law into the form of absolute unconditional commands, that in many cases it is absolutely necessary to have recourse to conditional, relative commands, commands in which the legislature simply lays down the general conditions of administrative action and leaves to the administration the expression of the will of the state in minor details, allowing it, in its discretion, to ascertain the existence of the conditions necessary for its action in the execution of the law. Where the administration has, in order to execute these rules, to apply to the courts— that is, where execution by judicial process is provided, no special judicial control is, in many cases, necessary, for the courts, as in the case of the imposition of penalties, may, when the administration applies to them for the power to act, refuse to grant the power on the ground that the case is not one of those provided for in the law. But for all cases where summary administrative proceedings are provided, or where the action of the administration is not reviewable collaterally by the courts, some method must be devised which will insure that the administration will act only in the case and only in the way in which the law has said that it may act. Special judicial remedies must be devised which will provide an effective judicial control.

III.—Kinds of judicial control.

The judicial control thus proves, on analysis, to be of a three-fold character. In the first place, it is exercised by the civil courts, first, in the power which is almost everywhere given to them to entertain suits of a private legal character against or by the government or some one of the public corporations of the government ; second, in the power to refuse to issue an order or warrant applied for by administrative officers ; and, third in the power to entertain suits against officers of the administration for the damages which they have caused by their illegal acts or the negligent performance of their duties.

In the second place, the judicial control is exercised by the criminal courts, first, in the power which they have to pass upon the validity of the acts of administrative officers when the individual is prosecuted by the administration for the violation of these acts; and, second, in the power which the courts have to punish officials for the commission of ordinary crimes or for the criminal violation of their official duties.

In the third place, either there have been formed special courts or there has been given to the ordinary courts a special jurisdiction to hear appeals directly against the acts of the administration. As a result of the possession of this jurisdiction, these courts may even annul or amend the acts of the administration which are complained of.

CHAPTER II.

I.—Suits by or against the government.

THE power of the courts to entertain suits in contract or tort to which the government or one of its legal corporations is a party depends upon the extent to which the government in its central or local organization is recognized as possessing corporate rights and as subject to corporate liabilities—in other words, upon the extent to which the government is recognized as a juristic person. As a general rule of law, it may be said that the government is a juristic person so far as concerns its power to bring suit,[1] but it is by no means fully settled in this country that the government is to be treated as a juristic person in case the wrong or breach of contract is committed by its officers. The idea that the government cannot be sued in the ordinary courts seems to have arisen from the application of the principles of the Roman law,[2] and the adoption of the monarchical

---

[1] *Cf.* Dillon, *Mun. Cor.*, 4th ed., vol. i., p. 55 ; see also United States *vs.* Maurice, 2 Brockenbrough (U. S.), 96, 109, opinion by Marshall, C. J. ; United States *vs.* Tingey, 5 Peters, 115 ; United States *vs.* Bradley, 10 Peters, 343 ; Dugan *vs.* United States, 3 Wheaton, 172.

[2] *Cf.* Mommsen, *Römisches Staatsrecht*, 2d. ed., vol. i., pp. 170, 679 ; vol. ii., p. 712.

principle that the "sovereign can do no wrong." This rule seems not to have been applied to the local incorporations of the government, which are liable to suit in the ordinary courts, although not to the same extent as private corporations. On account of the difference in the position of the central government and of the local governmental corporations, it is necessary to consider the control of the courts over the administration in the case of suits to which it is a party, from the standpoint of the individual and from that of the government, and also from the standpoint of the central government and from that of the local governmental corporations.

1. *Suits by the government against individuals.*— So far as the local corporations are concerned, it may be said that they occupy as plaintiffs in a suit against individuals about the same position that individuals occupy. In the case of the central government, however, we find that its position as representative of the sovereign has quite an appreciable effect on its position as plaintiff. In some cases its position as representative of the sovereign is carried so far as to permit it to enforce claims against individuals without recourse to the courts at all and by means of summary administrative proceedings. This is particularly true of claims which it may have against its disbursing officers.[1] In such cases the only control that the courts can have over the private legal relations of the government is to be found in their power of applying special remedies at the instance of some individual against the enforcement of sum-

[1] Murray's Lessee *vs.* Hoboken Land and Improvement Company, 18 How., 272.

mary administrative proceedings.   Further, even where such summary proceedings have not been provided for the enforcement of government claims, the government has privileges not possessed by the ordinary suitor, as, for example, where it is accorded the position of a preferred creditor, its claims taking precedence of all other claims.

In case the government sues an individual, it is generally admitted that the courts, although they have not the right to entertain suits against the government directly, may make allowances in their judgments for any counter-claim or set-off proved by the defendant to the suit.[1]   Use may not be made, however, of this power to give a judgment against the government.[2]

2.   *Suits against local corporations.*—As a result of the desire to facilitate the conduct of the private legal relations of the government, many of the important localities into which the state is divided are, as has been shown, regarded as corporations, and individuals are permitted to bring suits against them in contract and even in tort.   There is, however, a distinction made between what are known as *quasi*-municipal corporations and municipal corporations proper, in accordance with which suits in tort, except when permitted by express statute, may not be brought against the former, inasmuch as they are to be considered as agents of the central government, and, as such, share in the immunity possessed by the sovereign whom they are regarded as

[1] United States *vs.* McDaniel, 7 Peters, 1 ; see also United States *vs.* Ringgold, 8 Peters, 150, 163.

[2] DeGroot *vs.* United States, 5 Wall, 419, 431 ; United States *vs.* Eckford, 6 Wall, 484.

25

representing.[1] Suits in tort may, however, be brought against municipal corporations proper, since they are believed to be formed for the peculiar advantage of the inhabitants of the locality, and, not representing the sovereignty of the state, are subject to the rule of the private law that the superior is responsible for the acts of his agents.[2] But it is to be noticed that even municipal corporations proper are not generally responsible for damages resulting from the execution of what are regarded as governmental powers.[3]

Further, while the local corporations may thus be sued and judgment obtained against them in the usual way, it is to be noticed that such judgments are not commonly collectible in the usual way—that is, by sale on execution of the property of such corporations. The usual means of enforcing such a judgment in the United States is to apply to the courts for the exercise of their power to force the local authority to insert the necessary appropriation in its budget and to provide by taxation or otherwise for the payment of the judgment. While this is the usual method of enforcing a judgment against a municipal corporation, it is still true that the common law, where no change has been made by statute, permits the sale on execution of all purely private property of such corporations which is not devoted to a public service.[4]

3. *Suits against the central government: First,*

---

[1] Morey *vs.* Town of Newfane, 8 Barb. (N. Y.), 645 ; see also Hill *vs.* Boston, 122 Mass., 344.

[2] Bailey *vs.* Mayor, etc., 3 Hill (N. Y.), 531; see also Dillon, *Mun. Cor.,* 4th ed., vol. i., p. 45.   [3] *Ibid.*   [4] Dillon, *op. cit.,* vol. ii.. § 576.

The national government.—The English law, basing itself upon the principles that the sovereign can do no wrong and that when the government enters into private legal relations the sovereign acts through it, denies in principle to the individual the right to sue the central government except with its consent or in the special way which the government may have indicated. To prevent this privilege of the government from resulting in gross injustice, the individual was from time immemorial allowed respectfully to petition the Crown, which was historically the sovereign, that right be done him. Such a petition was called the petition of right.

In this country, the maxim that the sovereign can do no wrong is not a part of the law.[1] At the same time there is by the common law no remedy in case an individual desires positively to sue the government. The petition of right is regarded as inapplicable, inasmuch as the executive in this country is not regarded as the sovereign, and inasmuch as it does not have control of the purse-strings. The original practice, therefore, was for the individual having a claim against the government to petition the legislature for a special appropriation to pay his claim, and in case this petition was well founded, it was the custom of the legislature to pass a special appropriation bill which was regarded as mandatory upon the disbursing officers of the government.[2]

In the national government, on account of the

---

[1] Langford *vs.* United States, 101 U. S., 341. This is seen from the fact that in a suit brought by the government against an individual, he is permitted, as has been shown, to interpose a counter-claim.

[2] Kendall *vs.* The United States, 12 Peters, 524.

magnitude of its operations and the great number of special claims which were presented to Congress for settlement, this method proved to be an inconvenient one, and in 1855 an act was passed[1] providing a court for the investigation of claims against the United States government based upon a law or a contract. At first the decisions of this court had no legal effect whatever, since they were drawn up in the form of a bill which was afterwards to be laid before Congress for its approval. The act was afterwards amended so as to make the Court of Claims a real court whose judgments are of themselves mandatory upon the secretary of the treasury, and binding upon the individual suitor, and are to be paid out of any general appropriation for the payment of private claims. Appeal may be taken from the Court of Claims to the United States Supreme Court.[2] The act organizing the Court of Claims has not, however, vested it with jurisdiction over all suits against the government. Thus, for example, the Court of Claims has no equity jurisdiction and therefore may not decree specific performance of a contract or the restitution of property,[3] and has no jurisdiction over claims for torts committed by the government.[4] In order, however, to afford greater justice to claimants against the government, the Court of Claims and the United States Supreme Court, when cases have gone to it on appeal, have given quite a wide extension to the doctrine of *quasi* or implied contracts, and the

[1] 10 Statutes at Large, p. 612.   [2] 12 *Ibid.*, p. 766.

[3] Bonner *vs.* The United States, 9 Wallace, 156 ; United States *vs.* Jones, 131 U. S., 1.

[4] Gibbons *vs.* United States, 8 Wallace, 269 ; Langford *vs.* United States, 101 U. S., 341.

Court of Claims will take jurisdiction of suits which closely resemble suits in the nature of torts. Thus it has been held that if the government uses land to which it asserts no title, there is an implied contract to pay for it.[1]

The success of the Court of Claims was such that Congress in 1887 passed an act known as the Tucker Act, which extended the jurisdiction of the court to all claims founded upon the constitution of the United States or any law of Congress except for pensions, or upon any contract, express or implied, with the government of the United States, or for damages liquidated or unliquidated in cases not sounding in tort, in respect of which claims the party would be entitled to redress against the United States, either in a court of law, equity, or admiralty, if the United States were suable.[2] The Tucker Act, in addition to extending the jurisdiction of the Court of Claims, gave the circuit and district courts concurrent jurisdiction of all claims against the government of the character enumerated, under a certain amount.

In the cases both of the Court of Claims and of the circuit and district courts, when acting as courts of claims, the procedure is somewhat different from that which is followed in the ordinary courts when hearing cases between individuals. In the first place, the judges decide questions both of law and of fact. There is no jury. In the second place, the procedure before the Court of Claims is largely in writing,

[1] See United States *vs.* Great Falls Mfg. Co., 112 U. S., 645. The same rule is applied to patented inventions. United States *vs.* Palmer, 128 U. S., 262.

[2] As to the extent of the jurisdiction of the court under the Tucker Act, see Dooley *vs.* United States, 182 U. S., 222.

in order that the suitors in the court may not be obliged to appear in person or to send counsel a great distance, for the Court of Claims sits only at Washington. In the third place, the government is given certain privileges. Thus, it has always the right to appeal to the Supreme Court, the individual only in special cases. Thus again, any attempt fraudulently and wilfully to demand excessive damages from the government will result in voiding the whole claim. The same is true in case false evidence is adduced.

In addition to the Court of Claims there are one or two special courts for special classes of claims. Thus there is a court for private land claims.

In many cases special acts are passed which authorize the Court of Claims to hear cases which otherwise would not be within its jurisdiction. Such are the claims arising from collisions due to alleged negligence in the navigation of public vessels.[1]

Second, The state governments.—There is no general rule with regard to suits against the state governments. By the original constitution of the United States, a state might be sued by a citizen of any other state or by a foreign nation in the Supreme Court of the United States. This liability to suit, however, was removed by the eleventh amendment, which has been so interpreted by the Supreme Court as to make it well-nigh impossible to make a state a defendant in a suit in which an individual is the real plaintiff.[2] It has been held, however, that a state may be sued in

---

[1] See 14 Court of Claims, 435; 25 Statutes at Large, 1334; 24 Court of Claims, 372.

[2] See New Hampshire *vs.* Louisiana, and New York *vs.* Louisiana, 108 U. S., 76; Hans *vs.* Louisiana, 134 U. S., 1.

the United States Supreme Court by another state.[1] Further, the fact that a state owns some or all of the shares of stock of a corporation will not prevent the United States Courts from taking jurisdiction of suits against such corporation brought by individual plaintiffs.[2]

Some of the state constitutions expressly provide for the bringing of suits in the ordinary state courts against the state. Others expressly forbid that the state shall ever be made a defendant in any suit at law or in equity. In the majority, however, the old common-law rule prevails, that no suit can be brought against the state without its consent. In one state, namely, New York, the state has consented to being sued in a court of claims similar to that to be found in the United States government. Other states have, by general law, granted the right to the individual to sue them in the ordinary courts. Among them may be mentioned Virginia, of which it is said, "it has ever been the cherished policy of Virginia to allow to her citizens and others the largest liberty of suit against herself, and there has never been a moment since October, 1778 (but two years and three months after she became an independent state), that all persons have not enjoyed this right by express statute."[3] Another state, California, by act of February 28, 1893, provides for bringing suit for all "claims on contract or for negligence against the state." The provision of the statute of California

[1] South Dakota *vs.* North Carolina, 192 U. S., 286.
[2] U. S. Bank *vs.* Planters' Bank, 9 Wheaton, 904; Bank of Kentucky *vs.* Wister, 2 Peters, 318.
[3] Higginbotham's Executrix *vs.* Commonwealth, 25 Grattan, 637.

for suits against the state for negligence is almost unique, the usual rule being that the jurisdiction of either the general courts or the special courts which may be established is limited to claims arising upon contracts.[1] In New York, also, it is to be noted that the jurisdiction of the Court of Claims extends to claims arising out of negligence in the management of the canals operated by the state.[2]

4. *Suits indirectly against the government.*—Finally, it is to be noticed in the cases both of the United States national government and the state governments, that suits which are practically against the government are permitted where they are brought nominally against officers of the government. The theory, of course, is that in these cases the courts really enforce the will of the state against the unlawful refusal of its agents to perform their duties, but as a matter of fact the jurisdiction is sometimes admitted, even where the state really asserts adverse rights. In certain instances, the courts have seen that the real party in interest was the state, and in their more recent decisions they hold that they will look behind the parties of record and hold the suit to be against the state where the property and the interests of the state are directly involved. On the other hand, they hold quite universally to the rule that they will sustain the action where a distinct and specific right of person or property is asserted and protection or relief is sought against the threatened or consummated invasion by the act of officers assert-

---

[1] See The Murdock Parlor Grate Co. *vs.* Commonwealth, 152 Mass., 28.

[2] See Sipple *vs.* The State, 99 N. Y., 284; Splittorf *vs.* The State, 108 N. Y., 205.

ing an authority which is held to be void. "The distinction," it is said, "has been carried to such a point of refinement that in some cases it seems to resolve itself into the question whether the relief sought is affirmative, when it will be refused, or negative, when it will be granted."[1]

One of the most interesting cases on this point is that of United States *vs.* Lee.[2]

This was an action in ejectment brought against officers holding on behalf of the government possession of land to which the United States claimed title. The United States appeared for the sole purpose of objecting to the jurisdiction of the Court on the ground that the real and proper party defendant was the government: The Court, however, by a bare majority, held the action maintainable and gave judgment in favor of the plaintiff. The decision really amounted to an evasion of a substantial principle of law by a technical expedient. For the prerogative of the sovereign power not to be sued in its own courts in an action of ejectment becomes worthless if its instruments of action, by which alone it can accomplish its purposes, can be substituted in its place.[3]

Notwithstanding these considerations, in order to do justice, the court maintained the action and issued the writ of ejectment. The same principle has been applied to an action brought in the United States courts against state officers.[4]

Finally, by special statute the government is made liable for judgments obtained against its officers in special cases. This is true, for example, of the collectors of internal revenue, where they demand more

---

[1] Freund, "Private Claims against the State," *P. S. Q.*, viii., p. 636, citing Board of Liquidation *vs.* McComb, 92 U. S., 531, and Louisiana *vs.* Jumel, 107 U. S., 711.   [2] 106 U. S., 196.

[3] Freund, p. 638.   [4] Tindal *vs.* Wesley, 167 U. S., 204.

than the taxes required by law. The statutes[1] permit the individual to sue the collector, and the government pays the judgment. This is in reality recognizing the liability of the government to be haled before the courts at the instance of a private individual.[2]

II.—*Execution of the law by judicial process.*

Attention has already been called to the principle that in the absence of some special statutory provision the officers of the administration are not in some cases authorized to proceed directly to the enforcement of the law.[3] In so far as summary administrative proceedings in the execution of the law are not authorized, the very methods provided for the enforcement of the will of the state make provision for a judicial control over administrative action, inasmuch as the courts to which application for an order or warrant is made by the administration have the right, before issuing such order or warrant, to determine as to the legality of the action which the administration has taken.

But the courts have, in their decisions, very seriously limited the powers of control over administrative action which this method of enforcing the law accords to them. They have, in the first place, very generally held to the rule that their control is, ordinarily, limited to the determination of questions of jurisdiction and regularity of action upon the part of administra-

---

[1] U. S. Rev. Stats., Sec. 3220.

[2] On the general subject, see King, " Claims against Governments," *American Law Register and Review*, vol. 32, p. 997 ; Freund, " Private Claims against the State," *P. S. Q.*, viii., p. 625.

[3] For a fuller statement of these rules of law, see *supra*, p. 352.

tive officers. They will not, as a general rule, make use of this power of control to interfere in any way with the discretion which may have been accorded to administrative officers. For example, where administrative officers have assessed property for the purpose of taxation and the method of collecting such taxes is that by suit brought before the courts, the courts on such suit will give judgment against the administration only because administrative officers have exceeded their jurisdiction in attempting, for example, to levy a tax not authorized by statute, or have, in the assessment proceedings carried on for the purpose of determining the amount of the tax, applied rules which are clearly contrary to law.[1] The courts will not, on such suit, review the determination of the assessors as to the value of the property, where such assessors have had jurisdiction and have applied right legal principles.

Furthermore, in a number of instances the courts have held that, where this method of execution of the law by judicial process has been adopted, they are precluded from reviewing the action of the administration except as to jurisdictional matters, if the law has provided a method of direct review of such action. The rule is generally said to be that officers are presumed to have acted in accordance with the law, and that therefore their action may not be impeached in any way in a collateral proceeding to which the officers arriving at the determination sought to be reviewed are not parties, or where, if such officers are parties, the individual complaining of their actions has

[1] Houston Co. Coms. *vs.* Jessup, 22 Minn., 552; McCrillis *vs.* Mansfield, 64 Me., 198.

not at the time such action was taken availed of the remedy of direct review of such action.[1]

III.—Suits for damages against officers.

Attention has already been called to the fact that the English law never regarded officers as possessing any particular immunities resulting from their position as officers. It has been shown that assaults committed against them are punishable only in the same way as assaults committed against ordinary individuals, except in the case of resistance to officers in the performance of their duties. This position, which English officers have always occupied, has been due in part to the influence upon the English law of the old Teutonic law. That law regarded officers as subject to the law of the land in the same way as ordinary individuals, and as liable for the damages resulting from actions done without authority, whenever such actions caused damage to individuals.[2]

The character of the administrative system which England developed, was also in part responsible for the position accorded to officers. This was a system which has been called a self-government system. Officers did not form a privileged class, but were chosen from the ordinary members of the community, and, after serving their terms, relapsed into the ranks of society. During the performance of their duties, they did not, as a general thing, receive large salaries, certainly not salaries large enough to enable them to live without other occupation or means of livelihood.

---

[1] McMahon *vs.* Palmer, 102 N. Y., 176; *cf.* Swift *vs.* Poughkeepsie, 37 N. Y., 511.

[2] Loening, *Deutsches Verwaltungsrecht*, 771–784.

The result was that the English officer was merely an ordinary person who happened, as the result of circumstances, to be discharging duties of a public character.

The same rules of law were therefore applied to officers which were applied to ordinary citizens. Officers were not in theory, subject to certain specific exceptions which will be hereafter mentioned, exempted from liability for non-observance of the law on account of their official position. If during the period of their discharge of public functions they committed an act not justified by the law, such act was regarded as *coram non judice*—that is, as an act of a purely private and personal character for which, like any citizen, they could be held responsible before the ordinary courts. The important question to be decided by the courts whenever the acts of an officer came up before them was therefore the question of jurisdiction. Did the law give the officer the power to perform the act, the result of whose performance was damage to an individual?

The significance of this relation of officers to the courts was to be found in the fact that the courts had the power to determine in each specific case whether an officer had jurisdiction to do a given act. Any act of an officer might give rise to a complaint which the courts would have to decide. In deciding the complaints coming before them, the courts had the power to delimit the sphere of administrative competence in all of its details. What the actual extent of the control which the courts might exercise was to be, would depend entirely upon the attitude of the courts. They might pass upon every act of every officer, or they might limit their power in the interest of the public, and might thus leave something to administrative discretion which they would not attempt to control.

This is actually what the courts of England and the United States have done. In both countries they have made most important exceptions to the rule that the jurisdiction of all officers of the government is subject to delimitation by the courts, and that through the exercise of this power the courts may hold officers of the government responsible for damages resulting from acts which in the opinion of the courts were in excess of the jurisdiction of such officers. These exceptions are as follows :

1. *Chief executive not liable in damages.*—In accordance with the maxim that "the Crown can do no wrong," the English Crown was exempted from all liability for tortious acts. Indeed, in the theory of the law it could not commit a tort. This rule of law has been applied by the United States courts to the President. It is said that

no case has as yet arisen in which it has been attempted to hold the President of the United States amenable to a private action for his official misconduct; and certainly so far as the performance of the great political powers which are conferred upon him is concerned, no such action could be maintained. . . . The same immunity extends also to the governors of the states. "The Governor of the State," says Judge Cooley, . . . "could not be made responsible to private parties without subordinating the Executive Department to the Judicial Department, and this would be inconsistent with the theory of Republican institutions: each Department within its province is and must be independent."[1]

[1] Cooley *On Torts*, 1st ed., p. 377.

. . . No case has been discovered in which an action for damages has been sought to be maintained against the Governor for his neglect or refusal to perform even a ministerial act.[1]

2. *Heads of executive departments not liable.*—The heads of executive departments in both England and the United States are practically guaranteed immunity from suits for damages at the hands of private individuals. Mr. Todd says:[2]

It may be stated as a general principle that in assuming on behalf of the Crown a personal responsibility for all acts of the Government, Ministers are privileged to share with the Crown in a personal immunity from vexatious proceedings by ordinary process of law for alleged acts of oppression or illegality in the discharge of their official acts. . . . Whether the alleged liability arises out of contract or out of tort or from any matter of private, individual complaint against a Minister of the Crown for acts done in his official capacity, the ordinary tribunals of justice will afford him special immunity and protection.

The same rule is true of the heads of departments of the national government. Up to 1870 there was only one action brought against the head of a United States executive department.[3] This case was the case of Stokes *vs.* Kendall,[4] and was decided adversely to the plaintiff. It is interesting as showing distinctly the attitude of the courts towards this class of cases. It was preceded by the case of Kendall *vs.* the United States,[5] in which the same plaintiff as in the case of Stokes *vs.* Kendall had endeavored to obtain a *mandamus* against the Postmaster-General. The Supreme Court there decided that a given act was

---

[1] Mechem, *Public Officers*, etc., p. 395.

[2] *Parliamentary Government in England*, 2d ed., vol. i., pp. 494–495.

[3] See Brown's case, 6 Court of Claims Rep., 171, 180.

[4] 3 How., 87. [5] 12 Peters, 524.

not discretionary, but ministerial in character, and therefore that a *mandamus* might issue. And seven years later, when the same plaintiff brought a suit for damages against the Postmaster-General, the court held that this same act, which it declared in the other case to be ministerial, was, when a suit for damages resulting from it was brought, a discretionary act, and, therefore, that the Postmaster-General could not be held liable for damages.[1]

It may be added that the immunity thus granted to the higher officers of the state does not really diminish the control possessed by the courts over the administration so much as at first sight it might seem, for these high officers must come into relations with individuals generally through the action of their subordinates, and by the American law such subordinates are generally responsible for their actions, and are not protected by the fact that they have acted according to instructions from their superiors.[2]

3. *Liability of judges.*—The courts, with that tenderness which all human beings appear to have for the members of their own class, have held that in the case of judges of the higher courts a distinction is to be made between acts done without jurisdiction and acts done in excess of jurisdiction. The leading case upon this point is that of Bradley *vs.* Fisher.[3] In this case it is said :

Where there is clearly no jurisdiction over the subject matter, any authority exercised is a usurped authority, and for the exercise of such authority, when the want of jurisdiction is known to the Judge, no excuse is permissible, but where jurisdiction over

[1] See also Spalding *vs.* Vilas, 161 U. S., 483.
[2] Tracy *vs.* Swartout, 10 Peters, 80.　　　[3] 13 Wallace, 335.

the subject matter is invested by law in the Judge or in the court which he holds, the manner and extent in which the jurisdiction shall be exercised are generally as much questions for his determination as any other questions involved in the case, although upon the correctness of his determination of these particulars the validity of his judgment may depend. Thus, if a Probate Court, invested only with authority over wills and the settlement of estates of deceased persons, should proceed to try parties for public offences, the jurisdiction over the subject of offences being entirely wanting in that court, and this being necessarily known to its Judge, his commission would afford no protection to him in the exercise of the usurped authority. But if, on the other hand, a Judge of a Criminal Court, invested with a general criminal jurisdiction over offences committed within a certain district, should hold a particular act to be a public offence, which is not by the law made an offence, and proceed to the arrest and trial of a party charged with such act, or to sentence a party to greater punishment than authorized by the law upon its proper construction, no personal liability in a civil action for such act would attach to the Judge, although those acts would be in excess of his jurisdiction, or of the jurisdiction of the court held by him, for these are particulars for his judicial consideration whenever his general jurisdiction over the subject matter is invoked.[1]

In the case, however, of an inferior judge or magistrate the rule is different. If he exceeds his jurisdiction he is liable in damages to the party injured thereby, even though he was acting in good faith.

4. *Liability of ministerial officers.*—Another limitation which the courts have placed upon their control over the action of the administration is to be found in the rule that purely ministerial officers will not be held responsible for damages where they have followed instructions, which are legal on their face, and which

[1] See also Lange *vs.* Benedict, 73 N. Y., 12 ; McCall *vs.* Cohen, 16 S. C., 445 ; 42 Am. Rep., 61.

26

contain nothing which will apprise them that such instructions have been issued in excess of the jurisdiction of the officer who issued them.[1] The weight of authority seems to be in favor of the rule that a ministerial officer is relieved from all responsibility for the execution of orders, fair on their face, even when he is satisfied that the officer issuing them acted in excess of his jurisdiction.[2]

This general rule is applicable, not only to civil officers, but also to military persons. The general rule of law of this country, which we have inherited from England, is to the effect that a person does not by becoming a soldier cease to be subject to the jurisdiction of the ordinary courts as a citizen. Nevertheless, in order to maintain that discipline without which a military force would amount to nothing, the courts are careful in the exercise of their jurisdiction over military persons, not to hold them to such responsibility as will cause them to have hesitation in obeying orders which are apparently within the jurisdiction of the officer issuing them.[3]

5. *Liability for negligence.*—Under the English as well as the American law, officers are held responsible not merely for acts done without jurisdiction, but in certain cases for the non-performance or negligent performance of duties within their jurisdiction, or for bad faith. No officer, however, is held responsible in damages for the non-performance or negligent performance of duties of a merely public character. In order to be made the basis of a claim for damages,

---

[1] Savacool *vs.* Boughton, 5 Wendell, N. Y., 170 ; see also Erskine *vs.* Hohnbach, 14 Wallace, 613, 616 ; Cooley *On Taxation*, 2d ed., 797, and cases cited.   [2] *Ibid.*, 798.   [3] Com. *vs.* Shortall, 206 Pa. St., 165.

the duty, the neglect of which has caused the damage, must be one which the individual suffering the damage has the right, not as a part of the public, but as an individual, to have performed.   Thus, a sheriff is not responsible for the damages suffered by an individual from the sheriff's failure to keep the peace.[1]

The law further makes a distinction between the different kinds of officers, affording a greater immunity to officers who are recognized as thoroughly judicial in character, than to officers who are merely ministerial in character.   While this distinction between the character of the office was of great influence upon the courts in the early history of the law, it is believed that at the present time the distinction that is to be made is rather between the duties which the officer is to perform than between the officers who are to perform the duties.   Thus in the case of Wilson *vs.* The Mayor,[2] the judge says :

The civil remedy for misconduct in office . . . depends exclusively upon the nature of the duty which has been violated. Where that is absolute, certain, and imperative, and every ministerial duty is so, the delinquent officer is bound to make full redress to every person who has suffered by such delinquency. Duties which are purely ministerial in their nature are sometimes cast upon officers whose chief functions are judicial.   Where this occurs and the ministerial duty is violated, the officer, although, for most purposes, a judge, is still civilly responsible for such misconduct.   But where the duty alleged to have been violated is purely judicial, a different rule prevails ; for no action lies in any case for misconduct or delinquency, however gross, in the performance of judicial duties.   And although the officer may not in strictness be a judge, still, if his powers are discretionary, to be exerted or withheld according to his own view of what is

[1] South *vs.* Maryland, 18 How. (U. S.), 396.
[2] 1 Denio (N. Y.), 595, 599.

necessary and proper, they are in their nature judicial, and he is exempt from all responsibility by action for the motives which influence him and the manner in which such duties are performed.

The difference between these two rules is a real one, inasmuch, as has been seen from the opinion just cited, a ministerial duty may be imposed upon a judge, while an officer whose duties are generally ministerial may be called upon to exercise judgment and discretion; but it is well to remember that judicial officers are for the most part confined to the performance of judicial duties, while ministerial officers very seldom are entrusted with the performance of such duties. At the same time there is a tendency, in the case of officers who are not discharging judicial duties in the sense that they are holding courts, to hold such officers to a greater liability than is imposed upon officers who are engaged simply in the holding of courts. There is a class of officers to whom the name of quasi-judicial is applied; such as assessors for the purpose of taxation, boards of health, election officers, and so on. There is a tendency in the United States in the more recent decisions to relax the strictness of the rule in the case of such officers, and to hold them responsible for bad faith and dishonest purposes, notwithstanding the judicial and discretionary character of the act that they performed.

In respect to such cases [says Judge Cooley [1]], though they may be out of harmony with the general rule . . . and the reasons on which it rests, yet we may perhaps safely concede that there are various duties lying along the borders between those of a ministerial and those of a judicial character which

[1] *Torts*, p. 411.

are usually entrusted to inferior officers and in the performance of which it is highly important that they be kept as closely as possible within strict rules. If courts lean against recognizing in them full discretionary powers and hold them strictly within the limits of good faith, it is probably a leaning that in most cases will be harmonized with public policy.

With this exception, however, the motives of officers in the performance of a judicial act will not in any way affect their liability. If the officers are in fact corrupt, the public has its remedy, but the individual is not permitted to obtain redress against them by alleging that the action complained of was the result of corrupt or malicious motives.[1]

It is difficult to lay down rules by which a judicial or discretionary act may be distinguished from a purely ministerial act. Thus an act does not become a judicial act merely because its performance requires "the ascertainment from personal knowledge or by information derived from other sources of the state of facts on which the performance of the act becomes a clear and specific duty."[2] It may, however, be said that the duty in order to be a ministerial one must be one which the officer is called upon to perform, and which he can perform. Thus, where the performance of a duty "requires the possession or use of particular means or agencies or the expenditure of money, it must appear that the officer had either the means, agencies, or funds required, or the facilities for acquiring them."[3] Further, it must be a duty which it was absolutely

[1] See Bradley *vs.* Fisher, 13 Wall., 335 ; Rains *vs.* Simpson, 50 Tex., 495 ; 32 Am. Rep., 609 ; Pratt *vs.* Gardner, 2 Cush. (Mass.), 63 Am. Dec., 652.

[2] Grider *vs.* Tally, 77 Ala., 422 ; 52 Am. Dec., 65.

[3] Mechem, *op. cit.*, § 669, citing Nowell *vs.* Wright, 3 Allen (Mass.), 166 ; 80 Am. Dec., 62.

imperative upon the officer to perform, a duty the non-performance of which does not lie in the officer's discretion.[1] This being the case, the officer is not excused for any mistake, notwithstanding it may have been made in perfect good faith.[2]

It is, however, to be remembered that it is a maxim of the law that officers are presumed to have done their duty. The burden, therefore, of showing a failure by an official to perform his duty is on the person alleging such failure.[3] But, while it is presumed that officers have done their duty, at the same time, except in the case of courts of law having general jurisdiction, this presumption is not made as to jurisdiction. In the case of all tribunals possessing special and limited jurisdiction, and all administrative officers are regarded as embraced within this class, inasmuch as their duties are either stated in detail by the decisions of the courts, if they are common-law officers, or by statute if they are statutory officers, the jurisdiction must appear affirmatively on the face of the proceedings.

Further, the distinction between absolute lack of jurisdiction and excessive jurisdiction, which applies to the higher courts, does not apply to the lower tribunals. Among these are to be included all administrative authorities. This brings it about that an act which might not in any way affect the jurisdiction of a tribunal of general jurisdiction so as to make the officer who performed the acts responsible for dam-

---

[1] Mechem, *op. cit.*, § 669.

[2] See Amy *vs.* The Supervisors, 11 Wall., 136.

[3] See Mechem, *op. cit.*, § 677, citing Bank *vs.* Herold, 74 Cal., 603 ; 5 Am. St. R., 476.

ages, may cause the subsequent acts of inferior tribunals to be invalid, and will result in an excess of jurisdiction which will make the person who is guilty of such excess of jurisdiction responsible in damages.[1]

6. *Liability of officers for acts of subordinates.*— Finally, "it is well settled as a general rule of law that public officers in the performance of their public functions are not liable to third persons either for the misfeasances or positive wrongs or for the non-feasances, negligences, or omissions of their official subordinates."[2]

This rule as to the non-liability of public officers for the acts of their subordinates is subject to two exceptions. In the first place, where it is owing to the negligence of the superior or to his positive action that the damage is done by the subordinate, the superior is responsible.[3] In the second place, an exception is made to the rule in the case of ministerial officers whose liability for the damage occasioned by their illegal acts is greater than that of judicial officers. It is held that the responsibility of ministerial officers

---

[1] Thus, take the case of French *vs.* Edwards, 13 Wallace, 506, to which reference has several times been made. In this case the sheriff in the sale of lands for taxation had not followed carefully the provisions of the statute. It was held that as soon as he ceased to follow the provisions of the statute, which in this case were regarded as mandatory, inasmuch as they affected the rights of individuals, he ceased to have jurisdiction, and his acts thereafter were invalid. Take also the case of Mygatt *vs.* Washburn, 15 N. Y., 316. In this case the assessors assessed a person who was not within their jurisdiction, and it was held that they were liable for the damages which such person suffered in being obliged to pay taxes on the illegal assessment.

[2] Mechem, *op. cit.*, § 789 citing Robertson *vs.* Sichel, 127 U. S., 507–513 ; see also Richmond *vs.* Long, 17 Grattan (Va.), 375, 378 ; 95 Am. Dec., 461.

[3] See Wiggins *vs.* Hathaway, 6 Barb. (N. Y.), 632, 635 ; Bishop *vs.* Williamson, 11 Me., 495. In this case a postmaster was held liable for the default of an assistant whom he had not required to take the oath prescribed by law. See also Ely *vs.* Parsons, 55 Conn., 83.

cannot be evaded by delegating the performance of their duties to another. The rule is therefore well settled that the ministerial officer who owes a duty to an individual is liable to that individual for the negligence of his deputies.[1] This rule, of course, does not make him liable for the extra-official acts or misconduct of his deputies[2]; nor for the omission or neglect of an act or duty which the law does not require him officially to perform[3]; nor for the acts which were directed by the complaining party himself.[4]

Finally, it is to be noted that a public officer of whatever grade is liable for the negligence or other defaults of his private servant or employee who is not regarded as an officer of the government. When the subordinate, whose acts are the cause of the damage, does not hold an office known to the law, but his appointment is private and discretionary with the officer appointing him, the principal is responsible for his acts. Thus, a selectman was held liable for the damages caused by a laborer employed by him to cut brush and trees in order to make the highway passable, who through mistake cut down some trees upon the land of an adjoining proprietor.[5]

---

[1] Robinson *vs.* Rohr., 73 Wis., 436. See State *vs.* Moore, 19 Mo., 369; 61 Am. Dec., 563; Flanagan *vs.* Hoyt, 36 Vt., 565; 86 Am. Dec., 670.

[2] State *vs.* Moore, 19 Mo., 369; 61 Am. Dec., 563.

[3] Harrington *vs.* Fuller, 18 Me., 277; 36 Am. Dec., 719.

[4] Gorman *vs.* Gale, 7 Cowen (N. Y.), 739; 17 Am. Dec., 549.

[5] Ely *vs.* Parsons, 55 Conn., 83; see also Robinson *vs.* Rohr, 73 Wis., 436. On the general subject see Mechem, §§ 788–802, *op. cit.*

CHAPTER III.

I.—Control of the courts over the prosecution of individuals.

THE control which the criminal courts exercise over the administration is exercised in two ways. In the first place, the courts are called upon to entertain prosecutions brought by the officers of the administration against individuals, for the violation of laws and administrative ordinances, whose violation has been made punishable criminally, or for unlawful resistance to officers in the discharge of their duties. In all such cases the criminal courts have the right to refuse to punish the person prosecuted on the ground that the administrative officers have exceeded their powers and have acted without jurisdiction. The criminal courts in this way delimit the sphere of administrative action and force the administration to keep within the bounds set by law.

In some instances the control which the courts thus have over administrative officers is of such a character that its exercise may prevent the administration from enforcing the law. This is particularly true of those cases in which the decision reached by the court is reached through the aid of a jury, the members of

409

which are, under our law, chosen within the locality where the violation of the law complained of is alleged to have taken place. The requirement of our law, that the verdict of a jury must be reached as a result of their unanimous action, brings it about that in many instances it is practically impossible for the administration to enforce a law which is unpopular in the district from which the jury is chosen. A most notable instance of this paralysis of the efforts of the administration in the enforcement of the law is to be found in the case of the attempt to enforce a prohibition law or a law providing for the closing on Sundays of liquor saloons in cities. In these cases the control possessed by the criminal courts over administrative officers is so made use of, in many instances, as absolutely to prevent the enforcement of the law.

In some instances the legislature has frankly recognized the effect upon the enforcement of the law of the existence of the right of a jury trial and has attempted to substitute therefor the action of the equity branch of the courts. Provision in these cases is made, in addition to the prosecution before the criminal courts of the violation of the law, for the issue of an injunction by the proper court to restrain the doing of the act which the law is attempting to prevent. In these cases refusal upon the part of individuals to obey the injunction of the court is made a contempt of court, which, in addition to being punishable criminally, is followed by the commitment of the person guilty of such contempt by the court itself without the aid of a jury. This method of securing the imprisonment of persons for violation of the law without resort to a jury has been upheld by the Supreme Court of the United States.[1]

II.—*Power of the criminal courts to punish officials. Method of prosecution.*

The second way in which the criminal courts exercise a control over the administration is by entertaining criminal prosecutions of officers for the violation of their duties. The extent and effectiveness of this method of control depend, in the first place, upon the content of the criminal law—that is, on the extent to which the violation of official duty is punishable criminally, and, in the second place, on the method of prosecution.[2] For, while the content of the criminal law may be such as to provide for a large control over the administration, if the method of prosecution provided by law gives the administration a large discretion as to when the control shall be exercised—that is, if the courts or individuals have little power of initiating and carrying on prosecutions against officers, the control of the criminal courts may amount virtually to nothing.

There are two methods of conducting prosecutions, the one through a private prosecutor, the other through the public prosecutor. So far as the control of the criminal courts aims at the protection of private rights, the system of private prosecution will undoubtedly produce the best results. So far as that control aims at the efficiency of the administration, the system of public prosecution is capable of producing

---

[1] Mugler *vs.* Kansas, 123 U. S., 623; see also Dunbar, "Government by Injunction," *The Law Quarterly*, October, 1897.

[2] For the content of the criminal law, see *supra*, 298.

the best results, since it is certain that private prosecutors usually initiate prosecutions only where their
private rights have been violated.

The American system of criminal prosecutions is a
development of the English system. The English
system was based upon the idea of private prosecution. The usual method of prosecution was a complaint by the individual against whom the crime
had been committed to a committing magistrate who
made the preliminary examination of the prisoner and
sent the case up to the grand jury in case the prisoner
was held. The grand jury then proceeded by indictment. The grand jury was not, however, confined in its action to the cases sent up by committing
magistrates, but was authorized, as well, to proceed
of its own motion in regard to matters of which it had
personal knowledge. In this way it was possible for
individuals to make their complaints directly to the
grand jury or to members thereof. The only important public prosecutors in the English system were
to be found in the attorney-general and solicitor-
general, who were authorized to proceed of their own
motion by means of a criminal information in certain
cases of great public interest.

During the course of the nineteenth century, there
developed in most of the states of the American
Union a public prosecutor, known in some cases by
the name of district attorney, in others by that of circuit attorney, state's attorney, or prosecutor of the
pleas. An investigation of the development of this
office will show that it is the result of an attempt to
disintegrate the office of attorney-general. As a
general thing, the first step in the development was

the provision for an assistant or deputy attorney-general, to be appointed by the governor of the state, with jurisdiction either over some particular county or some judicial district of the state. Later on this officer became, outside of the national administrative system, elective by the people of the district over which he had jurisdiction.[1]

The establishment of this office was apparently due in large part to the desire of preventing inconsiderate prosecutions. Great discretion was therefore accorded to the public prosecutors in the initiation of prosecutions, although a monopoly of the power seems in no instance to have been given them—that is, the individual injured was always permitted and is still permitted to make his complaint before a magistrate, when the grand jury will act in very much the same way as under the old English practice. Some of the cases, however, would seem to indicate that the individual has no longer the right to go before the grand jury and make his complaint directly to them.[2] This power has been replaced by the power given to the public prosecutor to present cases himself to the grand jury.

As the management of the case before the grand jury is largely in the hands of the public prosecutor, the result is that, for the punishment of almost all crimes which the officers of the administration may commit, the co-operation of the public prosecutor has become a practical necessity.[3] This is so, furthermore,

[1] See People *vs.* Supervisors, 134 N. Y., 1.

[2] McCullough *vs.* Commonwealth, 67 Pa. St., 30; Fout *vs.* State, 3 Haywood (Tenn.), 98.

[3] This is particularly true in those states in which the public prosecution **may** proceed without the grand jury, *i. e.*, by information.

because of the fact that the conduct of the prosecution after it has once been initiated is largely, indeed, almost entirely, in the hands of that officer. Some of the cases on this point go so far as to intimate that the participation of other counsel than the public prosecutor in a prosecution for crime is absolutely forbidden.[1] Others declare that though other counsel—that is, counsel representing some private individual interest—may be admitted, their admission is a privilege which may be granted or refused by the district attorney, and not a right which the individual may demand by application to the courts.[2] Finally, a few cases would seem to indicate that the courts possess an inherent power to appoint one of the attorneys of the court to carry on the prosecution where that is necessary to prevent a failure of justice.[3]

The liability that there will be a failure of justice owing to the refusal of the district attorney to conduct a prosecution has brought it about that in New York resort is had to the central administrative control to supplement the control possessed by the criminal courts. Here the governor is authorized to require the attorney-general to attend in person or by one of his deputies a criminal court or appear before a grand jury for the purpose of managing and

---

[1] See, for example, People *vs.* Hurst, 41 Mich., 328.

[2] See State *vs.* Kent, 4 N. D., 577.

[3] Dukes *vs.* State, 11 Ind., 557; 71 Am. Dec., 370; Mitchell *vs.* State, 22 Ga., 211; 68 Am. Dec., 493. In these cases it is held either that the court may appoint some one to conduct the prosecution, where the public prosecutor has been retained by the criminal, or in case he is unable to perform his duty. Neither of the cases, however, holds that in case the prosecuting officer refuses to perform his duty, or performs it in a negligent manner, the court may appoint a prosecutor to conduct the prosecution in his place.

conducting in such court or before such jury such criminal actions or proceedings as shall be specified by the governor. In such a case the attorney-general or his deputy as authorized by law shall alone exercise all the powers and perform all the duties in respect to such actions or proceedings which the district attorney would otherwise be authorized or required to exercise or perform.[1] In Pennsylvania a statute provides that if the district attorney shall neglect or refuse to prosecute in due form of law any criminal charge regularly returned to him or to the court of the proper county, or if, in case of the admission of the counsel of a private party, the district attorney shall differ with him as to the conduct of the proceedings, the court, on the petition of the private prosecutor may direct the private counsel of the prosecutor to conduct the entire proceeding.[2] It will be noticed that, different from the New York law, the Pennsylvania law attempts to reinforce the control of the criminal courts by calling to their aid the private prosecutor.

By the original English law the public prosecutors had the right of entering what is known as a *nolle prosequi*, the effect of which was to discontinue the action, without, however, exempting the prisoner from the liability to a subsequent indictment for the same offence. It is difficult to say exactly what power the American public prosecutor has at the present time to enter such a *nolle prosequi*. Apparently the better rule with regard to this matter is that, prior to the commencement of the trial in open court,

[1] See Laws of 1895, ch. 821; see also State *vs.* District Court, 22 Mont., 25.
[2] See Pennsylvania Law, March 12, 1868.

the public prosecutor has the right to enter such a *nolle prosequi* in his own discretion, but that, subsequent to the beginning of the trial of the prisoner, this right is conditioned upon obtaining the consent of the court.[1] In some states, however, as, for example, in New York, the district attorney has no power whatever to enter a *nolle prosequi*, but may move the court to dismiss the indictment.[2]

The method of prosecution which has been developed in the United States tends naturally greatly to relax the control which the criminal courts have over administrative officers, for the public prosecutor, in whose hands is practically the power both to initiate and to conduct prosecutions against officers of the administration, is, whatever may be the method of organizing the system, in more or less close affiliation with the administration, and is more than likely to overestimate the importance of administrative independence, even to the detriment of private rights and in some cases of administrative efficiency. Where the public prosecutor is dependent in tenure upon some superior officer, as is the case in the national administration, where he may be dismissed at any time by the President, the danger is very great that the administration may prevent the exercise by the criminal courts of their control over administrative officers through its power over the public prosecutors. Even in the case that public prosecutors are elected by the people of the district over which they have jurisdiction, which is the rule in the state administra-

---

[1] For an exhaustive examination of the powers of the district attorney in this matter see State *vs.* Moise, 48 La. Ann., 109.

[2] See New York Code of Criminal Procedure, sec. 672.

tion, the control of the party is so strong as to make it sometimes practically impossible to secure energetic prosecution of official criminals with whom the leaders of the party are in sympathy. We have had, in our administrative history, many instances of the refusal on the part of the district attorney to proceed with the prosecution of public officers, or of such negligence on his part in conducting a prosecution which he has been forced by public opinion to initiate that officers guilty of official and other crimes have been able to escape punishment for their actions. In the national administration, in addition to the power which the President has over the district attorneys, is to be mentioned another power, through the exercise of which almost any prosecution against an official may be blocked, namely, the power which the attorney-general of the United States says the President possesses of entering a *nolle prosequi* at any stage of criminal proceedings.[1]

[1] *Cf.* 2 Opinions of the Attorneys-General, 482.

CHAPTER IV.

I.—Necessity of peculiar judicial remedies.

THE direct judicial control over the administration, which has so far been considered, has been found in the remedies offered to individuals against officers as mere persons to obtain satisfaction for the commission of illegal acts. It has been seen how careful the law is to limit both the civil and the criminal responsibility of officials in order to protect them from vexatious suits. It often requires practically an absolute overstepping of their jurisdiction, or corruption where they have acted within it, in order to found the responsibility, and all but denies any responsibility on the part of the government for the acts of its officers.

But, even were this method of judicial control more easily exercised than it is, it would be found in many cases to be ineffectual. A civil suit for damages against an official may be an altogether inadequate remedy, because damages will not in some cases be an adequate means of relief, and because, even if they were, the official sued may not be the possessor of enough property to satisfy the judgment. Again, the successful prosecution of a criminal suit against an officer may have value in tempering the future conduct of officials, but does not result in any actual improvement in the condition of the individual whose rights have been violated. In both cases a right may have been violated and adequate satisfaction may not have been made by the application of ordinary judicial remedies.

Were the remedies which have been mentioned the only means which the courts had to control the actions of the administration in the interest of private rights, the judicial control over the administration would thus be quite incomplete. Some means must be provided by which the courts may directly control the acts of the administration. It may be of vital importance that a thing be done which the law says shall be done. It is not just to tell an individual that he must wait until his right has been violated and then sue the proper official for damages, or even prosecute him criminally. The individual desires a definite thing done by the administration which the law says shall be done. Again, it may be of vital importance that an officer be prevented from doing an act which he threatens to do, or that a decision which is regarded as unfair or illegal be reviewed and annulled or amended. Here, for the same reason as before, it is not right to force the individual to rely solely on his power to sue the officer in damages or prosecute him criminally.

In all these cases, if individual rights are to be adequately protected against the administration, some method of judicial control must be devised in addition to those already mentioned. Some means must be offered of reaching the acts and not the persons of the officers of the administration. The various remedies through which the courts ordinarily exercise a control over the acts of the administration are known to the American law as extraordinary remedies, since, as a general thing, the jurisdiction of the proper courts may be invoked in their application only where there is no other adequate means of relief. Special courts or special statutory remedies may also be formed for the exercise of this control. The former method is that which has been in the main adopted in England and the United States, although instances of special courts and special statutory remedies are to be found.

II.—*History of the English method.*

1. *History to the beginning of the eighteenth century.*—The English system of extraordinary remedies, whose main principles have been adopted in the United States, is simply an outgrowth of the original system of administrative control. The Norman political system made no clear distinction between governmental authorities. All powers of government were consolidated in the hands of the Crown. First to be differentiated was the legislative authority, the Parliament. But for a long time after the differentiation of Parliament there was almost no legal distinction between the position of the officers who administered justice and that of the officers who administered government. Indeed, most important officers discharged functions in both branches, and all alike were regarded as merely the servants of the Crown. Some, it is true, were engaged mainly in the application of the private law, others were engaged mainly in the application of the public and administrative law. But

all were officers of the Crown, which directly or indirectly could remove them all from office and could
dictate to them what should be the decision of the
cases which were brought before them.[1]

To the officers of one of these courts, however, *viz.*,
the court of king's bench, which was regarded as occupying a superior position, because the Crown by a
fiction of the law was supposed always to be present
in it,[2] was given a supervisory power over all other
authorities.[3]   If any one was aggrieved by an act of a
subordinate officer of the Crown, he had the right to
appeal to the Crown, which was the fountain of justice,[4]
and such an appeal went to the court of king's bench.
At first it seems to have gone to the *Curia Regis* or
King's Council, before the development of the court of
king's bench.[5]   Indeed, after the development of the
court of king's bench, when the members of this court
became very technical in their application of the law,
appeals went in many cases directly to the Crown
and were attended to generally by the chancellor or
the council.[6]   For the King at the time of the formation of the court of king's bench specially reserved
to himself the decision of particularly difficult cases.[7]
From these reserved judicial powers grew up the

[1] Gneist, *History of the English Constitution*, i., 390; High, *Extraordinary Legal Remedies*, 3d ed., p. 5. As to the influence of the Crown over the decisions of the judges even, witness the famous case of John Hampden in the
court of the exchequer.

[2] See as to the origin of this fiction, Stubbs, *Constitutional History*, i., 487,
ii., 267 ; *cf.* Blackstone, iii., 41.

[3] Gneist, *History etc.*, i., 384.

[4] See Stubbs, *op. cit.*, i., 421 ; Palgrave, *An Essay upon the Original Authority
of the King's Council*, p. 61.

[5] 1 Ryley's *Pleadings*, 534   *Abbreviatio Placitorum*, 21.

[6] Stubbs, ii., 267.

[7] *Ibid.*, i., 525.

court of chancery as well as other courts.[1]   In answer
to such appeals, the court of king's bench issued in the
name of the Crown certain writs directed to the officer
whose decision was complained of, and so framed as to
afford the desired relief.   Though these writs were
originally issued under the king's great seal from the
office of the chancellor,[2] the courts soon obtained the
right to issue them directly.[3]   These writs were named
from the most prominent words in them—words which
largely expressed the purpose of the writ.   Thus, if
any one appealed to the Crown to force a recalcitrant
officer to do something which the law of the land com-
manded the officer to do, the writ which was issued in
answer to the appeal was called a writ of *mandamus*.[4]

At the same time that the court of king's bench
was developing these special remedies, which became
known as extraordinary legal remedies or prerogative
writs, the chancellor, the keeper of the King's con-
science, was, through the exercise of the reserved
judicial powers of the King, also developing a series
of special remedies called equitable remedies, the most
important of which, from the point of view of administrative law, was the bill of injunction.   Originally, however, the injunction does not seem to have
been made use of commonly against officers.

While most of the writs issued by the royal courts
were ultimately issued to litigants upon proper demand as of course, and were known as writs *ex debito*

[1] Stubbs, ii., 275, 601–603.

[2] Palgrave, *op. cit.*, pp. 8, 16, 17.

[3] Gneist, *Hist.*, i., 393.   See also Reeves, *History of the English Law*, Fin-
layson's ed., ii., 394, 507, 605.

[4] The word "mandamus" was applied originally to all the commands of the
King, but was later confined to the writ issued by the court of king's bench.—
High, *op. cit.*, p. 5.

justitiæ, the writs by means of which the court of king's bench exercised its supervisory powers over the other authorities do not seem to have become, in early times at any rate, writs of rights, writs *ex debito justitiæ*, but were issued only in extraordinary cases when some injustice was done which could not be remedied in the ordinary way. They were known, therefore, as "prerogative writs." The same was practically true of the equitable remedies, and particularly of the bill of injunction.

On the return to these writs, generally only questions of law were considered. They were made use of simply to keep the lower authorities within the bounds of the law, and could not be used, after the practice in regard to them became crystallized, to review any question of fact or of expediency. It therefore became necessary to develop some further remedy, unless the lower authorities were to be permitted to decide such questions free from all control. Such a method was found in the power which was granted to the individual to appeal to the Privy Council. Such appeals the council might hear as a result of the fact that the King granted to a division of it, *viz.*, the Star Chamber, a portion of his reserved judicial powers. This body acted as the administrative superior of the royal authorities in the localities, and on appeal to it questions of fact and expediency, as well as of law, could be considered.[1] Formed in the time of Henry VII. to control the nobility, who had grown turbulent during the wars of the Roses, it served at first to protect the weaker classes of the

[1] Blackstone, *op. cit.*, iv., 266; Palgrave, *op. cit.*, 57–61, 101–108; Stubbs, *op. cit.*, ii., 603.

community against arbitrary action on the part of
the administrative authorities, which were largely re-
cruited from the nobility ; but it was later, *viz.*, under
the Stuarts, used in such a way that it was abolished
on the occasion of the revolution.[1] In order to offer
an appeal similar to the one which disappeared on
the occasion of its abolition, it was provided in a
series of statutes that the court of quarter sessions of
the justices of the peace, which had been theretofore
mainly an administrative authority for the purpose of
county administration, should hear and decide appeals
from those decisions of the justices of the peace, acting singly or in petty and special sessions, which
affected property and the right of personal liberty.[2]
There was thus formed for the decision of questions
of fact and expediency, as well as of law, an administrative court in each county, which came finally to
have a very wide power of control over the acts of subordinate administrative officers.   Its members were
naturally well fitted for the exercise of this control,
since they had a special knowledge of the law they
had to apply and of the conditions of administrative
action.   For they were engaged in other capacities
as administrative officers.

Further, the commission of the justices of the peace
enjoined upon them in difficult cases to take the advice of the royal courts. This came finally to be
done by "stating a case" which was agreed upon by
the justices and the parties before them, and which
was then submitted to the royal courts, and finally

[1] 16 Car., I, c. 10.
[2] See Smith, *Practice at Quarter Sessions*, London, 1882, title, " Appeals ";
Gneist, *Das Englische Verwaltungsrecht*, 1884, 397.

decided by them.[1] In consequence of these facts, one
of the writs which were originally issued by the court
of king's bench, *viz.*, the *certiorari*, lost much of its
earlier importance in England, and we find that
statute after statute was passed which prohibited its
use as a means of appealing from the acts of administrative officers.[2]

But up to the coming to the throne of the Orange-
Stuarts in 1689, all officers, whether members of the
courts or administrative officers, held their offices at
the will of the Crown. In this fact, and in the existence in the Crown of reserved judicial powers, are
probably to be found the reasons why the Crown permitted such a control over the administration to be
given to the courts. For the Crown could exercise at
any time a strong personal influence over the judges
of the courts ; and if it was found that the administration of the law was becoming so technical as to ham-
per the action of the administration, the Crown could
at any time exercise its reserved powers and transfer
any matter to a newly created and more pliable
authority.[3]

In 1701, however, all this was changed. The Act
of Settlement made the judges independent of the
royal power, and the whole tendency of English development was to make the justices of the peace actually, though not legally independent of the Crown.
An attempt by Lord Somers during the reign of
William III. to coerce, through the power of dismissal from office, numerous justices of the peace raised

[1] Smith, *op. cit.*, 518.

[2] Gneist, *Das Englische Verwaltungsrecht*, 1884, 406.

[3] This was actually done in several instances, as has been shown. *Cf.* Palgrave, *op. cit.*, 57–61.

such a storm of opposition that no later ministry has dared to make use of such a power.

At the same time that the tenure of the judges and the justices became independent of the Crown their jurisdiction remained essentially the same, with the result that the control, which before might have been regarded as merely a part of the administrative control, became absolutely judicial in character—*i. e.*, was exercised by authorities independent of the administration which was to be controlled.

2. *History in the United States.* — Such was the condition of the control of the courts over the acts of administrative officers at the time the American colonies were founded. At first, indeed, the American judges, like the English judges of the same period, were both in tenure and action under the control of the executive which they were to control, but soon their tenure was assured both against the executive and the legislature, so that from a very early time the higher courts exercised a really judicial control over the actions of the administration. The justices of the peace did not, however, at first become independent in tenure of the administration. And this was probably the reason why our courts of sessions were not able to develop any very large jurisdiction. The appointment early in our history of other officers for purely administrative purposes relegated the justices to the position of inferior judicial officers who have a police jurisdiction and a minor civil jurisdiction. They were left very few administrative duties to perform. Notwithstanding the fact that the justices of the peace in the United States later on obtained a tenure independent of the administration, in that

they became generally elected by the people for a fixed term of office, they never got anything like the same jurisdiction that was given to their English brothers. It is true that in special instances we find appeals from the decisions of administrative officers allowed to the courts of the justices or their successors, the county courts. But it may be safely said that there has never been, and is not now in the United States, any at all important system of remedies against the acts of administrative officers except such as is to be found in the writs which the higher courts, as the result of their being the heirs of the English court of king's bench, have the right to issue. We have lost an important part of the English system of remedies, particularly important because by its means a host of questions of fact and of expediency could be reviewed on appeal. With us such questions are often decided finally by the administration, with the result that a most precious means of protecting individual rights has been lost.

In the United States, however, there have been in some instances established special courts to which appeal may be taken from the acts of administrative officers. These are found particularly in the tax administration under the name of tax appeal courts or boards of review or relief. A most notable body of this sort is the board of general appraisers in the national customs administration which hears appeals from appraisals and classification decisions.

III.—The present jurisdiction of the higher courts.

1. *The special remedies.*—The most important of the special remedies developed by the royal courts

were five in number, each one corresponding to a particular need which experience had shown to exist. They were the *mandamus*, to force the administration to do what it had illegally refused to do ; the prohibition or the injunction, to prevent the administration from proceeding to act where it ought not to act ; the *certiorari*, to review a decision made by the administration, to the end that such decision might be annulled or amended ; the *habeas corpus ad subjiciendum*, to bring the matter of an arrest up before the courts, so that the person arrested might be set at liberty in case the administration had acted illegally ; and the *quo warranto*, to prevent the usurpation of a franchise or privilege. This was later so shaped as to be made use of to decide the question who was rightfully entitled to an office of trust and profit. Logically there was no need for the development of these last two remedies, as the same result might be reached through the use of one of the other remedies.[1]

But the questions of illegal arrest and imprisonment and the usurpation of franchise or office were believed to be so important as to make expedient the adoption of special remedies for them.[2]

What was originally a somewhat informal complaint on the part of the individual that injustice had been done, became finally, as in the case of all the writs issued by the royal courts, a demand for the issue of a special remedy or writ such as the court had

---

[1] Thus in New York the *habeas corpus* has, as a result of the provisions of the Code of Civil Procedure, been somewhat replaced by the *certiorari* to inquire into the cause of detention. Sec. 2015 *et seq.; cf.* Church, *Habeas Corpus*, 330 *et seq.*

[2] The *habeas corpus* can be used only to relieve from actual physical restraint as the other remedies are sufficient to nullify the illegal order upon which the restraint is attempted to be justified. Wales *vs.* Whitney, 114 U. S., 564.

fallen into the habit of issuing. It was but a short step under such conditions for the courts to hold that the demand for a special remedy did not justify the court in issuing any other writ than the one demanded. While the appeal to the court might be made against any act of the administration and the jurisdiction of the courts was not enumerated in the sense that a special statutory authorization was necessary in each case of its exercise, the remedies which could be asked for in particular cases were gradually enumerated in the decisions of the courts. A simple complaint of the denial of justice was finally insufficient.[1] The decisions of the courts have thus become quite technical in their character and hold that a writ which may be properly made use of for one purpose may not be made use of for another. Thus the *mandamus* is not the proper writ to try the title to office.[2] Neither the *mandamus* nor the injunction is the proper remedy to review the decision of a subordinate administrative authority ; this is to be done by the *certiorari.*[3] It has therefore become necessary for the applicant for the exercise of the jurisdiction of the higher courts to make it certain, before he applies for the issue of any particular writ, that he is asking for the proper remedy. For, if he does not, he will be non-suited.

2. *Prerogative character of the writs.*—In the second

[1] Viner's *Abridgement,* 2d ed., xv., 185, citing Barnwell's Chancery Rep., 377, *anno* 1740, where the plaintiff asked for a bill in chancery and was told to ask for a *mandamus ;* also p. 201, citing Queen *vs.* Hungerford, 11 Mod. Rep., 142, where *quo warranto* was asked for and the applicant was told that he could have a *mandamus.* See also p. 206, citing 12 Mod. 196; and p. 208, citing 11 Mod., 254.

[2] People *vs.* Corporation of New York, 3 Johnson's Cases, 79.

[3] Mowers *vs.* Smedley *et al.,* 6 Johnson's Chancery, 28; People *vs.* Police Commissioners, 43 Howard's Pr. (N. Y.), 385.

place, owing to the fact that these writs were developed as a result of the exercise of the reserved judicial powers of the Crown they have never become writs *ex debito justitiæ*—that is, the individual may not have them merely for the asking, as is the case with writs beginning ordinary actions. The courts may refuse in their discretion to issue them.[1] From a very early time, however, on account of the importance of maintaining in its integrity the right of personal liberty, the *habeas corpus* has been regarded as a writ *ex debito justitiæ*—*i.e.*, to be issued on probable cause shown[2]; and the *Habeas Corpus* Act,[3] provided that the judges should issue it under a penalty for refusal. With this exception the rule was for a long time that these writs were, as the law expressed it, prerogative in character. The tendency of the more modern decisions as well as of the statutes passed on this subject has been, however, to assimilate these writs more and more to ordinary actions.[4] In some cases, too, the writs have been abolished altogether and ordinary actions substituted for them. This is true in New York of the *quo warranto*, and the information in the nature of a *quo warranto* which soon took its place. Here, however, the individual, before the action can be brought, must get the attorney-general to move, who, it would seem, has the monopoly of the action ; and it has been held that the courts may not force the attorney-general to bring such action.[5]

[1] See Viner, *op. cit.*, *sub verbo Certiorari*, iv., p. 345, citing 8 Mod., 331; also King *vs.* Barker, 1, Wm. Blackstone, 352.

[2] Church, *op. cit.*, 94 *et seq.*

[3] 31 Car. II., cap. 2, x.; Church, *op. cit.*, 109.

[4] See Kentucky *vs.* Dennison, 24 How., U. S., 66.

[5] Code of Civil Procedure, §§ 1948–1956; People *vs.* Fairchild, 67 N. Y., 334.

But notwithstanding the limitation of their prerogative character the courts have large discretion in granting or refusing the application for the issue of most
of the writs. In some cases the preliminary decision
refusing the issue of the writs is not appealable even [1];
and in no case will they issue where there is any other
adequate remedy.[2] What is an adequate remedy is to
be decided by the courts. They have held that a suit
for damages against an official is not an adequate
remedy,[3] but have intimated, at any rate, that a suit
for damages against a municipal corporation, where
damages are in the nature of things a perfectly competent means of relief, is an adequate remedy.[4] They
have also held that the remedy by indictment of an
officer is not an adequate remedy.[5]

3. *The purpose of the writs.*—The purpose of the
writs is twofold. In the first place, they are issued
mainly with the intention of protecting private rights ;
in the second place, some of them may be made use
of also for the purpose of the maintenance of the law
regardless of the fact whether in the particular case a
private right is attacked or not. Thus in the case of
the *certiorari* it has been held that this writ may not
be made use of simply for the maintenance of the law,

[1] See People *vs.* Stillwell, 19 N. Y., 531 ; County Commissioners *vs.* Jack-
sonville, 36 Fla., 196 ; People *vs.* Commissioners, 82 N. Y., 506 ; People *vs.*
Westbrook, 89 N. Y., 152 ; Sage *vs.* Fifield, 68 Wis., 546.

[2] Wampler *vs.* State, 148 Ind., 557 ; People *vs.* Board of Apportionment,
64 N. Y., 627 ; People *vs.* Betts, 55 N. Y., 600 ; High, *Injunction,* 2d ed.,
§ 28.

[3] Fremont *vs.* Crippen, 10 Cal., 211.

[4] People *vs.* Green, 58 N. Y., 295.

[5] People *vs.* Mayor of New York, 10 Wendell, 393 ; *In re* Trenton Water
Power Co., Spencer, N. J., 659 ; Fremont *vs.* Crippen, 10 Cal., 211 ; see also
Mechem, *Law of Public Officers,* § 941, note 3.

that no one may apply for it unless he has some particular interest in its issue which is greater than that possessed by the ordinary citizen.[1] The courts, however, have held with regard to the *quo warranto* that it may be issued on the demand of any citizen of responsibility[2]; and the better rule would seem to be that in matters of public concern any citizen or taxpayer may apply for the *mandamus*.[3] Further, in the proper cases the officers of the administration may apply to the courts to force by these writs inferior officers to perform their duties.[4] Finally, as a result of the *Habeas Corpus* Act passed in the reign of Charles II., any one may apply for the writ of *habeas corpus* whether he has any particular interest or not—that is, whether his own private rights are involved or not.[5] This rule has been very generally adopted into the law of the United States and is undoubtedly due to the necessity of affording as complete a protection as possible to the right of personal liberty—to the necessity of the maintenance of the law on this subject.

4. *Questions considered on the writs.*—As a general rule the courts may not on these writs consider or review the questions of fact or expediency which have

[1] Davis *vs.* County Commissioners, 153 Mass., 218 ; People *vs.* Leavitt, 41 Mich., 470 ; People *vs.* Walter, 68 N. Y., 403 ; People *vs.* Phillips, 67 N. Y., 582 ; State *vs.* Lamberton, 37 Minn., 362 ; Granville *vs.* County Commissioners, 97 Mass., 193.

[2] Commonwealth *vs.* Meeser, 44 Pa.St., 341 ; State *vs.* Hammer, 42 N. J. L., 435 ; State *vs.* Martin, 46 Conn., 479 ; see People *vs.* Londoner, 13 Col., 303.

[3] People *vs.* Collins, 19 Wendell, 56 ; People *vs.* Halsey, 37 N. Y., 344 ; State *vs.* Railway Co., 19 Wash., 518. As to injunction to restrain improper expenditure of public money, see Crampton *vs.* Zabriskie, 101 U. S., 601.

[4] People *vs.* Canal Board, 55 N. Y., 390 ; People *vs.* Trustees, 54 Barb., N. Y., 480 ; Attorney-General *vs.* Boston, 123 Mass., 460.

[5] 31 Car. II., cap. 2, x.; Church, *op. cit.*, 93.

been decided by the administrative authorities. This is one of the most important general principles affecting the use of the writs and lies at the basis of nearly all the cases.[1] The principle is applicable whatever be the rank or character of the officer who is to be controlled. Be he never so humble, if he have discretion, that discretion he is to exercise free from any control; be he never so influential, he must act in accordance with the law. Thus the decision by a board of local highway commissioners as to the route to be taken by a highway may not be reviewed by the courts,[2] while the refusal of the United States secretary of the interior to issue a patent for lands after all questions of discretion had been decided in favor of the applicant has been held to be the violation of a ministerial duty and may be overcome by application to the court.[3]

This rule is, however, subject to one or two exceptions. The questions of fact which have been decided by an administrative authority in deciding as to the title to office may be reviewed by the courts on either *mandamus* or *quo warranto*.[4] Further, the courts of some states will not permit administrative officers so to make use of their discretion as to make a decision which is absolutely unsupported by the

[1] United States *vs.* Seaman, 17 Howard, U. S., 225; Gaines *vs.* Thompson, 7 Wallace, 347; *Ex parte* Hurn, 92 Ala., 102; Burch *vs.* Hardwicke, 23 Grattan, Va., 51; People *vs.* French, 110 N. Y., 494; Harrison *vs.* New Orleans, 33 La. Ann., 222; Davis *vs.* Mayor, 1 Duer (N. Y.), 451. An important exception is made in the case of the *habeas corpus*, see Church, *op. cit.*, ch. xiii.; see also *In re* Martin, 5 Blatchford, 303.
[2] People *vs.* Collins, 19 Wendell, 55.
[3] United States *vs.* Schurz, 102 U S., 378. See also People *vs.* Beach, 19 Hun., N. Y., 259; and Kendall *vs.* United States, 12 Peters, 524.
[4] State *vs.* Garesche, 65 Missouri, 480; People *vs.* Pease, 27 N. Y., 45; People *vs.* Van Cleve, 1 Mich., 362.

28

evidence, but will on *certiorari* quash such decision.[1] The courts of some states also hold that where a statute provides that an officer may be removed from office for cause only, they have the right to control the discretion of the removing officer in deciding what is cause.[2]

Finally, in several instances special statutes have been passed which expressly give to the courts a control over the discretion of the administration. Thus the present customs administrative act gives to the circuit courts of the United States the power, on a sort of statutory *certiorari*, to reverse or amend the decisions even of fact of the board of general appraisers as to the classification of articles for duty under the tariff acts.[3] Thus also the legislature of New York has provided[4] that in case any person is aggrieved by the decision of the assessors as to the value of his property for the purpose of taxation, he may have a *certiorari* on which the courts may reverse or amend the decision of the assessors on the ground both of illegality and of unfairness or disproportionality.[5]

Finally, for political reasons the courts have very generally laid down the rule that they will not exercise their jurisdiction where it brings them into actual

---

[1] People *vs.* Board of Police, 39 N. Y., 506; People *ex rel.* Hogan *vs.* French, 119 N. Y., 493; People *ex rel.* McAleer *vs.* French, *ibid.*, 502.

[2] *Ibid.* See also Lawrence, "Police Removals and the Courts," *P. S. Q.*, March, 1905.

[3] U. S. Law of June 10, 1890, c. 407, § 15. Here the *certiorari* is probably a remedy *ex debito justitiæ*.

[4] L. 1880, c. 269.

[5] See also New York Code of Civil Procedure, § 2140, which provides that the court in deciding on the writ of *certiorari* may consider the weight of the evidence.

conflict with the chief executive.[1] The rule is clear
as to the President of the United States, but is not
so clear as to the governors of the various commonwealths.[2] Most of the cases where the *mandamus* has
been issued to the governor have been friendly suits
where the governor has not objected to the jurisdiction; indeed one of them holds expressly that the
court will issue the writ of *mandamus* to the governor
if he does not object.[3] Where, however, the courts
may issue the writs without coming into direct conflict with the executive they seem to have no objection to issuing them, even if they will be forced on
the return to the writs to annul the acts of the executive.[4] Thus they have issued a *habeas corpus* to
consider the validity of an act of the governor in
the extradition of a fugitive from justice, and have
decided that such an act was not in accordance with
the law.[5] In the case of *ex parte* Merryman, a case
of *habeas corpus*, however, the writ absolutely failed
of its purpose because the officer to whom it was
issued was supported in his action by the President,
and the court refused to take any further step on
account of the danger of a conflict with the executive.

[1] State of Miss. *vs.* Johnson, 4 Wall., 475; Grier *vs.* Taylor, 4 McCord, 206;
People *vs.* Morton, 156 N. Y. 136; High, *Extraordinary Legal Remedies*, 3d
ed., § 118 *et seq.* and cases cited.

[2] As to the *mandamus*, see Cotton *vs.* Ellis, 7 Jones, N. C., 545; State *vs.*
Chase, 5 Ohio St., 528.

[3] People *vs.* Bissell, 19 Ill., 229. As to the *quo warranto*, see Attorney-
General *vs.* Barstow, 4 Wis., 567; State *vs.* Bulkley, 61 Conn., 287. The rule
here is different on the theory that the courts issue the *quo warranto* not to
the governor but merely to one claiming the right to act as governor.

[4] Dullam *vs.* Wilson, 53 Mich., 392; People *vs.* Platt, 50 Hun., 454.

[5] People *vs.* Curtis, 50 N. Y., 321; People *vs.* Brady, 56 N. Y., 182; see also
Ex parte Merryman, Taney's Decisions, 246; *Ex parte* Field, 5 Blatchford,
63.

Some of the state courts have endeavored to extend this exemption from the operation of the jurisdiction of the courts to the heads of the departments. But this is not the best rule in the United States, and is in conflict with the decisions of the United States Supreme Court.[1]

5. *Distinction between legal and equitable remedies.*— Besides these general rules, which are applicable in a general way to all the remedies by which the jurisdiction of the courts is exercised, there are a number of special rules with regard to each one of the remedies. Thus there is quite a distinction between the extraordinary legal and the equitable remedies. While the former are almost always issued where the act of the administration is absolutely illegal in character, the latter may be issued only in those cases where the applicant for the remedy can bring his case under one of the recognized heads of equitable jurisdiction, such as that the act complained of is a breach of trust, will result in irreparable mischief to real property, or will lead to a multiplicity of suits.[2] Further, if we compare the injunction with the prohibition, whose purposes are largely the same, we find that the injunction appears to be, in the United States at any rate, the more popular remedy. This is due to the fact that while the prohibition may be made use of to prevent the commission of only judicial acts by administrative officers [3] the injunction may be made use of to restrain almost any kind of administrative action. In-

[1] See United States *vs.* Schurz, 102 U. S., 378.

[2] Green *vs.* Mumford, 5 R. I., 472, 475; Dows *vs.* Chicago, 11 Wall., 108; Hilliard, *Injunction*, 3d ed., 486.

[3] People *vs.* Supervisors, 1 Hill, N. Y., 195; Speed *vs.* Common Council, 98 Mich., 360.

deed, in some of the states the courts have made use
of the preliminary injunction with such freedom as to
paralyze almost completely the action of the administration. Thus in New York City police officers
have in several instances been by the injunction
restrained from preventing palpable violations of the
law.[1]

6. *Jurisdiction of the United States courts.*—In the
case of the state courts, the general rule is that the
jurisdiction to issue these extraordinary legal remedies
is possessed by all those courts which have inherited
the jurisdiction of the court of king's bench—and
most courts of general common-law jurisdiction have
inherited such jurisdiction. This rule prevents
courts with a mere appellate jurisdiction from issuing these special writs[2] and results also in the fact
that the equitable remedies may be issued only by
courts possessing equity jurisdiction. The jurisdiction of the United States courts is not, however,
governed by these general principles, but is so fixed in
detail by the constitution and the statutes that it becomes necessary to have reference to these and to the
decisions made in interpretation of them in order to
understand what exactly is the jurisdiction of these
courts. It has been held in a series of decisions that
the United States courts generally have no power to
issue the *mandamus* or *certiorari* except to aid an
already acquired jurisdiction : the supreme court, because the constitution does not include this power

[1] A good collection of these cases was made up in an editorial of the New York *Times* of April 23, 1886.

[2] Morgan *vs.* Register, Hardin (Ky.), 609; State *vs.* Biddle, 36 Ind., 138; State *vs.* Ashley, 1 Ark., 513; Memphis *vs.* Halsey, 12 Heiskell, Tenn., 210; see also Perry *vs.* Shepherd, 78 N. C., 83.

within the original jurisdiction given to that court [1]; the circuit and district courts, because such power has not been granted to them by the judiciary act.[2] The supreme court of the District of Columbia may, however, as a result of the fact that it has inherited for the territory of the District of Columbia the jurisdiction of the court of king's bench, issue the *mandamus*,[3] and, probably as a result of the application of the same principle, the writ of *certiorari* also. It will be remembered, however, that the national customs administrative act gives the power to the circuit courts to issue a sort of statutory *certiorari* to the board of general appraisers in customs matters. Where, however, it is necessary to issue such writs in order to aid a jurisdiction already in other ways acquired, the United States courts may issue the *mandamus*, and, as a result of the application of the same principle, the *certiorari*.[4] In some of the cases laying down this rule, a *mandamus* was issued by a circuit court to a municipal corporation to compel it to provide for the payment of a judgment obtained in the court against such corporation. Further, as a result of the provisions of the United States constitution, the supreme court, it would seem, has such power in cases where a state or a foreign diplomatic or consular officer is a party.[5] The rules are about the same with regard to the prohibition. The supreme court

[1] Marbury *vs.* Madison, 1 Cranch, 137; *In re* Kaine, 14 Howard, 103; *Ex parte* Vallandigham, 1 Wallace, 243.

[2] McIntire *vs.* Wood, 7 Cranch, 504; United States *vs.* Smallwood, 1 Chicago Legal News, 321; *Ex parte* Van Orden, 3 Blatchford, 166.

[3] Kendall *vs.* United States, 12 Peters, 524.

[4] Lansing *vs.* County Treasurer, 1 Dillon, C. C., 522; see also Rees *vs.* City of Watertown, 19 Wall., 107.

[5] Const., art. iii., sec. 2, par. 3; Commonwealth *vs.* Dennison, 24 How., 66.

has no right to issue a prohibition except in admiralty matters,[1] and it is very doubtful whether the circuit courts may issue a prohibition at all.[2]

The rules are, however, more liberal with regard to the injunction, the *habeas corpus*, and the *quo warranto*. The power to issue the *habeas corpus*, even to the administrative authorities of the commonwealths, is given to all the United States courts, except the supreme court.[3] They have also the right to issue the *quo warranto* when the question at issue concerns the denial of the right to vote on account of race, color, or previous condition of servitude for any officer other than presidential elector and legislative officers, or concerns the disqualification for other than legislative office resulting from the violation of the official oath, by engaging in insurrection or rebellion against the United States or giving aid and comfort to its enemies.[4] The supreme court may not issue the injunction except to aid an already acquired jurisdiction, and except in cases where a state or a foreign diplomatic or consular officer is a party.[5] The other United States courts have a large power to apply the equitable remedies in proper cases against the action of both national and state officers.[6] Congress has, however, forbidden the courts of the United States to make use of the injunction to restrain the collection of taxes by the officers of the United States government.[7]

---

[1] U. S. Rev. Statutes, sec. 688; United States *vs.* Peters, 3 Dallas, 121; *Ex parte* Christy, 3 Howard, 292; *Ex parte* Phenix Insurance Co., 118 U. S., 610; see also United States *vs.* Hoffman, 4 Wall., 158.

[2] U. S. Rev. Stats., sec. 716; *In re* Binninger, 7 Blatchford, 159.

[3] U. S. Rev. Stats., secs. 751-766 ; *Ex parte* Barry, 2 How., 65.

[4] Amendment XIV., sec. 3; U. S. Rev. Stats., sec. 563, par. 13, 14.

[5] U. S. Const., art. iij., sec. 2., par. 2.

[6] U. S. Rev. Stats., sec. 629, par. 2.   [7] *Ibid.*, sec. 3224.

These rules apply as well to the issue of these remedies against state officers as to their issue against the officers of the United States government. If the United States courts have not an already acquired jurisdiction in the cases where this is necessary, they may not issue the writs except in the cases provided for by the constitution or statutes. If they have they may.[1] On the other hand, the courts of the states may never exercise the jurisdiction which they may have over state officers in order to control the actions of the officers of the national government. For the United States courts have exclusive jurisdiction of all cases arising under the constitution and laws of the United States.[2] The result is that the officers of the national government are not nearly so subject to the jurisdiction of the courts as are the state officers. But this control is not nearly so necessary as in the state administration. For the administrative control is so strong in the United States administrative system that the mistakes of subordinate administrative officers are quite easily corrected on appeal to higher administrative officers.[3]

IV.—Special and statutory jurisdiction of the lower courts.

The special and technical character of the common-law jurisdiction of the courts has made it seem advisable in certain rather exceptional cases, where no one

[1] Graham *vs.* Norton, 15 Wallace, 427; Commonwealth *vs.* Dennison, 24 Howard, 66.

[2] U. S. Const., art. iii., sec. 2., par. 1; Brewer *vs.* Kidd, 23 Mich., 440; Ableman *vs.* Booth and United States *vs.* Booth, 21 How., 506; Tarble's Case, 13 Wall, 397.

[3] Butterworth *vs.* Hoe, 112 U. S., 50, 57.

of the writs affords the proper relief, to provide by statute for special appeals, generally to the lower courts, from the decisions of administrative officers, when either questions of law alone or questions of both law and fact may be considered. It has been shown that after the abolition of the court of star chamber, which served as an appellate court on questions of both law and fact for the decisions of the subordinate English administrative officers, it was provided in a series of statutes that appeals should thereafter be taken to the court of quarter sessions of the county, which was composed of the justices of the peace of the county.

While in the United States the statutes granting a power of appealing from the decisions of the administrative officers to the courts of quarter sessions or county courts, which have largely taken their place, are not nearly so numerous as in England, still we do find not a few instances of them. Thus in New York any one interested may appeal to the county court from the decision of the superintendent of the poor as to the settlement of a poor person.[1] An instance of a similar power of appeal, though in this case the appeal does not go to the county court, is the power given to any individual, who has been refused a patent for an invention by the commissioner of patents, to appeal from this decision to the supreme court of the District of Columbia.[2]

---

[1] L. 1872, c. 38.

[2] U. S. Rev. Stats., sec. 4911. This is in place of the administrative appeal to the head of department; Butterworth *vs.* Hoe, 112 U. S., 50, 57.

DIVISION III.—THE LEGISLATIVE CONTROL.

CHAPTER I.

HISTORY OF THE LEGISLATIVE CONTROL.

THE history of the legislative or parliamentary control must be studied in the history of English institutions, since England developed the modern legislative body. One of the most important functions of Parliament was from the earliest time to redress grievances. Even so late as the latter part of the middle ages, much of the time of Parliament was taken up in the discharge of this function. The grievances which Parliament sought to redress not only were notable abuses in the government, but were found in the most minute details of the government. Indeed at first the main means of controlling the administration, not only in the interest of society at large but also in that of individual rights, was to be found in this parliamentary control.

As a result of the government of the Stuart kings two facts, however, became apparent. The first was, that the party conflicts which are so apt to arise in Parliament made it an improper authority for the exercise of such an extended control ; the second was, that the parliamentary control was altogether insufficient for the protection of individual rights against an arbitrary and corrupted administration. These defects in the

system of control over the administration were remedied by increasing the independence of the local
organs and of the courts, and the consequent increase
of the judicial control over the administration.[1]   The
parliamentary or legislative control was in this way
reduced to the position of a subsidiary but at the same
time a necessary control.   The general redress of
grievances was therefore made by the courts, and Parliament redressed only grievances of an extraordinary
character.   Petitions for redress of grievances from
this time on took on the character more of propositions *de lege ferenda.*

At the same time Parliament began to increase its
control over the administration in other directions.
Thus it began to specify in its appropriation acts the
purposes for which money might be spent by the administration.   The spending of money had been before
1676, altogether an affair of the royal prerogative with
which the Parliament had not interfered.   But it was
led to assume this power as a result of the wasteful
administration of the kings, and as a result of the fact
that through this power it could exercise a very efficient
control over the general policy of the executive.

Further, in order that this power might be of any
value, it was necessary for the Parliament to assure
itself in some way that the administration had con-
formed in its actions to the provisions of the appropriation acts.   It therefore, somewhat later, began to
examine the accounts of the administration.   Again,
while Parliament still retained its former power of
impeaching the ministers of the Crown in case of their
continued and wilful disobedience of the resolutions

---

[1] Gneist, *Das Englische Verwaltungsrecht*, 1884, 345.

of Parliament and violation of the law of the land, it added very much to its powers of control by insisting that the ministers of the Crown should be such persons as could obtain and retain the confidence of Parliament. The result of the development of this principle of the responsibility of the ministers was a further increase of the control of Parliament, which is not capable of exact juristic determination, and which has practically resulted in the abandonment of the power of impeachment.

The formerly all-embracing parliamentary control was reduced thus practically to the exercise of three powers which are largely subsidiary to the other methods of control. These powers are: first, the power to remedy special abuses in the interest of the social well-being by entertaining propositions *de lege ferenda* and by investigating the conduct of the administration; second, the power of controlling the general policy of the administration through the voting of the appropriations and the examination of the accounts of the administration after the execution of the budget, in order to see whether the provisions of the appropriation acts have been observed; and third, in the extraordinary power of impeachment, to be made use of only when all else fails to bring the administration within the bounds of the law. This power is supplemented by the principle of the responsibility of the ministers to Parliament, and is largely replaced in actual practice by that principle.

Such was the form of the parliamentary or legislative control in England at the time the general English system of constitutional government was adopted in this country.

CHAPTER II.

THE exercise of this power may result from petitions which have been sent to the legislature by
individuals. For almost all American constitutions
guarantee to the individual the right to address
petitions to the government, and the legislature is the
place where most of such petitions go. The legislature may further act of its own motion and is generally on the watch for administrative abuses. The
means of exercising this control are the putting of
questions to the officers of the administration, and
the undertaking on the part of the legislature, through
committees appointed by it, of investigations which
may have in view either the unearthing of abuses which
have been suspected or obtaining information *de lege
ferenda*. In the United States there is usually one
such standing committee for each administrative
department. The main function of such standing
committees is to scrutinize carefully the way in
which the business of the particular department is
transacted. The special committees are formed for
the purpose of investigating some particular abuse
in the administration whose existence is alleged by

individuals or has come to the notice of the legislature. Real authority such committees do not have, except where the legislature may have the power of removal or impeachment. Their action can result simply in new legislation. Further, their power of obtaining information either from the officers of the administration or from private individuals is often not a great one. This is true, particularly of the committees of the national Congress. For quite a time it was supposed that, as a result of a decision of the United States Supreme Court,[1] Congress and its committees had full power to punish witnesses for contempt who refused to answer questions put to them ; but the same tribunal in a more recent case has limited very greatly this power. It has decided[2] that a congressional committee has no power to punish a witness for contempt in refusing to answer questions in regard to matters over which Congress has no jurisdiction ; and, while the Supreme Court has expressly refused to decide whether Congress has the power to force a witness to testify in cases where it desires information for its use in legislation, it seems to indicate in its opinion that Congress has no such power. At the same time the court indicated that Congress and its committees have the power to punish for contempt in the case of impeachment proceedings.[3] Nothing, however, prevents Congress or its committees from gathering testimony from willing witnesses.

When we come to the states it is not easy to say

[1] Anderson *vs.* Dunn, 6 Wheaton, 204.
[2] Kilbourn *vs.* Thompson, 103 U. S., 168.
[3] See also *Ex parte* Chapman, 166 U. S., 661.

exactly what is the power of the legislature in this respect. It is easily conceivable that the legislatures of the states might have this power although it is not possessed by the national Congress. For there is no principle of our constitutional law which is clearer than that, while Congress is an authority of enumerated powers, the legislatures of the commonwealths may do anything which they have not been expressly forbidden to do by the constitution. And seldom do we find in the state constitutions any provisions which clearly take away any such power from the state legislatures. Indeed in the constitutions of twenty-four of the states[1] such power of punishing for contempt would seem to be granted. The constitutions of several of the states provide that the legislature shall have " all other powers necessary for the legislature of a free state."[2] The constitution of Massachusetts has been so interpreted by the supreme court of the commonwealth as to give a committee, appointed for the simple purpose of investigation, the power to punish witnesses for contempt.[3] Finally, in the case of those states whose constitutions contain no provision as to this point, we have several decisions which throw light on the subject. Most of these are in the courts of New York, which has apparently exercised this power more frequently than the other states. Here it has been decided that the

---

[1] Alabama, Arkansas, Colorado, Connecticut, Delaware, Florida, Illinois, Indiana, Iowa, Louisiana, Maine, Maryland, Massachusetts, Minnesota, Missouri, Nebraska, Nevada, New Hampshire, Oregon, Pennsylvania, South Carolina, Tennessee, Texas, and West Virginia. See F. W. Whitridge on " Legislative Inquests," in *P. S. Q.*, i., 84, 89.

[2] *Ibid.*, 89.

[3] Burnham *vs.* Morrissey, 14 Gray, 226.

legislature or its committees, to which it has delegated the power of investigation either by statute or
by resolution, have the power to punish for contempt.[1]
The latest case on the point [2] imposes an apparent
limitation on this power in that it says that the legislature or one of its committees may only punish for
contempt witnesses who refuse to answer questions
put with the desire of obtaining information for future
legislative action; but, as it at the same time admits
that the court cannot impugn the expressed motives
of the legislature, all that the legislature has to do in
order to bring itself under the rule stated in this case
is to declare in the resolution appointing the committee that it desires such information.[3]   But even
if the legislature does not possess this power, still as
a matter of fact the officers of the administration will
usually comply with the summons of an investigating
committee of the legislature, and will answer all reasonable questions put to them, since " desiring legislation and always desiring money [they have] strong
motives for keeping on good terms with those who
control legislation and the purse." [4]

[1] People *vs.* Learned, 5 Hun., 626; see also Wilckens *vs.* Willet, 1 Keyes,
521, 525.
[2] People *ex rel.* McDonald *vs.* Keeler, 99 N. Y., 463.
[3] See also the case of *Ex parte* Dalton, 44 Ohio St., 142, which holds that
the legislature may punish for contempt in election cases.
[4] Bryce, *American Commonwealth,* i., 154.

CHAPTER III.

THE LEGISLATIVE CONTROL OF THE FINANCES.

THROUGH its control over the finances the legislature exercises a control over the general policy of the administration, for the conduct of the entire administration is closely connected with the amount of money which may be spent. The control over the finances is to be found in three powers: first, in the power any given legislature has to fix the total amount of receipts from taxes which the officers of the administration may collect for the coming budgetary period; second, in the power it has to fix the amounts of money at the disposition of the administration, and the purposes for which such money is to be spent; and third, in the power it must have, if the second power is to amount to anything, to ascertain, after the expenditure of the money, whether the administration has acted in accordance with the provisions of law fixing the amount of money to be spent and the purposes for which such money is to be spent.

I.—Control over receipts.

The legislative control over the finances in its modern form was, like the other methods of legislative control, developed by England. Originally the only way in which the English Parliament endeavored to control the financial administration was by fixing the amount of money which could be raised by the Crown by means of imposing taxes upon the people. The Parliament did not attempt to control the amount of money which could be spent nor the purposes for which it should be spent.[1] This was also true of the early American colonial government. The later development has reversed this condition of things. At the present time most of the receipts— *i. e.*, taxes—are fixed by permanent law. No given Parliament has much to do with receipts, for its action is no longer necessary in order that the receipts shall come in. So long as the law establishing the taxes is not repealed, which will require the combined action of both houses of Parliament, the administration may go on collecting the taxes regardless of Parliament, providing it acts in accordance with existing law.[2] This principle has been introduced into the United States. Thus in the national government the customs duties and the internal-revenue taxes, from which two sources most of the revenue of the national government is obtained, are both fixed in amount by permanent law in that the rates which may be levied are so fixed. The amount of money which is received from these sources is independent of the action of any particular Congress and depends rather upon the business and prosperity of the country. If the houses of Congress take no action on these matters the duties provided by law

[1] Cox, *Institutions of the English Government*, 199.

[2] Gneist, *Das Englische Verwaltungsrecht*, 1884, i., 431 ; ii., 715. At the present time almost the only tax which is fixed in amount by each Parliament is the income tax.

are still levied. This is true also of the other receipts of the national government, such, for example, as tonnage dues and the receipts of the post-office and from the sale of public lands. A given Congress has generally therefore nothing to say as to the amount of the receipts of the government. In order to change them in any way, either the two houses and the President must agree, or the two houses of Congress must act by a sufficiently large majority to overcome the veto of the President.

We find, however, instances of the annual vote of taxes by the legislature in some of the states. Indeed this seems originally to have been all but the universal rule as a result of the kind of tax which was adopted. This was the general property tax, and the way in which it was levied was to ascertain the amount of money to be spent and then apportion it among the counties of the commonwealth. This of course necessitated action by the legislature at each of its sessions. But with the recent changes in the tax system the control each legislature has over the receipts has been considerably lessened in many of the states. For some of the taxes are now fixed as to rate by permanent law—*e.g.,* the corporation tax and the inheritance taxes—and the action of any particular legislature is no longer necessary to their collection.

II.—*Control over expenses.*

It has already been pointed out that the English Parliament originally contented itself in the exercise of its control over the financial administration with fixing the amount of the supplies obtained from taxation which were to be placed at the disposition of the Crown. It did not attempt in any way to exercise a control over the disposal by the Crown of the money in its control, regarding the spending of money once raised as peculiarly a part of the royal prerogative. But the abuses of the financial administration particularly by the Stuart kings led the Parliament to begin soon after the Restoration, *viz.*, in 1676, regularly to designate the purposes for which the money should be spent, by the insertion in the grant of what was known as an "appropriation clause."[1] This clause not only designated the purposes for which money was to be spent, but also forbade the Crown to make any other use of the money granted than that expressed in the clause.[2] It must be remembered, however, that this clause at first affected only the extraordinary revenue of the Crown,—*i. e.*, the revenue coming from taxation,—and also was of a very general character. But with the gradual increase of the extraordinary revenue and at the same time the decrease not only in importance but also in actual amount of the ordinary revenue (*i. e.*, the revenue from the royal domains, *etc.*), the legislature got into its hands the control of most of the expenses of the government as well as that of the receipts which at this time had not become permanent. The result was a very unstable condition of the finances. This, it was felt, weakened the power of the state particularly since, as a result of the foreign policy of England during the reign of

[1] Cox, *Institutions of the English Government*, p. 199. Cox cites here much earlier instances of such appropriation clauses, but says that they were of rare occurrence.

[2] In 1680, Sir Edward Seymour, the Treasurer of the Navy, was impeached for not observing such clauses. *Ibid.*, 200, note (*a*), citing 8 State Trials, 127.

William III., a large debt had grown up. This instability was remedied in the following ways : In the first place, the receipts were made stable by establishing the taxes by permanent law instead of making the action of each Parliament necessary in order that they might flow into the treasury. In the second place, in order to insure the stability of certain at any rate of the expenses, it was provided that such expenses should be paid out as a result of a permanent law. Such was particularly the case with the interest on the public debt, which, it was felt, should not be dependent on the annual action of the Parliament.[1]

In the United States a somewhat similar method of insuring the stability of certain of the expenses has been adopted. As has been shown, the receipts are permanent. The statutes of Congress have also provided for quite a number of appropriations which are based upon permanent law. The growth of the national debt at the time of the civil war made Congress feel the same fear that had been felt before in England as to the effect on the public credit of the country of the dependence of interest and sinking-fund payments on congressional action. There was therefore adopted a system of what were called permanent annual appropriations established by permanent law which should be sufficient authorization to the administration to make the necessary payments without any special action on the part of the Congress. Among these permanent annual appropriations are to be mentioned, in addition to the debt payments, the expense of collecting the customs duties, and the salaries of judicial officers. Finally, as a result of the decisions of the

---

[1] See 3 Geo. I., c. 7; Gneist, *Das Englische Verwaltungsrecht*, 1884, 686.

supreme court,[1] the fixing of salaries by permanent law, which is often the case, is regarded much as a permanent annual appropriation. For the officer whose salary is thus fixed may sue the government for it. The salaries would thus have to be paid regardless of the action of Congress, unless such action was by a majority sufficient to override the President's veto. This decision of the supreme court has vastly increased the independence of the administration.[2] It is indeed true that the act organizing the Court of Claims provides that judgments against the United States shall be paid out of the appropriation for private claims; but in time of conflict between the Congress and the President it is very probable that the President would conduct the government and would have salaries paid without annual appropriations, and be able to do so successfully. The result of these permanent annual appropriations is that a large part of the current expenses of the government, inclusive of pensions and salaries, is beyond the reach of any particular Congress. That is, it is not necessary, in order that these expenses be paid, that there be any action at all on the part of Congress. The failure of Congress to act or to agree with the President will not affect the action of the administration in the carrying on of the government through the payment of a large part of the expenses. The expenses of the government which are particularly under the control of each Congress are those of the army, the navy, and

---

[1] United States *vs*. Langston, 118 U. S., 389.

[2] See also Antoni *vs*. Greenhow, 107 U. S., 769, in which it is said that the declaration by the legislature that money shall be spent is an appropriation by law.

of the other branches of the administration with the exception of the customs.

Congress has never, as has the English House of Commons, divested itself of the right to make appropriations other than those proposed by the administration. Indeed in practice many of the most unwise appropriations of the national government are made on the proposition of Congress and not on that of the administration. Congress further always makes use of its undoubted right to cut down or amend in some way the estimates sent in by the administration. It has also attempted, by tacking to appropriations provisions objectionable to the administration, to force their acceptance by it, under a threat of the refusal of the estimates, but the determined stand made by one of the Presidents and the absolute impossibility of refusing important appropriations to the administration have finally convinced the Congress that this is not a proper use of its control over the finances.

When we come to the control of the state legislatures over the expenses, we find such a variety of systems that it is impossible to say what is the general rule. In some states we find that the amount of the appropriations is fixed almost altogether by the administration in accordance with general and permanent laws over which a given legislature has practically little control[1]; and it has been held that without any special appropriation the payment of salaries fixed by permanent law may be enforced by *mandamus.*[2] In other and indeed in most cases most of the appropri-

[1] The courts seem to regard this practice as perfectly proper. See People *vs.* Supervisors, 1 Hill, N. Y., 195 ; John J. Townsend, Trustee, *vs.* Mayor, *etc.*, 77 N. Y., 542.

[2] Nichols *vs.* Comptroller, 4 Stew. and Port., Ala., 154.

ations are made annually or biennially by the legislature.[1] In all the states the legislature has the power to make appropriations other than those proposed by the administration if the administration is to submit estimates to the legislature. Generally also the legislature, where such estimates are submitted to it, has the right to cut them down and often exercises this power. But as a result of the very general power of the governor to veto items in appropriation bills the legislature may not force the administration to take action not approved by it as a result of tacking objectionable provisions to an appropriation bill.

III.—Examination of accounts.

In order that the control which the legislature possesses over the administration through its control over the receipts and expenses may be of any value, it is necessary that it have the further power of examining the accounts of the administration after the execution of the budget. In this way and in this way alone can it satisfy itself that its directions relative to the receipts and expenses have been observed. In the United States the legislature acts in its investigations unaided by any other authority. Great care is taken both by the national constitution and by the statutes of Congress to ensure the full publicity of the accounts of the administration, while the secretary of the treasury has to report to Congress in full the entire receipts and expenditures of the preceding year.[2] The rules of

[1] In some cases this is required by the constitution, Stimson, *op. cit.*, p. 320 B. This is so in Arkansas, Kansas, Louisiana, Missouri, Ohio, and Texas.

[2] Constitution, art. i., sec. 9, par. 7; U. S. R. S., secs. 260, 261, 266, and 267.

the House of Representatives have usually provided[1] that such accounts shall go to the Speaker of the house and be submitted by him to the house for reference. They are then to be referred[2] to one of the eight standing committees on expenditure, which shall examine, together with the manner of keeping them, the economy, justness, and correctness of the expenditures, their conformity with appropriation laws, the proper application of public moneys, the security of the government against unjust and extravagant demands, retrenchment, the enforcement of the payment of moneys due to the United States, the economy and accountability of public officers, the reduction or increase of pay of officers, and the abolishment of useless offices. Each of the eight standing committees on the expenditures of the departments has one or more of these subjects within its purview, and after making the necessary examinations is to report to the house. What the legislature will do in case of unauthorized expenditures or of failure to observe the provisions of the budget, the laws and the rules do not say ; and it is not the habit of the house to pass any law or resolution settling and affirming the actions of the administration in case they are in conformity with the appropriation acts, and releasing the officers of the government having control of the execution of the budget from all further responsibility for it.

[1] See Rule 42.

[2] Rule II, sec. 35.

CHAPTER IV.

IMPEACHMENT.

IMPEACHMENT proceedings, like the other methods of legislative control, are derived from England. The method of impeachment seems to have been necessary in England because the English law did not allow a civil or criminal suit to be brought against the highest officers of state except with extreme difficulty. It was thus developed mainly to fill up a gap in the judicial control. A further reason for its development is to be found in the impossibility of obtaining a conviction of the great nobles before the ordinary courts,[1] and in the necessity of some means of legislative control in the days when the principle of the parliamentary responsibility of the ministers had not been developed.[2] Since its development in England it has been adopted to some extent in almost all constitutional countries, and in some cases is made use of against not only the ministers but also all civil officers of the government.

The ordinary English method of impeachment was formed on the model of the ordinary criminal procedure, the House of Commons taking the part of

[1] Blackstone, *Commentaries*, iv., 360.
[2] For its history see Cox, *Institutions of the English Government*, 229, *et seq.*, 468.

the grand jury and thus bringing forward the impeachment or indictment, the House of Lords acting as the court.[1] The grounds for impeachment were originally abuse of office from corrupt, partial, or oppressive motives, violation of the law, and treason, which was usually defined by the court of impeachment to suit itself, and depended very much upon its feelings towards the accused,[2] but later came to include, especially during the reigns of the Stuarts, offences political in nature.[3] The punishment originally was death, banishment, fine, or imprisonment in the discretion of the court of impeachment. Soon after this method was developed there grew up the habit of exercising this control through the ordinary process of legislation—*i. e.*, by the passage of a bill of attainder in accordance with which no fair trial was granted the person attainted. This seems to have originated with the Tudors and was quite frequently employed during the constitutional struggle of the seventeenth century.[4] This method has, however, in practice been abandoned as grossly unjust. Parliament still, of course, has the power to pass a bill of attainder if it wishes to, although in the United States such action by either Congress or a state is forbidden by the national constitution.[5] The method of impeachment has, however, with the development of the principle of the parliamentary responsibility of the ministers, rather fallen into disuse, the last case being that of Warren Hastings, which occurred about the end

[1] Cox, *Institutions of the English Government*, 229, 470, 471.
[2] Gneist, *Das Englische Verwaltungsrecht* (1884), 436.
[3] *Ibid.*
[4] Cox, *op. cit.*, 235, 465.
[5] Art. i., sec. 9, par. 3; sec. 10, par. 1.

of the eighteenth century. The other methods of legislative control are so complete that it is difficult to see in what cases the method of impeachment could be applied with advantage. The power still remains in Parliament and may be made use of in an extreme case where all other means of control fail to bring the administration to an observance of the laws or customs of the land.

This method of impeachment has, however, been adopted in the United States both in the national and in the state governments. The national constitution provides that the House of Representatives shall have the sole power to impeach the President, Vice-President, and all civil officers of the United States [1]; that the Senate shall, with the chief justice of the United States as presiding officer in case the President is impeached, have the sole power to try impeachments and shall convict only as a result of a two-thirds vote of the members present,[2] and that the punishment in case of conviction shall be removal from office and disqualification to hold any office of honor, trust, or profit under the United States in the future, with the impossibility of pardon, but that the person so convicted shall be liable to indictment, trial, judgment, and punishment according to law.[3] The causes of impeachment are treason, bribery, and "other high crimes and misdemeanors."[4] There have been two views as to the meaning of this phrase. One is that the only cause for impeachment is a crime—*i. e.*, an act for which a person may be indicted

[1] Art. i., sec. 2, par. 5; art. ii., sec. 4.
[2] Art. i., sec. 3, par. 6.
[3] *Ibid.*, par. 7.
[4] Art. ii., sec. 4.

and punished in accordance with the law[1]; the other assigns a much wider meaning to the phrase and claims that the phrase was purposely left vague at the time of the formation of the constitution, so that it might by construction be made to include political offences.[2] The cases in which the article in the constitution relative to the causes of impeachment has been construed are few in number and some of them have been decided for jurisdictional reasons and are therefore of little value in throwing light on the meaning of the article. Thus the first case, *viz.*, that of Senator Blount, decided that a senator of the United States could not be impeached inasmuch as he was not a civil officer of the United States in the meaning of the constitution, while one of the latest cases, *viz.*, that of a cabinet officer, was decided largely on the ground that, as such officer had resigned and his resignation had been accepted by the President, he was not subject to the jurisdiction of the impeachment court. The only cases in which the person impeached has been convicted are those of Judge Pickering, who was convicted of offences distinctly not political; Judge Humphreys, who was convicted of treason in the beginning of the war, his treasonable acts being the making of a speech in favor of secession and acceptance of the office of judge in the southern confederacy. On the other hand, Judge Chase, who was impeached for "highly indecent and extra-judicial" reflections upon the government of the United States, made to a grand jury during the time when the alien

[1] See opinions of Mr. Senator Davis and Mr. Senator Trumbull in "Impeachment Trial of Andrew Johnson."

[2] See opinion of Mr. Senator Sumner. *Ibid.*

and sedition laws were in force; President Johnson, who was impeached for a political offence which had been made a high crime and misdemeanor by act of Congress; and Judge Peck, who was impeached for arbitrary conduct in committing for contempt of court an attorney who had published a criticism of one of his opinions, were all of them acquitted.[1] It would seem therefore that the phrase "high crimes and misdemeanors" does not include political matters. This is largely due to the large majority which is required for conviction in the court of impeachment. For in the case of an impeachment for an act of a political character party feelings will be arrayed against each other, and in the state of political parties in the United States it will be very unusual for any party to have such complete control of the court of impeachments as to be able to get the required two-thirds majority.

The constitutions of most of the states recognize the right of the legislature to impeach and convict the officers of the state government, but the provisions differ somewhat in their details. One constitution, *viz.*, that of Oregon, expressly forbids impeachment. The majority of the constitutions provide for the impeachment of all civil officers. Some expressly refer to the governor.[2] The cause for impeachment in most of the constitutions is crime, but some provide that immorality, official corruption, or misconduct, and even incompetence, incapacity, or neglect of official duty, and favoritism will be sufficient cause.[3] All the states

[1] See *Cyclopædia of Political Science, etc., sub verbo* "Impeachment." Article by Alexander Johnson; see also *Am. and Eng. Encyc. of Law*, 2d ed., vol. xv., pp. 1066 *et seq.* Article by Walter Carrington.

[2] Stimson, *American Statute Law*, p. 63.

[3] So in Louisiana, West Virginia, Virginia, and Florida. See *ibid.*, 64.

in which provision is made for impeachment, with the exception of Nebraska, provide that the lower house of the legislature is to initiate the impeachment generally as a result of a majority vote. In Nebraska the impeachment is to be initiated by the legislature in joint assembly of the two houses. In all but two states the impeachment is to be tried by the senate, a vote by two-thirds of whose members or two-thirds of whose members present, being usually necessary for conviction. In New York, however, the judges of the court of appeals, the highest court, are joined with the senate, and together with it form the court of impeachment, while in Nebraska the supreme court is the court of impeachment.[1] The effect of conviction is in almost all cases removal from office, and in most cases also disqualification to hold office. But generally persons impeached may be at the same time indicted and punished in the usual way.[2]

[1] So in Louisiana, West Virginia, Virginia, and Florida. See *ibid.*, 64.
[2] *Ibid.*, p. 65.

LIST OF AUTHORITIES.

Abbreviatio Placitorum, 421
Adams, *Works*, I., 237
Allison and Penrose, *Philadelphia*, 204, 208, 210
Anson, *The Law and Custom of the Constitution*, 180
Ash, *Charter of the City of New York*, 206
Aucoc, *Conférences sur l'Administration et le Droit Administratif*, 66
Baldwin, *Modern Political Institutions*, 94
Barbour, "The Value of State Boards," in *Conference of Charities and Correction*, 1894, 141
Beard, "The Office of Justice of the Peace," in *Columbia University Studies in History, Economics, and Public Law*, XX., 181
Benton, *Thirty Years' View*, 123
Bernheim, "Party Organizations and their Nominations to Public Office in New York State," in *Political Science Quarterly*, III., 244
Bishop, *Criminal Law*, II., 298
Black, "The History of the Municipal Ownership of Land on Manhattan Island," in *Columbia University Studies of History, Economics, and Public Law*, I., 207
Blackstone, *Commentaries*, 421, 422, 458
Blue, *New York State Library Bulletin*, 1901, 157
Blue, "Tendencies in State Administration," in *Annals of the American Academy*, XVIII., 155
Bondy, "The Separation of Powers," in *Columbia University Studies in History, Economics, and Public Law*, V., 31, 35
Bowman, "Administration of Iowa," in *Columbia University Studies in History, Economics, and Public Law*, XVIII., 63, 141, 157
Bryce, *American Commonwealth*, I., 209, 448
Chicago Conference for Good City Government, 251
Church, *Habeas Corpus*, 428, 430, 432, 433
Clarke, *Debates of the Convention of 1821*, 99
Commons, *Proportional Representation*, 243
Cooley, *Taxation*, 343, 358, 402
Cooley, *Torts*, 398, 404
Cox, *Institutions of the English Government*, 450, 452, 458, 459
Dallinger, *Nominations for Elective Offices in the United States*, 244
Dicey, *The Law of the Constitution*, 2

Dillon, *Municipal Corporations*, 4th ed., 165, 169, 203, 204, 208, 210, 211, 343, 383, 386

Dockery Commission, 53d Congress, Second Session, *House Reports*, 49, 1893, 120

Documents Relating to the Colonial History of New York, IV., 110, 184, 185

Ducrocq, *Cours de Droit Administratif*, 25

Dunbar, "Government by Injunction," in *The Law Quarterly*, October, 1897, 411

Dunning, "The Constitution in Civil War," in *Political Science Quarterly*, I. 47

Eaton, "Right to Local Government," in *Harvard Law Review*, XIII., 168

Eliot, "One Remedy for Municipal Government," in *The Forum*, October, 1891, 230

Elmes, *Executive Departments*, 75

Fairlie, "The Administrative Powers of the President," in *Michigan Law Review*, II., 47, 76, 87, 94, 114

Fairlie, "American Municipal Councils," in *Political Science Quarterly*, June, 1904, 218

Fairlie, "The Centralization of Administration in New York State," in *Columbia University Studies in History, Economics, and Public Law*, IX., 63, 139, 140, 147, 198

Fairlie, *Municipal Administration*, 100, 210, 212

Fairlie, "State Administration in New York," in *Political Science Quarterly*, XV., 195

Fisher, "Suspension of Habeas Corpus," in *Political Science Quarterly*, III., 75

Ford, *The Rise and Growth of American Politics*, 14, 24, 48, 236

Freund, "American Administrative Law," in *Political Science Quarterly*, IX., 43

Freund, "Private Claims against the State," in *Political Science Quarterly*, VIII., 393

Gitterman, "New York Council of Appointment," in *Political Science Quarterly*, VII., 231

Gneist, *Das Englische Verwaltungsrecht*, 371, 372, 450, 453, 459

Gneist, *History of the English Constitution*, 421, 422

Gneist, *Self-Government, Communalverfassung und Verwaltungsgerichte*, 199, 205

Goodnow, *Comparative Administrative Law*, I., 189, 221

Goodnow, "Local Government in England," in *Political Science Quarterly*, II., 179

Goodnow, *Municipal Home Rule*, 171, 172, 173

Goodnow, *Politics and Administration*, 4

Goss, "History of Tariff Administration in the United States," in *Columbia University Studies in History, Economics, and Public Law*, I., 62, 142

Guggenheimer, "The Development of Executive Departments," in Jameson, *Essays in the Constitutional History of the United States,* 120

Hammond, *History of Political Parties in the State of New York,* I., 102

High, *Extraordinary Legal Remedies,* 421, 422, 435

High, *Injunctions,* 431

Hilliard, *Injunction,* 436

Holland, *Elements of Jurisprudence,* 2

Howard, *Local Constitutional History of the United States,* I., 182, 183, 184, 185, 186, 187, 188, 189, 191, 195, 197, 198

Impeachment Trial of Andrew Johnson, 461

Johns Hopkins University Studies in Historical and Political Science, V., 206, 207, 210

Kent, *Commentary on the City Charter,* 206, 208

King, "Claims against Governments," in *American Law Register and Review,* XXXII., 394

Laférrière, *La Juridiction Administrative,* I., 299

Lawrence, "Police Removals and the Courts," in *Political Science Quarterly,* March, 1905, 434

"Local Self-Government in the Southwest," in *Johns Hopkins University Studies in Historical and Political Science,* XI., 190

Loening, *Deutsches Verwaltungsrecht,* 396

Lowell, *Government and Parties in Continental Europe,* 8, 69

Macy, *Party Organization and Machinery,* 5, 48

Maltbie, *English Local Government of To-day,* 328

Mechem, *Law of Officers,* 136, 222, 226, 263, 283, 297, 310, 314, 315, 341, 342, 344, 345, 399, 405, 406, 407, 408, 431

Messages and Papers of the Presidents, II., 265

Meyer, *Nominating Systems,* 246, 248, 249, 250

Mommsen, *Römisches Staatrecht,* 383

Montesquieu, *Esprit des Lois,* 24

Morehouse, *Supervisor's Manual,* 193

New York State Library Bulletin, 72; "Review of Legislation," 1902, 156

New York Times, April 23, 1836, 437

Oberholtzer, *The Referendum in America,* 37, 42

Orth, "The Centralization of Administration in Ohio," in *Columbia University Studies of History, Economics, and Public Law,* XVI., 63, 139, 140, 198

Ostrogorski, "Woman Suffrage in Local Government," in *Political Science Quarterly,* VI., 677, 264

Palgrave, *An Essay upon the Original Authority of the King's Council,* 421, 422, 425

Parker and Worthington, *The Law of Public Health and Safety,* 340, 348, 360, 363, 364, 365

"Penn's Charter," in *Johns Hopkins University Studies,* V., 206

Powers, "Railroad Indemnity Lands," in *Political Science Quarterly,* IV., 81

Powers, "The Reform of the Federal Service," in *Political Science Quarterly,* III., 302

Rawles, "Centralizing Tendencies in the Administration of Indiana," in *Columbia University Studies of History, Economics, and Public Law,* XVII., 63, 198

Reeves, *History of the English Law,* 422

Rollin, *School Administration,* 209, 219

Rowe, "The Financial Relation of the Department of Education to the City Government," in *Annals of the American Academy of Political and Social Science,* XV., 219

Ryley, *Pleadings,* 421

Sarwey, *Allgemeines Verwaltungsrecht,* 43

Sites, "Centralized Administration of Liquor Laws in American Commonwealths," in *Columbia University Studies of History, Economics, and Public Law,* X., 63

Smith, *Practice at Quarter Sessions,* 424, 425

Snow, *The Administration of Dependencies,* 121

Sparling, "Responsible County Government," in *Political Science Quarterly,* XVI., 191

Stubbs, *Constitutional History of England,* 179, 421, 422

Todd, *Parliamentary Government in England,* 399

Viner, *Abridgment,* 429, 430

Webster, "Recent Centralizing Tendencies in State Educational Administration," in *Columbia University Studies in History, Economics, and Public Law,* VIII., 62, 140, 198

White, "State Boards and Commissions," in *Political Science Quarterly,* XVIII., 156, 157

Whitridge, "Legislative Inquests," in *Political Science Quarterly,* I. 447

Whitten, "Public Administration in Massachusetts," in *Columbia University Studies of History, Economics, and Public Law,* VIII., 63, 141

Wilcox, *The American City,* 211

Wilcox, "Party Government in the Cities of New York," in *Political Science Quarterly,* December, 1889, 261

Wilcox, *The Study of City Government,* 320

Woodburn, *The American Republic and its Government,* 94

Wyman, *Administrative Law,* 2, 87, 90, 123, 142, 143

Young, "Administration of City Schools," in *Annals of the American Academy of Political and Social Science,* XV., 219

Zueblin, *Municipal Progress,* 211

INDEX.

A

Acceptance of an office, 255; when incompatible vacates first office, 309; at common law obligatory, 255

Accounts, examination of, by legislature, 456

Act of settlement, 24, 423

Administration, administrative control over, 373, 383; branches of, 120; bureaucratic system of, 228; central, 62, 64; in colonial period, 71; controlled by politics, 8, 29; control over, 367; county, 60; defined, 7, 14; delegate of the sovereign, 317; differentiated from politics, 6; end of, 229; expresses will of the state, 325; executes will of the state, 324; of financial affairs, 20; of foreign relations, 18; a function of government, 3, 13; governor not head of state, 107, 131; influences politics, 15; influenced by political parties, 12; of internal affairs, 21; of judicial affairs, 19; judicial control over, 376, 378; legislative control over, 377, 445; local, 162; of military affairs, 19; participation of local communities in, 55; regulated by the legislature, 43; subjected to judicial control, 22.

(See also Administrative law; Executive.)

Administrative abuses, power of the legislature to remedy, 445

Administrative action, classified, 317; in conditional and unconditional statutes, 325; differentiated from administrative directions, 316; methods and forms of, 316

Administrative acts, judicial in character, 333; of the executive, 50; special, 331

Administrative authorities, procedure to be followed by, 340; subjected to the control of the courts, 355

Administrative control, over administration, 373; disciplinary power of, 374; power of supervision of, 375

Administrative determinations, and the constitution, 334; when "due process of law," 356; final, when, 339

Administrative function, 14; of the executive, 67; territorial distribution of, 55

Administrative law, aims of, 371; defined, 1, 17; distinguished from constitutional law, 3, 370; exists in all highly developed governments, 3; extent of the study of, 5; in England, 1; interests protected by, 373; rules

469